CONTENTS

THE LIFE OF DAVID BUTLER

SULTAN OF SWING

BY MICHAEL CRICK

Biteback Publishing

First published in Great Britain in 2018 by
Biteback Publishing Ltd
Westminster Tower
3 Albert Embankment
London SE1 7SP

ISBN 978-1-78590-438-7

10 9 8 7 6 5 4 3 2 1

A CIP catalogue record for this book is available from the British Library.

Set in Adobe Caslon Pro

Printed and bound in Great Britain by
CPI Group (UK) Ltd, Croydon CR0 4YY

INTRODUCTION

YOU HAVEN'T MUCH TIME!

'Good night,' said the old man in the black velvet siren suit. He'd taken his young guest up the winding staircase to show him his overnight quarters in the attic of the red-brick country house. 'And in bidding me goodnight,' the visitor would recall, 'he spoke like any other worldly host, about not forgetting to turn out the lights.'[1]

It was well after midnight and, as he sat in his garret bedroom, the Oxford student was still in a bit of a daze, unable quite to believe the encounter he had just had. He took out several sheets of paper and quickly tried to scribble down everything that his famously eloquent host had said. There was so much to remember. The elderly gentleman must have spoken for at least two hours over the course of their evening together. Yet it was with some dismay that the awestruck visitor reached just six pages of notes and could recall nothing more.

The invitation had come out of the blue earlier that very afternoon, the first Monday of February 1950. David Butler, a 25-year-old research student from Nuffield College, Oxford, was in the middle of meetings at the BBC in London, planning the first ever television results programme for the coming general election, which was just seventeen days away.

Could Mr Butler please drop what he was doing, the caller asked, and go immediately that night to talk to the Leader of the

Opposition at his home in Kent? 'Well, obviously, one accepted that sort of invitation,' Butler recalled years later. 'And I had an evening which had an enormous effect on my life.'[2]

Winston Churchill wanted to discuss a long article he'd read in *The Economist* magazine while enjoying the New Year break in Madeira, writing and painting. The article, entitled 'Electoral Facts', had been written by David Butler, but under an anonymous byline – 'By a Correspondent'. It explored the possible outcome of the looming general election, which at that point Labour Prime Minister Clement Attlee had not yet called (but was constitutionally obliged to call by the summer of 1950). Butler's article was well-written and thorough. It discussed recent by-election results, Gallup polls (then still a novelty), the effect of turnout on the outcome, and the new constituency boundaries. Most important, though, the article concluded by unveiling what appeared to be an astonishingly precise formula for calculating the ratio of seats to votes in elections – what soon became known as the Cube Law.[3] Butler had spotted that in the three previous British general elections – 1931, 1935 and 1945 – as well as in recent elections in New Zealand, the ratio of the number of seats achieved by the two main parties was related in a cubic way to the number of votes they polled. Churchill was intrigued; it seemed a revelation.

When the election was called by Attlee a few days after publication, and Churchill was obliged to make an early return from Madeira, he was curious to know more. Could the unknown author of this interesting *Economist* article be tracked down and invited to shed more light on his Cube formula? And, furthermore, to assess Churchill's chances of returning to Downing Street?

It seems extraordinary today, when general elections are intense, high-activity affairs in which leaders' long daily diaries are controlled almost to the exact minute, that the Leader of the Opposition in 1950 had a whole weekday evening to himself at home, almost on his own. Why wasn't he out campaigning, or addressing public meetings, or at least busily preparing his next speech? The relaxed approach is especially curious when one remembers that the election was expected to be very close, and there were only two and a half weeks left for campaigning. Yet here was a 25-year-old Oxford research student taking a commuter train from Charing Cross to brief someone he regarded as 'the greatest man in the world'. Although he was leaving the bustle of television production for an evening of quiet seclusion in the country, it was surely a daunting prospect.

David Butler was met around eight o'clock at Oxted Station by a driver who took him the short journey to Chartwell, Churchill's famous country home overlooking the Weald of Kent. He waited nervously in the drawing room for the great man to appear:

> I think that he had just come from his bath for he was looking implausibly flesh-tinted and flabby. The croak of many frogs rasped through his voice and so marked was the impediment in his speech ... that at the beginning I had difficulty in understanding him. The evening was full of evidence of his kindness and his idiosyncrasies. 'How very kind of you to come,' he said as he shook hands.[4]

Yet the meeting didn't get off to a promising start, Butler recalls, for Churchill 'got very quickly bored with my attempts to explain the Cube Law to him – he was not very mathematical'.[5] Most senior politicians in such circumstances today would simply thank their young visitor and dismiss them politely – there was, after all, an election to be won. But instead, Churchill expected Butler to spend the whole evening there, listening to the celebrated raconteur 'showing off'. Butler remembers Churchill 'enjoying himself and neglecting the campaign in a manner unthinkable for a party leader today'.

They ate dinner together, and were alone for almost the entire evening. They also listened to the radio election broadcast being given that night by Churchill's colleague Anthony Eden, and Butler was then asked for his verdict. It was too academic, Butler replied, not enough of a fireside chat. Churchill responded that he had never talked over people's heads in his election campaigning. Butler records him saying:

> I remember in Dundee in 1908 talking on the highest level about free trade to a working-class audience, and being carried on the shoulders of the mob back to my hotel. And in 1940 I never talked down to the British people. I offered them the hardest programme a Prime Minister has ever offered them, and it proved the most popular programme ever propounded: the programme of 'blood, toil, tears and sweat'.[6]

The visitor from Oxford told the former Prime Minister he had been only fifteen when he heard the famous speech in 1940, and it had never then occurred to Butler that Britain might be defeated by the Nazis. 'What? Only fifteen in 1940?'

At that point Churchill counted on his fingers. 'Fifteen, and that was ten years ago? Ten years ago.' And Churchill smiled. 'You haven't much time, you know. Napoleon was twenty-six when he crossed the bridge at Lodi' – a reference to the military triumph in Lombardy in 1796, which the French leader subsequently thought launched him on the road to imperial greatness.[7] 'Better hurry up, young man, better hurry up,' Churchill urged, or words to that effect.[8]

David Butler stayed overnight and left after breakfast the next day. It would be many years before he spoke publicly about that astonishing evening in February 1950 (and more details can be found in Chapter Five). Yet the Chartwell visit, he says, was 'terribly important' to his subsequent career. 'I have never been able to be in total awe of any situation or person I have encountered since then. And it all came about through the Cube Law.'[9]

Winston Churchill had already been an MP for almost half a century in 1950, having been elected in 1900, the final year of Queen Victoria's reign. He would remain in Parliament for another fourteen years. His young guest would enjoy similar longevity and would still be plying his trade almost seventy years later.

I first became aware of David Butler as a schoolboy and student in the 1970s when I started becoming interested in politics and elections. As I scanned the rows of Butler books on the politics shelves of Oxford bookshops, I wondered how one man could be so prolific and also so ubiquitous, with his regular appearances on television and in print, not just in Britain, but in America and Australia, too, and later in India. When I started attending his Friday night seminars at Nuffield College, I don't think I ever spoke to him – I was too much in awe of this famous figure. It was only when he started working as a pundit for *Channel 4 News* a few years later that I got to know him, and to appreciate how generous he could be with a very junior journalist.

The great historian Sir Lewis Namier once said: 'General elections are locks on the stream of British democracy, controlling the flow of the river and its traffic.'[10] This is the extraordinary story of the man who effectively founded the science of elections in Britain – what became known as 'psephology'. David Butler didn't confine himself to an audience of academic colleagues, however, but was determined to make elections understandable for a mass audience – to combine scholarship with journalism. It is the account of a life which has been extraordinarily busy and happy, and always lived to the full – many lives, in fact.

CHAPTER ONE

BORN TO ELECTIONS

How fitting. The man who would make his name explaining elections to the British public entered this world right in the middle of a general election campaign.

On 17 October 1924, the day of his birth, Britain was twelve days from going to the polls in the UK's third general election in less than two years. Ramsay MacDonald's first Labour government would be ousted after just nine months in office and replaced by the Conservative Party under Stanley Baldwin. Labour's election chances may have been badly dented in the final few days by the publication of the Zinoviev letter, which suggested the party was getting orders from the Bolsheviks in Russia – an early example, perhaps, of 'fake news' in an election, since the letter is now widely thought to have been forged.

The Butler family were themselves heavily involved in the electoral contest. This was still the era when graduates of Britain's most established universities elected twelve of their own Members of Parliament. David's maternal grandfather, the historian A. F. (Albert) Pollard, was standing as Liberal candidate for the University of London seat, which he'd fought unsuccessfully in both 1922 and 1923. But when the election was suddenly called, Pollard found himself stuck on a lecture tour in America (in the middle, incidentally, of the US presidential contest that saw Republican Calvin Coolidge returned to office).

Unable to return to London, Pollard delegated the running of his university campaign to his daughter, Margaret – known as Peggie – even though she was about to have a baby. In truth, her duties weren't especially onerous – mainly dealing with Pollard's election correspondence. He came a poor third, having twice been runner-up (and so abandoned his parliamentary ambitions). When the baby was born, the family sent a clever and very brief telegram to A. F. Pollard in America. It contained no text, and was addressed to 'David Bothwell', which meant she had had a baby boy called David, and that both he and his mother were well. But Peggie was slightly disappointed. 'She liked babies, but didn't want another boy,' says Butler.[1] Her first son, Michael, had been born in 1922, following two girls, Christina (1919) and Honora, known as 'Nora' (1920) – four children in less than six years.

They called the new baby David Henry Edgeworth Butler (though he would abandon the Henry as soon as he got to university). Edgeworth was from his Irish ancestors, who included the nineteenth-century novelist Maria Edgeworth and the economist Francis Edgeworth, on whose knee David was dandled as a baby. Both were substantial figures in their different ways. David's father had 'Edgeworth' as a middle name, and two of his sons would get Edgeworth as part of their names, too, almost as if the family had the double-barrelled surname 'Edgeworth-Butler'.

His Butler ancestors were so distinguished academically as to earn inclusion as one of the nine great English intellectual families identified in an essay by the historian Noel Annan.[2] The family included numerous Oxbridge dons and four headmasters of top public schools. The future Conservative Deputy Prime Minister 'Rab' Butler was David's second cousin. Rab was still studying at Cambridge in 1924, having just been president of the Union. The social reformer Josephine Butler was David's great-aunt. (See the Appendix for more details of David Butler's extraordinary ancestry.)

Harold Butler, David's father, was Professor of Latin at University

College London (UCL), where he'd succeeded the poet A. E. Housman. At Oxford, he'd been something of a poet himself, having in 1899 won the prestigious Newdigate Prize, whose previous winners included John Ruskin, Oscar Wilde and – the year before Butler – John Buchan. Harold had become a lecturer at New College at the age of just twenty-three, before moving to UCL ten years later. He was known for having an extraordinary memory, and it was said that if Harold read an article in *The Times* twice, he could then recite it verbatim afterwards. Although he served as a lieutenant and then captain in the Royal Artillery during the First World War, he never saw action. 'As a teacher,' said his *Times* obituary many years later, 'he was kindly and encouraging, providing that a real effort had been made to attain his own exacting standard of scholarship, but he had no patience with slipshod work, and his disapproving silence could sometimes be, as it was meant to be, intimidating.'[3]

It was in 1917, when he was thirty-nine, that Harold Butler married Margaret 'Peggie' Pollard, just twenty-two, who had previously been one of his students, and worked during the First World War as a nurse in various London hospitals. Since 1919, the family had lived at 16 Taviton Street in Bloomsbury, in the area around UCL, a short walk from the University Senate House. It was a tall, Georgian terraced house, for which Harold Butler had acquired a 32-year lease from the Duke of Bedford, whose estate owned many of the properties in Bloomsbury. (A modern block today stands on the site – part of the School of Slavonic and East European Studies, now subsumed into UCL.) In the early part of the twentieth century, this area was home to the Bloomsbury Group, the famous set of talented bohemian artists and friends who shocked people with their liberal lifestyles. They 'lived in squares, painted in circles, and loved in triangles', observed the American writer and wit Dorothy Parker, though the Butlers were never part of that geometry.[4]

Fifty yards south of where the old Butler home once stood, Taviton Street leads into Gordon Square, which can perhaps be regarded as the spiritual home of the Bloomsbury Group. The writer Virginia Woolf and her artist sister Vanessa Bell had lived briefly at 46 Gordon Square during the early 1900s, and the house was occupied during the 1920s and '30s by one of the most influential men of the twentieth century: John Maynard Keynes, the foremost example of an academic who exercised great influence on government affairs, not just in Britain, but globally. When David was a baby, the Butlers' nanny would trundle him in his pram down to the enclosed garden in the middle of Gordon Square, for which the family paid seven pounds a year for access. Later, David would ride his tricycle along the pavement. He recalls seeing Keynes on occasion, but the family never had any dealings with the economist. Harold Butler disapproved of his lifestyle (though he probably didn't know the extent of Keynes's bisexual promiscuity). His father was on far better terms with another member of the Bloomsbury Group, the historian Lytton Strachey, who lived at 51 Gordon Square. Today, a blue plaque on the house commemorates the whole group.

Among David Butler's early memories are occasional glimpses of George V, when the King's car passed through the streets of Bloomsbury en route to Sandringham in Norfolk. His first political memory is, at the age of six, standing outside a school polling station in St Pancras in the 1931 general election, while his mother went inside to cast her vote for the Conservative candidate in support of the National Government, the coalition led by the former Labour leader Ramsay MacDonald.

It's hard to think of a more academic milieu outside of Oxford and Cambridge. Harold Butler walked home every lunchtime from his office on Gordon Square, though despite the proximity Peggie Butler invariably complained of him being late. Nearby were the offices of the Institute of Historical Research, founded by her father, A. F. Pollard, in 1921.

Like most middle-class families of that era, the Butlers employed several servants as well as nannies. As Butler recalls, 'My father earned £1,200 a year, then up to £1,600 a year. There was little money in the family, though we were comfortably off. The servants were each paid about £200 a year. School fees were £15 a term for each of us.'[5] During one tight family squeeze in the late 1920s, they had to get rid of one of the nannies, together with a housemaid and the cook. After that, Peggie Butler cooked the family meals herself. When David went to school, she started doing voluntary social work at the Lady Margaret Hall Settlement in Lambeth, which had been founded by Harold Butler's oldest sister Olive. The settlement tried to ameliorate medical conditions for deprived children in local state schools, and she dealt with non-attendance and other social problems.

David recalls how he told his sister Nora one day, 'Mummy hasn't exactly got great beauty or charm, but she's what Daddy would call a "thoroughly good fellow".' Nora then related these remarks to their father, who was reportedly very pleased.[6] Harold Butler loved spending time with his family, and while Peggie wanted him to go lecturing in America – so that she could go too – he declined because he didn't want to be apart from his children.

David Butler's earliest recollection is of weeping (about something long forgotten) on a beach in Aberdovey in Wales in the summer of 1927, when he would have been approaching his third birthday. Harold Butler hated London and got out as often as he could. In the long summer break, the family would leave the capital for several weeks to go and stay with aunts at Beechwood, a house near Birdlip in Gloucestershire. Butler's paternal grandfather had bought the property in 1882, and then extended it, and the home seems to have been as close to a rural idyll as one could imagine. 'It was an extremely happy place,' Butler says. 'There were lots of books acquired over forty years; a large garden; but no car.' The house had no mains water. 'We had rain water accumulated and had to pump it to make sure the loos worked. It didn't have electricity either, so I learnt about trimming lamps and tidying up candles and that sort of thing.'[7]

In the evenings, like most middle-class families in the pre-television era, they played cards and their parents read to the children. 'Daddy usually read to Christina and Nora while Mummy read to Michael and me,' he says. 'Most of Dickens, some Scott, and some Shakespeare. The rhythm of the English language at its best was subconsciously absorbed by me.'[8]

The garden contained a huge sycamore tree, which stood boldly as if it were marking the very top of the Cotswolds. 'It had a rope on it and I could climb the rope rather well,' says Butler.[9] The family would go for long walks, or for rides on bicycles, which they'd brought with them on the train from London. Every day they'd visit the local farm to collect milk and eggs, and in summer they'd often help out in the fields.

Another regular holiday destination was A. F. Pollard's large home at Milford-on-Sea in Hampshire, which also held an extensive library. The house was just eighty yards from the cliffs, which looked out towards the Needles off the Isle of Wight. 'Grandfather Pollard' was a strong swimmer, and the family would change in the house then clamber over the cliffs to go swimming in the sea. Butler was 'slightly frightened' of Pollard. 'He was rather strict,' he says, 'but I didn't have a dislike for him. He would express strong views on a large number of things. He was a very wide-ranging scholar but was caustic in his views about other scholars.'[10] Pollard was a clear influence on Butler. 'I saw him, and talked to him, and heard him, and picked up books from his shelves – from the age of ten to fourteen.'[11]

Family holidays also included trips to archaeological excavations in St Albans and at Maiden Castle in Dorset, which were being carried out by Sir Mortimer Wheeler, a friend of Harold Butler at UCL. In both 1931 and 1933, they spent several weeks on the Isle of Eigg in the Hebrides, an island some of his ancestors had once owned in its entirety.

David went to Camden House Prep School in Baker Street for four terms, and he remembers one occasion when the street nearby was covered in straw to dull the noise of traffic while the famous writer Arnold Bennett lay dying in his local flat. Since Harold Butler was a governor of St Paul's, the distinguished boys' independent day school in Hammersmith, it seemed an obvious choice for the Butlers to send all their children to St Paul's and its sister school for girls. But first, from about the age of seven, David and his older brother Michael attended Colet Court, the St Paul's preparatory school, which had about 400 pupils. This involved a simple journey from Euston Square every morning along the Metropolitan Line. It provided the boys with exciting train-spotting opportunities at Paddington Station, where the line comes out of the tunnel into the open air and runs parallel to the Great Western tracks for about a mile. The Tube train would pass King-class steam locomotives at the end of the Paddington platforms, stoking up to start their journeys west, and there was also an engine stabling yard just outside the mainline station. David and Michael, like many young boys of that era, would then underline the numbers and names of locos they'd seen in published handbooks which listed every railway engine in Britain.

Among David Butler's contemporaries at Colet Court was the future actor, broadcaster and comedy performer Nicholas Parsons, who was a year older, and recalls the ten- and eleven-year-old Butler walking with him round the playground earnestly discussing great political issues of the day, such as the abdication crisis, and the build-up to what would become the Second World War. 'Obviously from a very early age he was deeply interested in politics. He had great knowledge for a youngster,' says Parsons. 'It fired me up to be interested in current affairs. I remember talking to him about Abyssinia, and the Italian invasion, and what would happen next.'[12]

When Conservative leader Stanley Baldwin, Prime Minister of the coalition National Government, called an election in 1935, Colet

Court held a mock election. David says he voted Conservative (as his parents probably did that year) but was rather disappointed that an older boy was chosen as Tory contender instead of him. The Conservative candidate at Colet Court collected almost 80 per cent of the vote, he remembers. After that, 'I was hooked on elections. I absorbed all the 1935 constituency figures, and then went back to 1931 and 1929. I looked for close results and lost deposits.'[13]

It was also around 1935 that Butler began his long relationship with broadcasting – through listening to the BBC. 'When Grandmother Pollard died in 1934, my mother inherited some money, and we bought a radio. I would sneak in and listen to the news or to variety programmes.'[14] Although the BBC began broadcasting its television service in 1936, it would be another decade before he actually saw a TV set in operation.

David Butler also recalls 'going out with the Silver Jubilee crowds' in May 1935, and then, eight months later, he got 'tangled up in the funeral of George V, but didn't see very much'.[15] Butler was at Colet Court on 11 December 1936 when Edward VIII delivered his abdication speech on the radio – the headmaster had installed loudspeakers in the school hall so that everyone could hear the King's live broadcast. 'I remember being told about it a few days ahead. We didn't see the popular papers at home – they had started hinting about it in October. So, we only knew about a full-scale crisis for about ten days. We were not insiders. It came out of the blue.' There was no sense of shock, he says, but later 'there was a sense that Wallis Simpson would not have been a desirable queen'.[16] The day after Edward VIII abdicated, he recalls, 'our maid came up to our bedrooms at 7.15 a.m. and showed us *The Times* with black borders'.

The following year, 1937, David visited the House of Commons for the first time, and he recollects how he and his father looked down from the public gallery to see Prime Minister Neville Chamberlain on the green benches below, along with his most famous living predecessor, David Lloyd George.

David also took prominent roles in school drama, acting alongside Nicholas Parsons and the future broadcaster and Liberal MP Clement Freud. It seems astonishing today that a national newspaper should have been interested in the drama productions of prep schools, but in March 1936 the *Daily Telegraph* published a short review of Colet Court's *A Midsummer Night's Dream*. 'The result was charming,' wrote the reviewer, who concluded with the words, 'D. H. E. Butler was a most puckish Puck.'[17] David Butler was still only eleven, and this was probably his first ever mention in the national press. The Butler family were keen theatregoers and often visited the Tavistock Little Theatre in Bloomsbury, or the Old Vic in Waterloo, where they saw the rising star Laurence Olivier on several occasions.

Butler says he didn't know he was 'reasonably clever' until he came first in arithmetic around 1936, when he received the *Complete Works of Shakespeare* as a prize.[18] English was another of his best subjects – he came fourth out of twenty-one boys in his first year, 1932, and third out of fourteen in his final year, 1938. He was also an excellent story-writer. In January 1936, he wrote a long detective mystery called 'The Glass Bird, or Murder, Money and Monomania', about a series of strange deaths. The story is extremely advanced for an eleven-year-old, with a good plot, extensive vocabulary and a surprising knowledge of London and institutions such as the Royal Academy and coroners' courts.[19] The central character is Henry Augustus Jade, a Royal Academy member who seems to be loosely based on Augustus John, the bohemian artist who was a fellow of UCL. Harold Butler was so proud of his son's story that he typed it up himself and bound the work in a hardback folder.

David Butler was quite fond of sport, too. He even won two school gymnastic contests at Colet Court, and played rugby fives, and then occasionally for a school XV when he went to St Paul's, though he was never a dazzling success at team games. In cricket, his highest score was just eight and, rather than on the pitch, it was as team scorer that David excelled, reflecting his passion for numbers.

Harold Butler would regularly take his son to the Varsity match at Twickenham or to Test matches. Almost eighty years later, Butler would retain extraordinarily detailed memories of going with schoolmates to the Ashes Test at Lords in 1938, where they saw Wally Hammond rescue England with an innings of 240. 'England were 31–3, then Hammond got 70 between 11.30 and 1 p.m.; 70 between 1.45 and 4.15; 70 runs after tea, and then he got 30 the following day.' Every spring, David bought a copy of *Wisden*, the distinctive yellow almanac of first-class cricket over the previous twelve months; he loved juggling with cricket statistics and calculating batting and bowling averages. 'I knew all the cricket statistics from 1935 to 1939, then statistics dried up when war broke out.'[20] He even claims to have had the knack of recalculating a batsman or bowler's average ball by ball as the game progressed.

In 1938, after six years, David left Colet Court. His father had put his son down for Rugby, where Harold himself had gone, but the family instead chose St Paul's, where brother Michael was already a pupil, and David was awarded a scholarship. This should have relieved the family of school fees, but Harold Butler disapproved of scholarships and so carried on paying them. The St Paul's uniform was 'suitable for the late Victorian City', recalled contemporary Denis Gildea, with 'black coat, pinstripe trousers, white shirt, stiff white collar, black tie and black and white school cap. In summer, we wore straw boaters with a school ribbon.'[21] Boys who were more than six feet tall, or who were in the final year, could wear bowler hats – but if they did so, they had to carry an umbrella too.

In his first two years at St Paul's, Butler concentrated on his father's field, classics, but switched at the age of fifteen to what the school called Modern Special. This involved classes in literature, languages and history, but also more advanced subjects for secondary schools at that time, such as economics, politics, philosophy and psychology. Another contemporary, Richard Mayne, who was in the same class as Butler (and went on to work for Jean Monnet, one of the architects of modern Europe), described it as being like the Oxford University PPE course – philosophy, politics and economics. In his memoirs, Mayne wrote that 'one exciting term', an opinion poll was held in class, 'chiefly organised by a quick, darting boy called by us "Fanny" Butler, though properly known by his initials D. H. E.' Sadly, Mayne's book didn't explain where 'Fanny' came from.[22] The poll sounds highly innovative given that the first professional opinion polls – by Dr George Gallup – arrived in Britain only in 1938. Butler remembers the exercise, and says it was inspired by Gallup's early polling work, though he merely asked thirty or forty boys in the playground a few non-political questions.

Mayne and Butler have both said that one of the most impressive and influential of their masters was W. H. Eynon Smith, 'a totally eccentric teacher', says Butler, 'who would make a monstrous statement, and then say, "Now, prove this is false." I think he had thirteen boys in his history class and ten got awards to Oxford or Cambridge. He was seen as a genius.'[23] Smith would usually wear a grey check jacket and often a garish red tie, along with bottle-green corduroy trousers tucked into black boots. 'Eynon's voice was normally quiet, calm, and civilised,' Richard Mayne wrote,

> and the tone of our time with him was essentially 'rational' – one of his favourite words … For us, rationality became a catchword for the intellectual integrity he sought to instil, basing judgement on all the available facts, or suspending it if the facts were insufficient … He urged us to exclude all but the cogent, relevant arguments, to ask pointed questions, and not to be put off by emotional pressure or self-regarding temptation. He encouraged open discussion, but refused to let it degenerate into an argument or a merely two-sided debate.[24]

Sadly, Eynon Smith would be killed in a London bombing raid towards the end of the Second World War.

Another great influence on Butler was Walter Oakeshott, who was high master – the St Paul's equivalent of headmaster – throughout the war years, and later became Rector of Lincoln College, Oxford, and Vice-Chancellor of the university. 'He was incredibly energetic,' Butler says, 'very much a hero to me – a super man, wise and interesting.'[25] Oakeshott was tall and scholarly looking, known for his beaming smile and natural courtesy, and despite his heavy workload as high master, he tried to teach as many classes in school as he could for one period a week.

> And he was exciting. I remember during the Norway campaign in 1940, he gave a beautiful exposition of how we were going to lose Norway, quite early in the campaign. If I was asked for the person in my life I had most admired, I think it would be Walter Oakeshott.[26]

Walter Oakeshott's biggest achievement at St Paul's was successfully overseeing the school's wartime evacuation and its return to Hammersmith six years later. By 1938, war with Nazi Germany looked highly likely, though the Munich Agreement that September at least gave schools time to plan for the possibility of hostilities, and to prepare an operation to evacuate from London. Oakeshott arranged for St Paul's to occupy Easthampstead Park, a Victorian mansion near Crowthorne in Berkshire, which was rearranged to house classrooms, the library, dining facilities and school offices. And Wellington College, the public school which was about four miles away, let St Paul's share their science laboratories and playing fields. The plan was that once war was declared, everyone would be moved to Berkshire immediately. During the run-up to war, the assumption was that London would be attacked almost at once, and, in Denis Gildea's words, 'We all expected to be blasted to smithereens by Guernica-style bombing in the first week, so that transport would be in chaos.'[27]

Accordingly, St Paul's organised pupils to get to Crowthorne by bicycle from a series of meeting points in west London, and even carried out dress rehearsals, which involved David and Michael Butler completing half the journey by cycling out as far as Staines. Boys without bikes were expected to walk to Crowthorne, with an overnight stop en route. Spare clothing and emergency food rations for each pupil were sent ahead to Easthampstead and stored there in readiness.

In the event, when Britain declared war on 3 September 1939, the Butlers were on holiday in Shropshire, so they simply cycled the eighty or so miles down to the house in Birdlip in Gloucestershire, and remained there while Peggie Butler looked after a family who had been evacuated from London, and David and Michael did a milk round for a local farmer. It was two weeks before the boys set off for Crowthorne by train.

St Paul's acquired about ten houses in the Crowthorne area to accommodate around thirty pupils and staff in each, with five or six to a bedroom. These were large, comfortable properties, some of which belonged to retired colonels who had been at the military academy at nearby Sandhurst or the staff college in Camberley. Butler, though, was assigned to Meadhurst, the home of a warder at Broadmoor Criminal Lunatic Asylum, as the high-security psychiatric hospital was known at that time. In effect, St Paul's had become a temporary boarding school. Having people spread over a large area, with everyone relying on bicycles, was far from satisfactory, and during the heavy snows of 1940, pupils were confined for several weeks to their houses, receiving very little tuition.

Even in tranquil Berkshire, St Paul's knew it was vulnerable to attack. Trenches were dug in the school grounds, for use in case of air raids, and sandbags were filled for emergencies. Easthampstead Park was also used by the Army, which erected several Nissen huts.

And, in 1941, the Army's presence may have been the reason a series of German bombs were dropped along the main drive, one of which hit the lodge at the front gate. The school's long-standing Officer Training Corps was renamed the Junior Training Corps (JTC), and in 1941 even had an inspection from Old Boy Lt General Bernard Montgomery, who was reportedly extra-rigorous and 'looked at everyone's haircut'.[28] St Paul's also set up its own Home Guard platoon, comprising about sixty boys. 'We were issued with new American rifles with a jutting barrel and .300 bore,' said Denis Gildea.

> We wore the normal Second [World] War battledress and kept our rifles at home. We had to take turns to guard the company headquarters at night. It was an old shed in the middle of Crowthorne where our ammunition was stored. We each did nearly two hours alone outside on sentry duty.[29]

David Butler recalls being out on patrol one night as a lowly assistant ARP warden. 'I was bicycling along the edge of the grounds and saw a bomb go down. And the next thing we heard was that the headmaster of Wellington had been killed.'[30] The German bomb had landed directly on his home.

While David was boarding in Crowthorne, his parents had moved to mid-Wales, as Harold Butler was placed in charge of a part of University College London that was evacuated to Aberystwyth. The family's London home was left deserted for three years before they sold it in 1942. So for almost four years David Butler's family home was in the Welsh seaside resort, until his father retired and his parents moved to Leatherhead in Surrey in 1943. This was as far from London as Peggie Butler would allow Harold to live, as she decided to return to her social work at the Lady Margaret Hall Settlement in Lambeth.

In his final years at St Paul's, Butler took part in several extracurricular activities that gave small clues to his future career as a public performer who was fascinated by politics. The school magazine, *The Pauline*, gave a hint of Butler's later lifestyle when it described him in the Union debating society as a 'Puritan … crusader against nicotine and lewdness'.[31] Acting in the farce *Old Moore's Almanac*, he was considered 'a very sinister Evelyn Tent'.[32] And in the Essay Society he read 'a lengthy treatise' on 'conflict'.[33]

School reports sent to his parents from his final term at St Paul's, autumn 1942, suggest, however, that David Butler was not an outstanding pupil. His history master, Charles Lillingston, wrote:

> He has many very nice traits, but he is a bit whimsical, puerile, & I think probably suffers from having elder sisters! Some also think he is a trifle selfish. Personally I think he is essentially a very nice but shy person who only needs confidence to bring him out.

To Frank Parker, who taught French, David was 'still bright but has lost liveliness & not come up to the promise of last year. Does not take the same trouble he used to. I have too little time & contact with him to hazard the cause.' Another history master wrote:

> He appears to have latent talent, which occasionally emerges in his written work or in his remarks in form. But on the whole, he has struck me as rather erratic in his style, slightly superficial in his argument, and generally nervous in his all-round behaviour. He is still generally somewhat puerile – both mentally and physically – and has passed through a bad phase altogether; this, no doubt, is responsible for the comparatively low standard of his work while I knew him. But, as one very good essay he produced demonstrates, he has got the stuff, and it is to be hoped that it will not be long before he will show it.

'Chalky' Lancaster, who ran the Junior Training Corps, concluded: 'A bit lumpish in JTC – just waking up (too late) to the chances it offers to develop oneself. Passed Cert A – Lance Cpl (*honoris causa*).' As for sport, T. C. Martin wrote that David was 'an undistinguished athlete, but has been keen on cricket and played loyally for his club'.[34]

To be fair, David faced stiff academic competition from his contemporaries. Then, as now, St Paul's educated many of the sons of the London upper-middle-class elite, people whose parents did not wish, or could not afford, to send them away to board at one of the country's top public schools.

Despite such discouraging remarks from teachers in his final year, David Butler applied to the Oxford college where his father had once taught classics (and where Michael was already an undergraduate), and he travelled to New College that December to take the scholarship exam in history. He won an exhibition, or half-scholarship. While Harold Butler seems to have pulled a few strings, David would probably have been admitted to Oxford or Cambridge anyway on the strength of his exam performance.

A week before Christmas 1942, David Butler got a letter from L. G. Wickham Legg, a senior history fellow at the college who had known his father, formally saying the college would accept him. But the correspondence in the college archive suggests David showed rather a casual attitude to the whole thing, for he then gave the letter to his father to send back a formal reply, and to confirm he would be taking up his place. In his response, Harold Butler then explained to his old colleague how David had actually handed over Legg's original letter to him while they were out at the theatre.

If one ex-fellow of the college writing to a current fellow wasn't incestuous enough, Harold Butler actually used a piece of New College headed paper to write the acceptance letter on behalf of his son (even though he had not been a fellow of the college for many years). Unusually, because of wartime, David wasn't going to wait until the start of the academic year to go up to Oxford, but would go almost at once, in January. And yet, only four weeks before the start of term, David wasn't sure whether he was going to read modern history. 'He will probably wish to take Modern Greats,' Harold Butler reported, 'but has not definitely made up his mind.'[35]

Butler did indeed pick Modern Greats, better known these days by its proper title, philosophy, politics and economics – PPE. The course had been founded as recently as 1920, initially as a way to teach philosophy outside the traditional 'Greats' course, which also involved Greek and Latin literature and classical history. Hence PPE became known initially as 'Modern Greats'.

Studying PPE at New College would bring David Butler into contact with one of the greatest minds of the twentieth century. It would also start a close lifelong friendship with one of the most controversial figures in Labour Party history.

CHAPTER TWO

GUNG-HO FOR WAR

Arriving at New College early in January 1943, Butler was given a room on the top floor of the Robinson Tower, above the main gate to the college on Holywell Street, a steep climb of 104 steps. They're said to be the highest undergraduate rooms in Oxford, with a majestic panorama over the city's ancient spires and famous quadrangles.

Butler has often described how, in his first week, 'a man charged into the room and said, "Ah, you're Butler, aren't you? I'm Benn. We're doing tutorials together."'

It was Anthony Wedgwood Benn, son of Viscount Stansgate, who had been Secretary of State for India in the 1929–31 Labour government, having switched from being a Liberal MP to Labour. Benn, who had also gone to a top London independent day school, Westminster, would attend economics tutorials with Butler at New College on and off between 1943 and their final graduation in 1947. They would keep in touch for more than seventy years, until Benn's death in 2014. Although David Butler didn't have much time for Benn's increasingly left-wing politics in later years, he has always said Tony Benn was his closest lifelong friend.

Oxford in 1943 had around 2,600 students, barely a tenth of the university's population today, and even in wartime more than two-thirds of them were men. David Butler had to cram three terms of work into two terms in order to catch up with Benn and other colleagues at New College who had gone up in October 1942. Butler did both politics and economics that year, and in the summer of 1943, he got a second on his preliminary papers in both subjects (in an era when firsts were rare). He did no philosophy, however – that was a challenge for later.

Because of the war, many normal procedures at Oxford had been suspended, and David Butler knew his undergraduate career would almost inevitably be interrupted by military service, but he was keen to make the most of his time. Despite the pressure to catch up with colleagues who had started PPE the previous term, he still pursued various outside activities. Like many students who enjoy seeing a variety of political speakers, he joined all three main political clubs – Conservative, Labour and Liberal – and also the renowned Oxford Union debating society. He spoke twice in debates in 1943 but chose not to stand in Union elections. 'I didn't altogether like the scramble,' he says, preferring to leave that to his New College friend Anthony Wedgwood Benn, and another New College man, Peter Blaker (both of whom subsequently became presidents of the Union and, later, MPs). And, on two days a week during 1943, Butler also did military training for his Certificate B qualification to become an Army officer.

It was under the shadow of war that David Butler took up poetry, following in the steps of his award-winning father. His earliest surviving poem, entitled 'A Glimpse of Reality', was produced after only a few weeks at New College. Written, in his words, 'from the top of the Robinson Tower', it suggests he felt somewhat aloof from his undergraduate colleagues and rather enjoyed the life of a scholar in a garret. The opening verse reads:

> Far underneath the sounds of ribald mirth,
> The trivial fooleries of youth at play.
> But what care I? They know not what I think.
> I am alone apart, halfway to heaven,

Perceiving things to them invisible.
All common things are naught and naught exists
Save moon and stars and lofty towers and I.
– 'A GLIMPSE OF REALITY', OXFORD,
FEBRUARY 1943[1]

After just two terms at New College, and still only eighteen, Butler duly joined the Army in September 1943 and spent much of 1944 at the Military Academy at Sandhurst in Berkshire, only a few miles from the evacuated St Paul's.

In later life, David Butler rarely talked about his brief war service unless prompted, though he admits his Army career was far from traumatic. He simply feels his two-year stint as a soldier had no influence at all on his subsequent life. His six months at Sandhurst were a 'quite congenial' experience, he says, training with friends he'd got to know through military activities at Oxford. And he learnt to drive before he passed out from Sandhurst in September 1944; he then went to Kirkcudbright in the Scottish borders for tactical work. But his papers got lost in the system, which meant he couldn't actually start active service in his assigned regiment – C Squadron of the Staffordshire Yeomanry.

The weeks and months of waiting were surprisingly anguished. 'I was very enthusiastic,' he says – indeed, he often uses the term 'gung-ho' – and he was extremely disappointed about the bureaucratic delay which was excluding him from the action. 'I was going down to Great Yarmouth in a train, and I saw the Arnhem operation going on, with gliders being towed to drop troops there. And I was horrified – I thought the war was going to end before I could get into it.'[2]

The famous Battle of Arnhem was part of Bernard Montgomery's ambitious Operation Market Garden in September 1944 to try to end the war by Christmas, by taking a series of eight bridges in the Netherlands and Germany, including bridges over the Rhine.

This had been part of a pincer movement by British and American forces to encircle the industrial Ruhr, but, as shown in the film *A Bridge Too Far*, the Allies met stiff and growing German resistance over the last bridge at Arnhem. Market Garden was a serious failure which meant that, during the winter of 1944–45, Dutch people suffered terrible famine in those parts of the Netherlands that were still in German hands. Allied victory still looked inevitable, but the end of hostilities was probably delayed by about six months.

At least that gave David Butler more of a chance to take part in the action. Some of his experiences are documented in the censored letters he sent home to his parents, and which his father – ever the secretary-cum-historian – typed up for posterity.

'Life is now a strange unreal dream,' he wrote from Southampton in November 1944, as he prepared to set sail, relieved that his war was under way at last. 'I don't really believe it. I don't really believe it. I write from the unknown and can give no address.'[3]

A day or so later, having finally departed, he told of having spent his last night in England 'under canvas in the most utter frigidity and misery'. Later that day, he lamented, 'I have eaten nothing – merely superintended the feeding of hungry troopers in an overcrowded ship.' He admitted to a 'complete failure to feel sentimental at leaving England', only to add once they set foot in Belgium, 'If my departing from England was uninspiring, my welcome to the Continent was worse. An icy driving drizzle beat in our faces. Miserable houses and the twin spires of a cathedral peered through the mist … Now I am in a German barracks eating grapes at 18 [francs] a kilo.'[4]

The cathedral with 'twin spires' was almost certainly the Belgian port of Ostend. What astonished Butler most was the abundance of products in the shops: 'The temptations were very great – fountain pens and fruit, washing cases and clothing – all in the utmost profusion.' Nor did there seem any shortage of food. 'The bakeries had plenty of bread,' he noticed, and the people didn't look either ill-fed or ill-clothed:

> Plenty wore only clogs or wooden-soled shoes, but on the other hand, the women all wore what to my unskilful eye appeared to be silk stockings. Outwardly at any rate this town and its people appear to have recovered from the worst privations of war … It's odd to be living in a German barracks, cooked for and served by waiters who three months ago were doing precisely the same for their enemies. Life is still a dream. I am not sure that I believe it.[5]

A few days afterwards, Butler tells of going into Brussels with a companion from the regiment, on an errand in search of someone who knew his friend's uncle. But the contact had moved, and so they spent most of the evening chasing all over Brussels by tram:

> In three hours wandering in the dark – we made seven tram journeys (trams are free to us) and had twelve major conversations with all sorts … from a black-marketeer to an underground worker reluctantly carrying a bazooka to hand over to the police. Every single person we spoke to was charming to us – if we asked the way nothing would content them unless they set us on what they thought was the correct tram – fortunately they were generally wrong, so that our wanderings were delightfully protracted … discussing the war and the Flemish problem – explaining the latter in comparison with Wales – discussing the Boche and the resistance movement, discussing the black market and the bombing, discussing the tramway system and the differences and practicalities of our languages.[6]

It was an early sign of the inquisitive journalist in David Butler, eager to talk to and question everyone he meets, curious about the lives of others, and how they fit within the political and historical framework. Butler seemed overwhelmed by the sense of camaraderie, exhilarated at the way the hardship of war bred friendship. He felt his trip into Brussels was one of the most worthwhile and memorable evenings of his life. 'There is an element of intoxication about everything over here,' he wrote. 'The nearer to the battle-line, one finds everyone on the top of their form, talkative, joyous, active.' Normally he was 'rather shy' of strangers, he wrote. 'But here I have no inhibitions. We tried the policy of universal friendship with incredible, riotous success.'[7]

In his early weeks in Belgium and southern Holland with the Staffordshires, Butler seems to have been underemployed. His only real task was to censor the men's letters:

> At first it was quite interesting and, while it's still better than doing nothing, one gets rather tired of it. Not five people in a hundred write anything of any interest to anyone outside their families and sometimes not even to them … I shouldn't sneer. Actually, they're usually pleasant little pictures of various types of home, blurred only by their inarticulateness. But to the censorer [*sic*] there's an insufferable sameness about the lot, or almost the lot.[8]

Butler had gone out to the Low Countries as a second lieutenant and a tank commander. The Staffordshire Yeomanry, also known as the Queen's Own Royal Regiment, had been founded in 1794 as a volunteer force, and it always remained part of the part-time Territorial Army. Butler's section of the regiment – C Squadron – was based in Burton-on-Trent in Staffordshire, though he had no personal connection with Burton or the county.

The Staffordshire Yeomanry had spent the early part of the Second World War in the Middle East, initially in Palestine, using cavalry to quell the fighting between Arabs and Jews. The horses were soon replaced with tanks and armoured vehicles, and the Staffordshires then played a leading role in the North Africa campaign, and the battles of Alam El Halfa and El Alamein in 1942. This was followed by their participation in D-Day in June 1944, and six weeks of fighting, before the regiment was ordered back to England for specialist and highly secret training on a lake near Great Yarmouth in Suffolk.

Men who had gone through all this fighting and risked their lives on numerous occasions were now suddenly under the command of a young man fresh from training who had no experience of real war at all. Butler says:

> It was an astonishing thing, and I can never understand how the troops I commanded could tolerate it. They were battle-hardened; they'd been through the Western Desert; they'd been in the Normandy Landings, and here was this extremely green young man commanding four tanks … Mercifully, I didn't manage to kill any of my people.[9]

A poem Butler wrote, 'In Bitterness of Spirit: Christmas 1944', suggests he found it as difficult to join the men he commanded in social activity as he had his undergraduate colleagues at New College:

> They drank, they shouted, roistered. I,
> Being inexperienced, looked on amazed
> And drank with them. I learnt how time could fly
> On sodden wings. I watched and found new ways
> Of wasting health and wealth, of squandering life,
> How they think all this good, look back with pride
> On bygone nights of noise and drunken strife
> With self-control, intelligence denied.
>
> I watched and shared till, in a flash of light,
> The bitter hopeless self-escape stood clear.
> The hollow laughter and the futile fight
> Against themselves lay pitifully bare.
> Yet they are decent citizens and free.
> I may not judge. But such is not for me.
>
> – 'In Bitterness of Spirit: Christmas 1944',
> Sluiskil, Zeeland, 1944[10]

The Staffordshire Yeomanry's specialist assignment was to operate a group of DD [Duplex Drive] amphibious tanks – converted Sherman tanks which were known as 'Donald Duck tanks' and proved to be one of the great secret successes of the D-Day landings. Each tank was kept afloat by a screen, or skirt, which was inflated by compressed air. As Butler relates, 'These amphibious tanks were great canvas buckets, strung on top of a kind of curtain above the tracks of a Sherman tank. And at the back, driven by the tank tracks, but standing outside the tracks, were two propellers.'[11]

On D-Day, many of these tanks had plunged into the sea several miles from the French coast and sailed towards the Normandy beaches with very few mishaps. Now the fleet of amphibious tanks was to be greatly expanded to help the Allied armies cross the great rivers of north-west Europe, notably the Rhine, where passage was very difficult after all the bridges had been blown up by the retreating German Army.

The idea of using floating tanks for river crossings was clever in theory but physically complicated in practice, and more difficult than landing from sea on a gently sloping beach. A tank couldn't just trundle down to a large river and sail across. There was often a wide, very muddy shoreline to consider, and ramps might be needed to reach the water. Once on the river, the vehicles could easily be swept downstream by strong currents, or impeded by unexpected obstacles below the surface. Landing the tank on the opposite bank could be even more perilous. To help overcome these problems, the amphibious tanks would be aided by DUKWs – known as 'ducks' – amphibious trucks of the type which still operate as 'Duck Tours' on the Thames in London.

When David Butler finally joined his regiment in Belgium, they were based at Den Abeele, just inland from the port of Ostend. As a tank commander, he was in charge of both his own tank of four people – comprising himself, driver, gunner and radio operator – and three other tanks as well, putting him in charge of sixteen people in all. During the final weeks of 1944 and early weeks of 1945, they visited several different locations for training exercises, both on land and on water. Only rarely did they suffer enemy attack.

In January 1945, they were sent to the small village of Meers on the river Maas (or Meuse) in Limbourg, a strange crooked finger of territory in south-east Holland which pokes southwards between eastern Belgium and Germany. The stretch of the Maas here, just north of what would become the politically famous town of Maastricht, was reckoned to be very similar in topography to the spot where it was planned they would eventually cross the Rhine.

It was a time for experimenting with the tanks and DUKWs, for testing new devices, and for gradually putting together plans for the Rhine crossing. The Yeomanry's historian describes how the river at Meers was full of hazards, 'for there was a very fast-flowing current throughout the many acute bends, which resulted in one stretch of its course being something akin to rapids, and on which many a tank ran into trouble'.[12] Worse still, Butler and his colleagues experienced atrocious weather at that time, as a thaw melted the ice and snow, and the rapidly rising waters flooded adjacent fields, and C Squadron's entire tank park at one point, leaving behind sticky mud. The regimental war diary related almost daily mishaps. One tank was stranded in midstream overnight and couldn't be dislodged; another got out of control and floated downstream and crashed into the ferry at Maasband, the next town.

Then, in a similar incident, on Tuesday 6 February, Butler was commanding his tank through the flooded fields and across the river. The official war diary reported:

> Calamity occurred when Lieut. Butler, with Lieut. Biddle aboard, took up some obstacle into his props [propellers], and his steering went wrong. The tank went sailing down-stream with the DUKW in attendance, but could not land or gain hardly any control over the steering. Recovery vehicles and the ambulance

> went shooting off along the bank towards Maasband, and by this time the drifting tank was in the area of Maasband. It hit the protruding groyne broadside on, and immediately tipped over and eventually capsized. The Tank Commander & Lieut. Biddle and the operator were thrown into the water – the driver got out of the tank after a struggle and without being able to use the A&EA [breathing] equipment. The whole crew were picked up by Capt. Stewart in the DUKW, and the subsequent heavy rum ration soon put them to sleep!!! Remainder of the training was cancelled.[13]

David Butler's own recollection is that:

> As we went over the flooded fields, my propellers got tangled up with barbed wire, and when the tank got into the river I couldn't control it. I had a big tiller at the back which would direct the propellers, so we were swept down the Maas for about a mile. We were going sideways, and the tank tracks hit a groyne where they go out into the river, and it tipped over, and I was flung into the Maas.[14]

Butler managed to stand up on the tank, which was now on its side, but he feared his rather portly driver, 'Smudger' Smith, might be stuck inside the vehicle, until suddenly he emerged unscathed. Disaster was averted, and everyone returned to base safely. Butler was summoned before Major General Percy Hobart, the man who, in preparation for D-Day, had developed amphibious tanks and various other ingenious armoured vehicles, which acquired the nickname 'Hobart's Funnies'.

> He said, 'Mr Butler, you know that was very gallant in trying to stay with your tank, but you know what happens when a man in the Navy loses his ship? He never gets command of another ship

> again.' And I said, 'But I didn't. I was told to stay with my tank, and I couldn't control anything, so it wasn't steering. It was totally immobile.' He said, 'I wasn't told that.'[15]

Butler was sent away, brought back and told he would be all right. 'So, my great achievement was sinking a tank, but it was not an enemy tank; it was one of our own!'[16]

Fortunately, once the waters of the river Maas receded, Butler's tank was recovered, and the incident did him no lasting harm. Less than a month later, he was appointed signal officer for the squadron.

C Squadron was participating as part of the 21st Army group in Operation Plunder, Montgomery's attempt to succeed where Market Garden failed, and to cross the Rhine on the night of 23 March 1945. It was planned as the last great Anglo-American military operation of the European conflict, and it would prove to be David Butler's only substantial war engagement. Earlier that week, preparations were already in full swing to cross the river near the town of Rees, about twenty-five miles east of Nijmegen. The regimental war diary reports how their brigadier visited C Squadron that day while the men were 'in the middle of a meal of pork, provided by two pigs who wandered into the squadron area and dropped dead!!!'[17] At midnight 'on a cold moonlit night', the tanks moved into the 'inflation area', where their skirts were due to be filled with air, only for them to suffer 'heavy shelling' almost immediately, and for three tanks, including Butler's, to have their skirts 'ripped by flying shrapnel'.[18]

An hour earlier, thousands of infantrymen in amphibious Buffalo transporters and assault boats had already crossed the river. C Squadron followed three hours later at 2 a.m., 'under the constant whine of the thousands of shells streaming from our guns which lined the west bank'.[19] But the operation did not go entirely to plan. Three tanks sank in the river and eight more got stuck in the mud on the far bank, and it was hours before they could be pulled out.

'Fighting all day was hard and bitter,' according to the officers' diary. Two captains from C Squadron were killed, both by shrapnel, and five men were wounded. Yet the intense spell seems to have lasted only about twenty-four hours, and the squadron's work was broadly a success. A bridge was built across the river, and by 25 March 'a flood of vehicles and guns etc. commenced coming across'.[20]

Some tank crews suffered the small humiliation of having to cross the Rhine by ferry. These included David Butler's group. His account is that the driver of his amphibious tank claimed the vehicle wasn't working. Butler suspects this was a lie and that the real problem was that the driver was nervous of his leadership skills. So, they were given a non-amphibious tank to cross by ferry instead. Ahead of his vehicle, two other tanks rolled onto the ferry, only for it to sink, and so the tanks then had to be pulled out of the water.

The advance across the river by Butler and his men had been just a tiny part of Operation Plunder, which involved tens of thousands of British, Canadian and American troops, as well as vehicles, artillery, equipment and supplies, crossing this stretch of the Rhine – British forces on the north-western stretch of the river, Americans on the south-eastern – backed by planes, gliders and parachute drops. Winston Churchill visited several locations during the operation, including a brief excursion to part of the German riverbank.

A historian of the Staffordshire Yeomanry's role in Operation Plunder claims:

> We initially achieved complete surprise, for it was proved that as soon as the enemy found that tanks were supporting the leading forces at such an early hour in the operation, they lost a good deal of their taste for battle, and the following support divisions were able to break out of the initial bridgehead much earlier, and with far fewer casualties than had been anticipated.[21]

Even after the successful crossing of the Rhine, there were still parts of north-eastern Holland under German occupation. David Butler and his men took part in the liberation of several towns and villages along the Dutch–German border, and around the river Ems. In Enschede, the liberation took only a few hours, and they met little resistance, but the owners of the famous Bols gin factory in the town thanked their English liberators generously. 'I was doing something else,' Butler recalls, 'and I came back and found three of my tanks and my soldiers were all flat-out drunk. Each trooper had been given a case of gin.'

Despite the problems with his driver on the Rhine, he experienced few other difficulties commanding men who were generally older and more experienced than him in the ways of the world. 'The men were good to me, and I was obviously so young. I was a totally green twenty-year-old,' he says. 'My driver had some contempt for me, but I had no humiliating memories from my Army career.' As for the lifestyle of the men under his command, Butler says he was 'aware of the sexual activities of others, but for me it remained a virginal two years in the Army'.[22]

His war was really 'trivial', he insists, only nine months' service – seven of them in Europe – and just three days of what he calls 'blood and thunder', just as victory was within the Allies' grasp. 'We knew we were winning. There's nothing brave about my war record. I could have gone on fighting. I enjoyed my war, and was very gung-ho.'[23] He says he was never frightened, though did occasionally reflect that he 'might be dead tomorrow'.

In one incident, just after Enschede and beyond the German town of Lingen-on-Ems, he is fairly sure he killed someone. Coming under heavy artillery fire while going along a sparsely populated road, the tank suffered a 'ping' to its turret from the direction of a breeze-block shed. 'It was a mechanical thing,' he says.

> I said to my gunner, 'Traverse right. Knock that shed down.' It was an absolute necessity, an automatic action ... The shed was in

> some woodland to the right of the tanks, which were advancing in a column. It just collapsed completely. The man might have survived for all I know, but I doubt it. It was to save anybody coming behind me being shot by this man.[24]

'There was no alternative,' Butler wrote in 2000. 'But I am sometimes, perhaps all too rarely, troubled because for the only time in my life, I killed a fellow human being.'[25]

A few days later, Butler was assigned to assault a village in pursuit of retreating Germans. As infantrymen advanced across open ground, he and his men gave covering fire with machine guns and 75mm shells, and he fired towards the village church. 'I don't think the shells did much damage, but the foot-soldiers seemed grateful. There was no resistance – it was late April 1945 and the war was nearly over.' Then, to his horror, an hour later, he heard a *Te Deum* coming from the target church, where it suddenly became clear that all the villagers were huddled together. It was Butler's last day of action.[26]

A section of C Squadron had been assigned to take part in another river crossing – of the Elbe – but Butler wasn't among them. Instead, he spent the final weeks of the war in Europe in the riverside village of Stedden, about forty miles north-east of Hanover, from which the local population had been cleared out of their homes. Here, David Butler took very little part in the final hostilities of the war, and after VE Day, on 8 May 1945, the soldiers had even less to do. Most days were taken up with kit inspections, boating and swimming on the river, football and other sports and concerts. Towards the end of May, the regimental diary reports, 'Routine parades during the morning relieved by a lecture by Lt. Butler on New Zealand, which was well received.' Quite how Butler had suddenly become an authority on New Zealand, he can't recall.[27]

Back in Britain, a general election was under way – the first since 1935 – with polling day set for 5 July 1945, although the counting and results would be delayed for three weeks because of the elaborate arrangements for the millions of servicemen overseas to cast their votes, and for their ballots to be returned to Britain. The political parties had no facilities, of course, to campaign in far-flung military bases, so rudimentary efforts were made for the Army to put the parties' case for them. 'As a stop-gap,' the war diary notes on 23 May, 'a political discussion was held during the morning at which the Conservative and Labour candidates for Little Stedden addressed the constituents'. The account explains that for the two major parties, Lieutenant Butler acted as the mock candidate.[28] 'I was thought to be the most politically conscious person in the squadron,' Butler says. 'It was the biggest intervention I've ever made in an election! And yet I was too young to vote myself.'[29] British troops overseas are thought to have contributed to Labour's unexpected 1945 landslide.

The diary shows that a week later Butler 'held a discussion on the social security programme', and two weeks after that he gave 'an excellent lecture' on 'The Structure of Politics'.[30]

David Butler's term of military service was due to last three years, but he didn't fancy the idea of remaining in Germany as part of an army of occupation. So, instead, he volunteered for the continuing war in the Far East against Japan.

On 20 June 1945, Butler received orders to move the next day to the collecting area 'in preparation for posting to SEAC' – South East Asia Command. But things were pretty chaotic. Butler left after lunch the next day, only to return when he found no arrangements had been made for him at his new location. It was a similar story the following day. Finally, on 24 June, the regimental diary records Butler left 'this time for Bruges, and so far has not returned'.[31]

In the end, his offer to fight in the Far East was never taken up, as Japan surrendered in August 1945 after the atomic bombs on Hiroshima and Nagasaki. It meant he never completed his three years. After one month's leave he was sent to Catterick camp in North Yorkshire. Then, one day in early September, he was summoned to headquarters. What had he done wrong now, he wondered.

Nothing, it seems. He was being discharged.

He was told to collect a demob suit from a depot in York. But when he arrived back at the family home in Leatherhead very late that night, the doors were locked. So, he had to climb a drainpipe to get into his bedroom, where his mother was astonished to find her demobbed son next morning.

CHAPTER THREE

IN THE ABSENCE OF CRICKET

Behind the front door of David Butler's small flat in north Oxford is a bookcase with some of his most cherished volumes. He reaches to a rather battered, small, blue cloth-covered book and pulls it from the shelf. *The Times Guide to the House of Commons 1945* was published only a few weeks after the election that year, the latest in a series of reference books *The Times* newspaper had published for almost every British general election since 1880, giving results seat by seat, together with biographical details of both elected MPs and their vanquished opponents.

The Times Guide cost David Butler just five shillings in 1945, but today copies fetch £75 or more when they become available. The battered volume in Butler's possession, however, should be especially valuable for its historical significance. This single book could be said to mark the very start of election science in Britain, what soon became known as psephology. David Butler can be considered the father of that science.

He bought the book while preparing to return to New College after war service, where he planned to resume his PPE course as a second-year undergraduate. Yet within a few months he would have developed new thinking that would revolutionise the analysis of British election results. He was just twenty years old.

Reading the collection of results for the historic 1945 contest,

Butler was keen to make comparisons. Since his schooldays, Butler had been a bit of what people today might dismiss as a 'nerd' or an 'anorak'. Every summer before the war he'd engross himself in cricket statistics, regularly calculating the latest batting and bowling averages, but in the summer of 1945 there was no English county cricket to report – the game still hadn't properly resumed after its wartime break.

So in odd moments over many weeks in the late summer and autumn of 1945, David Butler applied his cricket methods to candidates in the newly minted *Times Guide*. He remembers, for example, working on the project while on a train on the old line from Oxford to Cambridge, where a New College rugby XV was due to play a scratch team from Trinity College at the rival university.[1]

Publishers had been compiling election statistics in Britain for more than 100 years. After the Great Reform Act in 1832, many areas saw the publication of parliamentary poll books, setting out results seat by seat. In 1853, a man called Frederick McCalmont started publishing the results nationwide, and *The Times* began its publication after the 1880 election. *The Times* soon faced competition from the Conservative Party's own *Constitutional Year Book*, the rival *Liberal Year Book*, and directories published by the *Pall Mall Gazette*.

But the 1945 *Times Guide*, and all the other directories before it, as well as the newspapers up to that point, gave results only in raw numbers, not in percentages. Today, it's easy to overlook that until the second half of the twentieth century, British election results were simply presented publicly as numbers of votes, as, for example in 1945 in Stepney, the seat of the incoming Prime Minister, Clement Attlee:

Attlee, C. R. (Lab.): 8,398
Woodward, Lt. A. N. P. (C.): 1,618
Lab. majority: 6,780

David Butler felt simple totals like these weren't enough. Today, more than seventy years later, opening the book in his hallway, he points to columns of small numbers that he inked in the margin of each result, which he'd calculated with his slide rule – each candidate's vote as a percentage of the total votes cast in that seat.

Like many scientific breakthroughs, what David Butler did was a remarkably simple step, so basic as to seem glaringly obvious nowadays. Yet until 1945, nobody in Britain had ever really presented or analysed parliamentary voting figures in percentage terms.[2]

Percentages eventually became universal, thanks largely to Butler's pioneering work, though *The Times Guide* only began including them from its 1955 edition. Other directories such as *Whitaker's Almanack*, the *Constitutional Yearbook* and *Dod's Parliamentary Companion* did the same, but it was only from 1959 that percentages were routinely given with the constituency results published in newspapers. (The Americans were only slightly quicker: the 1952 presidential and congressional elections, for example, were the first time that the *New York Times* used percentages in their results tables.)

But simple percentages for each candidate in just one election were of only limited interest. Butler 'stole' – his word – from the library of his grandfather A. F. Pollard, copies of the *Times Guides* for 1929, 1931 and 1935 and did the same exercise with the constituency results for these years, too. He still possesses these volumes as well.

Back at New College, Butler happened one day to mention his work playing with election statistics to one of his tutors, Philip Andrews, an economist, who later made his name for his studies of business behaviour and the structure of British manufacturing industry. Andrews suggested to Butler that he ought to talk to R. B. (Ronald) McCallum, a history don at Pembroke College who had just been commissioned to write an account of the 1945 contest, the first ever history of an individual British general election. Andrews had provided Butler with a vital connection, one which proved crucial not only to Butler, but to the whole study of elections.

McCallum was born in Paisley in 1898 and had been at Oxford almost continuously since arriving as an undergraduate in 1919, after service in the Great War. Alongside his teaching at Pembroke, McCallum had also just been made a part-time fellow of the new Nuffield College, which had been established in 1937 as a postgraduate institution which would concentrate on social studies.

Years later, McCallum would explain in a letter to a colleague how this first Nuffield election study had been initiated. One afternoon in March 1945, while reading in the library of the Oxford Union, McCallum suddenly realised he was due at a 3 p.m. meeting at Nuffield to discuss ideas for political research projects once the war had ended. He quickly set off for the college, which in those days occupied merely a couple of adjacent houses on the Banbury Road.

'I walked up St Giles thinking hard,' McCallum wrote. 'It was a matter of *amour propre* to find something by the time I got there. Suddenly a revelation came to me. For all I know I may have cried aloud: "Keynes and all that rot. We must have no more of that."'[3]

What had troubled McCallum for many years was John Maynard Keynes's worldwide bestseller *The Economic Consequences of the Peace*, published in 1919 immediately after the Treaty of Versailles, where Keynes had been a British delegate to the peace talks after the First World War. The book had helped cement Keynes's reputation as an economist, but it also influenced public opinion in Britain and America towards the view that Germany had been treated harshly by the peace treaty. This may have encouraged the subsequent appeasement of the Nazis in the 1930s.

In his book, Keynes devotes a mere four pages to the 1918 contest, which David Lloyd George announced just three days after the Armistice that November. The Prime Minister hoped his military victory would secure a quick election victory for his wartime coalition government ahead of the peace conference at Versailles, due early in 1919. The Armistice had been agreed on the understanding that the Allies would not exact revenge on defeated Germany. But

Keynes claimed that as polling day approached, coalition campaign managers grew more and more worried about their chances of electoral success, and Lloyd George became increasingly belligerent towards Germany. At one campaign rally, the former Labour leader George Barnes, who had been a member of Lloyd George's War Cabinet, had cried, 'I am for hanging the Kaiser!'[4] According to Keynes, politicians from other parties then joined the clamour to punish Germany.

Lloyd George's 'natural instincts… were right', Keynes wrote, but 'the progress of the general election of 1918 affords a sad, dramatic history of the essential weakness of one who draws his chief inspiration not from his own true impulses, but from the grosser effluxions of the atmosphere which momentarily surrounds him'. So Lloyd George took a much tougher line. In a six-point manifesto issued three days before election day, he finally pledged to put the Kaiser on trial, and to make Germany pay 'fullest indemnities'. Keynes concluded:

> A vote for a coalition candidate meant the crucifixion of Antichrist and the assumption by Germany of the British national debt … This was the atmosphere in which the Prime Minister left for Paris, and these the entanglements he had made for himself. He had pledged himself and his government to make demands of a helpless enemy inconsistent with solemn engagements on our part, on the faith of which this enemy had laid down his arms.[5]

John Maynard Keynes didn't see himself as the chronicler of the British general election of 1918: he was merely trying to explain the background to Versailles in terms of British politics. In the absence of alternative accounts, however, and with the extraordinary international success of *The Economic Consequences of the Peace*, Keynes's almost instant narrative quickly became the unchallenged conventional wisdom.

Ronald McCallum thought, however, that Keynes's brief account of the 1918 contest had been dangerous and played a part in encouraging the rise of Nazi Germany. *The Economic Consequences of the Peace*, McCallum later said, was 'a book about which I lost my temper at the time and kept it lost. I felt that the short, slight and sketchy remarks about the 1918 election had been absorbed and accepted widely because the book was in so many other ways celebrated.'[6] David Butler says McCallum felt his twenties and thirties – the 1920s and '30s – had been 'locust decades', which had been 'wasted under the shadow of the lost peace, Versailles'.[7] For the 1945 contest, McCallum wanted a more sober, academic analysis (though today, a hundred years after the 1918 election, a thorough scholarly book on that contest has yet to be published).

Indeed, Ronald McCallum felt very little was known about most general elections in times past. 'They take their course with much partisan excitement, produce a vast amount of ephemeral literature and oratory, and in the end it remains very mysterious as to what exactly the issues were and what was most prominent in the minds of the electors,' McCallum wrote later. He was also troubled about the perceived effect of the Zinoviev letter on the 1924 election and, in 1931, a scare whipped up about deposits in the Post Office Savings Bank. The only books about British elections in the past were the directories of results, such as *The Times Guide*. The appeal of such volumes probably did not extend beyond party insiders, and they lacked any academic analysis of either the chronology of each campaign or the votes cast and outcomes in each seat. 'It seemed very important that the first election after the war of 1939, the first election to be held after an interval of ten years, should not pass without some careful study,' McCallum later wrote.[8]

So, Ronald McCallum proposed to the Nuffield committee an account of what was likely to be the British general election of 1945. He didn't see it as a sociological account, but pure, traditional, contemporary history. He thought that the election 'must be photographed in flight, studied and analysed'.[9] They should get it right now, he argued, before people got it wrong later.

The Nuffield committee was an extremely distinguished group, and included the Warden of Nuffield, Henry Clay; the historian Robert Ensor; the socialist intellectual G. D. H. Cole; and, in the chair, the renowned long-standing Master of Balliol College, 'Sandie' Lindsay. 'There was general enthusiasm,' McCallum said,

> and I was at once told that I had to undertake it. I shimmered a bit and expressed doubts. I was silenced at once by Lindsay in his rather hectoring way. 'No, no, McCallum, you cannot have as good an idea as that and not go through with it.' So, it was settled really in a moment of time.[10]

Thank goodness Lindsay did intervene. For the Nuffield election studies books have continued for more than seventy years, from 1945 to 2017, covering twenty general elections, as well as the 1975 European referendum and several elections to the European Parliament.

As his main researcher, Nuffield provided McCallum with Alison Readman, who had just got a first in PPE at Oxford. 'I had expected from Nuffield by the law of probability a Labour Party girl,' McCallum later wrote. 'I did not expect this elegant young lady, daughter of a colonel of the Scots Greys ... She was, as might have been suspected from her origin, a Conservative.' McCallum, himself a keen Liberal, was eventually so indebted to Readman, in fact, that he made her his co-author, but, he later wrote, 'The most important discovery I made was an approach from a young New College ex-gunner, David Butler, who had worked out all results in percentages ... As you know, he did the statistical appendix and has never looked back.'[11]

When David Butler turned up at McCallum's rooms in Pembroke, the historian asked a few questions about his background and was delighted to hear that Butler's grandfather was the great

A. F. Pollard. He could certainly do with some statistical help, for McCallum, according to Butler, was 'totally innumerate' and admitted he knew nothing about statistics. Yet he was keen 'to give authority to his text' by analysing the election figures in detail.[12] 'It will look better with some figures in,' Butler would recall him saying. 'He sounded like Molière's *Le Bourgeois gentilhomme*, ordering books for his library on the basis of their binding, not their content.'[13] Rather than enlist a fellow don, or a graduate with mathematical expertise, McCallum was happy to delegate the work to this second-year undergraduate who had turned up on his doorstep. Despite his fascination for playing with numbers, Butler was hardly a great statistical expert, although his PPE papers did include statistics. Oxford University in 1945 would have included scores of maths dons and students better qualified than him.

> It wasn't statistics so much. I mean, I could just work out a percentage… It was very, very elementary. It was not clever statistical stuff of the sort that is done by people – some of my pupils – nowadays … I just had the great luck of being first in the field. Nobody had done this sort of thing before, and I did it. I had enough training, and a very good memory.[14]

That good memory, inherited from his father, would be crucial to Butler's future success. And a clever maths don with little interest in politics might not, of course, have pursued the project with the same dogged enthusiasm.

One day, while engaged on his work for McCallum, David Butler bumped into a PPE colleague in New College: a junior lecturer, Andrew Ensor, who had a room on the same staircase in the historic front quadrangle. Ensor, too, had been enlisted as part of the team on the McCallum book – analysing candidates' election addresses – after his father, R. C. K. (Robert) Ensor, had sat on the Nuffield committee that commissioned the project. Looking through

Butler's percentage work, Ensor floated the notion of 'swing' – that the main parties' share of the vote might 'swing' by a similar amount in every constituency, and that in turn might be linked to the change in the number of seats. It was just a spur-of-the-moment suggestion by Ensor. He wasn't interested in exploring it any further himself, and was quite happy for Butler to develop it on his own. (Ensor didn't remain in academic life, and later moved to America, where he achieved great success in the oil industry.)

Butler seized on the idea of swing with gusto and worked it up to remarkable effect in his work for McCallum. He finished his contribution to the Nuffield book by the spring of 1946, and once again his father kindly typed up the manuscript for the publisher.

Butler's contribution comprised two appendices, in fact, and together they are the foundation stones of modern British election science. The first was a sixteen-page section entitled 'The Relation of Seats to Votes'. This was the real analytical breakthrough.[15] The second appendix involved six pages of statistical tables which included the swing in major cities of the UK, as well as counties and regions.[16]

It was brave of David Butler to attempt what he did. Someone with a reputation to maintain might have been more cautious. In the '20s and '30s, the British party system had undergone great turmoil, partly through the split and decline of the Liberal Party, the rise of Labour, and then the formation of the National Government, a coalition which dramatically divided Labour and saw National candidates aligned to each of the traditional parties fight the elections of 1931 and 1935. Those two contests, and the previous election in 1929, had produced several serious distortions in the results for the main parties, and inconsistencies in the relationship between votes and resulting seats.

In 1929, Labour came to office in a minority government under Ramsay MacDonald having received almost 267,000 *fewer* votes than Stanley Baldwin's Conservatives, but having won 28 more seats. In 1931, Labour candidates who opposed MacDonald's new National Government racked up 6.6 million votes between them, but won only 52 seats, whereas the three strands of Liberals got 72 MPs, on the basis of just 2.3 million votes, barely a third of the vote for the anti-coalition Labour contingent. And in 1935, Labour suffered again, getting 154 MPs for 8.3 million votes, while the Conservatives got almost three times as many MPs – 432 – for 11.8 million votes.

So, in the decades before 1945 there seemed to be very little relationship between the number of votes a party obtained and the seats it harvested. And, of course, memories were still fresh from what had happened in Germany's federal election of November 1932. This led Adolf Hitler to come to power the following January with less than a third of the popular vote, even though the Nazis significantly lost both votes and seats compared with the previous federal election in July that year.

Other factors that would previously have impaired statistical analysis of British elections were the double-member constituencies (of twice the usual size, with two MPs) which existed in several cities and major towns until 1950; and the twelve university seats, where party affiliations were weak and independent candidates were often elected. Election analysts also had to cope with the added complication that before the war many candidates were returned unopposed – so dozens of MPs were elected having received no votes at all – thirty-two in 1924, for example; seven in 1929; sixty-seven in 1931; and forty in 1935. Yet most unopposed returns were in very safe seats, so if these MPs had been opposed they would probably have received very handsome totals. Fortuitously for Butler, the number of candidates elected in 1945 with no opponent was down to just three, though Labour still chose not to fight thirty-six constituencies across the UK, while the Tories opted out of seventeen contests.

Statistical analysis of elections would have been much harder in the decades immediately before 1945, had anyone sought to try it.

The process that linked votes to seats often looked random, and any forecasts would have seemed foolhardy or reckless. This was also an era when political polling was still in its infancy in Britain.

Yet David Butler argued – very presciently, and perhaps courageously – that by 1945 British politics had returned to a two-party system. Indeed, Britain was about to enter a period of extraordinary political stability, in which the Conservatives and Labour dominated votes and seats to the exclusion of almost anyone else, until the Liberals, the SDP and the nationalist parties began to 'break the mould' in the 1970s and 1980s. Butler confidently declared in his appendix that 'it is possible to indicate graphically the swing in popular opinion necessary to oust a majority government'.[17] One of the graphs in his first appendix set out how many seats either Labour or the Conservatives could expect to win according to each percentage of the combined vote they achieved, with Labour faring slightly better at each stage than the Tories. 'With very few exceptions,' he wrote, 'the swings in individual areas are within 6 per cent of the national swing of 12 per cent.'[18]

And he took a swing, as it were, at those who argued election forecasting was a hopeless activity, and that it was better to go by instinct:

> If politicians and journalists would pay less attention to straws in the wind and 'general impressions' of public feeling, and more to the statistical facts, their published prophecies as well as their wagers might be nearer reality … Above all this appendix has sought to provide a solution of a problem of even more fundamental importance – to find out how far a British election is a gamble, or how far it is based upon a system which, though it is arbitrary and unfair to minorities, and though it grotesquely exaggerates majorities, can be guaranteed to produce a particular result, given the proportion of people in the country who support each of the two major parties.[19]

Certainly, there were still some distortions in the electoral process when it came to the distribution of seats between the two main parties, but these were nothing like those in the inter-war years. They could largely be explained by differences in constituency size, and the fact that the average Labour seat was significantly smaller in population than the average Tory constituency. However, the boundary review expected during the 1945 parliament was meant to reduce this problem.

> If the unfairness of unequal constituencies is removed, a major party receiving a given percentage of votes can be guaranteed to win a certain number of seats, with a margin of error of not more than 20 or 30. Certainly the lamentations of those who suggest that it is possible for a party with 40 per cent of the total votes to triumph over a party with 50 per cent are falsified.[20]

So long as Britain remained a two-party system, he argued, then any party which got more than 2 per cent more than its main rival could be assured of governing with an outright majority. 'It is hereby submitted that, within reasonable limits, when the system is called upon to return to power that party which commands the most votes in the country as a whole, it will very rarely fail to do so.'[21]

And Butler's prediction has proved pretty accurate in the nineteen general elections since 1945. Only on three occasions – in February 1974, 2010 and 2017 – did no party get an outright majority. And only twice has the party that won most votes failed to win most seats – when the Conservatives beat Labour on seats, but not votes, in 1951, and when Labour did the reverse in February 1974.[22] Butler concluded his groundbreaking essay with the words: 'It is hoped that this appendix has opened up a totally different path for certain and exact analysis of election results.'[23]

It was an astonishingly bold claim for a 21-year-old who had not yet completed the second year of his university politics degree, and whose Oxford academic career had otherwise not been especially distinguished. But then it was hardly as if David Butler were challenging an established army of election scientists. There *were* no election statisticians at Oxford – or anywhere else in Britain. He had the field to himself.

Years later, the distinguished anthropology professor Mary Douglas would recall how, around 1947, she'd been lodging as a student in north Oxford with David's aunt, Violet Butler, who'd told her, 'You must meet my brilliant young nephew, who has devised a method of forecasting the result of general elections based on bowling averages.'[24]

The *Manchester Guardian* spent much of its long review of the McCallum/Readman book discussing Butler's statistical observations, welcoming the new approach of applying scientific methods to elections.[25] In fact, there had been a few attempts at analysing elections statistically in the late nineteenth century – the previous period in which two major parties dominated British politics – when the *Journal of the Royal Statistical Society* published several articles on the subject. By 'happy accident', one of these was written by Francis Edgeworth, one of David Butler's distant cousins in the Irish branch of the family from which he gets his middle name. Edgeworth was a brilliant all-round philosopher, economist and statistician, who served as Drummond Professor of Political Economy at All Souls College, Oxford from 1891 to 1922, and is best known today for inventing the Edgeworth box in economics. In 1898, Edgeworth had analysed the three previous general elections – 1886, 1892 and 1895 – and developed a complicated formula which linked the number of votes for what were then the two main parties (Unionist and Gladstonian, i.e. Conservative and Liberal) to the number of seats they achieved in Parliament.[26] (Unfortunately, many years later the formula was shown to contain a basic error.[27]) The same edition of the journal also included an article by Jervoise Baines, a retired Indian civil servant and census expert who had become an alderman on the London County Council (LCC). It was not a major feature of his article, but Baines used percentages to examine voting patterns in the 1898 LCC elections and the previous LCC contests in 1895.[28]

The idea of swing wasn't entirely new, of course, to British politics in 1945, at least as a general concept about the change in power between parties. Indeed, earlier in *The British General Election of 1945*, McCallum and Readman wrote that the result that year came from 'the old … hallowed … phenomenon of the swing of the pendulum, so familiar to students of British politics'.[29]

Another example came a half-century before, in 1897, when the Prime Minister Lord Salisbury wrote to his junior foreign minister George Curzon warning that government plans were greatly affected by the electoral cycle. 'In terms of practical politics,' Salisbury wrote, 'foreign policy is now dependent on the swing of the pendulum at home … no foreign policy can succeed unless it can be completed within one beat of the pendulum.'[30]

The one previous *statistical* reference to electoral swing, however, was much more obscure. In 1906, a former Liberal MP, Sir Richard Martin, became president of the Royal Statistical Society and entitled his presidential address: 'The Electoral "Swing" of the Pendulum'. Martin tried to quantify the 'swing' in the recent Liberal landslide of 1906, and suggested it was about 10 per cent.[31] (On the modern method of calculating swing, the 1906 result would, in fact, be just under 6 per cent.)

Before David Butler in 1945, the academic analysis of British election results, and attempts to link movements in votes to movements in seats, seems to have been confined to a handful of eminent statisticians in a very small social and intellectual circle. What Butler did was to address a wider, educated audience, and to turn swing from a rather recherché concept into something that was quantifiable and could be linked to contemporary outcomes, in terms of how votes translated into membership of the House of Commons and the formation of governments.

Butler's work went hand in hand, of course, with groundbreaking ways of measuring public opinion, which had long excited him. Before the Second World War, the most common way of assessing the popularity of governments or opposition parties was through by-elections caused by the resignation or death of MPs. These were much more regular than today. By-elections occurred, for example, at the rate of twenty a year in the four years before the outbreak of the Second World War (compared with just six by-elections in the whole four years of the 2001–05 parliament). So, the parties and the press had regular snapshots of how voters were thinking: outside holiday periods, by-elections would occur every three to four weeks, and it wasn't unusual for several to take place on the same day.

But, as David Butler had spotted as a schoolboy at St Paul's before the war, there was now a new measure of public support for the political parties – opinion polls. The practice came from across the Atlantic, where George Gallup set up his American Institute of Public Opinion in Princeton, New Jersey in 1935, after several years of conducting experimental unpublished polls to check their accuracy. One of his earliest private polls was to test whether his mother-in-law should stand again for re-election as Secretary of State in the state of Iowa. Gallup's poll suggested she should. So she did and duly won. Then, in 1934, ahead of the midterm US congressional elections, and having inspected voting records for every county in the United States, Gallup sent out mock ballot papers to a carefully chosen mix of voters in each state. The results of his poll were within 1 per cent of the actual figures. Two years later, in 1936, having launched Gallup Polls, he successfully predicted that Roosevelt would be re-elected President. His forecast margin of 8 per cent was well short of the actual 24 per cent, but established Gallup's credibility, since the other main forecaster, *Literary Digest* magazine, had predicted Alf Landon would win.[32]

Gallup employed two methods. The first was random sampling, whereby, for example, one in every 40,000 voters on the electoral register was contacted. The other was the quota method, whereby voters were chosen according to age, gender, location and so on, to reflect proportionately the country as a whole.

Soon Gallup polls were franchised overseas and the British Institute of Public Opinion, run by Henry Durant, published the very first Gallup poll in Britain, ahead of the Fulham West by-election in April 1938. It correctly forecast – against expectations – that Labour would take the seat. Gallup published their first national poll in the *News Chronicle* six months later, and further polls every few months until the end of the war. But with no general elections between 1935 and 1945, there was no way of testing the accuracy of these national surveys, though Gallup successfully forecast several more by-elections during the war years.

During the 1945 election, Gallup carried out two polls: the first forecast a 45–37 percentage win for Labour; the second a 47–41 percentage win. But not even the *News Chronicle*, which again published the polls – in the second case as its lead story – dared to suggest that this entailed a handsome Labour victory.

David Butler, already inspired by Gallup's work while at St Paul's, became increasingly interested in polling during his final two years at New College from 1945 to 1947, when he completed his PPE degree. Butler initially made contact with Robert Cruikshank, the deputy editor of *The Economist*, who in turn gave him an introduction to Henry Durant. Butler wrote to Durant at the end of 1946, telling him of his statistical work on the Nuffield book, which had not yet been published, and his findings on the 'strict correlation' between the number of votes a party gets and the number of seats it achieves in the Commons. 'If this argument is valid,' he told Durant, 'then, granted a prediction of voting as accurate as you seem able to provide, it is possible to forecast the outcome of a general election in terms of seats far more closely than has yet been done by anything but guess work.' Butler bombarded Durant with questions: had the nature of Gallup's samples changed over the years? When did public opinion swing to Labour during the war? Was there any variation in political consciousness between different parts of the country?[33] Henry Durant invited Butler to visit him at Gallup's offices in Regent Street, and the two struck up an important relationship.

Meanwhile, David Butler was completing his degree in philosophy, politics and economics, which was not entirely simple. In the autumn of 1946, Butler was assigned as his philosophy tutor Isaiah Berlin, who was then just thirty-three, and destined to be regarded as one of the greatest Oxford thinkers of the twentieth century. On Berlin's death in 1997, his obituary writer in *The Independent*, Henry Hardy, listed some of the superlatives regularly applied to him: 'The world's greatest talker, the century's most inspired reader, one of the finest minds of our time – even, indeed, a genius.'[34] Born to a Jewish family in Latvia in 1909, Isaiah Berlin had moved to Petrograd in Russia and witnessed the 1917 revolutions first-hand, before his family moved to London. Berlin then attended St Paul's School, fifteen years before his New College student.

Berlin had spent most of the Second World War working for the Foreign Office, and specifically at the British embassy in Washington DC, sending highly informative and astute despatches back to London – intelligence that was regularly relayed directly to Winston Churchill.

Butler took little advantage of the extraordinary privilege of being tutored by 'the cleverest man I had ever encountered' and someone known as the most interesting conversationalist of his age.[35] Berlin could be a highly eccentric tutor, and would often play with his wind-up gramophone or mechanical toys while teaching his students. One of them recalls Berlin teaching students while lying on the floor behind a sofa. Week after week, the freshman undergraduate struggled with Berlin's demands, and Butler recalls that after five tutorials, he confessed to his tutor that the essay he had written that week was 'nonsense'. Butler explained that he couldn't hold firmly in his mind 'for more than ten minutes the difference between inductive and deductive'.[36] Berlin responded kindly, but Butler merely repeated that his work was 'nonsense'. 'Then why are you doing it?' Berlin asked.[37] Butler said that he wanted to get a PPE degree. Berlin then explained that under the relaxed rules introduced for students during the war, he could take a PPE degree by studying only two of the three subjects (and indeed Berlin himself had long questioned whether it was possible for most PPE students to study all three subjects and be proficient in them all). David Butler quickly exploited this opt-out clause.

'Has decided to abandon Philosophy this term,' Berlin typed on a small card which still survives in Butler's internal New College file. 'Quite an able man to whom the subject is excessively uncongenial. Signed IB.'[38] Many students who suffered such embarrassment would have carefully avoided their tutor ever after. Not David Butler.

There was no subsequent ill-feeling between the two men at all. Indeed, Isaiah Berlin would prove a helpful contact in Butler's later career, especially in America, where he would casually drop into conversations a reference to 'my tutor Isaiah'.[39] 'And later in life, when I met Isaiah at parties, he would say: "Ah, there is David Butler. My greatest tutorial triumph! I liberated him from philosophy! The most unphilosophical pupil I ever encountered."'[40] And in telling the story, Butler imitates Berlin's distinctive deep voice.

Yet the episode also perhaps exposes Butler's greatest weakness as an academic: not only is he uncomfortable with pure philosophy, but he has never been very interested in political theory, in concepts, or in abstract ideas generally, nor even in the details of particular party policy. Butler has always been a man for facts, figures and statistics, some might say with a trainspotter or anorak approach to political science. This exclusively empirical, 'nuts and bolts' approach would prove something of a handicap in later years.

The revised PPE syllabus allowed returning servicemen to complete their degrees by taking just five papers in their final two years compared with the normal eight. Remarkably for a man who was to play such a major role in the history of political science, only one of Butler's five PPE finals papers was politics. The other four were economics, in which he sometimes shared tutorials with the future Cambridge economist and leading Keynesian Wynne Godley. One of Butler's economics papers was statistics, which he was taught by distinguished mathematical economist David Champernowne. His tutor for economic history, Ernest Phelps Brown, reported that Butler was 'keenly interested' and had 'imagination', but was 'not so good at marshalling his material on paper'.[41]

New College after the war comprised two separate generations of undergraduates. First, there were those like Butler who had matured through doing war service, some of whom had been recruited by the Warden without having to pass normal exams. Then there was a much younger generation, not long out of school. In his second year, Butler shared a suite of rooms with Avrion Mitchison, the future immunologist, who was four years Butler's junior, and the son of a Labour MP. They both recall how their shared ground-floor sitting room was an unofficial route into the college once the gates were locked. Around midnight, their window was often opened from the outside and a fellow student would pass through, having climbed over the college wall outside Butler and Mitchison's window. Mitchison was impressed that Butler never used his age and war service to lord it over his room-mate. In contrast, Butler was considered an 'intellectual snob' by Frank Smith, who also did PPE at that time. Smith explains, 'I had an inferiority complex because I was from the north and a grammar school. He was far above my intellectual standard.'[42]

For someone who would become famous for his energy and extraordinary output, Butler seems to have been remarkably relaxed as an Oxford student. 'I decided rather early', he later revealed, 'that if I worked very hard I might get a first, and if I didn't work hard I wouldn't fail to get a decent second, and so I stopped working, but

I didn't actually do anything very positive with my leisure.'[43] Aside from his rugby and a bit of cricket, and attending the three main political clubs, he often went to debates in the Union, though he never spoke again after his first two forays, and decided he didn't want the 'emotional strain' of standing for office.[44] He did, however, act as scrutineer in Union elections for his close New College friends Tony Benn and Peter Blaker, who later became ministers on opposite sides of the Commons (acting as each other's 'pair' when they wanted to miss a vote).

David Butler was awarded only a second-class degree when he graduated from New College in the summer of 1947, in an era when firsts were much rarer than today, and seconds at Oxford were not yet divided into 2:1s and 2:2s (and people still got thirds, fourths and mere pass degrees). A few days after finals, Butler and four of his friends, including Benn and Blaker, visited a booth in Cornmarket in the centre of Oxford which offered the novelty of an audio recording on a disc. The five recent graduates sat around predicting what they would each be doing in thirty years' time. Butler was going to be dull and bookish, they agreed, while he himself forecast that Benn would follow his father in becoming a government minister, but only at the lowest rank, of parliamentary under-secretary. When Tony Benn played the recording at David Butler's 75th birthday party in 1999, fifty-two years later, it caused much hilarity.

CHAPTER FOUR

SURVEYING AMERICA

'It was a grand tea party,' David Butler recalls, 'in the Victorian style.'

He tells the tale of how, in 1947, while still an undergraduate at New College, he was invited out to tea one Sunday in Boars Hill, the small village that overlooks the city of Oxford. Through his family connections, David Butler found himself among a glittering guest list from the Oxford elite. Others round the tea table included the biologist Julian Huxley, and the English literature don Lord David Cecil.

And their hosts that afternoon were no less distinguished. Gilbert Murray, the classics scholar and active Liberal, had been a friend of Butler's father at New College. Murray's octogenarian wife, Lady Mary, daughter of the Earl of Carlisle, was a formidable woman who half a century earlier had been the model for George Bernard Shaw's idealistic, young, aristocratic and redoubtable heroine Major Barbara, in his famous play of that name.

At one point during the gathering, Lady Mary turned to Butler and asked, 'What do you want to do?'

'I don't know,' he replied.

'You don't know?'

Butler relates how Lady Mary then rapped the table, stood up and interrupted the gathering: 'Gilbert, Gilbert, isn't this perfectly dreadful? Here's a young man of twenty-two who doesn't know what he wants to do!'[1]

Indeed, he didn't know what to do in life. Butler was wracked with doubts as to whether he was clever enough, or hard-working enough, to follow most of his ancestors into academic life. Three weeks working in the economists' unit of the textile manufacturers Courtaulds in the summer of 1946 had put him off a career in industry. So, in search of adventure, he applied for grants to study in America. First, he was awarded a scholarship worth $1,500 to go to Columbia University in New York. But a colleague had done some research into obscure overseas awards that were available to Oxford students and discovered the Jane Eliza Procter Scholarship at Princeton University in New Jersey.

Butler had been urged to go to Princeton by Gallup's London pollster, Henry Durant, since Gallup's worldwide headquarters was located there, and Butler was keen to do more work around polling, analysing why people voted the way they did. Butler applied to Oxford University for the Jane Eliza Procter Scholarship, worth $2,500, and won it for the academic year 1947/48, on completion of his PPE degree. He suspects he may have been the only candidate.

It was bound to be an exciting time politically, for 1948 was due to be a presidential election year, and nobody could forecast the outcome. Harry Truman, who had occupied the White House for three years, having succeeded to the presidency on the sudden death of Franklin D. Roosevelt just before the end of the war in 1945, would be severely tested. Gallup polls suggested Truman might easily be beaten for the Democrat nomination, and even if he won, he could still be defeated by any one of several possible Republican contenders in November. To add further spice, there was talk of war hero General Dwight Eisenhower entering the contest, and later came further challenges to Truman through breakaway Democrats of both left and right.

On 30 August 1947, David Butler set sail from Southampton, and almost immediately began the first of scores of long letters he would write back to his parents over the next sixteen months. His first began with this verse as he sailed westwards:

Ah me, my native land
Receding in the haze,
I shall not see thee more
For many many days.[2]

'The Atlantic is large but David is placidly enjoying himself,' he wrote the next day.[3] His ship, the SS *Marine Tiger*, was still fitted out for war service, which meant he had to sleep on a troop deck which had row upon row of canvas bunks. Meals involved long queues at a cafeteria where passengers were served food in compartmentalised trays, though the food was a big improvement on the post-war rationing back home. 'The tea is abominable and the coffee poor,' he wrote. 'But real ice-cream and quantities of real milk, butter and jam more than atone for other failings.' The other passengers were mostly Americans, largely students, with some Europeans and perhaps half a dozen Englishmen. 'The first impression one gets of Americans [is] of immense vitality and sartorial unconventionality.'[4] For much of the voyage he was seasick.

On arrival, Butler spent several days in New York. Having seen Columbia University, he was glad to have chosen Princeton. 'Thank God, thank God I am not going to Columbia ... it seems to be a huge office building in the middle of Manhattan Island.' Manhattan was 'nearly half filled by Jews', he observed to his parents. 'Anti-Semitism is one of the few things I feel strongly about, though I am sometimes guilty of it myself in a mild and unthinking way: however, I might well change my views if I had to live in New York.'[5]

His visit included a trip to New York's Museum of Modern Art. He felt it contained 'a lot of mush ... a lot that is of doubtful merit (Picasso's 'Guernica' for example) and some remarkable paintings...'

After a week, he moved to Princeton, and his letter home included a small pencil diagram of the set of rooms he'd been given in a modern block in the graduate college at Princeton, which was located about half a mile from the main university buildings. After a few days he ventured into Trenton, the nearby capital of New Jersey, where he attended a meeting of the Progressive Citizens of America addressed by Henry Wallace, who had been Franklin Roosevelt's Vice-President from 1941 to 1945 (only to be replaced by Harry Truman a few months before FDR's death) and who would go on to run as the Progressive Party candidate for President in 1948. Butler found Wallace 'very impressive. He didn't say much. His speech was not closely reasoned. But he spoke with great dignity and unmistakeable sincerity. I may perhaps have fallen a little under his spell, but I saw no strong weakness in his case, which was unmarred by hyperbole.' Wallace was followed by the black singer and political activist Paul Robeson, who began by singing two black spiritual songs. 'Unmusical as I am,' Butler recorded, 'I was deeply impressed … Robeson spoke briefly and what he said threw a new light on the Negro problem for me at least.'[6]

Butler's letters home show how, in the late 1940s, he was essentially a liberal Democrat in American terms, or on the Labour right in British politics (what today might be called a social democrat). He had thought that the return of the Conservatives in 1950 'might not lead to utter disaster. But if then they are led by a man who can seriously advocate following the American example of throwing off controls, God help England.'[7] And he wrote of being 'depressed' by Labour's poor performance in local elections.[8] When a by-election occurred in his home seat of Epsom, he urged his parents 'to reduce what will be an overwhelming victory for the Tories as far as lies in your power'. (His letter hinted that his father had voted Conservative in 1945, and his mother Labour.)[9]

Within a month, Butler began to find Princeton dull and earnest. Some of his fellow graduate students were excessively conscientious in their studies, to the exclusion of all else. During the week, he said, 'there tends to be a certain lack of that social intercourse and those outside activities which made life at Oxford so pleasant …

The life both of the University and of the Graduate College is the poorer for the fact that graduates do not participate in political, dramatic or literary societies.'[10]

Butler told people in the US how he'd discovered at Oxford that politics was 'his thing', that he was there to see how America ran its politics and to compare the two systems. But suddenly, after about six weeks at Princeton, 'I had a sort of Road to Damascus experience, and I said, "This is all wrong."'[11] Comparisons didn't really work; America was totally different and should be considered in its own right. After that, he was pretty sceptical about comparative government, though it wouldn't stop him from teaching the subject on both sides of the Atlantic for decades.

Butler decided the focus of his work at Princeton – public opinion – was the future. 'There are enormous opportunities for opinion research in England both in politics and sociology that have as yet been quite untouched,' he told his parents. 'The Americans are many years ahead of us in their exploitation of it. It is too late to be a prophet ... but there is great scope for Crusaders in this field.'[12]

In December, Butler attended a meeting at Gallup's offices in Washington DC to discuss a big survey that they were proposing to conduct across the USA. Once the questions had been settled, the exercise involved Butler and other members of the group going out and testing the process on ordinary members of the public. He managed to talk to three people in a local post office, and two in a café – some of whom he already knew vaguely – but found the whole exercise agonising:

> The most awful question that I had to ask was 'What did you argue (or quarrel) about most with your husband?' I hadn't the courage to put in the words in brackets. The first victim replied tartly that she loved her husband very much and never disagreed with anything that he said ... The remaining guinea-pigs bore up nobly under the interrogation – except for the only other

> stranger who told me exactly where Dr Gallup got off and why each question was a bad one … My skin will harden, I suppose … Of course, the whole business is anonymous and does no-one any harm. But Opinion Pollers [*sic*] have found that interviewer morale is one of their main problems. The temptation to cheat, to invent the answers or to prompt the respondent is very great, especially when the ballot is long and tedious. As with hitch-hiking, it can be great fun if the public is co-operative, but hell if one meets two or three refusals or unfriendly consents in succession.[13]

In December 1947, David Butler gave his impressions of America and its people in another poem. The last lines read:

> Afraid though they have all to hand
> Parochial in the vastest land
> Equal men with rights endowed,
> Unfair, intolerant and loud.
> Vigorous citizens and free
> Bluster concealing decency,
> The prop and ruin of their state,
> The whole world's violent love and hate,
> Men in extremes loved and abhorr'd.
> Riddles lie here; in a word
> Here lies a nation; let it lie
> A riddle still and never die.
> – PRINCETON, DECEMBER 1947[14]

There was an innocent, naïve air to many of his letters home. 'This evening I was given a glass of Crème de Cacao, topped with a thin layer of real cream,' he told his parents on one occasion. 'I am not a bibulous person because I don't like alcohol, rather than because I have strong moral principles. But if all alcohol was like this I would have to indulge in powerful moral gymnastics to build up my resistance ... I have never tasted so delicious a drink.'[15] In early December, he admits he has 'in the last three months consumed more alcohol than in the preceding 22 years; and yet, while here, I have drunk sociably and never, as in the Army, in quantity'. Drink was more available and cheaper than in post-war Britain, yet he found the range of drinks in academic circles very limited.

> Cocktails have become a conventional necessity in a large segment of American society. I have tasted no wine over here apart from the universal sherry – often from California and rather horrible; the staples are Scotch or Rye whiskey, and Martini and Manhattan cocktails. The war prevented my learning the least discrimination in alcohol in England, and the customs of the Americans prevent me doing so here.[16]

Socially, he was a bit of a fish out of water, though he tried his best. Where most people in their early twenties would have been too embarrassed to discuss issues such as drink and sex with their parents, Butler felt no inhibitions. Early on, he mentioned the 'American system of "dates" – a strange phenomenon that I must expand upon when I understand it properly'.[17] He frequently refers to rather tame parties as 'orgies' and admitted to having 'inherited from somewhere a strong streak of the puritan and I have been shocked by some descriptions I have heard of Princeton Saturday evening debauchery'.[18]

Butler also took to dancing, and in the spring of 1948 acquired what one might call his first girlfriend. Jane Cooper was the daughter of a Princeton professor and, after what seems to have been an energetic evening on the dance floor, David wrote her a poem:

> Dear Jane,
>
> I know not what the music plays,
> What pattern guides the myriad hurrying feet.

The couples twirl in labyrinthine ways,
Tread nameless dances to an unsensed beat.

I cannot tell why conduct such should bring
To ears to music deaf, to feet untaught
To waltz, to foxtrot or to anything
So deep a pleasure as last night it brought.

But naught escapes strict philosophic laws.
The scholar is their slave, the dancer too.
Since we have learnt 'To each event a cause',
The cause for this, dear Jane, must lie in you.

Remembering thus the pleasure that you gave
I must remain
A deeply grateful
Dave.

– PRINCETON, 25 APRIL 1948[19]

David Butler was under no obligation to stay at Princeton during term time, and in November 1947, his itchy feet took him on his first trip to Washington DC, where he had tea with the British ambassador. The next day, he enjoyed an hour and a half with William Fulbright, a former pupil of Ronald McCallum at Oxford who had been a Democratic senator from Arkansas since 1945 – and later served a record fifteen years as chairman of the Foreign Relations Committee. Fulbright forecast that in 1948 the Republicans would nominate Eisenhower for President, since polls suggested he would win 5–6 per cent more votes than any other Republican – a sign of how much polling was already influencing American politics. Fulbright was sure Eisenhower wanted to stand. 'You only have to talk to him for a few minutes to be convinced of that,' he told Butler.[20] (Fulbright was right, of course, though Eisenhower didn't run until 1952.) Their discussion ranged far and wide through economics and US foreign policy before Fulbright drove his visitor back to the YMCA, where he was staying. 'He was a very friendly, wholly unpompous person,' Butler told his parents. It was probably the first interview Butler had ever conducted with a senior politician in Britain or America.[21]

Harold and Peggie Butler regularly kept their son in touch with events back in Britain, posting letters, cuttings, magazines and even books to him, but in January 1948, in a sign of the times, he had reason playfully to rebuke his mother over one recent package. Against the backdrop of the House Un-American Activities Committee's anti-communist hearings, Butler told her:

> The envelope, being bulky, was opened by suspicious customs officials. They stamped on it 'nothing to pay'. But I fear that their eyes must have lighted on the Communist pamphlet you included. What will become of me? The FBI will be notified. My movements will be watched. Inquiries will be made. The indiscreet moments when I have vaguely defended some aspects of Russia or Communism from extremist attacks will be unearthed and set down against me. My visa will be withdrawn or at least my freedom of movement will be restricted and my stay in these delectable shores will be ruined. Mummy, how could you?[22]

Butler clearly made a good impression at Princeton, for his politics professor, William Ebenstein, offered to get him a job teaching comparative government at the University of Wisconsin. Butler might have been tempted, but he feared that accepting the work would have disrupted his plans to travel the country observing the closing stages of the 1948 presidential race. He also wanted to get back to Britain in good time for the next general election, which it was thought would most likely occur in 1949.

By February, Butler was back in Washington, where he spent nine days in the office of another Arkansas Democrat, Brooks Hays, hoping 'to learn, perhaps, how American government really works'.[23] His tasks included writing a 'speech' for Hays on Abraham Lincoln and the South, though the congressman never actually delivered it – it was simply published in the *Congressional Record* in Hays's name. 'I don't imagine that the people of Arkansas would take well the fact that their representative had his speeches ghost-written by a God-damn limey,' Butler wrote.[24] Other politicians he met included Estes Kefauver from Tennessee ('quite impressed'), who would be elected to the Senate in 1948 and became Adlai Stevenson's Democratic running mate in 1956. And his last call was to a young first-term Democrat congressman from Boston, of whom he wrote, with some prescience:

> Mr John Kennedy... is 30, looks 24 or less, is a millionaire, a son of the ambassador to Britain before the war. He is a Catholic and a progressive liberal. I spent an hour with him and I liked him greatly. He talked very freely about Boston politics and the nature of liberalism. He was the least cynical and least disillusioned liberal that I met in Washington. This was not because he was young and optimistic; it was rather because he had a more philosophical and long-term approach to politics. The outcome in 1948 did not worry him greatly. On the whole he thought that a defeat would be good for his party. He was not as unhappy as the others were at the fact that the liberal cause could not thrive in America until a depression came; he accepted the situation calmly. I felt for the first time that I was meeting a man who accepted to the full the newfound strength of America.[25]

In April 1948, Butler was commissioned to write a series of articles on American politics by *Time and Tide*, the British political and literary magazine owned and, in effect, edited by the former suffragette Lady Rhondda. The first of these, on the presidential election, for which he was paid seven guineas, was published in May 1948.[26] It was his first ever article in the British press, and he asked his parents for 'destructive criticism'.[27]

Yet Butler often felt he was being lazy. 'I'm in a bit of a trough of stupid depression and I'm not getting much work done,' he told his parents in April 1948.[28] 'I'm feeling very stupid,' he reported a couple of weeks later. 'I have been doing too little work, too little intelligent reading and my mind is working very slowly. I've drugged myself too much with idle conversation and, in weather as warm as this, it is very hard to break oneself to industry.'[29] It's not unusual for postgraduate students to harbour such feelings of failure. The unstructured day and lack of indicators of performance mean the student needs to be strongly self-motivated, and it is easy to feel guilty about any time spent away from studying.

Butler looked forward to the presidential conventions due to be held in Philadelphia that summer and hoped to attend as an assistant to the Washington correspondent of the British *Daily Herald*, Arthur Webb. He also pursued plans to write a book about the 1948 presidential campaign, similar to the Nuffield study of the British election of 1945, though these plans fizzled out after a few weeks. It was just too big an undertaking.

Four months later, Butler had a second meeting with Kennedy, who gave him several introductions to political figures in his home city of Boston. Kennedy was annoyed at the way some British Labour politicians denounced the Marshall Plan as 'American imperialism', and the way they dismissed the programme as a clever way of soaking up US surplus production. Butler, showing an instinctive sympathy for the Attlee government which permeated many of his letters at the time, wrote:

> I agreed that British misunderstanding of America was deplorable, but I suggested that Labour's misunderstanding American purposes was a natural reaction to the widespread American misunderstanding of Labour's motives and aspirations. I think that Kennedy, though a 'pleasant person', is a bit of an Anglophobe himself.[30]

During his stay in America, Butler frequently found himself defending the post-war Labour government from Americans who feared Clement Attlee and his colleagues were too socialist, and who were anxious that Marshall aid was simply being used to help nationalise private industry in Britain, most notably iron and steel.

Butler was greatly helped in making political contacts in US politics by the Oxford tutor who had deemed him to be a hopeless philosopher. Isaiah Berlin was a famous networker, with an extraordinary range of friends and contacts around the world, but especially in the USA, where he had worked at the Washington embassy in the early years of the war. On hearing of Butler's trip to the United States, Berlin had generously suggested he get in contact with several friends.

The most remarkable and fruitful of these contacts was Felix Frankfurter, one of the most distinguished lawyers in American history. In the 1930s (during which time he spent a year at Oxford), Frankfurter had been a friend and adviser to President Roosevelt, who in 1939 had appointed him to the US Supreme Court (where he would serve until 1962). Frankfurter was one of the most liberal members of the court, having been one of the founders of the American Civil Liberties Union (the ACLU) in his earlier life. 'I went very diffidently to the Supreme Court to see the great man,' Butler later wrote.

> He proved to be very small with a sweet face and an impish grin. He asked me what I was studying at Princeton: 'public opinion research'. 'What a terrible subject. I regard Dr. Gallup and his techniques as wholly inimical to the interests of democracy.' I was too awed by being in the presence of a Supreme Court Justice to contradict, but made some mumbling defence of polling. Frankfurter's eyes glazed over.

Still, Frankfurter arranged a second dinner later in the week, and Butler felt the judge had taught him a lesson: 'When we dined two days later, I fought back.'[31] In his contemporaneous letter to his parents, Butler gave more detail:

> Frankfurter resembles Isaiah rather, both in appearance and in speed and in manner of speech; like Isaiah his mind works faster than his tongue and he is continually tossing aside ideas that he hasn't time to develop... I did like Frankfurter. He was charmingly friendly, and a most stimulating person to talk to – a man continually generating ideas, revealing profound depths to his thought.[32]

The Supreme Court Justice was clearly impressed by the young Oxford student, and he and his wife invited Butler to dinner at a local restaurant, where they spent three hours together. Butler reported back to his parents:

> He has very considerable warmth and charm. He is afflicted by a slight impatience in everyday matters, irritated by delays in service. He is nervously tidy, pushing crumbs aside from the tablecloth with his spoon ... Frankfurter was much excited by the death penalty controversy in Britain. He is strongly for abolition and he was dismayed by the appeal to public opinion and the influence of Gallup polls in changing the Government's stand. He was horrified by the attitude of both judges and bishops to the issue ... He deplored the legalistic hypocrisy of the LCJ [Lord Chief Justice] and of [former Lord Chancellor, Lord] Simon whom he despised. He launched a well-argued tirade against Gallup poll democracy and in particular against its influence on this question. He cross-questioned me about my attitude towards Gallup polls and urged me to write a well-argued attack on them.[33]

In the summer of 1948, Butler attended the two main party conventions, Republican then Democrat, which were both held, two weeks apart, in Philadelphia. He returned to the city a third time for the convention of Henry Wallace's Progressive Party. In one of a succession of reports on the conventions for *Time and Tide*, he lamented the dull nature of the 1948 campaign.[34] Yet, at the Republican convention, Butler witnessed several days of turmoil and excitement as the party again picked Thomas Dewey, the New York governor who had been decisively defeated by Roosevelt in 1944.

Only then did Butler embark on his long hitch-hiking tour. 'Armed with $400 in travellers' cheques and about twenty letters of introduction I set forth really to discover America.'[35] The letters had been written by several of the congressmen he knew, and also by Felix Frankfurter.

Butler was inspired for his expedition across America by the well-known travel and political guide *Inside USA*, which had been published the previous year by the writer and journalist John Gunther.[36] Gunther had spent thirteen months on an extraordinary tour which encompassed each of the then forty-eight states, spending several days in each state talking to numerous people so as to paint a panoramic picture of the entire country. His hundreds of interviews included governors, senators and three US Presidents, as well as lawyers, journalists and businessmen, down to ordinary housewives, painters and policemen in the states and cities he visited. Gunther's book ran to 979 pages, far too bulky for Butler to take with him, so he would regularly visit local libraries to read the relevant chapter. Butler would often then compile a briefing paper for himself on whatever state he was visiting, which was very similar to how Gunther had worked when compiling *Inside USA*.

Remarkably, Butler hitch-hiked round with a bulky suitcase, although he claimed to find this helpful. Despite the difficulty of walking long distances with the case, it provided a ready-made seat when waiting at the side of the road and had another advantage too: 'It made people sorry for me,' he says. 'So, they'd give me a lift. Nowadays I would have a large rucksack, which would be more convenient. I had 157 lifts, and only three women picked me up, and I think two of those had a baby in the car.'[37] Occasionally people would ask Butler to take over at the steering wheel. 'I have met and talked with many Americans,' he wrote after his first day on the road, through northern New Jersey and upstate New York.

> I have driven a car at wild speeds through the long hours of darkness. I have engaged in petty larceny and political argument. I have been taken for a Frenchman, an Italian, a Jew, a black-marketeer and – many times – for an Englishman. I have been offered a business opening in Cuba.[38]

(The 'petty larceny' came during the night when his driver ran out of petrol in a small village near Buffalo, New York, where all the garages were shut, so they stole sixteen gallons from an unlocked petrol pump.)

From New York he ventured into Canada, visiting Toronto and Ontario, before crossing back into the US and spending several days in Ann Arbor at the University of Michigan. From there he crossed Michigan, then went steadily westwards through Wisconsin, Minnesota, South Dakota, Wyoming, Montana, Idaho and Washington state. After a second foray into Canada, this time into British Colombia, he hitched down the west coast through Oregon and onto San Francisco and Los Angeles in California. His return journey took Butler eastwards through Nevada, Arizona, New Mexico, Colorado, Nebraska, Iowa, Missouri, Kansas, Oklahoma, Arkansas, Tennessee, Alabama, Georgia, South Carolina, North Carolina and Virginia, before he finally took a train from Washington DC back to Princeton.

Towards the end, in South Carolina, Butler was involved in a serious crash. His driver, an Army sergeant, had picked up both whiskey and gin during the journey, and thought nothing of drinking at the wheel. Then the inevitable happened, and they hit the back of a lorry. The side of the car was smashed in, and glass was everywhere. Butler escaped unhurt, but the driver suffered serious facial injuries, and Butler's suitcase had a large dent. He also felt guilty that, having already driven for some of the journey, he hadn't insisted on taking the wheel again.

David Butler's summer tour took him to twenty-eight states. Typically for Butler, he totted up the figures. He had travelled 9,250 miles – 6,250 hitch-hiking; 1,490 by bus; 125 by boat; and 135 miles on a couple of short plane hops. And in his exploration along country roads and New Deal freeways, Butler pursued his own survey of American political opinion among the 157 drivers he met. People picked him up, he believed, because they wanted company, and so he felt no qualms about talking as a means of paying his way. It was also a chance to learn about the economic geography of America. 'What do people do around here?' he would ask. He learnt the skills of interviewing people, getting people to open up, and he would gently probe them about their work, backgrounds, families and politics. The conversational techniques he learnt while hitching across America in 1948 would prove immensely useful when interviewing important people in British politics years later. Many people at all levels like to chat about themselves, he soon realised, and to talk through their problems. They relish the chance to paint themselves as heroes, he found, and appreciate having a sympathetic listener. It was a contrast to his earlier shyness when asking opinion poll questions. Day by day, Butler conducted a straw poll, and kept a running tally of responses, noting how views changed over the weeks. Most drivers were asked who they would be voting for in the 1948 election and why; and Butler quickly deduced that President Truman would have great difficulty in retaining the White House that November.

But Butler was still interested, too, in formal surveys of public opinion. While in Ann Arbor he caught up with a friend from St Paul's and New College, Harry Field, who was working at the University of Michigan's Survey Research Centre (SRC) – Butler's first link with an institution that would be crucial to his subsequent career. He and Field discussed the idea of establishing a similar body in Oxford, and also a much less ambitious idea of surveying voters in one particular constituency at the next general election to establish why people voted as they did. (The constituency survey was never carried out, although a team from the London School of Economics conducted a similar project in Greenwich in south-east London at the 1950 election.)

Later, Butler spent an extraordinary day picking the brains of two future giants of American public life in quick succession. In St Paul, Minnesota, he enjoyed a two-hour interview with a local lawyer, Warren Burger, who would later become Chief Justice of the United States. At the recent Republican convention, Burger had been a floor manager for one of the unsuccessful candidates, Harold Stassen, and he explained the phenomenon of a 'bandwagon' effect in favour of the expected victor. 'When it looked that Dewey was winning, one often couldn't hold the most extreme partisans of Stassen – men who hated Dewey's guts – from switching their votes!' he told Butler. But Burger still thought Stassen a good prospect in the long term. 'I'm as sure as I sit here that Stassen will someday be President.'[39] Despite running nine times for President between 1944 and 1992 – a span of forty-eight years – Harold Stassen never made it to the White House. It was left to Republican Richard Nixon – not Stassen – to appoint Warren Burger as Chief Justice of the Supreme Court in 1969.

After meeting Burger, Butler went that same evening to see the Mayor of Minneapolis, Hubert Humphrey, campaigning at a St Paul country fair for election to the US Senate, and he got a long lift with the candidate back to Minneapolis late that night. He had not been 'in the presence of a great man', Butler concluded:

> He's clever, liberal minded, energetic, enormously ambitious, extremely attractive as a campaigner, an excellent speaker,

> apparently a very good administrator, yet I suspect something a little superficial about the man. It may be that he's done too much campaigning of late – the business of campaigning gives a man little time to think: it fosters an intelligence running in clichés. Perhaps after six months' rest Humphrey will no longer seem superficial. But he wants to be the Democratic nominee for President in 1952 and he'll have little time to rest.[40]

Humphrey failed to become the party's presidential nominee in 1952 and ran for the White House on three other occasions, most notably when he was the Democratic contender against Nixon in 1968, after four years as Vice-President to Lyndon Johnson.

Butler had already experienced, on a trip to Ohio that April, the terrible racism at that time of many white Americans. A reporter on the local paper in Cincinnati told him how reporting crime had made him 'firmly anti-negro'. The journalist claimed his local police commissioner had said that 'the chief ambition of 95 per cent of negro men was to rape a white woman'. Wasn't that 'putting it a bit strongly', Butler asked. No, the reporter insisted. The police chief, he said, had 'been dealing with the nigger for 30 years. He ought to know. You can never trust a negro. I'd never have one in our house.'[41]

Time and again, often unprompted, drivers would raise the question of race in America, and the position of black people, often with racist remarks. 'The negroes … think that if they have equal rights then they think they should mix with the whites,' one man told him in Virginia. 'I'm dead against that. They're untrustworthy folk!'[42] 'The only good nigger is a dead one,' said a Jewish driver in New Jersey. 'They've got the right idea in the South.'[43] Yet Butler also heard appalling comments about Jews. 'The trouble with Hitler was that he didn't kill enough of them,' said a driver in Pennsylvania. 'You can scarcely buy a thing in the US that hasn't been made or handled by a Jew at some point in its distribution. And now they want a country of their own,' said another driver in Pennsylvania.

Butler didn't know how to react. 'What does one do in these circumstances? Listen meekly as I did, telling oneself that one is learning a lot about one example of the ordinary American? Try to argue? Experiment by saying one is a Jew oneself?' Should Butler have kept quiet in gratitude for the lift? The danger of arguing was he might suddenly have been dumped in the middle of nowhere, with little prospect of another ride.

As Butler toured America that summer, polls suggested Dewey was winning. 'The result has long been taken for granted by everyone – except President Truman,' Butler wrote for *Time and Time* just before polling day. 'The chances are very heavily in favour of Thomas E. Dewey being next President of the United States.' Butler's conclusion after his 9,000-mile tour was that:

> Nobody likes Dewey while everyone thinks him able and everybody likes Truman while nobody thinks him able. For the first time in 24 years the American voter has no heroes or villains to choose between ... Truman presents to the public the picture of a likeable, well-meaning little man who, it has been said, proves the truth of the old American adage, 'Anyone can become President of the United States'. It is unfortunate for him that he has been long enough in office for the public to learn that he has neither the wisdom to formulate policies himself nor the ability to gather the most competent men around him.[44]

Governor Dewey, said Butler, was the 'City Slicker', an able man who would run a competent government, but who found it hard to persuade voters that he liked them, a man without warmth or any great principle. Had the Democrats found a candidate 'with a fraction of the Roosevelt stature', they would have stood a good chance.[45]

Butler had not been impressed when he initially saw Truman speak, in Denver, Colorado. His speech was 'stumblingly and uninterestingly delivered. There was scattered applause, friendly but not enthusiastic.' He found people saying, 'Well! He's a nice-looking guy,' and 'Gee! The President seems real human, doesn't he?'[46] This reflected the consensus among commentators that Truman improved his barnstorming speaking abilities as the campaign progressed. Butler then saw Dewey speak in Denver the very next day. 'Despite that smug smile which the poor man can't conceal he did very well,' he reported. 'He managed to put more warmth into his manner than I had thought possible and, though he had a fully-prepared text, he delivered it as though speaking naturally and easily from notes.'[47]

Butler was fortunate to spend election night, 2 November 1948, in high-powered company – at the Roosevelt Hotel in New York, which housed Dewey's campaign headquarters. Butler had been introduced by Felix Frankfurter to one of Dewey's speechwriters, McGeorge 'Mac' Bundy, a Republican who was subsequently National Security Adviser to two Democrat Presidents, Kennedy and Johnson. Butler found him 'a charming and exceedingly able man'.[48] The election party they attended – a floor above the Dewey HQ – had an even more esteemed host – Allen Dulles, another senior member of the Dewey team, who would later serve as director of the CIA under Eisenhower at the same time as his brother John Foster Dulles was US Secretary of State.

Butler was more interested in the election results than the drink and idle chatter. 'After a while,' he wrote, 'Bundy and I slipped out of the general conversation and huddled down in a corner of the room with pencil and paper, a political almanac and a portable radio. It was intensely exciting listening to the results.'[49] Early returns, from the big cities, suggested things might not go as well as these Dewey staff hoped, though 'even at 3 a.m. the odds seemed to be on Dewey'. Butler made a quick excursion to the nearby Truman HQ at the Biltmore Hotel, where he found a 'growing intoxication and exuberance' before returning to the Dulles party, where Dewey supporters were watching the ever more depressing results through the new medium of television. 'The television was very good,' he wrote. 'The cameras alternated between Dem and Rep HQ but spent most of their time showing the newsroom of one of the big radio stations and bringing one commentator after another to the microphone to give the latest results in Senate, House and Gubernatorial races.' As the Democrat tide grew more and more clear, Butler wrote:

> [Bundy] greatly shocked the other guests by not appearing distressed at the results and by saying outspokenly that the world would not come to an end if Truman were elected ... The dispirited guests left. Only Bundy and I remained, our ears glued to the radio, waiting for the issue to be clearly decided. Finally, at 7.30 a.m. there seemed to be little doubt.

When the final results were in, Harry Truman had 49.6 per cent of the vote to Dewey's 45.1 per cent, and won by 303 votes to 189 in the electoral college. Perhaps more than any election in history, 1948 went down as a defeat for opinion polls, symbolised by the famous photo of a grinning Harry Truman holding up the front page of the *Chicago Daily Tribune*, which even before the polling stations closed had hit the streets with its notorious banner headline 'Dewey Defeats Truman'.

When Butler visited Gallup headquarters a week after the result, he felt their excuses wouldn't save the firm from 'a great deal of disrepute and loss of custom'. But he thought 'the consequences of the election for the polling industry will be almost entirely for the good. It will make them a great deal humbler and make the public less credulous. But I think that polls will survive: on the whole I hope they do.'[50]

Butler's fifteen months in America were the start of the era when television took off rapidly. Just 0.1 per cent of US homes had a TV set in 1946; but only nine years later, it was more than half of households. Initially, judging from his letters home, Butler had not paid great attention to the new medium, partly because at this stage TV sets weren't very common in homes, though they were increasingly prevalent in bars, where people were attracted by the live sports coverage. Television at that stage was largely confined to the big cities, where stations could afford the high start-up costs. Shortly before polling day, however, Butler was invited to dinner by Felix Frankfurter's clerk, Elliot Richardson (who later held several Cabinet posts under Presidents Nixon and Ford, and famously resigned as Attorney-General during the Watergate scandal). Richardson then shared a house in Georgetown with six other young lawyers:

> It was a pleasant evening and the dinner was excellent. The conversation was limited by the fact that they had recently acquired a television set and that it occupied most of our attention. During the year that I have been in America television has made enormous strides … Many families of very moderate income now have sets (the cheapest now made costs only $99) … One can talk or read through a radio programme – television makes much heavier demands on your attention. When all major sporting events are televised men and children alike are chained indoors. Friends, acquaintances even, who haven't sets themselves feel free to come and look at their neighbours' contraptions. After listening to the American radio, I am very frightened when I think of what television will be like here in ten years' time.[51]

It was a time when America was still coming to terms with this extraordinary new medium. Whereas cinema and radio in the inter-war years were seen as positive forces which brought people together, television was much more controversial, quickly perceived as a force which might distract from traditional conversation between families and friends. Butler shared these concerns.

These were, in hindsight, surprisingly hostile observations from a man who would very shortly make his name on television and do so much to develop the medium in Britain as a forum for political analysis and debate.

David Butler would return to the United States every year or two for the next twenty years, often spending several weeks or more there. His first return trip came in 1951, when he went back to Princeton, Washington and New York. In 1952, he taught tutorials and seminars at a summer school at Cornell University in upstate New York, and this time watched almost every moment of that summer's party conventions on television. These resulted in a presidential contest between Dwight Eisenhower for the Republicans, and the Democrat Adlai Stevenson. 'I'm madly for Adlai,' Butler told his mother, using Stevenson's campaign slogan (which couldn't beat Eisenhower's 'I Like Ike' for simplicity). Stevenson's acceptance address as the Democratic nominee, Butler said, 'provided the only occasion in my life when I have been deeply moved by a political speech … I'm certainly happier than ever in my bets that Eisenhower won't win.'[52]

Five weeks later, while staying in Ohio with Anthony Wedgwood Benn and the family of Benn's new wife Caroline, the pair managed to secure a half-hour interview with Stevenson, though Benn asked nearly all the questions. It seems extraordinary that Stevenson could spare the time for two young English visitors in the midst of an election. 'On every issue that Anthony cross-questioned him about,' Butler reported, 'Stevenson's answers were overwhelmingly to my taste, and substantially acceptable to Anthony's more left-wing palate.'[53] In the end, Eisenhower won comfortably.

The new medium of television could also be deceptive, Butler felt. The star-struck Englishman had been convinced ever since the convention that Adlai Stevenson was going to win, thanks largely to this new means of political expression. 'If he remains as magnetic a television personality as he has shown himself to be, there can be little doubt about the outcome ... There is no doubt that the conventions settled television more firmly than ever in the saddle as the leading campaign medium.'[54]

David Butler's fifteen months in the USA in 1947 and 1948 had him hooked. He would later describe it 'as the best year of his life educationally', far more valuable than New College or the Army, and the period when he grew into adulthood.[55] He 'had ten times as much energy' in America than when he was in England, he once said, and soon created for himself the kind of transatlantic existence that is quite common in the modern world, but was not in the 1950s.[56]

> I am very lucky to be able to sustain two lives, one on each side of the Atlantic, related but totally different lives. Each time I come over here I am immensely entertained, educated, excited. Each time I learn more surely that England is my natural habitat – but that I shall be very unhappy if I can't get over here reasonably often.[57]

CHAPTER FIVE

INTO THE FAMILY TRADE

A hundred yards or so east of Robinson Tower, where David Butler first lived as a student at New College, is the junction of two age-old Oxford thoroughfares, Holywell Street and Longwall Street. Here, opposite the wall of Magdalen College, is one of the city's most industrially significant sites, the original garage of Morris Motors.

Today, the restored premises contain rooms for Butler's student successors at New College. Yet in the 1900s, this former livery stables was where 25-year-old bicycle-maker William Morris first moved into the exciting new world of motor engines. Morris had run a bicycle business here for some years, and David Butler remembers his father Harold telling him how, when he was a don at New College, he'd gone to get his bike repaired in the premises next door.

Morris then moved into motorcycles, and very nearly went out of business at one point, before recovering to feel his way into an industry which would make his name and vast fortune: motor cars. Initially, Morris did everything with cars *except* make them. He sold vehicles made by many of the early British manufacturers; he hired cars out; he ran a taxi service; and if you needed your car repaired, Morris was your man.

It didn't take long for Morris to see that everyone would soon want their own car. So, he designed the small, two-seat Morris

Oxford, known as the 'Bullnose' Morris. In 1912, he also acquired new premises in a former military college in Cowley, then on the south-east edge of Oxford, to manufacture cars in large numbers, using the same production methods pioneered by the great American Henry Ford. After the First World War, as Oxford developed from a university town into an industrial city, Morris was hailed as the greatest British industrialist of his age. He received public recognition with a baronetcy and later a hereditary peerage, as Viscount Nuffield, yet always retained his Oxfordshire burr. How many men could say that both of their names had embedded themselves so deeply into our history as Morris and Nuffield?

Until William Morris began giving away much of his large fortune, Nuffield was merely known as the Oxfordshire village where he lived. In 1937, Lord Nuffield allocated £900,000 (about £60 million today) to establish a new Oxford college bearing his name on a patch of waste ground which he had just bought next to St Peter's Hall (now St Peter's College), opposite the old castle mound and city prison. The site had previously housed coal wharfs and the terminus of the Oxford to Coventry canal. It would be established solely for graduates – the first Oxford college to take both men and women students on equal terms. Lord Nuffield had originally envisaged a college that would study engineering and accountancy, but was persuaded instead that it should concentrate on social studies – politics, economics and sociology. One of the early aims of the college, espoused especially by one of its founders, A. D. 'Sandie' Lindsay, the Master of Balliol and university Vice-Chancellor, was to 'bring members of the University into personal contact with men of affairs'.[1] Lindsay, a Labour supporter, who fought the famous 1938 Oxford parliamentary by-election as an anti-appeasement independent, hoped that the college would bridge 'the disastrous gap in our modern life, the gap between the theoretical student of society and those responsible for carrying it on'.[2]

Amidst David Butler's regular trips to America, his real base, from 1949 onwards, was Nuffield College, the institution to which he has belonged for almost seventy years, almost the entire life of the college. And perhaps no fellow of the college has epitomised the founding spirit of Nuffield – linking the academic world with public life – better than Butler.

Before 1945, Nuffield was tiny. At the start in 1938, it had just six part-time fellows – who included the controversial socialist academic G. D. H. Cole – and these all had fellowships with other colleges. There were also six visiting fellows, who included the long-standing general secretary of the Trades Union Congress Sir Walter Citrine. But the predominantly left-wing nature of the early founders annoyed Lord Nuffield – a free-market Conservative who had also backed the fascist leader Sir Oswald Mosley in the late '30s. (Indeed, for many years these strains endangered the whole project, as Lord Nuffield estranged himself from his college.)

It would be two decades before the Nuffield site could be developed properly, and so the early college was based in a large house at 17 Banbury Road – the location where the decision was taken in March 1945 for Nuffield to commission Ronald McCallum to write an account of that year's coming general election. Seminars were held in a hut in the back garden. By the time David Butler returned to Oxford in January 1949, following his fifteen months in America, the college was still very small in numbers. Nuffield had taken just two students in 1945, three in 1946, twelve in 1947 and fourteen in 1948. In the summer of 1949, when Nuffield accepted Butler, he was one of just twenty students – twelve from that year and eight from previous years.[3]

Butler had been accepted to write a DPhil thesis on 'The Electoral System in Britain Since 1918'. This was still an era when doctorates were treated with great suspicion by many people in academic circles. 'My father certainly had complete contempt for this German idea of a doctorate,' Butler later recalled. 'He said – and it sounds terribly snobbish, but he wasn't that sort of person – that people who get further degrees, it's just people who want an excuse to hang around in Oxford and haven't got their fellowship.'[4] Butler may have felt his second in PPE was inadequate for an academic career, especially when compared with the glittering prizes attained by his many scholarly forebears, but he also hoped a DPhil – what Oxford calls its PhD degree – would help him get teaching posts in America.

There was some literature on British elections before 1918, but remarkably little on the three decades since. His research consisted largely in consulting the limited number of primary sources: ploughing through parliamentary debates on electoral matters, and various committees and commissions on electoral procedure, electoral reform and parliamentary boundaries. He also combed through *The Times* newspaper and back issues of *The Economist*. Among the few academic articles, he was by happy chance fascinated to light upon the one by his distant cousin, the mathematician Francis Edgeworth, from the *Journal of the Royal Statistical Society* in 1898, which was among the first attempts to find a formula to relate seats to votes, through a study of the elections of 1886, 1892 and 1895.[5]

Butler's supervisor for his thesis was Herbert Nicholas, a fellow at Exeter College, who was to be a key part of the network of friends and colleagues who did so much to help Butler's progress over the next decade and became a visiting don at Nuffield in 1948. Nicholas, who came from the valleys of South Wales, was a small, dapper figure who, like Butler, had also been a protégé of Isaiah Berlin, having known him at New College in the 1930s and then in the Washington embassy during the war. Nicholas shared Butler's fascination with America and its politics. What's more, he had been commissioned by Nuffield to write the next general election book, after R. B. McCallum decided that the 1945 account was enough. Butler agreed again to write the statistical appendix, and essentially became Nicholas's deputy on the project, helping to draft and revise much of the text.

While supervising his thesis, Nicholas gave David Butler one important word of advice: 'Write.' He said that it was worthwhile starting writing even before one had completed one's research, as a means of working out what one still didn't know about a subject. It was a maxim Butler would apply to all his future work, and also pass on to the many research students whom he supervised himself. Owing partly to the paucity of research material, David Butler managed to complete his thesis very fast, in about fourteen months. He was awarded his DPhil in 1951, and in 1953 he published the thesis as a book.[6]

During Butler's fallow period – the six months between returning from America at the end of 1948 and being accepted by Nuffield in the summer of 1949, he had tried to continue what he'd done in America, touring the UK chatting to ordinary people to acquire a feel for local politics. But it didn't work with British people. 'People just wouldn't open up in the same way. They would clam up, and put me in a box around class and background, and just wouldn't talk.'[7] This kind of reportage continued more successfully with his work for Herbert Nicholas on the book for the 1950 election, when he travelled around the country questioning party organisers, agents and candidates, developing the style of instant history research that would become such an important part of Butler's activity.

This research dovetailed neatly with his continuing journalism. He did a report for *Time and Tide* on the Liberal Party Assembly in Hastings in March 1949, from which Butler predicted the coming election would be the party's last chance of serious revival and that afterwards it was 'likely that one hand rather than two will be adequate to count the Liberal representation in Parliament' (in fact, they won nine seats in 1950).[8] But gradually *Time and Tide* lost interest in his work.

Fortunately, Herbert Nicholas had introduced Butler to Alastair Buchan, home editor of *The Economist*, who asked him to write several articles on election topics from the spring of 1949 onwards.

The most important of these – and the one that caught Winston Churchill's eye – was commissioned towards the end of 1949 to mark the fact that 1950 would be a general election year. Butler remembers returning late in the evening on Christmas Day, 'rather drunk' after a family party, to write it.[9] Then, suddenly, having seen the names on an embargoed copy of the 1950 New Year's Honours List, Buchan realised that the election was likely to be very early in the new year. So, he rushed Butler's article into print in the first edition of 1950. He gave it extra prominence, although Butler remained anonymous.[10]

Butler forecast that the turnout at the coming election – due before the summer of 1950 – would be 'of record size'. He was right – it was an extraordinary 83.9 per cent, never exceeded before or since. As we have learnt, the most eye-catching feature of the article was to introduce to modern British politics the Cube Law. This was not Butler's own discovery or invention, but an idea that had lain dormant for decades. He had come across it a few weeks before, while researching his thesis, amidst the reams of evidence people had submitted to the Royal Commission on Electoral Systems back in 1909. In his submission, James Parker Smith, a former Liberal Unionist MP who took a great interest in election matters, had analysed the relationship between the number of seats each major party obtained and the total votes they'd received nationally. Smith had suggested that in a reasonably homogeneous country, which had a two-party system and single-member seats, the ratio of seats won by each party was proportionately a cube of the ratio of the votes cast for them. So, if the ratio of votes cast is A:B, then the ratio of seats is $A^3:B^3$. Smith, who acknowledged he had obtained the formula from the leading mathematician Percy MacMahon, maintained that it had broadly worked for the six general elections between 1885 and 1906.[11]

Butler then did some work on what he says was an old-fashioned hand-cranked calculating machine at Nuffield and found that this 'simple rule-of-thumb formula' had also worked 'with extraordinary accuracy' for the three most recent general elections in the UK – 1931, 1935 and 1945 – contests with which he was already very familiar, having already calculated the swing in each seat back in 1945.

Moreover, in the previous five elections in New Zealand (from 1935 to 1949), Butler observed, the formula had correlated with the final outcome with an average error of only one seat, admittedly in a House of Representatives of just eighty members. The performance in the three most recent British elections was even more remarkable. Since the return of a predominantly two-party system in the UK in 1931, 'the average error in calculating the division of the contested seats won by the major parties is – fantastic though it may seem – two seats' (in a House of more than 600 seats). So, Butler suggested, a 65–35 division of the vote between the two main parties would produce a division in seats of roughly 520 to 80.

A cubic calculation from a 65–35 vote split works out as follows:

0.65 x 0.65 x 0.65 = 0.274625
0.35 x 0.35 x 0.35 = 0.042875

A ratio of 0.274625 to 0.042875 strictly produces 519 seats for the more popular party, and 81 for the less popular. The calculation for a very narrow 51–49 split in votes is:

0.51 x 0.51 x 0.51 = 0.132651
0.49 x 0.49 x 0.49 = 0.117649

The cubic ratio here, 0.132651 to 0.117649, produces a division of 318 seats to 282 in a House of 600 seats.

'On the average in recent elections,' Butler wrote, 'between 15 and 20 seats have changed hands for every one per cent turnover in votes; a turnover of 15 to 20 seats means of course a change of 30 to 40 in the size of the Parliamentary majority.' But Butler warned readers not to assume this rediscovered rule was hard and fast: 'There is nothing magical about this formula. There is no reason why it should fit with such uncanny accuracy the results of the next election.'[12] Nor did Butler actually use the term 'Cube Law' at this stage.

Butler's unveiling – or rediscovery – of the Cube Formula, or Cube Rule, would make quite an impact in statistical circles. It was taken up in the inaugural lecture of the eminent statistician Maurice Kendall, who called it the Cube Law and used it for a series of articles in *The Observer*. Yet, after the election, in an academic article in the *British Journal of Sociology*, Kendall and his co-author Alan Stuart would be quite dismissive of Butler's discovery. 'On the face of it,' they said, 'the law seems to have been reached on very doubtful premises.'[13] When they applied the Cube Law to the results of the 1950 election (which occurred after Butler's article), Kendall and Stuart said it produced an error of forty seats in terms of the actual majority – 'a salutary reminder of the limitations of the cube-law in prediction'. Yet, by a strange quirk, applying the Cube Law to the final Gallup poll before the 1950 election was far more accurate: it overestimated the Labour outcome by just one seat, and underestimated the Conservative result by five seats.[14]

For a few weeks at the start of 1950, the new Cube Law caught people's imaginations as a new magic formula which could explain how elections worked. And thus it was that Butler's article in *The Economist* caught the attention of Winston Churchill while he was on holiday on Madeira. The Conservative leader was intrigued by the new possibilities of forecasting much more precisely the level of popular support through the new Gallup polls. And the issue became even more pressing when, only a few days into his holiday, Clement Attlee suddenly called a general election for 23 February. After just nine days on Madeira, Churchill was obliged to fly back to London to lead his party in that contest.

It was a few weeks afterwards, in the afternoon of 6 February, while he was in London, that David Butler suddenly received the request, with about three hours' notice, to come down to Chartwell for dinner with Churchill, and to stay overnight. 'This is not the sort of invitation that is refused,' he wrote in a long account he typed up the next day.

Even after the lapse of a few hours, Butler claimed to have a 'tragically short' memory of everything that had transpired between them at Chartwell, but he salvaged what he could. 'I, clutching at every moment of this brief glimpse of greatness, must indiscriminately record all that I can remember of the evening.'[15]

On election matters, Churchill's main concern was that his old party, the Liberals, were fighting around 125 more seats in 1950 than they had in 1945. The Conservative leader claimed it was 'undemocratic for this wanton little clique of Liberals to put up candidates who had no chance and who threatened the country with a Government elected on split votes'. Churchill told Butler that had the Liberals taken up the idea of an electoral pact which he had offered them three years before, they 'could have had what terms they wanted. They could have maintained their independence and had sixty seats and continued to be one of the great parties of the nation.' But they had dismissed Churchill's offer. 'They were deludedly self-important little men,' he said.[16]

But Butler suggested the Liberals would only have done a deal if Churchill had offered them proportional representation (PR). Churchill's response was to suggest having PR in the big cities, a policy he had long supported, and which he said would have the extra advantage of providing 'really safe seats for one or two really distinguished men' from each of the parties. Now, he said, safe seats went to 'unimportant little men chosen by local cliques'.[17]

Before dinner Churchill offered his guest the choice of sherry or tomato juice. Butler, worried about how much alcohol might be served later, chose tomato juice. 'I hope that you drink,' Churchill remarked. Butler says his host certainly did:

> He had three glasses of champagne with his dinner and two glasses of superb brandy, followed by a whisky and soda afterwards. And he had one, if not two, more whiskies before midnight. After dinner he smoked one huge cigar and was surprisingly inexpert in keeping it alight. An amusing touch at dinner came during the entrée when the maid gently pointed out to him that he had not fed his dog – a brown poodle. For a minute he went into ecstasies of foolish dog talk, apologising to the dog.[18]

Churchill explained that he was the only person allowed to feed the animal, who had only one meal a day, and ate it all in three minutes before belching very loudly.

Throughout, Butler had the impression that there was a large staff quietly hidden away but ready to respond to Churchill's every need. 'In particular, there were the discreet and anonymous young ladies who slipped in and out to accept his instructions and seemed to be kept permanently on call to take dictation when the mood should seize him.'[19]

Apart from the staff at Chartwell, the only other person occasionally present during the four-hour conversation was Churchill's long-standing friend and expert adviser Lord Cherwell – 'the Prof' – who had been the government's chief scientific adviser during the war. The former Oxford physicist was 'a strange uneasy figure with an over-intellectual forehead but an unimpressive manner', says Butler.

> He was a little embarrassed in his role as Churchill's intellectual keeper. Whenever Churchill made a statement on economics or statistics he would turn to Cherwell and say, 'That's right, isn't it?' And Cherwell would say 'Yes' and adduce reasons or, if it was obviously doubtful, would in a very deprecatory way skirt around to suggest that some people might, by very tenuous and roundabout reasoning, put forward a different conclusion. I could understand

> why Cherwell is disliked and why [journalist Alastair] Buchan could say that he goes around guiltily like an academic who has sold his academic integrity.[20]

At times, he wrote, Winston Churchill spoke of his 'extreme old age' – he was seventy-five – yet he 'gave the impression of greatness and of pettiness' from time to time as well:

> Always he spoke in the grand Churchillian phrases, by the mere timbre of his voice and the rounding of his sentences conjuring up crowded meeting halls or vast stadiums. But when one got used to that one stood astonished at the way in which he wavered between the perceptive epigram and the petulant explosion.[21]

Churchill had plainly made 'discreet enquiries' about his visitor. Lord Cherwell, for example, seemed to know of Butler's family relationship to Rab Butler – 'how he knew, I am unaware', David Butler wrote – and Cherwell also suggested Butler was a socialist. 'I said nothing to indicate my politics during the evening,' Butler recalled, 'except to make one protest about my relative neutrality.'[22]

During dinner, Butler recalled, Churchill warned: 'You'll have to listen to Mr Eden after this. You can stop your ears if you like.' A man brought in a wireless set, and Churchill interrupted his senior colleague's broadcast two or three times. 'He's speaking too fast,' he said at one point. Afterwards Churchill summoned an assistant: 'Get me Mr Eden at the BBC. Mention my name and you'll get him.' And when Eden came on the phone, Butler could hear Churchill from the next room duly praising Eden's speech: 'Anthony, excellent, excellent, capital.'[23]

It was only after his call to Eden that Churchill asked Butler what he thought of the address, and Butler described it as 'an admirable and honourable speech but not a very good broadcast'. It was 'too academic', Butler explained, and 'wasn't a fireside chat'.

Diverted onto the subject of fireside radio talks, Churchill 'for five side-splitting minutes' began a long mimicry of a trade union leader – probably Ernest Bevin – addressing the nation on radio in an intimate manner. 'I gets home in the evening after a hard day's work and I takes off my coat and I says to the wife "This isn't like the old days."' Churchill 'rolled on and on' in this style and, says Butler, 'if it had been given by a trade union leader it would indeed have been a most powerful speech'. And at the end Churchill claimed, 'I could go on like this for hours. I've been in the game for fifty-four years. But Anthony couldn't.'

Butler suggested lesser mortals might have difficulty holding an audience for thirty minutes. 'I never have any difficulty in holding them for half an hour,' Churchill replied. 'I find a twenty-minute broadcast much harder than a half-hour one … I am not unmindful of the need to broadcast to four or five people round a fire rather than four or five thousand in a hall.'[24]

And Butler got the impression that Churchill wasn't worried about the prospect of being defeated again at the polls. 'This election', Churchill told him,

> involves many problems for me personally – where I shall live, what will happen to my book, my whole way of life. They say I am ambitious. I do not know why I go on except that it is my duty as long as I am spared in my extreme old age, to maintain my health and vigour. But I could now very happily spend the winters in warmer climates and come back just for our glorious summers … The consolation of vigorous old age is that I still find so many new things to interest me, like your cube formula.[25]

At this point in their extraordinary conversation, Churchill seized on the fact that Butler was only twenty-five. He teased him that he had to hurry up since Napoleon had been only twenty-six when he crossed the bridge at Lodi, the advance in northern Italy that

Napoleon later regarded as the key turning point in his career. And this prompted Churchill to start comparing Napoleon with Hitler:

> You know Hitler has exploded the Napoleon legend. Napoleon achieved so little compared with him. Think, then to stand on a hill and deploy 70,000 troops in a battle was the summit of human grandeur, the biggest thing a man could do. Hitler never fought a battle but he mastered more of Europe much more completely than Napoleon and he commanded vastly greater armies.[26]

There would be 'dire consequences for the country' if Labour was returned to office, Churchill warned. 'America will abandon us. With the hydrogen bomb they don't need our Norfolk airstrip any longer … They will abandon us and our credit will go down and down.'[27]

Yet he had worked well with Stafford Cripps during the war, Churchill said, and got on well with all of his senior colleagues in the wartime coalition – except Labour's economic thinker Hugh Dalton. 'I could not think him honest. He caused me great trouble at the MEW [Ministry of Economic Warfare].' It would have been 'disastrous', Churchill said, if Clement Attlee had fulfilled his plan to make Dalton Foreign Secretary. 'But the King stepped in and refused. One of the advantages of the monarchy.' But Churchill insisted he didn't dislike the Labour Party. 'I only dislike Socialism which is a wicked evil foreign doctrine.' And later Churchill, '*a propos* of nothing', according to Butler, exploded: 'I hate tyranny. I hate tyranny. I will fight with all the vigour that is in me…' And, Butler wrote, he 'sailed unconsciously into a long series of Churchillian clichés about the glories of Liberty'.[28]

It was around midnight when their conversation drew to a close, and Churchill insisted on personally taking his guest up to his room. Yet first he took Butler into his own bedroom and 'demonstrated with childlike pride' a large recording machine, sent to him from

America, and supposedly the only one of its kind in the world. The machine could take an hour's dictation and turn itself on and off at the sound of a human voice.[29]

The next morning, after breakfast, Butler was summoned to Churchill's room to say goodbye. 'There in bed surrounded by newspapers, with his spectacles on the end of his nose, lay this improbable old man,' he wrote. Churchill thanked his visitor and concluded that Butler's analysis of the election was not 'very hopeful', though Butler tried to reassure him the election could go either way. Then Churchill's eyes fell onto the paper he was reading, and Butler quietly left.[30]

> I understood that the audience was over. As I moved through the next room I heard his voice saying yet again 'How kind of you to come!' I hesitated again for a moment. Then I caught the eye of the boy who was showing me out. His expression explained as plainly as could be that Mr Churchill was very vague about terminating interviews and that one was not meant to turn back merely because he shouted things after.[31]

Later that day, back in Oxford, Butler typed up a six-page account of his extraordinary trip for his parents:

> I hope that I behaved with outward self-possession, but I was conscious of an unsophisticated excitement of the 'Fancy this happening to little me' variety. And that perhaps is why I failed so completely to feel that the remarkable garrulous old man in whose company I spent four hours last night was the same as the world figure of whose personality and public characteristics I have so long been conscious.[32]

The encounter had a lasting effect on David Butler. Having spent four hours, one to one, with the man he considered to be the greatest in the world, he was never in awe of any politician ever again. He'd already spoken to substantial figures in America, of course, but 'this weird experience' with Churchill, he says, 'put the seal on it', and gave him the extra confidence to talk to anyone.[33]

A very different incident in Oxford also helped turn Butler from a rather timid young man into a confident networker. He was dining in Corpus Christi College one evening and reached over to greet a colleague, only for his academic gown to drape across the table and send several glasses crashing to the floor. Having survived the crash, the broken glass and all the embarrassment, Butler realised that he could cope with any social *faux pas*.

On his return to Oxford in 1949, Butler lived in St John Street and then shared a flat with his old New College friend Peter Blaker in Bradmore Road. Then, from around 1952, he took another flat in Banbury Road which he shared with Zbigniew Pelczynski, a Polish refugee at Nuffield who had fought in the 1944 Warsaw Uprising. Pelczynski, who was later credited by President Clinton as being his most influential tutor when Clinton was a Rhodes Scholar at Oxford in the late 1960s, recalls how he and Butler would organise joint dinner parties as they experimented with entertaining and cooking. Butler was characteristically practical in his approach, says Pelczynski:

> I would prepare a menu. 'Let's simplify it,' he'd say. 'Cut this out and that out. Limit the cooking to an hour.' He had his watch in his hand. I wanted delicious constructed things. It was very enjoyable and would last till 1 a.m., when I was dying to go to bed. 'Zbysek, my principle when cooking is you've got to wash up.' It was part of his routine-ised life.[34]

Butler bought a car and rented a garage in Walton Street from a young philosophy don at St Anne's College called Iris Murdoch. And every few weeks, for much of the 1950s, he would organise trips with friends to watch Shakespeare in Stratford-upon-Avon, just north of Oxford. 'Again, it was very well organised,' Pelczynski recalls.

> He came with a hamper full of food and a few bottles of juice. Half way to Stratford, just beyond Shipston-on-Stour, there was a clump of trees and some grass, and David always stopped there. His time was always measured. It was time to put down the blanket and have a good lunch, and we would then get to Stratford for the 2.30 performance. I saw more Shakespeare plays every two months with those trips than ever since.[35]

Despite the dinner parties, picnics and plays, Butler doesn't seem to have managed to attract a proper girlfriend. He was good-looking, but it was not easy in a university where men were in the overwhelming majority. Perhaps women also found Butler too earnest, too wedded to his narrow academic interests, and maybe a touch humourless. 'It just seems that on a personal level no one ever quite taught him what women are like and how to speak with them,' a younger member of his family says. 'I think he's always been ever so slightly scared of them.'

In the summer of 1952, while remaining a research fellow at Nuffield, Butler also got a one-term lectureship to teach politics at his old college, New College, standing in for his mentor Herbert Nicholas (who moved there from Exeter College in 1951). But he still wasn't sure he was cut out for academic life. He had started to dabble in broadcasting, with some success. And then there was the possibility of politics itself.

Tony Benn and another Oxford friend and contemporary, Sir Edward Boyle, were MPs already, both having been elected in 1950. Butler had voted Labour in 1950, but for the next three elections – 1951, 1955 and 1959 – he abstained from voting, on the grounds that he didn't feel right talking sympathetically to someone in politics while knowing he'd voted against their party. Nor was Butler particularly committed.

One evening in 1954, Butler was crossing Parliament Square when he noticed the lantern on top of Big Ben was alight, to signify that the House was sitting. He suddenly wondered what he would do if Edward Boyle were to write him a letter to say a Conservative seat was coming up, and that he could fix the selection for Butler. Would he accept? 'And I instantly knew that I would,' he thought to himself. 'The best club in London. The opportunity to have some say in all sorts of political issues – I couldn't resist it.'

A few days later, again outside Parliament, he remembered his earlier fantasy and wondered what he'd do if instead Tony Benn suggested he could arrange a Labour seat. 'Once again, I knew that I would jump at the opportunity, for just the same reasons.'

Then what if the letters arrived together? Which seat would he pick? He wrestled with the problem and decided he'd go for the Tory one. 'It was not that my sympathies at the time were more Conservative than Labour – rather the reverse. It was that I would be a hypocrite in either party. But, not being a true believer, I'd feel less guilty among pragmatic Conservatives than among Labour zealots.'

Five years later, Butler concluded he would accept neither offer. He recalled the words of another Tory MP he knew called Richard Fort, who said that every friend who'd taken ministerial office had been obliged to 'make some sacrifice of family or personal loyalty in pursuit of their career'. And he'd also observed Tony Benn at home one night being interrupted by the phone and immediately agreeing to speaking engagements on two successive Friday nights. 'And, as he spoke, I saw Carol's face. The Benns were, and continued to be, very happily married. Carol knew perfectly well what it meant to be a politician's wife. But, with four small children, I watched her seeing two more family evenings lost.'[36]

David Butler would choose a life of politics, of course, but in a rather different way.

CHAPTER SIX

TELLY DON

'By the magic of psephology we are able to predict what we think has happened tonight,' announced the BBC's David Dimbleby just seconds before 10 p.m. on the evening of the June 2017 general election. 'And what we are saying is the Conservatives are the largest party, but they don't have an overall majority at this stage...'

For decades, election nights, held every four years or so, have been high drama – occasions when careers are made and lost. For a few weeks, even the most powerful politicians in the land have had to cede centre stage to tens of millions of ordinary voters. To many of those involved in this extravaganza, general elections are the big test, the climax of years of preparation – the Olympic Games or World Cup of politics.

For a period of roughly twenty hours or so, from shortly before the close of polls on election day through to the following afternoon or evening, the closing drama is staged in TV studios and through their scores of outside broadcasts. The main players aren't just politicians, but teams of studio analysts and election experts, armed with computers and elaborate graphics, and under intense pressure to produce quick results. The test is the speed with which they get results on screen and forecast the right overall outcome.

Remarkably, immediately after the BBC was founded in 1922, it faced three general elections in just twenty-four months, and each time broadcast the results overnight on its new radio service. The corporation had no news-gathering operation of its own in those early days, so depended for results on the long-established news agency Reuters. But for its third election – in October 1924, just a few days after David Butler was born – it seems Reuters let them down badly. The BBC was pipped for speed by the nearest operation that one could describe at that time as a rival public service – the rolling illuminated 'sky signs' that flashed each result down to the crowds gathered in Trafalgar Square. Immediately afterwards, Reuters got an angry letter from Arthur Burrows, the BBC director of programmes, who had doubled up as the radio announcer:

> We are disappointed in last night's news services, in as much as we are informed that we were hopelessly behind on several occasions, and particularly in respect to the state of the parties. I am told this morning on good authority that at the moment (1.05 am) when I was announcing the state of the parties to be Conservatives 82, Labour 41, Liberals 13, Independents 1, the signs in Trafalgar Square were announcing Conservatives 113, Labour 50, Liberals 20, Independents 2 – a difference of nearly 50 in the returns.[1]

For the next four general elections – 1929, 1931, 1935 and 1945 – the BBC continued transmitting a simple overnight results service on radio. Although BBC Television started in 1936, it was taken off air during the war and didn't resume until 1946, so BBC TV wasn't present for the 1945 election. At the start of 1950, when the Labour Prime Minister Clement Attlee went to Buckingham Palace to ask the King for a dissolution of Parliament, with an election set for 23 February, the BBC faced the possibility of the first television election in British history.

At this stage it was still only a possibility because BBC TV was extremely wary of getting involved in the election at all. It seems a bewildering fact, but at that time broadcasters – and the BBC were the *only* broadcasters in those days – imposed a rule on themselves against covering the daily cut and thrust of election campaigns. This rule had been adopted on the understanding that the political parties would have been very unhappy had the BBC tried to cover campaigns as news events, through fears that the broadcasters might be biased one way or another. The BBC's assumption was that if they didn't apply their own internal ban, the politicians would impose one themselves.

And this restriction went hand in hand outside election time with the even more absurd Fourteen-Day Rule, whereby the BBC could not broadcast anything on any topic which was due to be discussed in Parliament over the next two weeks. This extraordinary rule, which was a serious restraint on BBC journalism, was not abolished until 1957.

So, in 1950, BBC news bulletins announced on 11 January that Parliament had been dissolved and an election date set, but the corporation refrained from any news coverage of the campaign for the next six weeks. The only sign on BBC radio or TV that an election was taking place were the regular election broadcasts which each major party was allowed to make setting out their case, but even then, in 1950, BBC TV carried them only as sound broadcasts, with no moving pictures.

In the autumn of 1949, the BBC had suggested to the three main parties that at the next election TV cameras should be allowed to broadcast a campaign speech made at one of their public meetings in the London area, or that representatives of each party might put their case in a TV studio. A BBC memo reported that 'every effort was made to interest [the parties] but the matter in their view did not even admit of argument'.[2] There were also concerns that allowing politicians who were constituency candidates onto the airwaves might breach the provisions of the 1948 Representation of the People Act, which regulated election expenses. The cost of the broadcast, it was feared, would be included as part of a candidate's expenses return, since such expenses had long been limited by law.

The ban on radio and TV coverage of elections seems extraordinary today, but it has to be understood within the historical context. In the late '40s and early '50s, British politicians were sceptical that the BBC could be trusted to be even-handed in its coverage. Memories were fresh of the pioneering way in which Nazi Germany had used radio, cinema newsreels – and, to a small extent, TV as well – for propaganda purposes; similarly, broadcasting was exploited by the Stalinist regimes of the Soviet bloc to extol the achievements of socialism and its leaders, while denying a platform to any alternative views.

But there was no restriction on the BBC reporting the *results* of an election once the polls had closed. So, five days after Attlee went to the Palace, the BBC assistant head of talks, Grace Wyndham Goldie, wrote a memo to her boss, the head of BBC television Cecil McGivern, about the coming election night. 'I take it', she wrote, 'that it would be impossible for television on that evening to ignore the elections altogether.'[3] Many senior figures within the BBC did indeed seem to think TV could ignore the 1950 election results, expecting people to rely on radio broadcasts. Since the 1924 election, the BBC had simply employed a radio announcer to read out constituency figures as they came in, with music played whenever the results dried up. Most senior BBC staff thought any results service should be confined to radio as before; and, as Goldie later explained in her memoirs, these colleagues thought television 'could add nothing to the detailed reading of figures. There was no point in putting a camera in front of an announcer and watching him read.' There were technical objections, too. Some warned it might be 'difficult, even dangerous' for transmitters at BBC television headquarters at Alexandra Palace in north London to carry on working beyond their normal closing time of 11 p.m. – they might get overheated and even explode. 'The general feeling at Alexandra

Palace', wrote Goldie, 'was that the chances of a fiasco were so great that the plan we proposed should not even be attempted.'[4]

After much internal argument, however, it was eventually agreed that the BBC TV Current Affairs department could broadcast a live programme from Alexandra Palace for about two hours and a quarter, from 10.45 p.m. until around 1 a.m., by which time, it was hoped, the outcome would eventually be clear. There would also be a fifteen-minute *Election Analysis* programme after the 8 p.m. TV news bulletin the following evening. This was a historic development – the first election results programmes on British television. And rather than just listing a long series of constituency results, Goldie wanted intelligent, neutral commentary. She had to do it all on a budget of just £400 (about £10,000 today).

Nobody who met Grace Wyndham Goldie ever forgot her. David Attenborough once described her as a 'small, vivacious bird-like lady – though perhaps with rather more of the eagle than the wren'.[5] The future BBC director-general, Alasdair Milne, who was then a young producer, says she was 'a lion of a woman', and he remembers her 'striking finely chiselled face', together with 'a sharp questing mind and great charm, though she did not deploy it on everybody in equal measure'.[6]

Indeed, Goldie was arguably the most important woman in the history of the BBC. Born in the Scottish Highlands in 1900, she'd been present at the very birth of television in Britain in 1936, attending the opening night at Alexandra Palace as a critic for *The Listener* magazine, when she immediately realised that TV was the future. Goldie then spent most of the war as a civil servant at the Board of Trade and didn't join the corporation until 1944. In 1947, after three years in radio, she joined the BBC's quaintly named Television Talks department, and over the next eighteen years presided over the pioneering golden age of BBC current affairs journalism.

Goldie was responsible for commissioning legendary flagship programmes such as *Panorama* and *Tonight*, and she nurtured a long string of distinguished broadcasters – all men – including Robin Day, Cliff Michelmore, David Attenborough, John Freeman and Ian Trethowan. Her off-screen recruits included Michael Peacock, Donald Baverstock and Alasdair Milne. Two of her protégés, Trethowan and Milne, would become BBC director-general, while three others became managing directors in ITV.

Goldie thrived in what was a strongly male world. Had she lived in later times, she might have become the corporation's first female director-general. She was a woman of extremely strong personality, who knew what she liked, and what she didn't. 'A lady of iron whim' is how the Oxford academic Herbert Nicholas once described her.[7] Goldie did little to help other women, though, and Alasdair Milne says she might dismiss a female colleague as 'just a chit of a girl'.[8] She liked to be surrounded instead by good-looking, clever young men. They included David Butler, who probably owes more to Grace Wyndham Goldie than to any other person in his career, with the possible exception of Ronald McCallum.

Without Goldie's strong lobbying internally, BBC TV would probably never have broadcast a results programme in 1950. But Goldie credits Chester Wilmot, an Australian who presented one of her existing programmes, *Foreign Correspondent*, with getting her to press the case within the corporation. 'We cooked up over lunch a plan, drawing pictures on the table-cloth,' she said years later, 'about where we should have things and how we should have maps doing this, and outside broadcast cameras doing that, and … inspired by Chester's enthusiasm, I put up a plan.'[9]

Wilmot had been a war reporter with the Australian Broadcasting Commission, and then, after D-Day, made his name with British audiences reporting for BBC radio from the war in Europe. Wilmot clearly merited a major role in Goldie's programme, but Goldie was also keen to include some analysis of the results, which she knew was likely to arouse deep concerns among her highly cautious bosses at Broadcasting House. Employing Wilmot as the main studio analyst, however, might be a step too far and could imperil the whole project. Instead, Goldie proposed that Wilmot should be the overall programme presenter, or compère:

> He was an Australian. He knew a good deal about British politics but such was the delicacy of the situation then, as always, between broadcasters and politicians, that the idea of having a running commentary on the results of a general election I knew it would make people's hair stand on end ... and the fact that the commentary was going to be given not by one of the BBC's own parliamentary experts but by an Australian war correspondent, and one who was a freebooting, enterprising sort of character would not be acceptable.[10]

Goldie quickly went in search of expertise outside the BBC. She feared, however, that print journalists would not be regarded as sufficiently neutral since they were invariably connected with newspapers which were partisan. The obvious alternative was the academic world, which would probably be cheaper, too. So Goldie tried to enlist Ronald McCallum, the main author of the 1945 election book (though, by then, he'd decided not to write its 1950 successor). A week after her memo to Cecil McGivern, Goldie went to Pembroke College, Oxford, to see the 51-year-old McCallum, but the academic was wary. 'He was courteous but reluctant,' she wrote later.

> He knew nothing about television. He was not prepared to give instant comment on individual results. This was not his métier. At last he said he would take part on two conditions. One was that he would be asked to give only two or three considered comments during the course of the evening. The other was that a young man who had worked with him on the book about the 1945 election, and who knew, he said, a great deal more than he did about detailed facts and figures, should appear on the programme too.[11]

So, three days later, on 26 January 1950, less than a month before polling day, Goldie wrote to David Butler to try to recruit him to her venture, addressing her letter to the 'Research Station' at Nuffield:

> We are considering putting out on the evening of February 23, as a prelude to showing the results, a short comment illustrated by charts and diagrams, on the difference of the conditions of this election compared with the election of 1945. We are also considering a comment during the evening of February 24, on the nature of the results.[12]

Goldie explained that she was hoping 'to persuade Mr McCallum to take part', and that he had suggested Butler's inclusion. She asked if Butler might be in London over the next few days, where they could have lunch at her club. Alternatively, she said she could arrange to be in Oxford. 'There are, I think, possibilities in television, for showing aspects of the election which it is difficult to make clear in "sound" broadcasting. But if we attempt this, we want to be sure that we have expert advice and so I am venturing to consult you.'[13]

Butler was just twenty-five. He was to be associated with election night results programmes for the next sixty-five years, on both TV and radio, and beyond the BBC and Britain, for a range of broadcasting companies on four different continents. For more than half a century, Butler would play a leading role not just on camera, but also behind the scenes, developing visual techniques and methods of rapid statistical analysis to make sense of a wealth of election numbers for a mass audience.

It was a step into the unknown. Indeed, in 1950, David Butler knew hardly anything about BBC television. Around 1948, his parents had bought a television set for their home in Leatherhead, but Butler very rarely viewed it. He'd caught the odd glimpse of television during his time in America and watched in high excitement an overnight results programme from the 1948 US presidential contest in a hotel in New York, but after his work for the 1950 BBC broadcast he would joke that he had now spent more time *appearing* on British television than watching it. It was probably true.

Yet David Butler wasn't totally new to the BBC. In 1949, after his year in the United States, he had contacted a former New College colleague, Paul Johnson, who had become a producer at the corporation, about the possibility of presenting a radio programme about his hitch-hiking journey round America. Johnson suggested Butler submit a draft script, but it took several months for Butler to respond. 'I am still unemployed,' he told Johnson, 'but, having a good many small irons in the fire, the script got pushed aside ... Do what you will with it ... The waste-paper basket may well be the proper destination.' The script was 'quite good', Johnson replied. 'I'm hawking it around ... I may find someone but it's always a chancy business.'[14] Nothing came of the idea, however.

Later, at the end of 1949, the BBC did employ Butler to present two editions of a radio programme called *Inside Britain*, for transmission in north America, and for which he was paid twelve guineas for each broadcast. After the second programme – and coincidentally the very day Grace Wyndham Goldie wrote her memo proposing the election results programme – the producer submitted an internal report on Butler's performances:

> The two scripts he wrote for us were very good, and my only criticism of them would be that possibly he has not had quite enough experience of writing for the microphone. This was fairly evident in his first broadcast when his voice lacked emphasis and he was ill-at-ease. However the second time after hearing a playback of his first effort, and a record of [BBC correspondent] Graham Hutton, he was very much better. He was quick to see where he had gone wrong and will I think improve even more with practice. He has a good deep voice, but tends to lisp. This can be completely eliminated by seeing that the vocabulary he uses does not include

> too many 'R's. For example 'scurry', 'flurry', 'celebrate', 'cerebrate' and so on. I do think he could and should be used again.[15]

The producer who wrote that memo was Anthony Wedgwood Benn, who had joined the BBC after Oxford (and would be elected an MP at a by-election later in 1950). Interestingly, Benn's rather positive report didn't declare that Butler was one of his closest university friends. Perhaps Benn's bosses were already aware of that.

Whereas Ronald McCallum had reacted to Grace Wyndham Goldie's request to contribute to the 1950 results programme with wariness and weariness, Butler's response could not have been more different. He immediately saw the historic nature of the project, and the potential of the new medium. Goldie wrote in her memoirs how Butler displayed 'characteristic energy'. Many people who had agreed to make their first appearance on national live television would have reacted with considerable nervousness, and waited to hear what the producers required. Butler, in contrast, acted with astonishing boldness for someone so young and inexperienced. Although he had never visited a television studio, nor yet seen a TV camera, he delivered a stream of helpful suggestions to Goldie about how the new programme might be made, trying to meet the challenges of making elections visual.

On 31 January 1950, just over three weeks before polling day, Butler wrote a four-page letter containing several charts and graphs which he had drawn in his own hand. This letter shows how Butler understood not just the politics and figures of an election night programme, but also the potential excitement and drama of the occasion. He sensed he was joining a team of pioneers.

Showing his background as a sports enthusiast, Butler began his memo with a mantra which has stood the test of time for election night broadcasts:

> The full result will be available tomorrow. If you insist on staying

> up tonight it's because you're impatient and want, like any sportsman, to spot the winner as soon as possible. This is to help in the game. But remember we're doing no more than trying to anticipate what will be common knowledge in a few hours or a few minutes time.[16]

Butler then explained how to forecast the outcome on the basis of just a handful of results, pointing out the importance of uniform swing: 'If one area is swinging against a party it is probable that all others are doing the same,' so that once they'd registered the swing in a few seats they would have a pretty good idea of the trend in Britain as a whole.[17]

But there was one big obstacle to this analysis: the redrawing of constituency boundaries in 1948, which had left very few seats unchanged, so it would be tricky to compare like with like. (Boundary changes was an issue to which Butler would return.) So, Butler put forward another way of assessing during the night which way the election was going – more than twenty 'barometer' constituencies which had a history in recent contests of going the same way the country went. Foremost were the two Salford seats, and his list also included West Fulham in London.

Grace Wyndham Goldie had told her bosses in her original memo that in some respects the TV results programme would be inferior to that of their radio colleagues (though there may have been a touch of office diplomacy in this, since she did not want to worry radio people, who still dominated the BBC hierarchy). BBC TV could not 'compete in speed' with radio, Goldie said, since radio had 'a team of twenty or thirty people working on checking and collecting results and getting them into deliverable form and they tell me that even then the rush is overwhelming.'[18] That winter's night in February 1950, the results did indeed come through to Butler and his colleagues rather laboriously. BBC Television had no teleprinter at Alexandra Palace to spew out tape from the news agencies. Instead, they had to rely on telephone messages from Broadcasting House (BH) in central London, where BBC radio had teleprinters. It meant the TV team had to trust radio staff at BH to interpret and prioritise the wire material, rather than assess it themselves. This inevitably meant that the TV service broadcast their results after they had been revealed on radio by the famous announcers John Snagge and Stuart Hibberd.

To help him in the studio for the 1950 programme, Butler had enlisted two assistants, Creighton Burns, an Australian from Nuffield (who years later became editor of the *Melbourne Age*), and Harry Field from New College. Their task was to help Butler work out the swing between the two main parties, using the fairly primitive tool of slide rules. On camera, it was only a matter of seconds before Butler could say how a result compared with 1945; whether it was in line with other results; whether there were variations from one region to another; and so forth. He would also mesh in local details about each constituency and its candidates:

> I found that I could talk spontaneously. I was doing, in front of a camera, what I would have been doing if I'd just been alone at home, or with friends – interpreting the election results – and it was thought to be a success. I just had the great luck of being the first in the field. Nobody else had done this sort of thing before. I had enough training and a very good memory.[19]

From the start, David Butler had been keen not just to fulfil his analytical duties in the studio, but to play a major role in designing the programme. He devised a grid system for the large map of Britain which Goldie erected in the studio, broken down into squares for each seat, which were painted black and white depending on the result. (This was long before colour television – how fortunate for TV graphics designers that the era of monochrome television roughly coincided with the age of two-party politics.)

Unlike modern election results programmes, which have the accumulated experience of previous broadcasts, and are usually planned and rehearsed over months, if not years, the BBC's 1950 election programme was cobbled together in barely a month. Assistants practised running from one studio to another in gym shoes; secretaries learnt systems for typing and checking results; and studio managers rehearsed the operation of the State of the Parties board in the studio. Chester Wilmot, the main presenter, was armed with a pile of index cards for each constituency, giving their past history and details on the candidates.

But the BBC hierarchy was very anxious about the manner in which McCallum and Butler might comment on results. And Norman Collins, the controller of BBC Television, wrote to Grace Wyndham Goldie instructing that 'though we are fully at liberty to analyse the results as they come through and draw such historic comparisons as may be relevant, we must scrupulously avoid anything that may be interpreted as political prophecy'.[20] This was a rule Butler seemed keen to ignore. And Goldie had little enthusiasm from some of her superiors. Cecil McGivern was pleased with the idea of live cameras in Trafalgar Square (where Richard Dimbleby was the reporter), but otherwise he reckoned it 'a waste of the limited resources of television to let a few people know tonight instead of tomorrow which politician had lost his seat and who had got in for East Walthamstow'.[21]

Much rode on the programme; the political dangers were enormous, especially at a time when the distinguished academic Lord Beveridge was chairing a committee to examine the future of the BBC. In the event, however, the programmes went without mishap, and stayed on air for an hour longer than planned. 'David Butler had been immediately impressive,' Goldie later wrote. 'His extraordinary memory, his knowledge of political facts, personalities and past records, his assistants with their slide rules, had allowed him to pour out, without self-consciousness and throughout the night, a continuous flow of informed comment.'[22]

David Butler was never an outstanding charismatic broadcaster, but the process did come naturally to him. He was relaxed and a quick thinker, and on live results programmes could speak fluently and spontaneously about each batch of figures as it arrived. Goldie wrote: 'He was not only highly informed about the machinery and history; he had a prodigious memory for detail, a taste for statistics, a total lack of nervousness of television cameras and an immense constructive and practical interest in methods of presentation.'[23]

Sadly, no recording seems to have survived of the 1950 results programme, though there are a few photographs taken for the BBC publicity department. 'Skilful and exciting' was the verdict of the radio critic of the *Manchester Guardian*: 'Probably nothing done by television so far has justified more the claim that once television is established it can, for some purposes, make the sound radio take a back seat.'[24] *The Listener* said, 'Chester Wilmot and David Butler pursued their gruesome tasks of analytical disembowelling of the returns with gusto.'[25]

'The young David had dark hair and the trace of a curl and magnetism on camera,' wrote the former BBC executive John Grist. Butler, he added, 'became a national celebrity overnight', which must be something of an exaggeration, since only about a third of a million households had TV sets in 1950, covering roughly 2 per cent of the population.[26]

Goldie called the 1950 results programme a 'watershed in the handling of British politics on television', which 'demonstrated that television could present to the nation the compelling drama of a great national political occasion in which every voter had participated'. And no party leader, she argued, knew what the result would be 'earlier than a shepherd in the Highlands or a housewife in Islington. The privilege of the few had once again been extended to the many.'[27]

Grace Wyndham Goldie soon came to see David Butler as her discovery, her protégé, and they quickly developed a close friendship, lavishing each other with praise. The Sunday after polling day, Butler wrote to thank Goldie for a 'not just memorable but enormously enjoyable' two days, with a 'warming atmosphere of teamwork', and he expressed his 'gratitude and admiration' to her.[28] Goldie replied the next day:

> You made a most tremendous personal success of the evening. Everybody is astonished that you managed not only to confront the cameras and the whole television machine with so much aplomb that you might have been doing it all your life but to combine this with working the most complicated statistics and putting over the results with complete authority and sureness of touch. I can't imagine how you did it.[29]

The success of the overnight results programme partly reflected the uncertain and gripping nature of the event, and the prolonged counting process. By Friday afternoon, Labour and the Conservatives were running neck and neck. Other programmes were regularly interrupted to announce new constituency results, and four times Labour seemed to establish a lead, only for it to be lost again. It was not until the following Monday, with figures from the last, furthest-flung seats, that the final result was known: Labour 315; Conservative 298; Liberals 9; Irish Nationalists 2; and The Speaker. Attlee's 1945 Commons majority of 146 over all other parties had now been reduced to just five seats, and it was widely accepted that his government couldn't survive long before another election.

David Butler had become one of the very first of a new species, the 'telly don'. They sounded like prehistoric dinosaurs; on the contrary, telly dons were pioneering university academics who were determined to reach a much wider audience through this powerful new mass medium. Other early examples, of course, included Isaiah Berlin, the historians A. J. P. Taylor and Alan Bullock, the polymath

Jacob Bronowski, and the art historian Kenneth Clark, all of whom were regular guests on the popular BBC show *The Brains Trust*, which moved from radio to television later in 1950. Many telly dons suddenly became celebrities and public figures, instantly recognised in the street in an era when viewers had little or no choice of channels, and even quite serious programmes could generate audiences of many millions. But telly dons were also the victims of much jealousy and derision from their academic colleagues. They were often dismissed as superficial and only interested in fame, and in what were presumed to be large appearance fees.

It was clear after the 1950 result that the BBC would be calling on the services of this young telly don again very soon. In February 1951, Gallup published a poll that showed the Conservatives with a handsome 13 per cent lead – 51 per cent to Labour's 38 per cent. A year after their four-hour dinner at Chartwell, the Conservative leader Winston Churchill phoned David Butler for advice on what to make of the figures. Butler's response was to suggest the poll would mean an outcome similar to 1935, with a huge Conservative majority of around 250. Immediately afterwards, Butler followed up the call with a two-page letter, in which he outlined the usual reasons for caution – sampling error, margin of error, undecided voters and 'considerable evidence' from the previous thirty years to suggest that 'usually an election campaign helps the party in power'. Butler concluded:

> I should be surprised if an election in the near future would give the Conservatives quite as overwhelming a victory as today's poll would suggest. But … I should be still more surprised if the Conservatives failed to win an appreciable majority of the votes. A lead of only 2 per cent, I am certain, would be sufficient to give the Conservatives a Parliamentary majority of over 50 seats. A lead of 5 per cent would give them a majority of well over 100 seats. In short … the poll results … give very strong reason

> to suppose that an early appeal to the country would return the Conservatives with a very comfortable majority.[30]

Butler's diary suggests he'd hoped to open up a good correspondence back and forth with Churchill, and that by sending such a long letter the Conservative leader might write back and ask for more. He also treasured the idea of a letter with the great man's autograph. Butler was therefore terribly disappointed when all he got in reply was a six-word telegram: 'Thank you so much = Winston Churchill.'[31] 'So ends that episode,' Butler lamented at the time.[32]

Anthony Wedgwood Benn, who had just become an MP in a by-election, was not very pleased when he heard that his friend had been helping the Conservative leader prepare for electoral hostilities. Benn wrote in his diary that Butler's letter had 'undoubtedly … strengthened the determination of Churchill to call for an election'.[33]

Clement Attlee managed to hold on, in fact, until the autumn of 1951, and he called an election for 25 October in the hope of increasing Labour's slender majority. Churchill invited Butler to see him at his London home in Hyde Park Gate on the Saturday morning before polling day. 'It was early and he rather shocked me by the offer of a glass of port at ten in the morning.' Butler was also struck by how much Churchill seemed to have aged in a few months:

> He was sitting in bed with a table across it, laden with fruit and biscuits and papers. We were interrupted by Mrs Churchill coming in with a toothache and he showed himself as an extremely gentle, sympathetic husband. But, alas, he did seem pretty gaga. When I tried to explain to him that, if you take one seat from a party and give it to the opposition, it makes a difference of two to the parliamentary majority, he started to test the arithmetic moving apples and tangerines across the table.[34]

According to Tony Benn's account written eleven days later, and based on Butler's recollections, Churchill 'asked several questions about his chances of success in the Election. David was cautious and indicated that an overall majority of forty or so was likely. Putting it into betting odds, he got a more lively response and they had a little backchat.'

And, Benn relates, Churchill recalled 'almost exactly' what Butler had said when they met in February the year before. Then, just as Butler was about to leave, he was given a very difficult question:

> Churchill asked him quietly and soberly, 'Mr Butler, do you think I am a handicap to the Conservative Party?' It was said without dramatic intent – indeed with a rather pathetic desire for reassurance. David did not answer for a while. 'Come Mr Butler, you need not be afraid to tell me.'
>
> 'Well,' replied David, 'I do not think that you are the asset to them that you once were … the public memory is short, you know.'

This was astonishingly bold, and yet also diplomatic, especially for somebody so young who was talking to such a legendary figure whom he greatly admired. Churchill replied: 'But the people love me, Mr Butler. Everywhere I go they wave and workmen take off their cloth caps to cheer me.'[35]

And indeed Winston Churchill won the election five days later by a margin of seventeen seats, rather short of the comfortable majority that Butler had forecast the previous February. Several months before the October 1951 general election, Butler was invited by the BBC to do the results programme again, and he put considerable thought into how the 1950 format might be improved. He contributed with his personal experience from America – indeed, Butler was probably the *only* member of the BBC team actually to have seen the presidential results coverage in 1948, and in the spring of 1951 the BBC representative in North America had introduced Butler to programme makers at CBS. 'They seem to live lives ten times more hectic than anything I've seen at Alexandra Palace,' Butler told Grace Wyndham Goldie.[36]

Every few weeks, Butler bombarded Goldie and her colleagues with suggestions. He wanted the programme to show more of 'the works', including calculators and teletype machines. He explained how when he watched television at home, 'I shall never be able to watch with the simple-minded curiosity of the rest of my family.' He wanted to see and know more – what was 'happening just off screen and in the producer's box'.[37]

A few weeks earlier, he had written a detailed nine-page report setting out possible visual graphics to make the results more intelligible. To avoid the backlog that had occurred in 1950 (with twenty results waiting at the busiest spell), he suggested showing seats two at a time, with one result in the top half of the screen, the other below; and he even drew a diagram of how the screen might look. And he argued that running totals of how many seats each party had won should be given 'at least once every quarter of an hour', perhaps on 'a simple scoreboard with revolving moveable figures', or by 'slots through which individually painted captions can be inserted' (giving two more diagrams of how it might look). He also proposed more outside broadcasts, possibly with senior party officials such as the Conservative chairman, Lord Woolton, and the Labour general secretary, Morgan Phillips. It might also be worth taking cameras to the best results-night parties, he suggested. 'Last time the Conservatives had a party at the Savoy and Labour, presumably, in the Meeting Hall at Transport House. The scenes here, if American experience is any guide, should offer superb television material.' But he also went into tiny details, such as whether results should be listed alphabetically by candidate name, and whether their initials should be omitted or not.[38]

Television was rapidly gaining popularity. Around 1.1 million households had TV licences by the time of the 1951 programme, three or four times as many as in February 1950.[39]

This time, Chester Wilmot was replaced by Graham Hutton as overall presenter, and Ronald McCallum was quietly dropped as one of the studio experts in favour of Herbert Nicholas, his successor as the author of the Nuffield election book. Interestingly, the *Radio Times* gave Butler higher billing than Nicholas, even though the latter was by far the more senior in academic terms, and was Butler's DPhil supervisor at Nuffield College.[40] This results programme was much longer, and came in four parts – from 10.15 p.m. to 4 a.m. on election night, and from 10 a.m. to 5 p.m. throughout the next day; followed by updates on the Friday evening from 5.45 to 6 p.m. and 8.15 to 8.45 p.m. – more than thirteen hours of output in all. This time, too, there were regular live reports from election counts – in Fulham, Birmingham and Salford (where Richard Dimbleby was the reporter). 'With three outside broadcasts,' declared the *Radio Times*, 'stationed in London, the Midlands, and in the North, the Television Service hopes to scoop the world by showing some results as they are announced.'[41]

At Alexandra Palace, the work was divided between the two television studios. To give the programme a sense of drama, the activity in the studio where the results arrived was covered by two live cameras, though there were no microphones, so that staff could talk 'at will without any of their comments going on the air'.[42]

At that time, long before digital technology and computer graphics, television visuals were primitive. As each result was phoned in from Broadcasting House, a member of staff would write it out on a slip, which had several duplicate sheets attached. Once the figures on the slip had been checked, it was matched with the relevant caption card from a large tray-like box containing, in alphabetical order, cards for all 625 seats in the UK, on which candidates' names and parties had already been carefully written. The slip and relevant caption card were then passed to a graphics artist, who neatly wrote in the figures for the result by hand with quick-drying paint. The cards were then clipped onto easels placed in front of two studio cameras. At the peak period, with results arriving fast, the cameras would cut from one caption to the next at intervals of just seven seconds.

Meanwhile, the duplicate slips for each result were passed to David Butler and his two Oxford colleagues, and also to the studio assistants who operated the squares on the large map of the United Kingdom. The state of the parties was also represented by two vertical chutes into which painted table-tennis balls were dropped for each seat the main parties won – lavender blue for Conservative, and black for Labour.

David Butler recalls how the output was very much determined by how long it took the ink on the captions to dry – about half a minute or so, which gave him and his colleagues time to think out what to say.

> And in that thirty seconds the swing figure could be calculated by somebody quickly with a slide rule, and so one could say, the moment the result came on screen: 'That's an exceptionally big swing,' or 'That's a very small swing,' or whatever. One could do all those things very fast, and the people in the BBC thought one was very clever.[43]

It was understood that Butler could just chip in at any time with a very brief remark such as 'Three per cent swing to Labour, a record so far' – ideally for no more than ten seconds, and often much shorter. In time, this would become a David Butler trademark on election results programmes.

After rehearsals in 1951, or after programme meetings, David Butler wrote long letters to Grace Wyndham Goldie with his views on what aspects had gone wrong, and how things might be improved – suggesting graphics, where on-screen people should sit, how the information should be got to the presenters, and so on. In effect, he became a TV producer as much as a studio pundit.

'David Butler was perhaps a little frustrated in the early stages,' said one critic. 'He had plenty to say but little chance to say it.'[44] 'Mr Butler's swift accounting of the statistics was almost miraculous,' wrote the *Yorkshire Post*.[45] 'Mr Butler kept his end up,' thought the *Glasgow Herald*, 'but he admitted, round about half-past three, that his mathematics were getting "a bit slow".'[46] According to the *Daily Herald*, the 'indefatigable' Graham Hutton and Butler would occasionally 'nibble a sandwich or sip a glass of milk. It was all very informal.' But while Hutton got a 'leg-stretch' by walking over to the large studio map from time to time, the 'imperturbable' Butler remained at his desk, 'a straying forelock creeping further and further down over his forehead as the hours went on'.[47]

These pioneering days of election analysis and television results programmes were one of the most exciting periods of David Butler's life. Both as a psephologist and as a television broadcaster, he was there at the beginning. And yet he was personally troubled by doubts. He didn't know where his future lay. On the one hand, like so many of his illustrious ancestors, he was trying to pursue an academic life. He had spent the summer of 1950 back in America teaching at university summer school. Finishing his DPhil, he told himself, would not only help get work in the USA, it would also reassure himself, he wrote in his 'commonplace book' (an irregular diary), 'that there is a place in the academic world for a person as muddled as I am'. He wondered whether he was any good at teaching. He was 'far from ideally suited' to being an academic, he wrote, or what he quaintly called an 'academe':

> I enjoy thinking myself an academe. I enjoy the social life of academe. I even enjoy teaching when I am sure of my subject. But I have not got the scholar's instinct. I don't love books or reading. I haven't great intellectual interest in the subtleties of

> my subject. I don't move happily among abstract ideas. I don't think clearly and my memory is far from certain … Am I being too perfectionist? Am I afraid of living in a community where I shall have colleagues doing the same job but being patently much better at it? Is there any other job in which I would do as well or be as happy? I wish I could assess better my capacities. If I am as incompetent academically, as blurred in mind as in my more depressed moments I suspect myself to be, I should certainly not attempt to pursue an academic career.[48]

It seems extraordinary that Butler should have harboured doubts about his memory, when his growing reputation rested on his recall of obscure and tiny details. He also spoke of the 'pressure of social temptations', and 'patterns of completely unsystematic idleness'. One of the great drawbacks of his life was he did 'no reading'; he hadn't read 'a serious book from cover to cover for months', he admitted.[49] (This has long been a problem for graduate students: they are expected to read hundreds of books, so just end up gutting them for good material.) Butler hoped that writing regularly in his diary would help discipline his thoughts, and also make him a more fluent writer.

Butler had achieved an extraordinary amount by the age of twenty-six, more than almost anyone of his Oxford generation, and yet his writings in his journal expose the anguish and self-doubt he suffered. 'If I could discipline my mind,' he wrote, 'if I could concentrate even on uncongenial tasks, if I could devote my full attention to any discussion – and I never can – I would certainly have much less ground for all these doubtings.'[50]

By now, Butler had begun giving PPE tutorials to students from other Oxford colleges. 'I have occasionally felt that I have fully succeeded in giving my pupils the illusion that they were learning. I have not yet experienced the satisfaction of feeling that I myself have really taught them anything,' he wrote at the time.[51] 'It is so much easier to teach good than mediocre pupils,' he noted, adding also that it was 'so much easier to teach men than women', without any explanation why.[52] He briefly toyed with the idea of getting a job for a couple of years at the University of Virginia; then dropped the idea on the grounds of his father's age – he died in June 1951 – and because it would mean missing a general election and might endanger the contacts he'd made in journalism and other fields.

Butler had wider anxieties too, especially as the conflict in Korea worsened relations with Russia. In December 1950, two days after President Truman declared a state of emergency against communist imperialism, Butler declared that the international situation could 'hardly be blacker'. His 'selfish anxieties', he wrote, didn't:

> centre on an early atomic death so much as on the dilemma that one would face living under a Communist government. I don't think that I should either be a hero or sell my soul – probably I'd seek if some escapist solution were possible – a menial clerkship with country walks and Shakespeare as the solaces.[53]

As the 1950s got under way, Butler was weighing up a very uncertain future. He had taken substantial strides in television, but it was an industry that was new and fickle. Pursuing what he called the 'family trade' – being a university don – seemed equally unstable but was the most natural and obvious thing to do. Yet David Butler would be a very different kind of academic to his illustrious ancestors – 'new money', as it were, to their 'old money'. Butler was moving into the new world of higher education in the latter half of the twentieth century. Political science was a very modern subject compared with classics and history, his father's and grandfather's subjects, while his personal speciality, election studies, was brand new. Where his forebears spent years writing for scholarly tomes and obscure journals read by a few hundred colleagues at best, this latest Butler academic wanted to use the new forms of communication, often at great speed, to improve understanding of his subject among millions of the general population. Above all, David Butler's approach was one of 'applied research' rather than the theoretical. His aim was to make an impact.

CHAPTER SEVEN

A SPEEDOMETER TYPE DEVICE

Not long after David Butler's success on the 1950 results programme, Grace Wyndham Goldie had written asking if Butler would like to take part in other TV programmes. A few days later he replied suggesting his own series on men who held powerful positions in Britain. 'I don't know what makes a "television personality" or whether they are particularly rare,' he wrote, though it's not clear how much he had himself in mind.[1] His idea was a series of programmes consisting of interviews with leading figures in different fields. In its own way, it was ahead of its time, foreshadowing the landmark *Face to Face* interviews that John Freeman conducted a decade later. Butler's initial list comprised a Cabinet minister, a top civil servant, an industrialist and a trade union leader, and maybe later a financier, a journalist and 'the common man'.[2] Butler felt a lot rode on the success of this project, believing that it might determine whether his future lay in journalism or academic life, and the worry seems to have caused him sleepless nights. 'I don't yet know if I'm to go in for a journalistic career,' he wrote in his diary in November 1950:

> but at least I hope for a semi-journalistic career and it behoves me to wield a readier pen than I have in my last few attempts at journalism.

> It is obvious that the next six months will go far to shape my whole career. The television interviews are going to be a severe test. Success in them will open large horizons. Failure will damage my self-esteem but will hardly do me serious or lasting harm.[3]

The series was commissioned, but preparations dragged on. The process of choosing potential subjects and then approaching them lasted well over a year. Among the names considered for the programmes were several elderly men who had played key roles in the run-up to war, including Lord Halifax, Sir Samuel Hoare and Alfred Duff Cooper. But, inevitably, most targets declined, and the final line-up of interviews was not that distinguished, though just as male and grey. His first live fifteen-minute interview in the series *Men of Authority*, in November 1950, was with the former Liberal leader and Home Secretary Lord (Herbert) Samuel. He was followed over the next six weeks by Lord Lyle, the boss of the sugar firm Tate & Lyle; Sir John Maud, a senior civil servant; and Lincoln Evans, the leader of the iron and steel workers' union. No recordings seem to exist, but reports in the BBC Audience Research files suggest Butler didn't fare too badly for someone who had never presented live TV programmes on his own before, especially in the first three programmes. On the Samuel interview, some viewers felt:

> David Butler's questions to Lord Samuel were not penetrating enough, failure to make them so being occasionally attributed to youth and inexperience. More generally, however, it was thought that he handled the interview with tact and aplomb and that he put some opportune questions while showing a becoming deference to a recognised great personality.[4]

With Sir John Maud a week later, viewers thought Butler was 'more at ease' and 'showed a greater facility in pursuing the points at issue'. The Samuel programme scored 61 per cent on the BBC 'Reaction

Index', lower than the BBC average of 66 per cent, but the Maud programme rose to 68 per cent and Lyle 72 per cent.[5]

Despite the favourable audience reaction, Butler thought his interview with the businessman Lord Lyle was 'disastrous'. He says he dried up in the first sentence of his introduction. Then Lyle was 'slow and rambling', ignored Butler's questions and answered 'totally irrelevantly' at times. Butler 'was very depressed about it – particularly as, under the strain, I tensed up a little, and wasn't as easy as I should have been'.[6]

The TV programmes seemed to knock Butler's confidence. He wrote of 'worrying about "my television personality". Have I been making a public fool of myself – pretentiously bullying these distinguished people in public, asking them unanswerable questions?' He'd been especially shaken by an abusive postcard along such lines which he'd received from a viewer.[7]

Sadly for Butler, the programme with the trade unionist Lincoln Evans fared badly too, with a research score of just 53 per cent, though the TV panel blamed the failure largely on Evans, who 'lacked the personality which made previous speakers in this series successful'. But the report concluded that Butler 'should have been quicker to realise this was a case for firmness rather than tact', though he conducted the interview with 'his usual patience and understanding, and it wasn't always his fault that he failed to elicit the information asked for'.[8]

Butler found the whole process quite difficult. 'I doubt if I've contributed one original notion to the series so far,' he wrote in his diary at one point. 'Lack of concentration, lack of flexibility, lack perhaps of brains,' he lamented.[9] He undoubtedly suffered from a dull line-up of elderly male guests who were inexperienced broadcasters and worried about giving too much away.

It was unfortunate for Butler that the final programme should have been by far the worst. Despite her overall admiration for Butler, Grace Wyndham Goldie was not impressed, and she seems to have concluded that Butler was not an exceptional TV performer on his own. He never presented his own on-screen programme again.

By contrast, the series went down well with another man of authority: Lord Nuffield, who in the early 1950s was pretty disaffected with the college he'd funded and which bore his name. Indeed, Butler recalls the future warden Norman Chester telling him that the *Men of Authority* programmes were 'the first time he'd ever heard Lord Nuffield say something nice about the college'.[10]

The *Men of Authority* series also seemed to lessen Butler's opinion of Grace Wyndham Goldie. 'She doesn't do things by the time she promises and when she does give her attention to a problem she wastes a vast amount of time on irrelevances,' he wrote. 'I wish she were a man. I'm sure she'd cope better with the programmes and I'm sure that I could cope better with her.'[11] His remarks sit uneasily with the more feminist Butler of later life.

Nonetheless, Goldie was still keen to use him as an on-screen expert. Later, in the summer of 1952, she recruited Butler to take part in a TV programme analysing the US presidential election contest between Dwight Eisenhower and Adlai Stevenson – probably the first time that American politics was ever covered in detail by BBC Television, though the broadcast lasted only twenty minutes. Butler recollects that the programme – which was based in London – had been the suggestion of Robert, or Bob, McKenzie, a Canadian sociology lecturer at the London School of Economics. McKenzie had done some broadcasting for small radio stations in western Canada before the war and was now doing occasional work for the BBC.

Butler recalls that he first met Bob McKenzie at a Liberal Party press conference in 1949, and before long they were close colleagues, both as broadcasters and as academics. Butler was much inspired by the work McKenzie had done for his doctorate, which was turned into his seminal book *British Political Parties*, published in 1955, which explained where power really lay inside the parties. Butler later described it as the 'most important book on British politics since the war'.[12] McKenzie saw himself primarily as a serious academic: the only reference to broadcasting in his entry in *Who's Who* was as a 'recreation'.

But Bob McKenzie was 'great fun as a person', says Butler.

> Politics was his hobby, his sport, his enthusiasm. He wasn't a very profound man as a historian or as a sociologist, and he really was barely numerate. But he had this colossal enthusiasm for whatever he was doing in conversation – a kind of obsessive thing, which sometimes drove him over the top. He knew politicians and he knew how to talk to them. He asked questions with great enthusiasm ... Bob's real genius, once he'd written *British Political Parties*, was to make politics fascinating to undergraduate audiences at LSE and to mass audiences on the telly.[13]

What Butler especially admired about McKenzie, who was seven years his senior, was the way he went out and interviewed the practitioners of politics – ministers, MPs and party organisers. This paralleled Butler's own inclination, honed in America and continued for the 1950 Nuffield book, for interviewing people 'on the ground'. McKenzie got to know them as contacts and friends, frequently inviting them as guests to address his seminars at the LSE. Before long, Butler and McKenzie became established as partners on election night results programmes, and their famous double act would last almost three decades, until McKenzie's death in 1981. The pair were always friends, Butler insists, but to many people working with them in the studio, and to viewers at home, they came across as competitors who gently needled and outbid each other.

To some extent BBC producers may have encouraged an on-screen rivalry to make more engaging television. There was always competition between them to forecast the election outcome first, and to come up with the most cogent analysis of what had happened in that particular general election. Where Butler loved figures and detail, McKenzie was more comfortable with the broad brush and the big picture.

* * *

Far from neglecting his academic studies, David Butler took command of another election project which would dominate more than half a century of his life. The 1945 Nuffield election books had been pioneered by Ronald McCallum and Alison Readman, while the subsequent volume, on the 1950 election, had been written by Butler's former politics tutor Herbert Nicholas. But Nicholas, too, wrote only a single edition, and in the summer of 1951, when Butler was just twenty-six, Nuffield College asked him to take charge of the next volume (for a contest that was officially due by February 1955, though everyone expected it much sooner). Nuffield promised Butler that in consequence, as soon as Clement Attlee went to the Palace and the next election was declared, they would make him a research fellow of the college. So, when on 19 September 1951 the Prime Minister duly went to ask for a dissolution, 'I was made a research fellow by royal proclamation and got into the family trade of being a don.'[14] It was a commitment that lasted more than half a century.

In the opening paragraph of the 1951 book, David Butler wrote that it seemed 'appropriate' to ask 'why elections merit study', and to examine 'how much has been or can be learnt from psephology'.[15] In a footnote at the bottom of the page, Butler explained: 'I am indebted to Mr RB McCallum for the invention of this word to describe the field of research in which he is so eminent a pioneer. It is derived from ψήφοS – the pebble which the Athenians dropped into an urn to vote.'[16]

Ever since, David Butler has always said the word 'psephology' was a 'high-table joke', coined during a discussion between McCallum and two brothers who were Oxford classics dons – the future

President of Corpus Christi College, Frank Hardie, and Colin Hardie, who taught at Magdalen. But a letter written by McCallum on 12 July 1949 suggests Butler's account is slightly inaccurate or incomplete, and that McCallum himself did not coin the word. McCallum's letter, written to his co-author on the 1945 Nuffield book, Alison Readman (whose husband C. W. Wright had studied classics), suggests the word may have had even more eminent origins. McCallum wrote:

> By the way, the correct name for the science which we have invented is psephology. (Ask your husband for the Greek derivation.) I was with Lewis and the Choice Spirits today and I told them I was the inventor of Electionology. This dreadful hybrid shocked them very deeply and indeed I should have known better. So they gave me psephology.[17]

It seems the real inventors of the word 'psephology' were McCallum's companions earlier that day. Yet who were 'Lewis and the Choice Spirits'? It is almost certainly a reference to the renowned literary and academic discussion group to which McCallum belonged, which was known as the Inklings. The leading lights of the Inklings included the two Oxford children's writers, J. R. R. Tolkien, author of *The Hobbit* and *The Lord of the Rings*, a former colleague of McCallum's at Pembroke College; and C. S. Lewis, who wrote the famous Narnia books. Colin Hardie was also among the nineteen formal members of the group. Until 1949, the Inklings held their main meetings in C. S. Lewis's room in Magdalen, but they also held more informal gatherings, involving a wider circle, on Tuesday lunchtimes in the Eagle and Child, the well-known pub in St Giles. The Inklings would meet in a quiet back room known as the 'Rabbit Room', where they would sit around the fire, supping their pints and discussing literary issues and other matters. Crucially, 12 July 1949 – the day McCallum wrote to Alison Readman – was a Tuesday.[18]

It seems pretty certain that C. S. Lewis, the man who created the magical, mystery world of Narnia, with its mythical beasts and talking animals, also played a role in inventing the word 'psephology'. Certainly, Lewis had studied Greek at Oxford, though it seems likely that Colin Hardie played a part in the discussion too, but there is no record of whether he attended the Eagle and Child that Tuesday.

In a way, neither McCallum nor Butler was right in thinking they had coined a new word. 'Psephology' had already been used in the early twentieth century by mathematicians who studied Pythagorean number theory – relating to the famous rule that in a right-angled triangle, the square of the hypotenuse is equal to the sum of the squares of the two shorter sides. In 1912, for instance, an article in the mathematical journal *The Quest* spoke of 'Pythagorean number-values or psephology'.[19] Although both versions of 'psephology' derive from the Athenian tradition of counting with pebbles, they mean very different things.

Moreover, Ronald McCallum beat David Butler in getting the word 'psephology' into print in an electoral context, albeit only by a few months. In a review of the previous Nuffield election book for 1950, McCallum concluded that it had 'made a notable advance for a subject for which it might be convenient to coin a new term, psephology'.[20] This review was written for the *Oxford Magazine*, a journal for Oxford academics.

But David Butler, with an eye for publicity, can at least claim credit for getting the word into public discourse, and for spreading it to America. The latter happened during the summer of 1952, while he was teaching at a summer school at Cornell University in upstate New York. Cornell's publicity department issued a press release based on an interview they'd done with Butler in which he described himself as a 'psephologist'. 'And', he told his mother, 'the word caught the fancy of a copy-reader of the New York *Herald Tribune* who couldn't find it in the dictionary.'[21] The result was a half-column on the back page under the headline 'All a Joke says British Visitor: Oxford Don Explains New Word', in which Butler insisted the term 'was coined purely in jest'.[22] It was too late. The word was out.

A day or two later, another reporter rang from *Time* magazine. The result was a six-line item in the education section, in which the word 'Don' had seemingly become part of his name: 'Cornell had a distinguished visitor last week—Oxford University Don David Butler, who calls himself the world's first psephologist ... Butler admitted that the coinage was a joke, "but for all I know, the word may someday catch on".'[23]

Catch on, it did. 'Psephologist' and 'psephology' went global. Back in Britain, the *Daily Express* picked up on the term, with the headline 'Psephologically Speaking: You may vote for a good-looking party'. This was over a review of Butler's 1951 election book, where the article cited a forecast by Butler that television would transform traditional election campaigning and might 'even affect the pattern of advancement in the party hierarchies'.[24] And the new word was cited in other reviews of Butler's book on the 1951 contest. The *Economist* review had the headline 'Psephology – The New Science', and another article was more acerbically entitled 'Psephological Dyspepsia'.[25]

The term 'psephology' gave the study of elections the air of a serious, scholarly science that had been around for centuries, whereas in reality there had been almost no full-length academic studies at all into elections before 1945. 'It is always a good thing,' Ronald McCallum wrote later, 'if you start a new form of study, to find a Greek name for it. It looks established and respectable and intellectual snobs wonder uneasily whether it has not been known long ago and whether they ought not to pretend to have known about it all their lives.'[26]

A few days after introducing the word to America, Butler wrote from Cornell University to his publisher Maurice Macmillan, the future MP and Cabinet minister, who had taken over running the family firm Macmillan from his father Harold. In his letter, Butler admitted that he had placed the word so prominently in the book with the 'vague idea' the new word 'might catch the attention of those reviewers who do not read beyond the first paragraph'. Now, after the publicity he had generated for the word in America, he concluded that it was 'even more seductive than I had hoped'.[27]

It wasn't long, however, before Butler had doubts about spreading the word 'psephology': it had a 'pompous sound', he felt, and had 'a slight flavour of bogusness' from which he feared psychiatry and psychology both suffered.[28] 'It has some of the verbosity that many of us associate with quite a lot of people who go under the general "psychological" label,' he once said. The word he deliberately promoted as a publicity gimmick he later regretted. 'I just made it that special thing,' he says. 'But it has hung, like an albatross, around my neck for the last sixty years!'[29]

Partly through the fuss generated by the new word, the 1951 Nuffield book made a bigger impact than its two predecessors and helped establish both David Butler and the Nuffield series as regular election fixtures. *The British General Election of 1951* had a more playful style and was less dry than the previous volumes. Of all the Nuffield books that Butler edited, or co-edited, the 1951 edition was perhaps the most personal. Chapters on candidates, the press and broadcasting, which in most future editions would be farmed out to academic colleagues, were written this time by Butler himself.

The most striking thing about the book is how Butler foresaw many of the themes and research issues of British political science over the next twenty-five years.

> Moving pictures are required as well as snapshots. There is a need to see how far long-term influences on electoral opinion can be traced. Local candidates and organisations may not sway many votes between two successive elections, but over a longer period

> of years local efforts may do much to build upon the tradition of voting for a particular party. Why, for instance, did the Liberal Party decline at such different rates in adjoining and relatively similar constituencies? How far was political organisation responsible for the long-continued strength of Conservatism in the working-class districts of Birmingham? How important will the varying efficiency of local parties today be in determining the results of elections in the 1970s?[30]

David Butler's interest in politics at the constituency level, and his experiences of the notorious 'redistricting' process in America, had led him to a lifelong interest in boundary reviews, which inevitably had an effect on the outcome of elections. It was a subject, however – like so much else in political science – which had attracted little attention from either academics or journalists. Until the Second World War, boundary changes were rare, but then Parliament agreed that in future boundary reviews would take place every five years. Butler had briefly written about boundary reviews in his thesis (later published as a book) and in 1955 he published his first major academic article on the process, and in particular the boundary review instituted by the Conservative government in the run-up to the general election of that year. For an academic article, and at a time when analysts were much more deferential to people in power, it was highly critical of all those involved: 'Parliamentarians, party officials, civil servants, and academic observers showed lamentably bad foresight,' Butler wrote.[31] 'I was made very angry by Gwilym Lloyd George, a very incompetent Home Secretary, making a botch of this,' Butler says. 'I'd written many journalistic things before, which had little impact, but this one made an impact.'[32]

Butler made several recommendations in his article, several of which were taken up, including the suggestion that holding reviews every Parliament was too frequent and every fifteen years or so would be more practical. Butler remained interested in the subject for the rest of his career. He would often scrutinise the Boundary Commission's proposed changes in minute detail, ward by ward. He would frequently make recommendations to the Commission on their work, and occasionally on specific plans, and would sometimes visit public hearings.

At the BBC, meanwhile, Grace Wyndham Goldie was thinking ahead to the next general election, due by October 1956, in the expectation that BBC Television might face competition for the first time. What's more, that competition would probably be far bolder in its coverage of politics. In 1954, Parliament would vote to allow commercial television in Britain, with the new ITV channel due to go on air towards the end of 1955. Goldie was keen to make big improvements to the programme formats of 1950 and 1951. A new presenter was introduced – Richard Dimbleby – who had made his name as a BBC radio reporter during the war, recording despatches, for example, from a bomber on a mission over Germany. Dimbleby was a serious journalist and a natural broadcaster who had delivered live reports from outside broadcasts for the 1950 and 1951 programmes. Richard Dimbleby, or his elder son David, would play a role in every BBC TV results programme from 1950 to 2017, except 1966, while his younger son Jonathan presented three results programmes for ITV, in 1997, 2001 and 2005.[33]

At the start of 1955, Goldie and her colleagues were still at the long-term planning stage; the eighty-year-old Sir Winston Churchill was hanging on as Prime Minister, and there was little thought of an election before the following year. That January, the BBC producer Michael Peacock had an innovative idea. His brother worked for IBM, and Peacock wrote to David Butler to suggest they use a computer for the next results programme. The machine would be as much for visual imagery, it seems, as to assist with analysing results. It should be 'as large, complicated and impressive as possible!' Peacock suggested.[34] American broadcasters had used computers on the 1952 presidential election, yet despite his

1951 memo recommending their use, Butler was now dismissive. 'If we used it,' he replied next day, 'it would be quite definitely as a stunt. I don't think there's anything an electronic computer could do which could not be done virtually as cheaply and conveniently by a couple of chaps with ordinary calculating machines.'[35] He also feared a computer might actually make things slower. In reality, Peacock wasn't really proposing a 'computer' in the modern sense, but a more modern electronic calculating machine which would replace, or supplement, the old-fashioned methods.

Butler's opposition didn't last long, however. 'I am now writing hurriedly to you merely to serve notice that I have changed my mind about electronic brains,' he wrote to Peacock the following month.

> If we could get a suitable one free I have, in the light of further information, come to the conclusion that it might be well worthwhile, both as a gimmick to tease the viewers and as a device for obtaining fuller and speedier statistical information to serve as a basis for comment.[36]

His enthusiasm for the new technology grew rapidly. Three weeks later, by now anticipating an election in October, David Butler wrote a ten-page letter to Grace Wyndham Goldie, in which he not only now suggested using at least four computers, but also showed he had done considerable research as to what computers were now on the market, how they might work and how they could speed things up. And before long he had taken the initiative and talked directly to IBM himself, although in the end the idea was dropped as IBM couldn't give any assurances about what would happen if the computers broke down.

Butler's March letter to Goldie bubbled with other helpful and imaginative suggestions about how her programme might be improved and he showed a keen awareness that they might lose their monopoly on coverage to the new commercial channel, ITV. Indeed, one gets the impression that Butler would have revelled in the role of TV producer – he loved the intellectual challenge of using the new visual medium to explain complicated information to a lay audience. Reading his letter, and Butler's subsequent correspondence in the months ahead, it is striking how much of what he suggested was taken up. Indeed, many of the features of the 1955 programme, devised by Butler, Peacock and Goldie, are still the basic ingredients of election programmes more than sixty years later.

But Butler's most eye-catching suggestion was tucked away in the middle of his March 1955 letter, on page eight: 'To show people how the tide is going, a simple pendulum might be used,' he suggested, and his letter included a small diagram, which he had drawn in pencil, of what this new pendulum device might look like. 'If the pointer is kept at the figure revealed by the electronic calculators as the average swing so far,' he explained, 'the total number of seats likely to change hands will always be available.'[37]

In a second letter, written two months later, Butler again mentioned his proposed device for relating the change in the percentage vote to the change in the number of seats, and sent Goldie a revised drawing, though sadly this picture does not seem to have survived. This time, Butler casually referred to his invention as a 'speedometer type device'.[38]

Only now the need was more urgent. That April, Sir Winston Churchill had finally stood down as Prime Minister, and had been replaced by Sir Anthony Eden, who almost immediately called an election for the following month. So the BBC TV results programme had to be put together rather hastily (though the snap election did at least mean ITV would not yet be on air to pose any competition).

Butler's two letters were, of course, the origins of the famous Swingometer, which for millions of viewers ever since has helped to explain the concept of swing. In time, it became the great totemic symbol of BBC election night programmes and was often parodied by satirists. David Butler wanted to operate his 'speedometer type device' himself in 1955, but in the end a revised version was given only a very limited outing. This is all the more surprising when, after BBC TV's failure to do a deal with IBM, their rivals in radio managed to link up with a 'computer' at the English Electric company in Stafford. 'Deuce', as it was called, was a vast machine which involved punch cards, a memory on a magnetic drum, and a series of mercury tubes. The BBC claimed Deuce was 'among the fastest' electronic computers in the world.[39]

Instead, the TV results programme merely tested a tiny Swingometer as part of regional input, operated by Stephen Milne, a politics academic from Bristol University, as he reported from the studio in Bristol on the two seats in Southampton. Milne's device, propped on a desktop easel, was just a half-moon graphic painted onto a piece of card, overlaid with a movable arrow to show the swing between the parties across the city. Though it appeared on screen only for a few seconds, it is widely recognised as the first use of the Swingometer, even though it didn't relate votes to seats. Although Milne was one of the most distinguished early analysts of British elections, who had conducted detailed studies of what actually happened in constituency campaigns, it seems a pity that the first Swingometer could not have been operated by the man who first suggested it to the BBC.

For the subsequent 1959 election programme, Grace Wyndham Goldie commissioned a full-size version of the Swingometer, measuring nine feet by six, which was operated by the inventor himself. From 1964 onwards, however, Bob McKenzie took over the Swingometer and did so for six successive general elections; later, Peter Snow operated the first electronic version; and in modern times it has been Jeremy Vine's toy. Modestly, David Butler has always given credit for inventing the Swingometer to Stephen Milne, who died in 2014. The correspondence from 1955 shows, however, that it was really Butler's invention.

The results programme for the election held on 26 May 1955 boasted twice as many cameras as the BBC had employed for the Coronation two years before, and by now about a third of British households had a TV set. It is also the first election programme for which a substantial recording survives (it is sometimes replayed on the BBC Parliament Channel, and has had more than 12,000 views on YouTube). What is striking to a modern viewer is the formal, stilted nature of the programme. Richard Dimbleby appeared as a bear-like figure whose head seemed to have been placed on top of his very broad shoulders without any sign of a neck; he wore a double-breasted suit with top handkerchief and waistcoat. Butler, in a lighter suit, sat immediately to Dimbleby's left, looking remarkably young for thirty, with striking dark hair, and when he addressed the camera he tended to incline his head slightly towards the right. He spoke with a very clipped upper-middle-class voice, as many people did at that time. Dimbleby usually addressed Butler, McKenzie and the BBC parliamentary correspondent Teddy Thompson by their surnames, as if they were his pupils at public school, and Butler himself occasionally called the BBC man 'Thompson' as well. The few interviewees were listened to respectfully, with no interruptions. Dimbleby seems to have had no earpiece; instead, the phone on his desk would ring now and then with details of what was happening next. At one point, Bob McKenzie addressed the camera with a cigarette in his hand.

The whole operation was notably wooden, jerky and unrelaxed compared with the swift and easy fluency of modern election programmes. A couple of the academic contributors outside London spoke to camera as if giving university lectures. People were reluctant to interrupt each other, and there were often gaps of two or three seconds when nobody said anything. Jokes and humour were much less common.

Although Dimbleby was a superb broadcaster, he readily conceded that he lacked any great knowledge of elections, which made Butler and McKenzie all the more necessary. At the start of the programme, having referred to 'a pretty hefty organisation … full to the brim with backroom boys and girls', Dimbleby introduced Butler as 'my constant companion', and Butler then directed the camera towards his six-strong team from Nuffield. Butler was very much the second voice on the programme – 'my other half', as Dimbleby called him at one point.[40]

'Dimbleby seemed interested but at the same time deferred to other people,' Butler says. 'He was absolutely splendid, the best person to sit beside in an election. He was so absolutely calm and certain. And so intensely competent. If one stumbled or anything, he picked up the pieces instantly, never in a reproachful way.'[41] Much of the programme consisted of result cards on screen, when Dimbleby would outline the basic facts and Butler would come up with some percentages that had been worked out by his Nuffield colleagues – usually the swing, or turnout, or very often whether or not weaker candidates had managed to save their deposits.

Butler's first forecast came thirty-six minutes into the programme, after just two results – a 2.2 per cent swing to the Conservatives in Cheltenham, and 2.4 per cent in Salford West. 'If the whole country behaves like that – a swing of two to two and a half per cent – the Conservatives will have a lead … of about 120 seats clear over Labour.' 'If the whole country behaves like that' would become a common Butler catchphrase in the years ahead, a kind of insurance policy against the pressure to produce an early forecast.

Butler pointed out that 'in the past, the country has behaved in an extraordinarily unified way', but Dimbleby noted the 120-seat prediction on a scrap of paper and explained that he believed in 'holding experts to account'. When Butler appeared again, four minutes later, he clearly feared he'd been a bit rash, and refused to elaborate on his prediction: 'I think I've stuck my neck out far enough for the time being,' Butler said. 'When four or five results are in I shan't be so worried about the extension of my neck. But for the moment I think I'd better hold my peace.'[42]

Richard Dimbleby queried whether it was really possible to forecast the whole outcome after just two results. Butler explained it was, because 'we in Britain are – perhaps thank God – so unified a country. What happens in one part of the country seems to happen in another. Past elections have shown an extraordinarily even turnover in votes between one constituency and another right throughout the country.'

'Is that what's called being a "psephologist"?' Dimbleby asked teasingly. 'I've heard that word used about you and I gather it's rather a controversial word?' Butler patiently explained how the word – which he pronounced with a long 'E' – had been thought up by R. B. McCallum, 'my mentor in the study of elections'.

Butler was right to fear being rash. The problem was that in 1955, the first two results were slightly untypical, and the actual swing nationwide turned out to be barely 2.0 per cent. So Anthony Eden's majority was sixty, exactly half Butler's initial forecast.

The broadcast programme lasted about seventeen hours in all, with a two-hour break in the middle of the night. It had been tiring, of course, but towards the end Butler didn't seem to have lost any of his enthusiasm, and he remarked that 'it would be interesting to see just how the results flowed in during this wonderful, strenuous twenty hours'. Then he checked himself: 'I don't say "wonderful" in terms of the results, by the way, just say it because it was exciting listening to the results, which is what I personally happen to find the most enjoyable thing in the world.'[43]

'No one had a greater personal success during the election than Mr David Butler,' *The Observer* remarked.

> His marathon television commentary ... was about the most lucid and apt thing in the campaign. As remarkable as his hoard of precise electoral information, both in his head and on his cards, was the talent he showed for imparting it, hour after hour, without ever seeming a pedant or an irritating know-all ... None of

> the other psephologists has quite such a passion as he has for the new discipline.[44]

The TV critic of the *Star* newspaper suggested Butler 'must claim the unwritten vote of many a woman'.[45] For a columnist on *The Scotsman*, Richard Dimbleby's three studio analysts looked rather like gnomes:

> especially Mr David Butler, that low-browed high-brow who, with unruffled composure and engaging charm, worked out everything for us on the instant with a slightly diffident authority. It may have all been a trifle egg-headed, but it was fascinating, as fascinating as running a toy electric railway system.[46]

David Butler was paid 100 guineas (£105) for his studio appearances and a further £50 for his intense activity in the weeks beforehand, when he played a major role in working out how the results system would operate – around £4,000 in 2018 money. Immediately after the programme, Michael Peacock wrote to Butler: 'The letters are still pouring in congratulating you and the rest of us … It appears to have made almost as great an impact on the viewers as did the Coronation.' But there was one small drawback, Peacock suggested: 'I am afraid that the prestige of sephology [*sic*] has suffered somewhat … I imagine you are busy trying to analyse why the swing was not as uniform as in the past, and why the turnout varied…'[47]

'I am not dismayed by the damage to the prestige of psephology,' Butler replied. 'We were wrong on a number of things, but only mildly. I shall be humbler in future.'[48]

Grace Wyndham Goldie was quick to write and thank Butler:

> First of all, my dear David, I must say how much I admire the recurring *tour de force* of yours. It really wins the admiration of the whole country. We have been inundated with letters of

> congratulation … They are all for the team as a whole and your name recurs with great frequency.[49]

No doubt thinking of the pending threat from ITV, Goldie immediately tried to recruit Butler for the subsequent election, even though it was not likely for another four or five years. 'Incidentally, how do you feel about signing a contract with us now for that event?' she asked. 'Don't take this as a joke! I was really asked to approach you seriously about it … I may say that I will have nothing to do with it next time unless you are on it too.'[50]

Butler responded positively, but he had one big regret about the 1955 programme. 'It was perhaps a pity,' he wrote in a five-page memo immediately after the broadcast, 'that we abandoned the Swingometer. In a simplified way the swing device used in Bristol (a pendulum on a semi-circular card) was a good one and I would have liked to have had a similar device lying on my desk.'[51]

CHAPTER EIGHT

GILDED YEAR IN GEORGETOWN

Despite being socially awkward in some ways, few people in his day were better at the art of networking than David Butler. One of his many friends and contacts in the early 1950s was William Clark, the diplomatic correspondent of *The Observer*, who was himself a gregarious host. He would often invite Butler over to Sunday lunch at his home at the foot of the Chilterns in Buckinghamshire, where he would entertain political friends on a large scale.

In 1955, Clark abruptly left journalism to become press secretary to the new Prime Minister, Sir Anthony Eden. And Butler thinks it was Clark who recommended him for a new role which would make use of his experience in America. How would he like to do a stint as personal assistant to the British ambassador in Washington, Sir Roger Makins, for whom his primary task would be to write speeches? It would be a great opportunity to get to know some of the most powerful figures in America, and also to test the possibility of moving into government as a career. (A personal connection was that Makins's outgoing speechwriter, Jake Carter, had once worked with Butler's uncle, Graham Pollard, on a famous exposé into the forgery of some nineteenth-century pamphlets.)[1]

Butler had never met Sir Roger Makins, but he seized this chance. Having quickly completed the manuscript for the 1955 general election book, he took leave from Nuffield and sailed that September on the *Queen Mary* to New York – first class. Though Butler was only thirty, and knew nothing of the diplomatic world, he was given the rank of counsellor – he'd have been happy to go as a second secretary, but Makins had wanted to attract good applicants.

The generous salary was well above what Butler had been earning in Oxford, and far more than contemporaries who had joined the Diplomatic Service. 'I was over-paid, and over-ranked,' Butler would recall, 'but I didn't do any particular harm while I was there.'[2] A young Washington colleague, Peter Marshall, recalls the embassy chief clerk telling him: 'I had no idea he was so young – I would never have agreed to [him] being paid at that level if I'd known!'[3]

Sir Roger Makins, the son of a former Conservative MP, was, says Butler, 'an extraordinary, self-contained giant'; an intellectual who had once been a fellow of All Souls. Isaiah Berlin, who'd known Makins at All Souls, described him as 'the best second-class mind in Britain', a description that would echo over the coming twelve months as Butler found his new boss 'almost never said anything original or profound or witty'.[4] Makins had served as ambassador in Washington since 1953 and was a great admirer of America following two previous stints in the US. His wife, Alice, was the daughter of Dwight Davis, who had been the US Secretary for War under President Coolidge, though he is probably better known as a distinguished tennis player who founded the Davis Cup tournament.

Makins had gone to Washington on the understanding that a large part of the job was public relations. Before he crossed the Atlantic, Makins had received training in how to do interviews for the new medium of television, and his new speechwriter had, of course, already established himself as a skilled TV performer. Much of the British ambassador's role involved touring the country selling Britain and British policy, and in his three years Makins managed to visit all of the then forty-nine states.

But Makins was 'no great orator', Butler recalls; he was a serious man, with little sense of humour.[5] According to Makins's daughters, Sir Roger didn't get on with Butler's predecessor, and Lady Alice disliked Jake Carter even more than he did. Carter was too much of a 'flowery man-about-town', they felt, while his American wife Ernestine, a successful journalist and fashion writer, seemed too interested in making her name in Washington society.[6]

So Butler faced the challenge of jazzing up Makins's speeches in a way the ambassador would accept, and which wouldn't make Makins sound unnatural. 'My predecessor tried to insert a line or two of verse into his drafts,' he says. 'I cut out all such literary flourishes; Roger was no good at delivering poetry.'[7] So, like any good speechwriter, he listened very closely to what Makins said in everyday discourse, and quickly learnt to write what sounded natural coming from the ambassador's mouth.

The arrangement worked. Early on, Butler reckons, Makins accepted about 85 per cent of what he wrote; by the end, it was more like 95 per cent. 'That's not to say Roger was becoming my puppet. He read it with extreme punctiliousness – he made corrections on the text that I wrote for him.'[8] 'I was becoming *his* puppet,' he later elaborated, 'increasingly aware of just what he liked to say.'[9]

But Butler found that while his boss was good with paperwork – 'a magnificent administrative athlete', according to one colleague – Makins didn't talk much, either to Butler or to anyone else.

> I used to see quite a lot of him whilst I was doing my job, but I wasn't intimate with him. I didn't have much conversation with him; he didn't volunteer much, and he didn't talk about diplomatic things to me at all. But people did come to me on the assumption that I was an intimate of Roger's, and I had to, not exactly brush them off, but say: 'Go and say it to him yourself.'[10]

Butler found Sir Roger had a 'wonderfully organised intellect'. If Butler asked a question or queried some plan, Makins 'would shrug his shoulders and either give me an answer, or say "I'll tell you tomorrow" – which he always did, unprompted. He didn't ever think aloud to test ideas. He didn't like meetings.'[11] Makins was a 'competent but not a brilliant speaker', Butler reckoned, especially at speaking unprepared, so Butler would always give the ambassador a draft which Makins would then study very carefully and learn almost off by heart.[12]

Writing speeches was a task that required extreme tact, such as when he had to prepare for Makins to open an exhibition of works by Barbara Hepworth. 'He and I disapproved of her works almost equally,' Butler confessed in a letter home. 'I managed to sound very enthusiastic without saying anything at all. I thought her carvings ... frightful. Her drawings were more passable.'[13]

And Butler spent much time looking after a constant stream of political visitors from London, from backbench MPs to the Prime Minister Sir Anthony Eden, who reportedly greeted him with the words, 'Ah, David Butler, the historian,' in acknowledgment of his new Nuffield election book. 'It was very flattering. He was absolutely charming to everybody.' And yet Butler also heard from embassy colleagues who'd been in other places which Eden had visited in his three stints as Foreign Secretary 'horror stories of his being such a capricious person and so difficult. So there were two pictures: Eden the charmer, and Eden the awful man that Foreign Office people knew him to be.'[14]

The new Labour leader, Hugh Gaitskell, visited Washington, too, accompanied by his wife Dora. 'He has created a *very* good impression,' Butler told his mother. 'Certainly he was very lively and very frank at this party and very friendly when I drove them from the party to the Embassy. She is much more intelligent and agreeable than I had thought.'[15] The following day, at the Overseas Writers' Association, Gaitskell 'spoke effectively and answered questions brilliantly with just the right amount of indiscretion for an off-the-record speech, not giving away anything vital, but flattering his audience by giving them the illusion that he trusted them'.[16]

But the outstanding impression from reading David Butler's letters home to his mother – and in contrast to his 1947–48 spell in America – is the extraordinary social life he led, a whirl of political cocktail parties and dinners which took up most nights of the week.

Butler rented a small house at 3009 Dumbarton Street, Georgetown, which he'd obtained through an agency. It was a neat, two-storey, red-bricked, terraced property which had been built around 1900, and whose female owner had survived the sinking of the *Lusitania* in 1915. Intentionally or not, Butler had placed himself geographically at the very heart of what Vice-President Richard Nixon disparagingly called the 'Georgetown Set', during what was the set's most influential period, the early years of the Cold War. All around him in the criss-crossed streets were a powerful network of politicians and government officials; journalists and lawyers; professors and publishers; diplomats and spies. Most had been educated at Ivy League universities, and by and large they were Democrats and liberals. They knew how power worked in Washington and they ran not just the United States, but effectively the whole of the Western world as it grappled with the threat from Soviet communism.

This political elite lived within an area of less than one square mile, bounded by Rock Creek to the east and the Chesapeake and Ohio Canal to the south (and, just beyond it, the Potomac River). To the west were the lawns, halls and spires of Georgetown University, and its northern boundaries were Montrose Park and the estate of Dumbarton Oaks, where in 1944 the wartime Allies had agreed to establish the United Nations. The dwellings weren't large by American standards, nor especially extravagant, and it was a true community, whose residents were regularly in and out of each other's homes and flats.

Gregg Herken, author of *The Georgetown Set*, says: 'Those who inspired, promoted, and – in some cases – personally executed America's winning Cold War strategy were not generals at the Pentagon but a coterie of affluent, well-educated, and well-connected civilians living in a fashionable Washington DC neighbourhood.'[17] The set's battles, Herken writes:

> were planned and directed not from the Pentagon's war room or the mahogany-panelled cloisters of Foggy Bottom [the State Department] but from Georgetown's cosy salons, where high policy was sometimes made between cocktails and dinner, in what was both a ritual and an institution in Washington: the Sunday night supper. There was even a word – 'salonisma' – coined to describe the power that the Georgetown set wielded in Washington.[18]

The community was an 'entity unto itself', remarked Phil Graham, the publisher of the *Washington Post*:

> In other cities, people go to parties primarily to have fun. In Georgetown, people who have fun at parties probably aren't getting much work done. That's because parties in Georgetown aren't really parties in the true sense of the word. They're business after hours, a form of government by invitation ... it's fair to say that more political decisions get made at Georgetown suppers than anywhere else in the nation's capital, including the Oval Office.[19]

In the autumn of 1955, the thirty-year-old David Butler was moving back to an America which, after the isolationism of the 1920s and '30s, had only just embraced its place as leader of the Free World. To people outside the Diplomatic Service, venturing into this world would have been a daunting prospect, but David Butler easily slipped into his new Washington surroundings. He was at home in a political community that attracted some of the brightest minds in the land. Five months after he arrived, he was invited to the home of one of Georgetown's most famous – or notorious – couples, Donald and Catherine Hiss, for a 'large and very congenial dinner party'. At the time, Washington was slowly recovering from

David's grandfather Arthur Gray Butler (1831–1909) (right) and great-uncle Henry Montagu Butler (1833–1918) (left), former headmaster of Harrow and Master of Trinity College, Cambridge.

A. F. Pollard, the Tudor historian, who was David Butler's maternal grandfather and encouraged his interest in contemporary history and his passion for facts.

Harold Butler, David's father, won the Newdigate Prize for poetry at Oxford and was a lecturer at New College at twenty-three before becoming Professor of Latin at University College London.

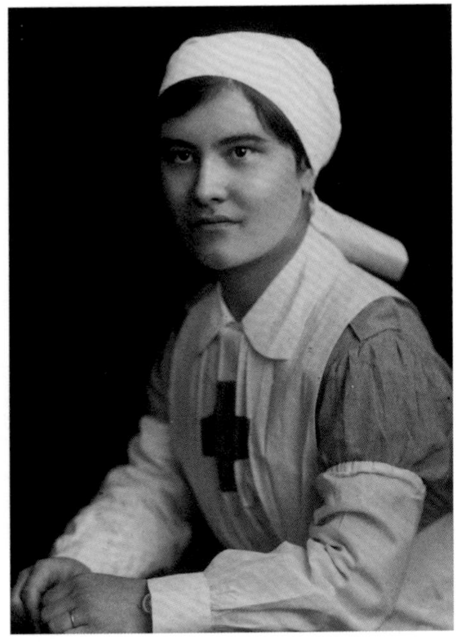

Margaret 'Peggie' Butler, David's mother, who married Harold in 1917 while serving as a nurse during the First World War.

David and Michael in the garden of Gordon Square, Bloomsbury, a few yards from their family home. The square's most famous inhabitant was John Maynard Keynes, whose contentious account of the 1918 election sparked the Nuffield general election studies. © BUTLER FAMILY

David (right) and his sisters Christina and Nora bury brother Michael during a family holiday on the island of Eigg. © BUTLER FAMILY

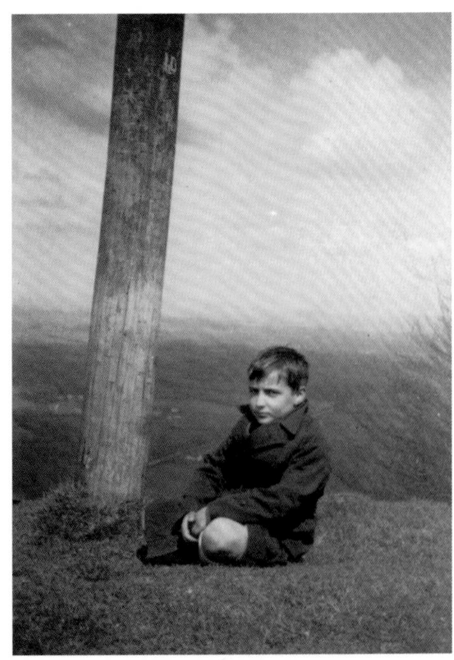

Young David, both pictures taken at or near his grandparents' country home in Birdlip in Gloucestershire, at the top of the Cotswolds. © BUTLER FAMILY

Butler was in the Officer Training Corps at St Paul's before serving as a lieutenant in the Staffordshire Yeomanry during the war. He was commander of a group of amphibious tanks but experienced only about three days of 'blood and thunder'. © BUTLER FAMILY

Election analyst at twenty-five, on the very first BBC TV election results programme in February 1950. Left to right: Butler, his mentor R. B. McCallum and the Australian presenter Chester Wilmot, as a studio hand paints in the latest results. © BBC PHOTO LIBRARY

By the 1955 election, Butler was well-established as a 'telly don' and number two on the programme to the great presenter Richard Dimbleby. Butler later worked as a pundit on BBC and ITV programmes presented by Richard's sons, David and Jonathan. © BBC PHOTO LIBRARY

Butler invented the BBC Swingometer in 1955, but rarely got to use it on air. Here, however, he wields the Swingometer on the 1965 BBC local elections programme. © BBC PHOTO LIBRARY

By the time of the February 1974 programme, Butler's hair was much greyer, but he dressed more in the fashion of the period. © BBC PHOTO LIBRARY

Butler, Angela Rippon, David Dimbleby and Bob McKenzie in 1979: it was Butler and McKenzie's last BBC results programme, and Dimbleby's first as presenter. © GETTY IMAGES/UNITED NEWS/POPPERFOTO

Marilyn Evans got a congratulated first in English at Oxford and was active in left-wing politics. © BUTLER FAMILY

Marilyn arrives at Kingston Register Office in March 1962 to marry David. She insisted on a very quiet wedding to which only a handful of close family were invited. © BUTLER FAMILY

The Butlers outside 151 Woodstock Road, Oxford: Marilyn, Gareth, Daniel, Edmund and David. © BUTLER FAMILY

David and Tony Benn shared economics tutorials at New College in 1943 and always remained the closest of friends, though they disagreed politically in later years. © BUTLER FAMILY

Butler in his study at Woodstock Road. © ANN ADDISON

David as supportive consort to Marilyn. He was hugely proud of her achievement in becoming Rector of Exeter College, the first female head of any Oxbridge college that had previously been only for men. © BUTLER FAMILY

ABOVE Gareth, seen here campaigning for Labour in the 1987 Greenwich by-election, was the most political of the Butler sons, and shared David's passion for elections and political facts. He died suddenly of a heart attack in 2008. © BUTLER FAMILY

LEFT A grotesque of Marilyn erected on the wall of Exeter College. © BUTLER FAMILY

LEFT Marilyn and David in 1994 with their first grandson, Jack. © BUTLER FAMILY

post-war McCarthyism, and it was just eight years after Donald Hiss and his more famous brother Alger had been denounced as Soviet spies, but never convicted (though in Alger's case the accusation was later thought accurate). 'It was very much a Georgetown affair,' Butler wrote to his mother, 'and I felt completely at home knowing all the other twelve guests in one milieu or other.'[20]

The next day, Butler attended a lunch with Joe Alsop, one of America's top newspaper columnists, and sat next to Alice Roosevelt Longworth, the daughter of President Theodore Roosevelt; widow of a House Speaker from the 1920s, and 'one of the great wits of her day'.[21] The political-cum-social round continued that evening as Butler hosted a dinner party himself in Dumbarton Street. His guests included General John Ackerman, vice-director of the National Security Agency; and Joseph Harsch, a well-known TV news analyst with the NBC network.

Joe Alsop was one of Isaiah Berlin's closest friends in Washington, with whom Berlin would often stay on his regular visits. And, very conveniently, Butler's new home was on the same street as both Joe Alsop and his brother Stewart, who was also one of America's top newspaper columnists. Butler lived roughly equidistant between the two men, who at that time collaborated on a column for the *New York Herald Tribune* which was syndicated to 200 papers across the USA. And just across the street from Butler was Felix Frankfurter, the Supreme Court Justice and friend of Isaiah Berlin whom he had got to know during his American stay in 1947 and 1948. Frankfurter lived at 3018 Dumbarton Street, in a large house which he later rented to Henry Kissinger, who once remarked that the 'hand that mixes the Georgetown martini is time and again the hand that guides the destiny of the Western world'.[22] The house was subsequently bought by Kissinger's immediate successor as Secretary of State, Cyrus Vance.

Frankfurter may have been considered a liberal member of the court, though he didn't always correspond to type – he voted for the internment of Japanese Americans in 1944, for example – but in 1955 America was still digesting the justices' decisions the year before in perhaps the most famous case in Supreme Court history: Brown *v* Board of Education, which outlawed segregation in American schools. Felix Frankfurter had played the leading role in a judgment that was a milestone in the history of civil rights in America.

Even though they had met several times before, Butler says it was during this year at the embassy that he 'really came to know and love Felix', despite their forty-year age gap. Butler found him 'in a way, a lonely old man', since his wife Marion suffered from mental illness and nearly always remained upstairs. Almost every Sunday, Butler would be invited over for a pre-lunch drink:

> He wanted an audience and, over a Manhattan, he would reminisce about Washington and Harvard in the 1920s and 1930s. I was lost at many of his anecdotes but I knew just enough of the allusions to keep him going. He had a wonderful gift for portraying his contemporaries – Franklin and Eleanor Roosevelt ... his enemies [Walter] Lippmann and Nixon. He had an eager, Anglophile, curiosity about the doings of Parliament. He demanded the latest news over the abolition of capital punishment.[23]

'Mr Frankfurter' – as Butler's letters usually called him – loved hearing about politics in America or Britain, and enjoyed the intellectual stimulus of a robust debate as he and his young visitor sipped their drinks. One evening, just before Christmas 1955, Butler had gone back briefly to Dumbarton Street to get ready for a couple of social engagements that evening:

> I met, passing my door, Mr Frankfurter. And he so obviously wanted to talk about British Cabinet changes that I weakly invited him in 'for five minutes'. He stayed talking brilliantly for 45. And I did not know how to turn a Justice of the Supreme Court

> out of my house. In the end, I had to transfer my watch from one wrist to another, and then, after a battle with lost cufflinks, and other evidences of the malignity of matter, I had to cut my cocktail party and even arrive late for my dinner...[24]

A couple of weeks afterwards, Butler went back to Frankfurter's home:

> We had a splendid time. I have never before known a man of over 70 who so loves controversy – and who plays so fair in argument, never intruding the weight of his own great eminence to support his case and never altogether losing sight of the ideal of disputation as a means to truth.[25]

On another occasion, after Sunday lunchtime drinks at Frankfurter's house, Butler wrote in his diary: 'I had to own myself defeated in my attempt to defend Herbert Nicholas's judgement that in some ways, because of his lack of deviousness, future historians would rate Truman's moral stature above that of Roosevelt.'[26]

'FF was very combative and sought disagreement at every point, largely with me,' he wrote after one Frankfurter evening dinner. 'I know better than not to argue back.'[27] Occasionally the pair would be joined for drinks by some of Frankfurter's former clerks. On another occasion, giving Frankfurter a lift home one evening, Butler found himself 'involved in a very vehement argument with him on how far a politician could compromise and yet keep his integrity. He is far more perfectionist than I, for all that he has seen forty more years of politics.'[28]

Despite living not far from the up-and-coming Senator John F. Kennedy in Georgetown, Butler says very little about the man who would be elected President four years later. On one occasion, he heard Kennedy deliver 'a cultivated and witty speech' to the Women's National Press Club on the relationship between politicians and writers. But Butler, who was a speechwriter himself, of course, saw no sign of the oratory that would soon captivate the world. 'He read it very badly, and I assumed that it was ghost-written until he answered questions when he was, speaking extemporaneously, equally cultivated and witty, and almost as bad in delivery.'[29]

Butler often held his own cocktail parties and dinners, financed by his embassy allowance. He was usually aided in the preparation by the cook and housekeeper who were also provided by the embassy, but whom he had to share with a colleague. Butler's first housekeeper, Termutus, was not a great success. 'Getting the house in order has been hard work,' he wrote early on, 'because, as I sadly discovered, Termutus doesn't like work and she thinks that brass should be cleaned with water and soda, and she expects one to suggest every menu, and her repertoire is restricted to chicken and lamb.' Butler also found, after talking to his colleague, that 'Termutus had a gift of always hiding herself in the other house whenever she saw some work threatening'. So, she had to go. 'Sacking someone is a terrifying experience for the first time,' he wrote, 'but I got over it quite painlessly.'[30] Termutus's replacement, Lucy, was an 'older and abler and much nicer Jamaican' who worked for Butler full time.[31] His relationship with Lucy, however, was not always comfortable either. She had the habit of drinking when he arranged dinner parties. And when Butler was ill one day, he wrote in his diary (in a way people might find racist today): 'After a day of dozing, with Lucy brooding ominously in the background, and, I suspect, chanting black magic spells, the evil passed from me.'[32]

Butler's biggest act of hospitality came in March 1956, when James Butler, a cousin who had briefly been MP for Cambridge University in the 1920s, was due to visit Washington to research a book about the wartime British ambassador Lord Lothian. James Butler had recently retired as Regius Professor of History at Cambridge. The young diplomat managed to acquire as his other guests two of the towering figures of 1950s Washington, who both lived only blocks away from his home, for what he described as 'the most portentous dinner party I have yet attempted'.[33] Dean Acheson had recently been Secretary of State under President Truman, when he was one of the chief architects of the post-war world – or *Present at the Creation*, as his memoirs rather immodestly put it. Indeed, Acheson was, along with Henry Kissinger, one of the most powerful Secretaries of State of the twentieth century and would remain an informal adviser to every President until Nixon. Walter Lippmann, whom Butler had taken to lunch several times, was then at the peak of his fame as a newspaper columnist, and probably deserves a place in the ten most influential and distinguished American journalists of the past hundred years. David Butler must have been delighted to get both men to his table, yet the glittering pairing was something of a diplomatic *faux pas*.

Everyone in Washington politics, it seems – everyone except Butler – knew that Acheson and Lippmann had fallen out badly, having once been good friends. Lippmann had been very critical in his regular syndicated columns of Acheson's central role in developing what became known as the 'Truman Doctrine' of American intervention around the globe, and the policy of containment to stop communism. Acheson never forgave Lippmann for the strength and persistence of his criticism. And Lippmann, in turn, would always refuse any social invitation if he knew Dean Acheson was going to be present.

Yet Butler's gathering in Dumbarton Street passed off remarkably peacefully. Acheson and Lippmann greeted each other with surprise, and spoke for the first time in years. 'Lippmann and he had a good argument on devolution of Presidential powers,' Butler wrote afterwards, 'in which I found myself entirely on Lippmann's side; I felt that Lippmann had a much sharper sense of the politically probable. But it was certainly a very successful evening.'[34]

Indeed, Butler didn't know of the bad blood between them until Felix Frankfurter teased him about it a week later. 'FF assured me that the Achesons really had enjoyed it,' Butler wrote:

> but pointed out that it was probably six years since Acheson and Lippmann had sat at a small table together. I gather that all Acheson's friends are far more unforgiving than Acheson himself for the way in which Lippmann treated him when he was Secretary of State. I'm very glad I only learnt this after the dinner party … I should have been an anxious host if I had known I was entertaining two reputedly irreconcilable public figures.[35]

Fortunately, Sir Roger Makins wasn't that bothered when his assistant apologised for his social gaffe. 'They're being very silly about these things,' Butler recalls Makins responding. 'It's our job to make them talk to each other.' Butler concludes that getting Acheson and Lippmann to talk to each other again was 'the most political thing I think I did while I was in Washington'.[36]

Although Butler was diligent on the Washington social scene – as both host and guest – there were some invitations he didn't accept. He was never much of a concert-goer or music-lover – whatever political benefits might ensue – and in April 1956 he caused great consternation among embassy colleagues when he turned down a much sought-after invitation from a Washington hostess to a concert evening at Constitution Hall to celebrate National Music Week (endorsed by President Eisenhower). 'The horrified reaction to his refusal appeared to call into question his respectability,' his colleague Peter Marshall later recalled. 'I sympathised with him on hearing of his misfortune. He asked whether, in that case, I was prepared to join in an "Enemies of Music" group, which would campaign to end such discrimination.'[37]

Marshall himself could hardly be called non-musical. He sang, in fact, in the choir of Washington Cathedral, but nonetheless he agreed to join a 'fictional society' for people who 'deplore the idolatry of music' in Washington, and suggested he consult a friend about it – Day Thorpe, music critic of the local *Sunday Star*.[38] Thorpe agreed to publicise the group but insisted on a better title.

So, Marshall came up with 'The Society for the Disestablishment of Music', which had, of course, connotations with the status of the Church of England. Butler had Marshall and Thorpe to dinner in Dumbarton Street and, the following Sunday, Thorpe entertained the two diplomats to dinner at his home in the suburbs, where, Butler says, 'time passed hilariously and argumentatively'.[39] The result was a half-page article in the arts section of the following *Sunday Star* – then Washington's leading newspaper – based on an interview with the society's chairman, 'Mr Byron D. Charles'. Thorpe explained this was 'a pseudonym he insisted upon', though the article didn't say that 'Charles' was English. Byron D. Charles supposedly claimed:

> What we propose to do is to relegate music to its proper position in modern society. We are not enemies of music – far from it … We realise that harmonious sound has a small though actually quite important place in the world … Our purpose is to attempt to seat music on its proper side of the salt, to expose it as expensive, time-wasting, debilitating, and while perhaps not intrinsically and essentially mean, certainly one of the most active causes of sham and hypocrisy.
>
> … Why should symphonies, operas and similar long-hair music purveyors be granted a Government subsidy in the form of remission of amusement taxes? Why should the Government distinguish between amusements? Does it not sour the man whose delight is Havana cigars and French cognac to remember that he is taxed heavily for his fun, and at the same time is forced to carry the load of the so-called amusement of the music-lover?[40]

The quotes from 'Byron D. Charles' are probably an amalgamation of what Butler and Marshall dreamt up over the two dinners, with much embellishment, no doubt, by Thorpe. It is hard to imagine either Butler or Marshall uttering lines such as: 'The fetish of music-worship is as incomprehensible as it is menacing.' It was all a big jape, of course, yet contained a serious examination of the significance of music. The *Sunday Star* article ended with Day Thorpe relating how, 'bleached by searing, but controlled anger', he rose up and told Charles: 'I can assure you that *The Star* will have no part in publicising your vicious, stupid, and uncivilised propaganda. Music is the most nearly divine achievement of centuries of human endeavour.'[41]

'Two or three times,' Butler explains, I had been invited to concerts by Washington *grandes dames*, and I thought: "I know that I will behave myself, but I also know I will be quite bored."'[42] Yet the episode shows a slightly mischievous side to David Butler, and demonstrates his constant temptation to stir things up, provoke debate and question basic assumptions. Why should people who don't love music be treated as inferior? Is it right for the state to subsidise music so heavily? Yet, as Peter Marshall recalls, the two British diplomats were taking a bit of a risk:

> I felt it necessary to ask for some amendment of the draft, so as to rid it of the more obvious indications that the chairman of this subversive body was British. We could not risk a trans-Atlantic incident. The article … aroused strong public reaction. Could such a monster really exist?[43]

There were also genuine streaks of David Butler in what 'Byron D. Charles' was quoted as saying. He has never been a great music lover. His family say the only music they can recall him enjoying are the satirical songs of Tom Lehrer, which are, of course, highly political. (Lehrer's sudden popularity in American liberal, academic circles also coincided with Butler's time at the embassy.)

While working in Washington, Butler acquired his own car, a large, old, 'gas-guzzling' Buick convertible, though his driving soon became a joke around the embassy. Twice in the space of two weeks he ran out of petrol, and Peter Marshall drew up a postcard which said 'Out of Gas', to place in the glove compartment to remind him to fill up regularly. And Butler had quite a serious accident when another car crashed into his vehicle from the side while he was driving the ambassador home from a diplomatic evening.

His diplomatic life was so busy that Butler found very little time for reading or keeping up with academic developments in his areas of political science. Nonetheless, it's clear from his diary that he spent plenty of time in contact with the network of academics and pollsters he'd got to know at Princeton in 1947–48 and on subsequent visits to the USA. He would frequently see the pollster Richard 'Dick' M. Scammon, who was probably the nearest equivalent America has had to its own David Butler. Scammon set up the Election Research Centre in Washington in 1955 and founded the series of books *America Votes*. Members of Congress whom Butler saw regularly included the powerful senator William Fulbright, and congressmen Richard Bolling of Missouri, Henry Reuss of Wisconsin and Brooks Hays from Arkansas, for whom he had briefly worked in 1948. All were Democrats of a liberal hue.

Yet, strangely, during his entire year in Washington, David Butler didn't once visit the US State Department. And while 1956 was a momentous year in Washington (and world) politics, one gets no sense of this from Butler's letters home to his mother, though the biggest events really occurred after Butler left in September 1956. Although it had been a presidential election year, there is surprisingly little reference to the contest in Butler's letters home. It wasn't clear until early in 1956 that Eisenhower would run again, though once he had declared, his re-election seemed assured. Nor, despite the Egyptian nationalisation of the Suez Canal in July 1956, is there any inkling of the build-up to the Suez Crisis. Roger Makins left Washington a few weeks after Butler, and later told his former speechwriter that he was deeply shocked by the Anglo-French invasion. He would have had to resign as ambassador, he claimed, had he still been in post, 'because the venture would have betrayed so many assurances he had given to American friends'. Butler wasn't sure he believed him.[44]

The ambassador spent about a quarter of his time outside Washington, and another of Butler's tasks had been to liaise with the various British consuls-general dotted around the United States to arrange interesting activities on the ambassador's various trips. Butler would sometimes describe himself to colleagues as Sir Roger's 'election agent'.[45] And occasionally, if Makins couldn't attend some event, or the occasion was considered too insignificant, Butler would go to speak instead.

Butler often accompanied Sir Roger on his tours around America. In Kansas City, he met former President Truman – 'that remarkable extrovert … a singularly chipper character' – and former Republican Governor Alf Landon, who, when he lost to Roosevelt in 1936, had suffered the biggest landslide (in electoral college votes) since 1820. 'To my surprise,' Butler wrote, 'I found him one of the most attractive politicians I have [ever] met – genial, amusing, well-informed, simple.'[46]

In September 1956, with the Suez Crisis brewing behind the scenes, he and Makins accompanied the Chancellor of the Exchequer (and, indirectly, Butler's publisher) Harold Macmillan on a trip to Indiana, where Macmillan's mother had been born. The ambassador's small plane hit a severe storm on the return flight and, while Butler felt very sick, Macmillan just kept on reading Thackeray's *Vanity Fair*, which he'd started on the outgoing flight the day before. 'Flying back on the Sunday he'd got to page 890. He just read fast, steadily, turning the pages – an extraordinarily unflappable figure with a great crisis going on. He talked a bit with Roger but he wasn't talking or doing much. He was just reading *Vanity Fair*.'[47]

David Butler had gone to the US not just to explore America and Washington politics, but also to sound out a possible new career.

Would being a public servant or a diplomat be more fulfilling than life in an Oxford college? He reached a conclusion just after half-way through his stint at the Washington embassy. While on a quick 48-hour trip to Harvard University, meeting up again with old friends and prominent politics professors, he felt a touch of nostalgia for Oxford. 'The other man's pasture is always greener,' he wrote to his mother, 'but I have found that seven months in the most delightful and gilded of bureaucratic jobs has cured me of any lingering doubts that the force of inertia, which kept me in the academic world, has led me to miss my vocation.'[48]

Whatever the superficial attractions of working in government, or in the media, or even in politics, many of the internal torments and doubts David Butler had suffered over the previous few years were cast aside. 'I knew that I was an Oxford don,' he says. 'I was happy to go on doing the job in Washington and I didn't make a fool of myself, but I wanted to come back to Oxford, having had this experience and found that this wasn't a sweeter pasture.'[49]

CHAPTER NINE

BUCCANEERING BUTLERS

Winston Churchill delivered only a handful of campaign speeches during the general election of 1950, but perhaps the most important historically came in Edinburgh, nine days before polling. It was the height of the Cold War. China had just gone communist, and Churchill spoke of the 'gravity' of our position, and that of the entire world. 'Soviet Russia – the immensely powerful band of men gathered together in the Kremlin – has ranged itself against the Western democracies,' he warned his election audience. 'At the other side of the world the 500,000,000 of China have fallen into the Communist sphere.'

Churchill looked back to the famous Potsdam conference of 1945, which had seen the leaders of America and Britain contain Stalin by agreeing the future of defeated Nazi Germany. And now Churchill, whose wartime leadership involved much 'shuttle diplomacy' between Allied heads of government, suggested 'another talk with Soviet Russia upon the highest level'. He added: 'It is not easy to see how things could be worsened by a parley at the summit, if such a thing were possible.'[1]

That, incidentally, was the first use of the word 'summit' to describe a meeting between high-level leaders. And Churchill's appeal for a get-together 'at the summit', involving Stalin, President Truman, and presumably himself if re-elected, was widely reported all over the world as a substantial news story. What Churchill said mattered globally. Yet, strangely, there was no coverage of Churchill's speech on either BBC radio or television.

Not even an announcement of this magnitude would persuade the BBC to relax its self-denying rule that from the day that a general election was called to the night of the results, there was a complete ban on politics in both TV and radio news bulletins. The BBC dismissed Churchill's idea of a 'summit' as election campaigning – which to a degree it was, of course – and so omitted his speech from any of their news bulletins. And yet Churchill's promise made an international impact. The 1950 Nuffield election book later reported: 'The next morning the newspapers of the world were carrying excerpts from his speech, which at one stroke made the British election world news.'[2]

Even Radio Moscow reported what Churchill had said, as did almost every serious newspaper and broadcasting station around the globe. What made the situation especially bizarre was that in 1950, the American broadcaster CBS took its microphones and recording equipment to many election meetings around the UK and relayed campaign reports back to the United States, while Britain's own broadcasting network was banned from such news coverage.

Similarly, in 1951, the BBC cancelled a TV programme about the birth of a baby since it included new facilities developed by the National Health Service. Even though all parties supported the NHS, it was feared the programme could help Labour, as the NHS was widely perceived as being one of the party's achievements.

Perhaps the most extraordinary thing was that this blackout on election news wasn't demanded by government, or legislated by Parliament, but imposed by the broadcasters themselves. The BBC governors and many senior editors were keen to avoid accusations of bias, and feared that if anything went wrong, they would be blamed. As has so often happened during almost a century of British broadcasting, decisions about programme coverage have been greatly influenced by the politicians' ultimate power to determine the broadcasters' future.

Yet below the corporation's most senior bosses, Grace Wyndham Goldie led programme editors and producers in seeing big possibilities to bring politics to life in front of the rapidly growing television audience. She was eager to prove they could be trusted not to favour one side or the other. And David Butler would play a central role in the transformation of television coverage of politics that occurred during the 1950s. That included the Swingometer and other innovations for election nights, but also public and private efforts to get the absurdly strict broadcasting rules relaxed.

Butler had seen first-hand how American broadcasters covered US presidential elections without being hamstrung by serious accusations of bias. And in the 1951 Nuffield election study – the first he edited – Butler began what would become almost a personal crusade to bring Britain in line with the much more liberal practices of American campaigns. His comments in the 1951 election study came close to anger:

> The BBC, by its charter and its traditions, has not only to be neutral, but to be seen to be neutral … It permits nothing which might conceivably affect the contest to be disseminated from its transmitters. All jokes and all allusions to politics or electioneering are rigorously excluded from the air … In the news bulletins election items are virtually confined to reports of formalities, such as the dissolution of Parliament and the arrangements for polling day. In short, for as long as the election lasts, the BBC abandons any attempt actively to meet the challenge of maintaining a fair political balance in its programmes; it solves all its problems by a policy of comprehensive omission. This policy is not confined to domestic broadcasting. The overseas services are similarly censored, lest presumably in some remote part of the world a soldier with a postal or proxy vote should be influenced unfairly.
>
> The present situation seems thoroughly unsatisfactory. The high standard of neutrality which the BBC maintains in electoral

'peace-time' would surely justify its being allowed a freer hand during the period of hostilities. Obviously, the greatest caution must be observed, but it is absurd that political subjects should be ignored by the main national medium of communications just when interest in them is at its peak.[3]

It was courageous for Butler to be so outspoken against the BBC when he himself was regularly engaged by the corporation, and he dearly loved the work he did on television. But he also knew that many senior BBC journalists quietly supported his position.

Strangely, while publicly recognising that the future of politics was in television, privately David Butler was more ambivalent and harboured concerns about the long-term effects of the new media.[4] His visits to America in 1948 and especially 1952 had shown how TV could be a powerful new tool. The 1952 election was the first time the American TV networks had broadcast the party conventions live and from coast to coast, devoting several hours on each of the five days to events in Chicago, where both gatherings were held. The network output seemed to be decades ahead of anything the BBC could – or would – do at that time, and Butler marvelled at how both the fixed TV cameras and those roaming around the convention hall – and beyond – could portray the raw drama of the presidential selection process. But this letter home to his mother also foresaw problems:

On occasion this roving of the camera had brilliant if brutal results. It would settle on a close-up of some unsuspecting member of the audience as he slept or picked his nose or looked infinitely bored or applauded wildly and unselfconsciously. It was a monstrous invasion of privacy but it made fascinating viewing. The inquisitive camera … brought off great coups sometimes, when over-sensitive microphones picked up private conversations on the platform and enabled one to identify the speakers…

> But I can't help worrying about the presumption, the claim to ubiquity of television. In America the press arrogates to itself fantastic rights: it may go anywhere and ask anything. In repeated battles last week television asserted and established its claim to go wherever the press goes ... It can prevent some underhand dealings by the singularly penetrating glare of publicity which it can direct almost where it chooses. But by the destruction of all political privacy it can also foster mob-rule. It is an instrument for still further exciting an already over-suggestible people.[5]

David Butler clearly had an eye for visual presentation and for style, and he was probably better placed than most of his academic contemporaries to exploit the revolutionary new medium. His excitement about the novel way in which US networks brought American party politics into tens of millions of homes found a receptive ear in Grace Wyndham Goldie. Even if British broadcasters were still not allowed to cover election campaigns, she was keen to develop new ways to explain politics through broadcasting other events. It would be three decades before MPs or peers would allow debates in Parliament to be televised, but there was an obvious third option. The nearest Britain had to the US presidential conventions were the annual party conferences, usually held in the early autumn over a period of several days, and where hundreds of ordinary activists would mix with well-known party grandees, ministers and MPs.

In August 1953, Goldie asked David Butler and Bob McKenzie to write a private report for the BBC examining whether the corporation should, and could, cover the annual conferences, and exploring how the obvious obstacles might be overcome.

Butler and McKenzie took three months to prepare their twelve-page document, and not surprisingly it concluded that televising these events was in the 'public interest'. Other media regarded party conferences as significant events, they said, and nine million people in Britain belonged to one party or another. 'As the newest of the great instruments of information, TV should seek to make its own distinctive contribution to public understanding of Party Government.'[6]

The two academics recognised that the presence of TV cameras would 'inevitably change the nature of the conference', but they weren't certain *how* they would change. 'It seems likely', they wrote, 'that the advent of television would induce greater – but not much greater – executive control of conference proceedings.' But they warned that an attempt to stage-manage events excessively might backfire on the parties.[7] They also expected a greater 'self-consciousness' of participants, and a greater 'awareness of acting on the national scene'.[8]

Yet Butler and McKenzie were realistic about the limitations. They acknowledged that if the BBC covered the closing session of the Conservative conference, which in those days was traditionally on a Saturday afternoon, then 'even the Prime Minister, whose speech occupies most of this session, might not be forgiven by frustrated sports enthusiasts', since Saturday was TV's big day for sport.[9] Also, how would BBC producers cope with footage of any unplanned incidents on the floor of the conference, or film which was unfavourable to an eminent speaker? And should film excerpts which might be repeated in a round-up programme that night simply reflect a microcosm of the proceedings, or should they concentrate on 'newsworthy speeches (which may mean speeches critical of the party executive or of the party's own representatives in Parliament)'?[10]

A bigger problem was persuading the two main parties to admit the cameras (although they were already allowed for short extracts for BBC news coverage, and for cinema newsreels). In July 1953, the BBC formally approached both the Conservative and Labour Parties for permission to cover their conferences in full each day, and for a daily summary programme later in the evening. Labour's National Executive deferred the matter to the conference itself, but recommended rejecting the idea, which the 1953 conference in Margate duly did. The strongest fear, it seems, was that 'delegates would be more than ever inclined to speak to the audience outside rather than to the issues before the conference'.[11] The Conservatives regarded the BBC request more favourably and complained that they didn't see why a 'Labour Party veto' should prevent the BBC from covering their proceedings.

Butler and McKenzie proposed that the best way to resolve the impasse would not be to pursue live daily coverage for the time being, but to extend the existing television news access to transmit a late-night thirty-minute round-up of proceedings. 'If the half-hour evening programme were successful,' they wrote, 'it might … establish a more confident climate that would lead to full coverage in two or three years' time.'[12] And a footnote to their memo reflected their US experience: 'The consensus of American opinion is that the net effect of televising the Party Conventions has been wholesome and in the public interest.'[13]

The BBC endorsed Butler and McKenzie's proposals and, in 1954, decided to broadcast for the first time a late-night summary of the Conservative conference in Blackpool, even though Labour still refused to let cameras into their proceedings. But Butler was upset to learn of the BBC's plans only from reading *The Times* while teaching at Berkeley in California, rather than from Grace Wyndham Goldie herself. 'As usual,' he wrote to his mother, 'that wretched woman hasn't written to Bob or to me, despite her solemn promise that she would as soon as things were settled.'[14]

Butler and McKenzie had, in fact, created a nice job for themselves, for it was decided that the three-man on-screen team for the conference programmes would involve both men, together with the *Observer* political correspondent William Clark. Grace Wyndham Goldie confirmed the contract to Butler in a telegram which also contained the forbidding words 'CONTROVERSY DISALLOWED'.[15] McKenzie would be the main presenter in

Blackpool, with Butler as 'expert adviser and additional interviewer', while Clark, based in London, would be the overall presenter of the output.[16]

The logistics were a nightmare, as the raw film of events had to be flown from the conference venue to London and then processed at great speed. In later years the BBC usually paid for David Butler to attend each conference, though they didn't always use him on screen. It was more for Butler's ideas and contacts – sometimes, for example, to help persuade a politician he knew to do an interview. Bob McKenzie remained the more attractive broadcaster, a presenter who bubbled with enthusiasm. He understood the drama of politics and the show-business needs of TV producers; he did incisive interviews, yet also had an engaging sense of humour. So the BBC increasingly employed McKenzie more on screen than Butler.

Labour relented and admitted cameras for its conference in 1955, although it would not be until 1965 that the main parties consented to live television coverage of each day's proceedings.

After the 1955 general election, in which Eden increased the Conservative majority from seventeen to sixty, Butler returned to his public campaign for British broadcasters to emulate their American colleagues in having the right to cover election campaigns. The BBC had shown it could be neutral when covering ordinary political news, he argued. 'It is absurd that at the height of that most important of national political events, an election, the BBC news bulletins should for all practical purposes ignore it.'[17]

Four months after the election, BBC television faced competition for the first time in the form of commercial television – or independent television, ITV – which was funded by advertising. The new ITV channel's news provider, Independent Television News (ITN), and some of its bolder new regional ITV stations, such as Granada in the north-west, were keen to bring politics to the television screen. The pressure for change began to build. ITN began testing the rules at a series of by-elections in late 1956 and early

1957 – in Melton in Leicestershire; North Lewisham in London; and Carmarthen in South Wales. The ITN presenter Robin Day had suggested that as a 'dry run' he and others should compile film reports which included interviews with the by-election candidates and voters. But bizarrely, to avoid accusations that they had 'influenced the result', these reports would not be shown until *after* voting had ceased at 9 p.m. on polling day.[18]

Butler decided to act, and made good use of his personal contacts. He admits he 'conspired' with Grace Wyndham Goldie, Tony Benn, and also with his fellow BBC commentator Bob McKenzie (who had written a chapter for the 1955 Nuffield study), to convene a two-day conference at Nuffield College, on Friday 10 and Saturday 11 January 1958.

It turned out to be the end of the week when the Chancellor Peter Thorneycroft, along with Enoch Powell and Nigel Birch, had famously resigned from the government over spending policy. There were only about sixteen people present at the Nuffield 'summit', but it was a star cast – 'everyone you could wish to have at a conference', Butler says. This was quite a coup for Nuffield, for the college was barely formed. Construction of the main quad was only just finished, and the college didn't receive its Royal Charter until June that year. This was not some grandiose event in high Oxford; it was instead quite a furtive place to be gathering.

Tony Benn, who had briefly been a BBC producer and now advised his party on broadcasting matters, enlisted the Labour leader Hugh Gaitskell, but only on the understanding that there would be somebody of equal status from the government side. With Harold Macmillan away in South Africa, David Butler duly persuaded the acting Prime Minister, his second cousin 'Rab' Butler (and Macmillan's long-standing Conservative rival), to represent the government (along with the Chief Whip, Edward Heath). They were joined by the widely respected Liberal leader Jo Grimond. And the directors-general of both the BBC and ITV, Sir Ian Jacob and Sir Robert Fraser, were there too, and Geoffrey Cox, the editor of ITN. 'It was all hush hush at the time,' recalls Martin Harrison, a young colleague of David Butler's, who is the only other survivor of the select group. 'The mere fact that these people were getting together at Nuffield required a high level of security.'[19] As well as Bob McKenzie, other academics present included Herbert Nicholas and the historian Alan Bullock.

The BBC team had been wary at first. Sir Ian Jacob felt that the pre-conference papers prepared by Nuffield were inaccurate, and he feared they suggested that the BBC had 'been absurdly over cautious' in the past, and 'timid or self-defensive' (as indeed they had been).[20] In a series of letters and a face-to-face meeting, David Butler had to placate Jacob's rather suspicious assistant, Harman Grisewood. 'The academics are supposedly neutral,' Grisewood warned his BBC colleagues, 'but in fact I believe they (Butler and McKenzie at any rate) are heavily in favour of relaxing restrictions all round. There are dangers in a free-for-all which I hope we will not be alone in having to point out.'[21] Sir Ian Jacob was kept on board by agreeing to let him make a statement at the start of the event.

The conference began on the Friday night with dinner in the Nuffield fellows' dining room – 'rather a dismal meal', Benn wrote in his diary. 'Sir Ian Jacob had been angered by one of the papers circulated and he was in his most bureaucratic mood. One felt he was lusting for blood and the best thing was to let him get it out of his system.'[22] Rab Butler, on the other hand, was in high spirits, Benn relates, and 'could scarcely forbear to cheer' at Thorneycroft's departure. 'I'd better not gloat, had I?' Benn quotes Rab Butler saying. 'It has been a wonderful week.' Indeed, it seems probable that Rab Butler's good mood following the demise of his ministerial adversaries may have changed the whole tone of the weekend and turned a potentially embarrassing flop into a triumph for Butler, McKenzie and Goldie. Benn's account continues:

> After dinner we gathered round the fire for coffee. It was rather exciting to think that the Deputy Prime Minister, the Leader of the Opposition, the Liberal Leader, the two Directors-General and three Heads of Oxbridge Colleges should be meeting together at this particular moment. No publicity has been given to the meetings and nothing has leaked to the press. But what a wonderful news story it would make.[23]

They spoke until eleven o'clock that night, during which time Rab Butler told David Butler that he supported the televising of Parliament. The deliberations resumed the following morning and continued until mid-afternoon, when Grimond gave Heath and Benn a lift back to London.

It was a great success, a pivotal moment in the coverage of elections on television and radio. 'It was largely a matter of mood music,' Harrison says, 'in broad terms to persuade the politicians that the broadcasters could be trusted.'[24]

A private report of the event related: 'It was argued, mainly by the academics … that public service broadcasting could not legitimately ignore what was the most significant news of the day [and] that the newspapers were already reporting the campaign, many of them in a highly tendentious fashion.'[25] This tension, between the broadcasters' duty to remain neutral and the freedom enjoyed by the press to be more opinionated, would persist through the coming decades. David Butler recalls that 'the two directors-general were very po-faced and negative in the first informal discussion' and seemed opposed to any change. But then, he says, Rab Butler intervened and said, 'Oh no, no, no. Let's have some buccaneering.' Butler remembers, 'Here was Rab – the most senior person there – and that liberated them, and people then talked much more freely because Rab was saying, "Let's do this." I'm still slightly amazed at how we put it together.'[26]

In the aftermath, broadcasters were suddenly allowed to cover elections in much the same way as they do today. TV and radio reporters could now act as proper journalists at election time, although still within constraints relating to time and balance which gave them less freedom in their coverage than the press enjoyed. 'It was actually quite important as the thing that liberated the BBC and the commercial television channels from being too bloody cautious,' Butler later recalled. 'This was the only time I feel I've been a real activist in politics.'[27] But the discreet Nuffield agreement almost came unstuck when news of the summit appeared in a feature item in the *Manchester Guardian*, though with almost no detail.[28] Hugh Gaitskell said he would never come to the college in future if what then transpired was leaked to the press. Gaitskell seems to have been in a difficult position because he'd failed to tell his shadow minister for broadcasting, Anthony Greenwood, about the event.

Senior politicians had met regularly with senior figures from broadcasting for several years through a small inter-party committee which discussed the system of regular party political broadcasts. But the BBC historian Asa Briggs pointed out that the 'neutrals' at the Nuffield weekend – Butler, McKenzie and other academics – had not served on this committee, and 'it was they who set an agenda at Oxford which covered a wider range of issues than the Meeting on Party Political Broadcasting had ever considered'.[29]

Asa Briggs's official history of the BBC glides over the decision to let broadcasters cover election campaigns, and instead argues that the Nuffield conference was significant for addressing the whole tone of political coverage on television *between* elections (though this is not reflected in the five-page account of the event which was produced, but not made public).[30] TV and radio producers could now choose the topics for campaign debates on TV or radio, decide how those issues might be covered, and pick possible representatives rather than having to wait for the parties to nominate their preferred choices.

'Nuffield College', said the offending *Manchester Guardian* article with prescience, 'may find itself rewarded by a significant footnote of its own in the history of political broadcasting.'[31] And a more relaxed regime, the article suggested, should start with film reports from the next by-election, which was due shortly in Rochdale in Lancashire.

And that's what happened. The ITV news service, ITN, ran a film report by George Ffitch which included interviews with voters, but only shots of the candidates – not interviews. ITN had a slight problem, since the Liberal candidate was Ludovic Kennedy, who had just resigned as an ITN newscaster, and they didn't want to be accused of favouritism. 'ITN's sally into by-election reporting – the first time it has ever been done – could do no harm, and might do much good,' said the *Manchester Guardian*, 'if only in making politics a little more real and down-to-earth for people far outside the range of Rochdale.'[32]

The local ITV station, Granada, felt less constrained and ran two whole programmes on the Rochdale campaign. The first involved the three candidates being questioned, one by one, by a panel of three newspaper editors; the second comprised speeches from each candidate, followed by another film report which included vox pops with voters. The ITV coverage was a significant breakthrough. 'After Rochdale the right of television and radio to report elections was never in any doubt,' wrote the editor of ITN, Geoffrey Cox.[33] Broadcasters had shown they could now cover election campaigns without serous accusations of bias, though the new rules were not announced publicly until a year later.

The following general election, in October 1959, was radically different in campaign style from any that had gone before. Indeed, David Butler sees it as marking a whole new era in British campaigning. It was 1959 which saw the first extensive use of polling and marketing techniques by the parties. But the biggest development was on the small screen, and 1959 can really be called Britain's first television election. The BBC and ITV covered events every night on their bulletins; they ran extracts from speeches by leading politicians on the hustings; broadcast film reports from key constituencies; and held live debates between leading spokesmen for the major parties – a mix of coverage which has remained broadly the same ever since. Most important, perhaps, voters were able to see and hear senior politicians engaging properly with each other in mike-to-mike combat in the TV and radio studios. Granada even ran a very ambitious *Marathon* programme in which they invited every candidate in the north-west to speak live for a minute each, seat by seat, with the right for each then to have a minute to reply to what their opponents had said. But if any candidate refused the invitation, then the debate from that seat was scrapped. In the event, only fifty-four candidates refused, and so sixty-three of their opponents were barred. Nonetheless, 231 of the region's 348 candidates got their two minutes of ITV exposure – around eight hours of television.[34]

David Butler has argued that between 1880 and 1955 the nature of British election campaigns changed very little. The party leaders, and perhaps a few senior colleagues, would travel around the country from area to area, addressing big rallies, and their speeches would be covered in the press the following day. And there was no interaction between the leading players at all, no debate or dialogue; instead, they concentrated on talking separately to voters. Winston Churchill was an exception, in that he did occasionally respond to something Clement Attlee had said the night before. Butler suggested that it was like watching two armies on separate battlefields fighting straw enemies of their own devising.[35] Nor was there much sense of general elections being 'national' events; local candidates enjoyed a lot of freedom to do their own thing, printing their own literature, stepping out of line on policy, and even campaigning in different colours from their party colleagues.

The Nuffield conference played a big role in changing all that. From 1959 onwards, television, not public meetings, was the primary forum for politicians to get their messages across to voters. David Butler deserves great credit for hastening that huge development.

And Butler confirmed his appetite for innovation and impact just as energetically on the election night programmes. In the same year as the Nuffield conference, he was commissioned by the corporation to liaise with the developers of early computers to procure a suitable calculating machine for the next all-night BBC results programme. A device was hired at very little cost, and nicknamed Ella for broadcasting purposes. When it came to the big night, Butler got second billing in the BBC's *Radio Times*, below Richard Dimbleby but ahead of colleagues such as Cliff Michelmore, Bob McKenzie and Alan Whicker. Butler had 'practically made himself Britain's Mister Election', the magazine boasted.[36] Although it was the first time that the BBC faced competition from commercial TV on election night, they easily trounced ITV, both in audience – 13 million – and in announcing most results first.[37]

Early on that night in October 1959, Butler said he'd 'never known an election harder to predict' and forecast it might be 'neck and neck'; he then revised this to say the Tories would get back in 'by a short head'. 'I'm much more at sea than I was at other elections,' he declared, and then, as if to illustrate this, five minutes later said, 'I want to rat on my prediction. It's a clear-cut victory for the Conservatives.' As the night progressed, Harold Macmillan did indeed achieve that 'clear-cut victory', amassing a Commons majority of 102 over Hugh Gaitskell's Labour Party – the fourth election in a row at which the Conservatives gained seats. The Ella computer, which digested individual constituency results and quickly calculated overall national figures, broke down at one stage, though the studio team managed to conceal this from the viewers.

Around 3.20 in the morning, with the constituency results having slowed down, Butler told viewers that it was always 'irritating' after 'these marathons' that people congratulated him on 'a feat of endurance'. It was no feat, he insisted, as 'I'm merely sharing the sort of thing I find fun, with as many viewers who are foolish enough to stay up until 3.18 in the morning'.

'You want to speak for yourself,' Richard Dimbleby interjected. 'No, I think Bob McKenzie is corrupted in this way too!' Butler replied. 'He enjoys elections for their own sake.'[38]

The 1959 general election is now widely accepted as marking a turning point, in which the BBC and ITV competed to try to catch up with the possibilities for covering politics through the new medium of television. A year later, the 1960 US presidential election was dominated by four television debates between Richard Nixon and John F. Kennedy. Butler had attended both American party conventions and spent several months following the campaign. On election night in New York, he again found himself in the role of TV pundit, as he was interviewed by the great Walter Cronkite during the overnight CBS results programme. It hadn't been planned. Butler was visiting the CBS studio to make comparisons with the BBC results output, and to give advice to an old friend, the CBS commentator Eric Sevareid. But the final outcome was hugely delayed and during the middle of the night, when few results were coming in, he was invited to join Cronkite in the studio for a discussion which he says lasted twenty minutes, a surprising length of time. An extract which was recently on YouTube, of the final three and a half minutes, showed him in rather an odd position physically. Perhaps CBS had no spare seats, for Butler seemed to be kneeling beside Cronkite's desk as they discussed the differences between British and American elections.

By that time in the morning, it seemed clear Kennedy would win, and Butler couldn't hide his satisfaction. 'Sometimes, I wonder whether we [in Britain] aren't too slow in recognising new talent and blood,' he told Cronkite. 'One of the virtues of the Convention system and the whole American structure of politics is that the forceful, aggressive individual who really has talent can show his talents fast and get to the top fast. I think we've seen this last night.'

Television, and the famous TV debates, had worked, he argued. 'It wasn't that [Kennedy] beat Nixon but he showed that he was of the same quality as Nixon – he couldn't be dismissed as an upstart, brash young man without the experience and quality. He was in the same league as Nixon.'[39]

Butler was surprised that his on-screen chat with Cronkite went on so long. 'I kept giving him obvious out-cues,' he says, 'to let him wind things up, but he didn't take them.'[40] It was probably because the CBS producers had no other item to go to.

The format of the BBC results programmes was well-established by the time of the 1964 general election, when Harold Macmillan's successor Alec Douglas-Home faced Labour's answer to John F. Kennedy: the down-to-earth Yorkshireman and former Oxford don Harold Wilson. But Grace Wyndham Goldie had moved on to higher things within the corporation and the programme was run jointly by Paul Fox and Michael Peacock. While Peacock appreciated Butler, Fox didn't rate the Nuffield man as a broadcaster, especially in comparison with Bob McKenzie. 'I'm not President of the David Butler Fan Club,' Fox said in 2016, and elaborated:

> His performances on screen, frankly, were second rate. He had a first-class mind, and was good at revealing information, but took an awful long time to say it. He had an awkward way of performing on screen. Bob was the better performer on the night. He understood TV much better. David didn't understand TV and perhaps thought it was beneath him. He sat awkwardly in the Richard Dimbleby programme, beside the presenter. Viewers see what it looks like on screen. Whereas Bob had his toy Swingometer to play with, David just had a pencil and a slightly mad stare.[41]

Fox feels that perhaps Butler 'looked down his nose' at him because of his background in BBC Sport. 'I didn't go to Oxford or anything like that.' But Fox insists there was never any question of dropping

Butler. 'I wouldn't have dreamt of getting rid of him. He was unquestionably an essential member of our election team. He had to be there because he provided wisdom.'[42]

Butler didn't always get things right, as viewers had seen in 1959. In 1964, he predicted a majority of forty for Wilson's Labour Party after the first result in Cheltenham, but this forecast was soon revised to 'not greater than forty, or less than twenty'. In the end, Labour scraped in with a majority of just four seats.

Keen as always to spot new themes, and influenced by his experiences with US politics, Butler seemed more willing than others in the studio to discuss the difficult new issues that emerged in 1964 – race and immigration, and the fact that the concentration of ethnic-minority immigrants in certain seats seemed to have boosted the Conservative vote there. This trend occurred most notably in Smethwick, near Birmingham, where the Conservative candidate ran an overtly racist campaign, and Labour's shadow Foreign Secretary, Patrick Gordon Walker, lost his seat on a remarkable 7.2 per cent swing against his party. 'This issue has counted for rather more than one would like to see in quite a lot of places,' Butler lamented. 'The racial issue has some very alarming dynamite in it from the political point of view.' And later he added: 'I'm afraid that we're going to see a certain number of other people who try to do what was done in Smethwick ... and we may get some extremely unpleasant politics in this area of exploiting race subtly or overtly ... a sad consequence of this election.' They were quite brave – and prescient – comments for Butler to make live on television, especially when none of his studio colleagues came to his aid.[43] Four years later, Enoch Powell, who was MP for a nearby constituency in Wolverhampton, would further exploit the issue with his famous 'Rivers of Blood' speech.

The 1960s, of course, were an era when everyday racism and sexism were still common, and Butler's condemnation of racism contrasts uneasily today with Richard Dimbleby's extraordinary remarks, during a lull in results, about the programme's female production assistants:

> Just as a change from politics and MPs, who to some extent, with some exceptions are not awfully pretty, viewers would like to have a quick look at some of the girls working around us in the studio who are doing such an invaluable job [camera roves to blonde woman] … There's Miren Cork, being very discreet and modest … We have in the background large numbers of the girls all wearing – I don't know what the colour is – it isn't salmon pink; it's sort of terracotta overalls, because we thought it would be less conspicuous than if they were allowed to wear their own clothes, poor little things. There are girls who've been flying backwards and forwards, there are charming girls on the telephones … Down here in the foreground you have some terribly hard-working girls who've been killing themselves on your behalf … I want you to see Jane Callender – she's working like a beaver just behind my back.

Dimbleby then announced that a viewer had rung in to say they'd seen a mouse run along the state-of-the-parties board. Dimbleby responded that if that were true none of the girls would be there. 'There is no mouse,' he insisted.[44]

More serious than the rodent for Butler personally was that the diversity of results in 1964 meant his 'theory of swing', on his own admission on screen that night, took 'a bit of a battering'. Results were 'nothing like as uniform' as had been expected. At this point a studio guest, the journalist Anthony Howard, pounced, saying, 'The thing that's given me the greatest single delight tonight is the number of household gods of psephologists' traditional orthodox wisdom that have been demolished. National swing's gone; Cube Law we haven't heard a word about … but above all personality has been proved to count for something in elections.'[45]

Butler defended himself, arguing that despite 'disparate results on swings and roundabouts' the actual formula of national swing had worked 'quite extraordinarily well'. Labour looked like getting a 3.5 per cent swing overall, enough for a small majority.

Anthony Howard's attack reflected quite a persistent critique on the left at that time – that political scientists were both interfering in the democratic process and also getting their forecasts wrong. Howard's words in the BBC studio mirrored an attack two years earlier from the *Daily Mirror* journalist Gerald Kaufman, who would later become one of Harold Wilson's advisers in Downing Street, before becoming a Labour MP and minister. In October 1962, Kaufman had attacked both David Butler and his friend and TV colleague Bob McKenzie in an article for the *New Statesman* magazine entitled 'The Witch Doctors'. He mocked Butler for saying the seat of Montgomeryshire was 'far from safe', four months before a by-election there in which the Liberals more than doubled their majority. More seriously, he claimed Butler and McKenzie's 'original, scientific platform' had become 'more and more rickety' underneath them:

> Its principal prop was 'the Cube Law' – that statistical formula (first enunciated by Dr Butler) which aimed at stating an exact mathematical relation between seats and votes in British general elections … For some years Dr Butler defended it gamely, but in the end even he had to give up. In his study of the 1959 general election, the famous law – destroyed by Liberals and maverick voting generally – does not appear in the index.[46]

Kaufman complained that much of the 'growing lack of flavour' in British politics in recent times was due to the 'merciless mulling over of procedures by self-appointed experts' like Butler and McKenzie 'whose loudly proclaimed neutrality from vulgar partisanship gives them the status of umpires of the game'. What a joke and revenge it would be, he declared, if, at the next election, voters defied their laws.[47] And to an extent in 1964, they did.

The 1964 election programme would be the last presented by Richard Dimbleby, who was suffering from cancer, and died the following year. He was replaced for the 1966 programme – just eighteen months after the 1964 edition – by the *Tonight* presenter Cliff Michelmore, whom Butler found lightweight in comparison with his predecessor.

In 1966, just as in 1964, David Butler overestimated the Labour majority on the basis of the first result. He forecast Wilson would get a majority of near to 120 this time. His actual majority was ninety-six.

CHAPTER TEN

COLLEGE MAN

On his return from America in October 1956, David Butler immersed himself fully in the life of Nuffield College. After his twelve months with the Diplomatic Service, he now knew that he preferred the scholarly life, but he didn't just want that. He again threw his energies into bridging the divide between scholarly and public affairs, in line with the intentions of the college founders: 'I wouldn't have liked to be an ivory tower academic ... I was going back to an academic *plus* public life... going around party conferences for the BBC, going and doing the election night stuff, and miscellaneous bits of journalism, and enjoying the *frisson* of being in affairs.'[1]

Nuffield also appointed Butler as dean and senior tutor, which for the next eight years gave him the overall role of overseeing graduate students, their research work, pastoral care and discipline. In 1956, this was not especially onerous, since Nuffield only had about thirty students, though the numbers gradually grew, but on the other hand, in such a small college, a large share of the college's reputation was bound up in each student and their research. Butler made a point of entertaining every student and fellow at his home.

Meanwhile, he secured a contract with Brasenose College, which didn't have its own politics tutor, to teach undergraduates for several hours each week in some of the basic history and politics parts of the PPE course, such as the Modern British Government paper and Political Institutions. The arrangement continued for ten years until Brasenose appointed an in-house politics tutor, Vernon Bogdanor, in 1966.

At Nuffield, Butler also acted as personal supervisor to a handful of students doing postgraduate research degrees. The general recollection is that Butler took a pretty hands-off approach to their work. But they also recall how he was brilliant in making good use of his political contacts. So the students he supervised would be encouraged to talk to people in the 'real world' about the subjects of their theses, and Butler would often tee them up with a phone call or letter to the expert concerned.

Appeals through *Oxford Today* magazine and through some of the colleges where Butler taught prompted several recollections of his teaching style. Scott Housley, at Brasenose in the mid-1960s – recalled how tutorials were 'interrupted by frequent phone calls' – in one case, he says, Butler 'apologetically [asked] me to leave the room as it was the Prime Minister (then Harold Wilson)'. Housley was impressed to get a handwritten good-luck letter on the eve of his finals even though he had not seen Butler for two years.[2] Jonathan Seagrave, at Brasenose at exactly the same time, recalls arriving at Nuffield with his essay, only for a very busy Butler immediately to tell him to dictate an article he'd written, over the telephone to the *Sunday Times*. 'Which I duly did. I don't think the essay got much attention. There were many digressions into current affairs. It was a great education in the best sense … I would not have missed it for the world. His tutorials were certainly the most entertaining I had.'[3]

Sheila Dunleavy recalls that when she married her husband Patrick (the LSE politics professor who was at Nuffield in the mid-'70s), Butler gave them a 'very special wedding gift'. It was a large pottery dish with the couple's initials entwined in the middle, and she says Butler often did the same for other students of his when they married.[4]

Stephen Brooks, a mature student at Lincoln College who'd previously been a trade union official, is less effusive.

> I was keen to have him as a tutor, as he was so well-known. Having waited two terms for him, I was disappointed, because he had no interest in undergraduates. But as soon as I could introduce him to somebody of note in the Labour Party, I was somebody worthy of attention.

Nor was he impressed by Butler's regular name-dropping.[5]

Butler was also notorious for his unfortunate habit at parties of constantly looking over the shoulders of whomever he was talking to, to see if there was anyone more interesting to talk to. On the other hand, Butler would also go out of his way at social gatherings to introduce newcomers and people who didn't know anyone to the important guests, often extolling their abilities and achievements while doing so.

Overall, Butler had a light teaching load, and over the decades Nuffield College gave him an ideal base for his growing empire of activity. Gradually Nuffield was getting more plugged into public affairs, a role which before the war had probably belonged to All Souls more than any other Oxford college. But where All Souls was all-male and had a reputation for being intellectually intimidating and elitist, Nuffield welcomed people of both sexes, and was a more relaxed setting where late at night the Warden, Norman Chester, might be found playing table tennis with his colleagues (for whom gamesmanship mattered more than skill). It became the college to go to for experts on politics, economics or industry, where scholars would mix with real players in such fields.

By 1963, Nuffield had two future British Prime Ministers as visiting fellows – Edward Heath and Jim Callaghan – while the future Indian Prime Minister Manmohan Singh had just completed his DPhil. Butler played a leading role in selecting the visiting fellows, though Heath was an awkward choice; sometimes charming, but sometimes difficult. 'More than once,' says Butler, 'I was lobbied by fellows asking to be spared sitting next to him, not because of his politics but because of his grumpy silences.'[6] Another visiting fellow in the early '60s was the Labour politician (and former New College don) Richard Crossman, who also wrote a column for *The Guardian*. After one dinner, Crossman wrote about what he'd been told by a senior Treasury official 'while dining in an Oxford college the other day'. The fellows were shocked, since the Treasury man would be clearly identifiable, and so Butler reproached Crossman. 'That was silly of me,' Crossman replied. 'I should have said "dining in a Cambridge college".'[7]

Nuffield's growing stature was illustrated on the night in January 1963 when the Labour leader Hugh Gaitskell suddenly died. Journalists were keen for reactions from the leading union leaders of the day, such as the TUC boss George Woodcock, Frank Cousins of the transport workers' union, and Les Cannon of the electricians'. It was eventually discovered they were all dining that night at Nuffield. 'This is one of the youngest of the Oxford colleges,' said a feature in the *Sunday Times*, 'yet it is already a precocious powerhouse of ideas which will have a potent hand in the policies re-shaping the country.'[8]

Nuffield also provided generous funds for research projects and gave Butler on-the-spot access to a pool of talented and enthusiastic research students who could act as assistants on his books and broadcasting work, and several of them ended up being his co-authors. The fellows of the Nuffield senior common room also supplied a small team of experts and friends with whom he could chew over ideas and political developments. 'One was all the time drawing on colleagues,' Butler recalls, 'particularly people like Philip Williams, who was an enormous influence on me as a close friend who was deeply interested in politics, and was linked to Roy Jenkins and Tony Crosland, and saw things through that. Our paths lay parallel … We were bachelors together in the 1950s.'[9]

Williams was a specialist in French politics who is remembered for his subsequent magisterial biography of the Labour leader

Hugh Gaitskell, which took him ten years to write. He was brilliant, Butler says, at understanding how politics worked, how politicians thought and operated across Europe. He and Butler twice went on Continental holidays together, and they would regularly read and comment on each other's manuscripts, but Williams shared none of Butler's gregarious nature:

> He was an odd man … he was a terribly hung-up, inhibited bachelor who didn't like talking to people. He wouldn't broadcast. He wouldn't do things that would have got him more into [the public eye] … His books on France are magnificent things, and it's quite odd that he didn't have any feeling for art or literature, and quite how he empathised in the way that he did with the French – he wasn't even a very good linguist – I don't know.[10]

Butler loved his intimate involvement in college life – what he would call 'one of the overwhelming plusses of being in Oxford' compared with other universities. 'I was in love with the college in the 1950s,' he once said, and gave it 'a very large amount of my affection and energies'. They were the most formative years in Nuffield's history, before and after it became a residential college in 1958, while it still occupied an incomplete building site.[11] In this period he also served as domestic bursar for a year, and as chairman of the common room, and he enjoyed college politics as much as national politics. 'When an issue comes up,' he once said, 'I guess at what the outcome's going to be, and sometimes I'm right and sometimes I'm wrong, but I'm testing my skills as a political predictor.'[12]

When Butler became dean of Nuffield in 1956, he was the first dean the college had ever had, since until then there had been too few students to look after. Effectively, he became deputy to the new Warden, Norman Chester, who would prove to be one of the most important influences on Butler's career. Chester, a Mancunian who retained his northern accent all his life, had a reputation for being blunt and abrasive, but also very kind. Unusually at that time for an Oxford or Cambridge head of house, he was not an Oxbridge graduate, having left school at fourteen to work for the treasurer's department of Manchester City Council before attending Manchester University as a mature student. After joining the civil service in 1939, Chester made his name as secretary to the historic Beveridge Committee on social insurance, and his academic speciality was public administration. Norman Chester, more than anyone, put Nuffield on the map, during his twenty-four years as Warden of the college from 1954 to 1978.

Butler was the first dean of a co-educational college at either Oxford or Cambridge, which entailed working out new rules to cope with male and female students living side by side. Butler sometimes took a rather puritanical approach. The chairman of the small junior common room one year was Jagdish Bhagwati, who went on to become one of the world's most distinguished economists. Bhagwati recalls that a couple of American students at Nuffield wanted to bring their wives into lunch. 'David was hesitant, while I pushed for it,' he says:

> Mixed corridors were also our demand and they came into effect. Once I wanted to put up my friend Padma Desai (whom I married later) on her way back to India from Harvard and asked David if I could. Amusingly, David said: 'You may if you promise to treat her the way you would a male friend!' I did put her up, but I will not say whether I did what David suggested![13]

Another Butler concern was that people coming into breakfast in their bedroom slippers were setting a sloppy precedent which needed to be stopped. On the academic side, Butler helped introduce a system of dual supervision, whereby each graduate student was given a supervisor from within the college alongside the supervisor provided by the university, even if their university supervisor was also a Nuffield fellow. This doubled a student's sources of advice, and also meant they got another referee for when they moved on. Today, this system is common in higher education.

Butler even got involved in choosing college furniture, communal decoration and artwork, as a long-serving member of the Premises Committee. Perhaps his proudest achievement, however, was to persuade his colleagues to install floodlights to illuminate the distinctive tower from dusk until 10.30 p.m. every night, an idea Butler copied from Christ Church after walking back from Oxford Station late one evening and noticing the contrast between Nuffield's dark tower and the illuminated Tom Tower. Thereafter, whenever he saw the flood-lit square tower of Nuffield, he got a 'slight egotistical sense of pleasure that other people will be getting pleasure from seeing this sort of version of a dreaming spire'.[14]

Years later, Butler was involved in commissioning a promising young Yorkshire artist to come and draw a portrait of the Warden, Norman Chester. Unfortunately, David Hockney turned up at Nuffield without his drawing materials, and so Butler had to accompany him to an art shop in Broad Street to get him fully equipped.

A big advantage to Nuffield was its location – being near to Oxford Station meant that visiting speakers and guests could get there remarkably quickly – in about an hour from London by train – without, Butler says, 'feeling that one is imposing a great deal on them'.[15] One drawback, however, was that in the 1950s Nuffield's facilities for entertaining were pretty limited. That all changed in the summer of 1958, when the Duke of Edinburgh came to present the college's Royal Charter and open the new dining hall (and Lord Nuffield heckled a correction to a point the duke made in his speech).

The following year, David Butler immediately took advantage of this new college attraction by starting one of the institutions for which he is most fondly remembered by many of his former students: the evening politics seminars with visiting guests. Butler had noticed how, in the early 1950s, his friend Bob McKenzie held seminars with distinguished political speakers at the London School of Economics, and decided to copy the idea. Yet Oxford is much harder for political people to get to than the LSE, which is only a mile from Westminster and Whitehall. So, as an incentive for people to visit Nuffield, Butler devised a simple package of a ninety-minute seminar plus drinks and dinner – only he put the emphasis on the latter, the hospitality. 'Dear xxx', his letter would start:

> May I invite you to dine in Nuffield one Friday next term? There is a snag to the invitation. For many years now I have run a university seminar on British Politics in which I try to show the young how far the actual practice of politics is like the textbook picture.

And, to make life easier, his standard letter set out a precise timetable:

> The seminar starts at 5 p.m. and ends just after 6.30 p.m. which leaves ample time for a glass of sherry before dinner at 7.15 p.m. There is a train from Paddington at 3.15 p.m. which arrives at Oxford at 4.18 p.m. After dinner there is a 9.20 p.m. from Oxford arriving at Paddington at 10.20 p.m. or a 10.25 p.m. from Oxford arriving at Paddington at 11.31 p.m. If you did not want to rush back to town we would be delighted to put you up in College overnight.[16]

Another simple but brilliant modification to McKenzie's LSE format also occurred to Butler. He knew from experience that speakers delivering a written text could often be ponderous, and badly misjudge their audience by pitching themselves too high or too low. And once a lecture begins at a certain level, it is difficult to adjust midstream. Butler ordered his visitors specifically not to work out in advance what they were going to say. 'I want you to guarantee that you will prepare nothing,' Butler would tell them. 'All I want is your genius. Just talk about your career, off the record.'[17]

This might cause some consternation, particularly in ministerial private offices, where civil servants felt they had a duty to draft speeches and briefs for their bosses and were naturally wary of their ministers venturing out on their own, unprepared and 'off-piste'. But many senior figures were delighted to accept.

The seminars were held as a series through one term, but not every term, depending on David Butler's overseas trips. The usual format was that either Butler himself or a graduate student he had chosen would read a five- or ten-minute paper to introduce the guest and outline some of the problems they appeared to face in their work. This would provoke thoughts, help relax the guest, and through a strange process help them to absorb the nature of the gathering. The visitor would then be invited to respond, and Butler would then pose a question or two – often very broad questions; often quite blunt and cheeky – and after a while the session would then be open to the audience. It was all 'off the record', so the speaker was guaranteed that he would not be quoted directly – what he said was merely to inform his audience's understanding of how politics and power work in practice. Butler later explained: 'You soon realise that, as long as you are not questioning them in a hostile way – which I have never done – your guests are rather flattered … I had made this very elemental discovery: people do enjoy talking about their problems.'[18]

Few people could resist the cachet of speaking to an Oxford college and dining at high table, even if the audience was mainly students, rather than 'the great and the good'. Many visitors found it valuable to reflect candidly for a few hours on their work, without the danger of an unguarded comment appearing in the press. People often made indiscreet comments, yet, remarkably, nothing seems ever to have leaked. (A rare exception occurred when Tony Benn – or one of his advisers – leaked his words to the press, but that hardly counts as a breach.) As Nuffield's fame and standing grew during the 1950s and '60s, so it became easier and easier to attract guests. And Butler was himself building up contacts through his journalism and research on the Nuffield election books. The 'enormous advantage' of Nuffield, he says, is that:

> you can invite anybody without embarrassment. You can invite a Prime Minister to come and dine in college, and 'Do you mind talking to a seminar for a few students?' You can give them a respectable dinner with safe company, and they know that they're going into a safe world, and they don't say 'No', on the whole.[19]

Many senior figures returned to the Nuffield seminars again and again. Regulars in the first decade included Labour politicians Roy Jenkins, Richard Crossman, Patrick Gordon Walker, Brian Walden and Butler's old friend Tony Benn; Tory front-benchers Bill Deedes, Sir Edward Boyle, Enoch Powell, Iain Macleod, Willie Whitelaw, and the Tory Chief Whip, Martin Redmayne; journalists included the editor of *The Times*, William Rees-Mogg, and Ian Trethowan of the BBC. Frequent guests in the 1970s included Shirley Williams, Norman St John-Stevas and Douglas Hurd, and the year 1976/77 saw visits from former Prime Ministers Ted Heath and Harold Wilson, followed by Jim Callaghan in 1981. In the 1980s, Tory ministers Chris Patten, Michael Heseltine, Geoffrey Howe, Ken Baker and Leon Brittan all attended.

The seminars attracted not just Nuffield fellows and students, but PPE students from all over the university, and other graduates and undergraduates. Nobody seemed to worry about who was in the room. This author's memories of attending Butler seminars during the 1979 'Winter of Discontent' are among my strongest recollections of studying PPE. Famous politicians would often address the political clubs or the Oxford Union, but those were semi-public events where visitors were partisan and usually quite careful in what they said. On Friday night in Nuffield, the guests would open up; one got a glimpse of how power worked in practice, and often heard speakers, such as senior civil servants, whom one would not normally encounter. Sir Robert Armstrong, for example, visited while he was still Cabinet Secretary, and Sir Ian Bancroft when Head of the Civil Service.

It wasn't just the college that attracted members of the political class, but David Butler himself. He did not make huge numbers of TV and radio appearances during the 1950s and '60s, but they were broadcast occasions that people remembered – most notably the election programmes.

David Butler also exploited his slowly growing reputation as a television personality to approach sources for the regular Nuffield election books. With the 1951 and 1955 volumes, he had spent many days touring Britain, interviewing regional Conservative and Labour organisers about the campaigns in their areas, getting a feel for what was happening at the grassroots. This was a springboard to expand the research effort, helped by sharing the organisation of the election books with others.

Whereas Butler had edited the 1951 and 1955 books single-handedly, the 1959 book saw a pattern that continues to this day. As an assistant, he recruited Richard Rose, who was then an American DPhil student at Magdalen College and says he began by accompanying Butler on his election tours, then volunteered to write a chapter for the book on public relations in the campaign and ended up as co-author. Butler and Rose wrote 'in a vivacious manner', declared the Labour MP Tony Crosland. 'In consequence, the book is entertaining as well as essential reading.'[20]

Butler credits Richard Rose with the suggestion that they interview many more key players in the campaign. At this stage they started to interview mainly national back-room strategists and advisers. Aside from that, the authors spoke to just a handful of Labour front-benchers – Jim Callaghan, Dick Crossman and Denis Healey.

The much greater emphasis on exploring recent history by interviewing real political operators reflected Butler's development of the Nuffield evening seminars: indeed, some people were interviewed when they came to the seminar. The interview programme was developed substantially with Butler's co-author on the 1964 and 1966 books, Anthony King, a Canadian who had been a student at Nuffield and was now a fellow at Magdalen, and the pair started doing interviews for what became the 1964 election book. Between 1963 and 1966, they conducted around 400 interviews, and in some cases spoke to people seven or eight times.

Generally, Butler and King would visit subjects at the Commons, or in their party offices or in their ministries; a neutral alternative might be Butler's club in London, the United University Club (later merged into the Oxford and Cambridge Club). Many subjects said they could be much more candid if questioned again after the election, and so the authors developed the practice of returning to people after polling day, though they weren't always as revealing as they'd promised. The interview process involved carefully typing up what people said afterwards, and diligent preparation in advance:

> One must reassure those one sees that one will not waste their time – to show that one already knows a lot about their central problems is a good way of encouraging frankness. One must also reassure them that one will not abuse their confidence. The technique of such interviewing depends upon personal relationships, upon the establishment of trust … It was appreciated that we had no interest in printing personal gossip or being *Time*-style inside-dopesters.[21]

Butler admitted that very little of the material they gathered in their exhausting interview programme appeared directly in print, but notes that by talking to the actors involved they gained the confidence to make bold statements about what had happened. In 1964, Butler and King managed to speak to most of the major players. The Prime Minister, Sir Alec Douglas-Home, who was at the end of the Conservatives' five-year term, was interviewed for forty-five minutes in Downing Street in April 1964. He told them that he would never agree to a TV confrontation with the Labour leader, Harold Wilson, as such events could be two-edged. 'You might be off your form,' Home explained, 'and you could not help but give publicity to the other fellow.' He said that having seen the Nixon–Kennedy debates in America, he had 'vowed never to take part in similar affairs'. Butler and King wrote in their notes that, 'far from being the boyishly self-confident figure portrayed in the press, [Home] seemed subdued, bewildered, unsure of his or his party's position, and generally pessimistic about the future. He frequently expressed his perplexity at the failure of the Conservatives to improve their position.'[22] Yet by the time of their next interview, a half-hour session during the 1964 campaign itself, with the parties now much more closely in contention, Home's 'morale seemed much higher'.

The election book interviews regularly exposed the personal acrimony that often existed within the high commands of both parties, and, in the case of the Conservatives in 1964, the strains that persisted following the 1963 leadership change. In his post-1964 election interview, party vice-chairman Lord (Oliver) Poole claimed that around the spring of that year, he 'had knocked together the heads of Maudling, Macleod and Heath, and had told them to stop bickering'.[23]

The Foreign Secretary Rab Butler, who had again failed to become leader, was interviewed by David Butler on his own, and was understandably scathing about Home and his colleagues. 'Poor Alec's not going over, is he? He's so amateurish,' he remarked in February 1964. 'The PM has no depth and fails to see the whole picture. Central Office people are not very bright,' he said in a second interview four months later, while saying it was time to sack Lord Poole – 'this millionaire's errand boy'. When Butler and King interviewed Poole themselves, about voting behaviour and what was happening in various seats, they felt Poole talked 'a great deal of intelligent nonsense'.[24]

The former Prime Minister Harold Macmillan also gave a notable interview, at the offices – suitably enough – of his publishing firm. He disclosed that he had warned the Queen, upon becoming Prime Minister in 1957, after Suez, that his government 'might not last six weeks'. Discussing his famous phrase 'You've never had it so good', Macmillan claimed it had not been aimed at the electorate as a whole but very specifically at a 'younger boiler-suited heckler' in the crowd at a meeting and was intended to contrast his position with that of 'pensioners and people living on fixed incomes'. Macmillan also gave Butler and King a detailed account of the 1963 leadership crisis which led to Home replacing Macmillan.

Material like this, never intended for public attribution, gave Butler key insights into the inner workings of politics. In particular, Butler continued to write the Nuffield studies' chapters summarising events of the previous parliament, and while these chapters rarely quoted the interviews, they were immeasurably improved because of them. This was part of David Butler's secret: the sheer breadth and depth of who he was listening to. And it became a two-way trade. Busy and senior figures were very happy to make time in their diaries to see him because Butler could feed them useful insights as to what was going on elsewhere in politics.

The substantial body of interviews radically changed the nature of the Nuffield books. Butler and King believed the 'problem of electoral strategy' had been 'neglected', with no scholarly work on the subject.[25] So the authors tried in their interviews not just to learn the details of month-by-month election planning, but also to discover what evidence party strategists had about the electorate and voting behaviour. And what is striking from the archive is how often some senior politicians seemed to have given little or no thought to such matters. The 1964 election book contained four chapters on the parties' election strategies: this analysis was greatly influenced by this new type of background interview work, though sources were rarely quoted by name.

It meant that David Butler was becoming even more of a political journalist than he'd been during the 1950s. Yet Butler was scathing about the standards of political journalism in Britain. In 1963, he wrote a long article for the American magazine *Harper's* on 'Why American political reporting is better than England's [*sic*]' and shortly afterwards presented a BBC radio programme on the same theme. Butler argued that American political correspondents got 'a great deal nearer to what was really happening at the heart of affairs' in Washington, and reached 'a level of intimacy and perception which is seldom matched even by the best of the British press'.[26] 'Scoops are surprisingly rare,' he complained.

> The leaking of a document is astonishingly rare … Whitehall's secrets go untapped by the press … our public life is conducted in a much more private fashion than that of almost any other democratic country. Rules and conventions prevent lobby correspondents from securing, or at any rate from publishing, the most elementary political information.[27]

Yet, by the 1960s, it was no longer true to say that David Butler had the field of British election analysis pretty much to himself. There was a growing body of academic and journalistic literature about elections, and the first direct competitor as a book chronicling an election campaign. *The Making of the Prime Minister*, by the political journalists Anthony Howard and Richard West, was very much based in title and format on Theodore H. White's classic, bestselling account of the 1960 US presidential campaign.

The people who rapidly chronicled the Kennedy era, especially after his assassination, were often dismissed with the disparaging, and apparently contradictory, term 'instant history'. But Butler delivered a stout defence of instant or contemporary history in a lecture in 1967, which was later reproduced in a New Zealand historical journal. 'As one who practises instant history, I am not prepared to accept that my occupation is in any essential way different from that of the traditional historian,' he declared.[28]

In producing an immediate account of events, Butler argued, the instant historian could gather a lot more written material and ephemera than would probably be available to future historians. The accounts he and King had given of the 1964 and 1966 elections had the huge advantage, he claimed, that the authors were able 'to test out our theses on so many of the people who were directly involved, both by interview and by asking for their comments on our draft manuscript'.[29]

Butler and King had risen to new levels with their 1964 and 1966 books. The 1964 volume is really the first comprehensive election study, with a much better mixture of tables, graphs, social surveys, cartoons, anecdotes and quotations from the new bank of background interviews. It was also the first in the series to contain a chapter analysing election candidates, and more chapters were farmed out to academic colleagues, allowing greater expertise. (Remarkably, these included three future members of the House of Lords: Alan Beith, a Nuffield student who wrote about the press; and Bernard Donoughue and Kenneth Morgan, who wrote about the constituency campaigns in Finchley and Swansea West respectively). Significantly, for the first time since 1945, David Butler did not himself write the statistical appendix, the section on which his psephological career had very largely been based. The work was given instead to a young Nuffield student, Michael Steed, who would continue writing the books' statistical appendices for the next forty-one years (combining this with being a very active Liberal; a candidate in five Westminster elections, and party president in the late 1970s).

The move was an acknowledgement not just of David Butler's growing workload, but also of a turning point in his career. He had originally made his name through establishing election statistics, or psephology, as a subject, but the science was now developing well beyond his capabilities. Butler had never been a 'proper' mathematician, and there was a limit to how far he could go with his limited grasp of calculus and statistics.

In the main text of the 1964 book, Butler and King had acknowledged that swing was no longer as uniform nationally as it had been immediately after the war, and they included a map to show how there were substantial regional variations, a trend that would continue further in subsequent elections. In his appendix, Michael Steed then argued that the formula for calculating swing, first developed by David Butler for the 1945 book, should now be modified. Butler's swing was simply a measure of the relative change between two elections in percentage votes for two parties – generally Conservative and Labour. But Steed argued that this was an imprecise indicator of electoral change and didn't allow for important factors such as variations in turnout (which were especially diverse in 1964) or for possible distortions caused by third parties – an unsurprising argument for someone who was a leading Liberal (and more Liberal candidates stood in 1964 than in any contest since 1950). Steed argued that a better measure of swing was the relative change in the votes for two parties *as percentages of the total vote for those two parties*, not the overall total vote. But 'Steed Swing', as he liked to call it, has never really caught on in public analysis, partly because it is much harder to calculate.

Since Labour scraped in with a majority of just four seats in 1964, it was widely assumed another election wouldn't be far off. So the 1964 post-election interviewing programme merged into the pre-election interviews for what became the 1966 campaign, when

Harold Wilson increased his majority to almost a hundred, despite the Conservatives replacing the old-fashioned Alex Douglas-Home with the more youthful Edward Heath.

Anthony King left the project after the 1966 election to take a post at the new University of Essex, and for the 1970 volume Butler originally recruited as his co-author Austin Mitchell, a student at Nuffield who later achieved fame as a television presenter and subsequently as a Labour MP.

Mitchell stepped down from the co-author role well before the 1970 election, but he did many interviews with Butler for the book. He would later recall how nothing was written down during questioning; the aim was to make the subject as relaxed and informative as possible, all on the understanding that, rather like the Nuffield seminars, what people said was not for direct quotation, but for background, to improve the authors' understanding of events. But, as Austin Mitchell later described, it required good memory 'to write it all down on the train back to Oxford, a humiliating procedure because David could always remember everything word for word while I struggled to get my few thoughts down and usually ended up with illegible notes'.[30]

Over time, the election book interviews built up a great archive of material covering sixty years of British political history, which was kept at Nuffield College. David Butler has always been generous in making the interviews available to other historians and scholars, on similar 'background' terms to those given to the subject originally, though the fact that the notes were compiled only from memory an hour or two afterwards, not made contemporaneously, makes the material slightly problematic as a historical source.

The Nuffield election studies started to be copied by academics around the world, and the format of the volumes (and variations on the basic title) were used for a series of five other studies (three by Butler's former students) which went way back beyond the first book from 1945. The first, by Trevor Lloyd, was on the great 1880 contest in which Gladstone trounced Disraeli. This was followed by books on the elections of 1906, 1910 (both contests), 1931 and 1935.[31]

David Butler also initiated another great resource for academics and journalists around the same time. In June 1960, he wrote to Reg Allen at his publishers, Macmillan, with a suggestion: 'I have for some time cherished the idea of compiling a *Handbook for Twentieth Century Historians* – a compendious but not vast dictionary' which would list facts, dates and references which might be of help 'to the growing army of young men [*sic*] writing theses on recent British political, social, and economic history'. Hoping also to generate sales to journalists and libraries, Butler proposed an alternative title: *Britain in the Twentieth Century – A reference book*. He envisaged that this would be another Nuffield project – with the college providing many experts who might help compile the material, as well as potential buyers and readers. He hoped the college would pay for a research assistant who 'would do the overwhelming bulk of the donkey work but I would take full responsibility for detailed planning and supervision'.[32]

Among the facts which Butler planned to include were the precise composition of governments, with the exact dates of all ministerial changes; election results; Gallup poll ratings; economic statistics; lists of permanent secretaries in every government department, and British ambassadors overseas; leading party and trade union officials; and potted political biographies. In each case these would cover the period from 1900 to 1960.[33]

Macmillan said yes; Nuffield said yes; and Butler recruited a PPE graduate from St Hilda's College, Jennie Freeman, to do the research. Yet the process of compiling the book was more onerous than Butler had expected. What proved most time-consuming was assembling complete lists of government ministers over the sixty-year period, especially when existing sources were sometimes inaccurate and lacked precise dates of ministers' appointments to office and their departure. Details of senior civil servants were even more elusive. The departure of southern Ireland from the United Kingdom in 1922 presented problems in statistical time-series, while the devolved nature of some institutions in Northern Ireland and Scotland also caused difficulty.

The manuscript of *British Political Facts 1900–1960* was finished in June 1962 and the 245-page volume was published in the summer of 1963. 'The scholar, the journalist, the politician, and the club bore were all in the authors' minds,' Butler and Freeman wrote at the start of their introduction. Butler explained how during his twelve years at Nuffield he had:

> noticed the amount of time that [I] and others wasted in searching for seemingly obvious facts about twentieth-century Britain … Experience of checking facts in newspaper offices and broadcasting studios and the anecdotes of friends in Whitehall and Westminster have made plain to us how much elementary political data is annoyingly elusive.

Moreover, many of the existing directories of political information were published only on an annual basis, which was 'frustrating' for people trying to compile facts or trends over many years. 'Nobody had ever done it longitudinally,' he later explained.[34] But the authors admitted an element of 'systematised plagiarism', as they put it, so were generous in citing sources. A footnote also appealed to readers to make 'suggestions of corrections and additions' in case there was a second edition.[35]

There was, of course. Indeed, *British Political Facts* was a valuable resource for academics, historians and journalists for the next half-century, bringing David Butler's name to a wider audience in yet another way, though it may not have done his personal academic reputation much good. It reinforced the image Butler had among some colleagues that he was a kind of political trainspotter, who was solely interested in facts and obscure details, rather than analysing and interpreting what they meant. Among both university colleagues and his wider audience, Butler was in danger of becoming a joke figure who only seemed to have one obsessive interest in life. His exceptional ability on live television to recall minute details about individual MPs and their constituencies led people to compare him with Leslie Welch, the 1950s celebrity who achieved fame on TV and radio as the 'Memory Man' who would ask audiences to challenge him with any question on sport, which he invariably answered. Butler also risked parody as a modern-day version of the schoolmaster who declares at the opening of Charles Dickens's novel *Hard Times*: 'Now, what I want is, Facts. Teach these boys and girls nothing but Facts. Facts alone are wanted in life.' Indeed, Butler was publishing his new directory at the very time when history teaching in schools was rapidly moving away from the simple learning of dates and recitation of key facts.

Yet David Butler never felt embarrassed by his love of facts, or accusations that he was a mere fact-gatherer. He saw himself following in the footsteps of his maternal grandfather, A. F. Pollard, who also thought history could succeed only on a bed of facts. Pollard had been a great believer in works of reference, and also contributed a hundred entries to the *Dictionary of National Biography*. His father, too, was equally committed to factual accuracy. There had been two sets of reference books in the Butler family home – one in the dining room and one in the sitting room – and Harold Butler always advised his children: 'Never argue about verifiable questions of fact.'[36]

David Butler has described *British Political Facts* as the 'most massive enterprise of my life', and he was involved in ten editions between 1963 and 2010, with the time period gradually extended to cover the whole of the twentieth century and beyond.[37] Jennie Freeman didn't work on the second and third editions, published in 1968 and 1969, and instead the effective role of co-author, updating information and adding new data, passed to Anne Duncan-Jones (later Sloman), who had worked on the 1966 Nuffield election book. It was a slightly awkward situation, as Freeman's name remained on the cover as official co-author due to her work on the first edition. Remarkably, Sloman says the two women never met. She, like Freeman, was a recent PPE graduate from St Hilda's, and recalls being one of two candidates for the job. 'One question he asked was "What would most irritate me about you?" and the other person said, "I smoke," so she didn't get the job.'[38] Sloman recollects how 'pedantic and careful' they were about authenticating every detail, which was a major operation in an era without the internet.

> David's energy was exhausting. He made me feel tired just listening to him, and he speaks extremely fast. He was never a don who sat at a desk and just ploughed through a load of documents. But he gave me a free hand in what I did. I introduced lots of new sections to the book.

These included subjects such as ministerial resignations; MPs switching sides; the administration of justice; the economy; and nationalisation. 'He was a wonderful boss,' says Sloman. 'He kind of gave you your head, always willing to discuss with you, never grand about anything.'[39]

Anne Sloman provides an excellent example of the way Butler would always try to help people with their future careers through his extensive network of contacts in the media and politics. In the late 1960s, Butler had suggested his old BBC boss Grace Wyndham Goldie come to Nuffield to work on her memoirs after she had retired, but they were in some chaos, and Sloman was assigned to help sort them out. 'She could be a terrible bully,' Sloman recalls. 'I had one of the worst evenings of my life at her flat.' And Butler also arranged for Sloman to do research work at the Commons for his old New College friend Peter Blaker, who was by now a Conservative MP.

In 1967, Sloman secured an initial three weeks' work with one of Butler's contacts in BBC radio, Stephen Bonarjee. 'I was in!' Sloman says, and she quickly started a stellar career with the corporation. By 1974, Sloman was editing the BBC radio election results programmes, and eventually she rose to become the corporation's chief political adviser. But throughout Sloman's early years in the BBC, she continued to help Butler with the *Political Facts* books and was named co-author for the fourth and fifth editions in 1975 and 1980 (for which Jennie Freeman's name was now removed from the cover, despite her earlier contribution).

Butler was very grateful to friends and colleagues writing to correct misprints and mistakes in previous editions. 'It would be wrong to suggest that the first edition was riddled with errors,' Butler wrote at the start of the second edition. 'The percentage of mistakes in the 50,000 or more facts and figures it contained was low. In this edition, thanks to our readers, it is lower. But some undoubtedly survive, and once again we beg those who use this book to send us their corrigenda.' Butler's approach was constant striving for perfection, hoping for 'new editions that will be more error-free and still more compendious'.[40]

Unlike some authors, Butler positively relished having mistakes brought to his attention. After the second edition, one reader, Paul 'PC' Thompson, wrote in to correct the date of death of a minor minister from the 1920s. 'More please, more,' Butler wrote in his thank-you note. So Thompson set to work and sent Butler long lists of corrigenda, only for Butler to urge him to find even more corrections. Eventually, Butler rewarded Thompson by offering the choice of dinner at Nuffield, or for Butler to visit the school where Thompson taught. Thompson chose the latter.[41]

British Political Facts was also influential in spawning other works. There was an Australian off-shoot, and one of Butler's former research students, Chris Cook, published several volumes of *British Historical Facts* in a very similar format.[42]

In 2018, Roger Mortimore and Andrew Blick brought out the directory in its latest incarnation, covering British history since 1900, almost twice as long a span as the original book. In tribute to the founder, they also changed the title slightly. It is now called *Butler's British Political Facts*.[43]

CHAPTER ELEVEN

THE LOVE OF HIS LIFE

'There is also a hint here and there,' Grace Wyndham Goldie wrote to Butler after the 1955 BBC results programme, 'that the ladies in the audience found you particularly impressive!' As we've seen, Goldie's letters also included the occasional suggestion that she herself had a soft spot for the young academic, even though she was married and twenty-four years his senior.[1]

David Butler was strikingly handsome as a young man, with dark hair which always stands out in photos and TV recordings. And he was intelligent, polite, generous, optimistic and sociable. He had abundant energy and passion. He may not have enjoyed music but was reasonably cultured in other respects: he appreciated fine art, loved going to the theatre and cinema, and he read plenty of novels, mostly English classics rather than modern literature. During his time in America, he'd come to adore parties and dancing; he could mix a decent cocktail and he was a regular and attentive host. He could boast plenty of friends and liked staying with young families.

Several of David's friends in these years knew of his longing to get married and have a family, and some of them worked hard to find a suitable partner. One friend feared he 'might slide off with anybody because he was so avid about getting married. We were dead worried he couldn't find a wife. He was getting quite edgy about it. He'd pursue women who were quite unsuitable.'

Perhaps it was because he was a touch gauche – awkward and

slightly ill at ease with women. He also came across as rather serious and over-dedicated to his work, even obsessive at times, while lacking a sharp wit, or much inclination to poke fun at himself. Yet when Butler was finally successful in his quest for love, his marriage was incredibly strong, enduring and touchingly romantic. And he became a model husband and father.

He'd left the Army a virgin and there is no sign of anybody one could remotely call a girlfriend until Jane Cooper at Princeton in 1948. 'Of all the female sex that I have encountered over here,' he wrote to his parents, 'Jane has unquestionably the most interesting – and incidentally the least American – mind.'[2] They exchanged letters for a few years, and generally met when David was in America, but the 3,500 miles across the Atlantic proved too far for a proper relationship, and Butler thinks she was 'slightly more fond of me than I was of her'.[3]

Then there was Benedicte, the first woman with whom he ever fell in love. She was Danish and a history student, about seven years younger than Butler, and had first come to Oxford in the early 1950s to study at Lady Margaret Hall. In 1956, Benedicte Hjejle switched to Nuffield College to do her DPhil thesis on British social policy in India during the early nineteenth century, including the work of the East India Company, and the horrors of slavery and the burning of widows. Benedicte remembers Nuffield as a 'family of students', and she was one of only four or five women in the whole college. David gave her considerable advice on her work, and they started seeing a lot of each other socially – attending parties together and punting on the Isis and Cherwell. She says most of the college thought they were having a romantic relationship, though it's clear it was nothing like as advanced as people assumed, even though he visited Benedicte and her family in Copenhagen. 'My companions observed that we were getting interested,' she says, 'but we didn't work it out.'[4]

Perhaps surprisingly, Butler's senior colleagues at Nuffield seem to have raised no objection to the relationship, even though the college dean and senior tutor had fallen in love with one of the students he was supposed to advise on both academic and pastoral matters. This was in line, of course, with the culture of the time. Nowadays Butler would almost certainly have been in breach of the strict rules that exist regarding staff–student relationships throughout most of higher education.

Judging from his letters and his sporadic diary – what he called his commonplace book – David Butler's relationship with Benedicte was more serious for him than for her. She first appears in his diary on 7 June 1957:

> About midnight on June 3rd, quite unexpectedly, what I had seen, not altogether optimistically, as a protracted siege, turned into a mutual admission of affection. What the future holds I do not know. There remains the delectable work-destroying present, the solemn routine front that has to be maintained in College, concealing the simple, tremulous, delight of thinking about her, and, far, far, more, being with her. How odd that 32 years of existence, novel reading, and talking with friends, should so little have prepared me for the possibility I remember envisaging some eight years ago – of being overwhelmed by 'some irrevocable cataclysm of love'. I had come to think that some day I might meet someone with whom I developed a sufficient fondness and sense of congeniality to consider a partnership for life … This isn't a rational matter. The world of emotion is very unfamiliar – and very wonderful. And I am so glad I never really fell in love before, because then I wouldn't have made the discovery with Benedicte.[5]

A month later he declared that he wouldn't write any more about Benedicte, 'perhaps because of an odd feeling that to record anything on these pages would be a species of treachery'. He explained also that the writing of letters and – 'God help me' – verse to Benedicte had 'syphoned off the urge to set my thoughts down here'.[6] But five days later he returned to the subject: 'I am in love in a way that brooks no doubt or contradiction.' But he knew that suffering lay ahead, since Benedicte had told him she did not feel quite the same way. 'She thinks, alas, that she will leave for Denmark in six to nine months' time, if not without compunction, without an impossible sense of loss,' he wrote.[7] He'd promised not to 'weary' Benedicte 'with importunities' or to burden her with guilt by his entertaining false hopes. 'Her fears of my being bitter against her are obvious nonsense, but whether I could altogether sustain so intimate and constant a relation with her, if I were not buoyed by the possibility of her relenting, I do not know.' He knew 'hours of unproductive worry' lay in the months ahead, and acknowledged:

> the infinite and desolating sense of loss that may face me next year ... I shall be a better and wiser person, a more useful counsellor as a result of it all, even if some very unhappy and solitary hours of pain await me ... I have said not once but several times that I want what she wants more than I want what I want myself.[8]

What partly went wrong with the relationship was that Benedicte felt she should soon return to Denmark for family reasons.

> My mother had a serious eye illness which made her almost blind – *retinitis pigmentosa* – and my sister was also ill at the time. It was tempting to settle in Oxford and I had true regard for David, but I also knew that as the years pass by you are better off in your own habitat.[9]

She feels that their coming from separate worlds and upbringings didn't help. 'After all, I wasn't English, and he wasn't Danish, and although we had a lot of academic interests together, we both stuck to rather different cultures.'[10]

By that autumn, having once more experienced the 'highest pinnacle of hope' and 'the depths of final despair', he decided things were hopeless. He would try to keep out of Benedicte's way, which can't have been easy at Nuffield, a close community of only a few dozen people. He hoped that with the rhythm of work and social distraction, the 'echoing pain that throbs through me so many times a day will die away'.[11]

His diary for the following April, however, suggests he was still very much in love:

> The vicissitudes of my private miseries continue … I must yet contend in silence with the simple longing for her, the irrepressible hope that perhaps in the end she will change her mind. I find myself praying to a God in whom I do not really believe, praying half nobly that I may do what is right and best, that her welfare should come first, half selfishly that I may yet be granted the thing I want more than anything else in the world.[12]

That summer, while teaching at Cornell in America, he wrote to his mother that he had received 'a letter from England that put an end to any surviving hopes'.[13] Benedicte Hjejle went on to a distinguished academic career at Copenhagen University, and she and David kept in touch for the rest of their lives, occasionally seeing each other on their visits to each other's countries.

Some couples tried to help David by match-making. These included John Fforde, a Nuffield economist who was a close friend, and his wife Marya, who had worked on the 1951 and 1955 election books. Another such couple who tried to help were the Whitbys. Joy Whitby was the sister of Harry Field, the friend of Butler's from both St Paul's and New College, who subsequently studied elections at the University of Michigan, and who also worked alongside Butler on the 1951 BBC results programme. Joy Whitby recalls an occasion during the war when David came for tea at the Fields' home: 'Mother put out on the table her prized box of chocolates – this was during rationing – and I was appalled as a little girl, as he was eating up all our ration! He was so concentrating that he was a bit awkward socially.'[14]

The early '50s saw the Whitbys at the heart of a classic example of Butler networking – or, less charitably, an illustration of the incestuous world he occupied. Joy got a job as a research assistant to Butler's old tutor Philip Andrews, who was now at Nuffield, and then she married Tony Whitby, a graduate student at the college who was being supervised by Butler. After Oxford, Tony Whitby joined the Colonial Office, but was bored there, so it was arranged for Butler to invite Grace Wyndham Goldie to the Whitbys' home in Bryanston Square, and she ended up offering Tony a job. It proved a fruitful encounter, for Whitby duly joined the corporation and went on to become editor of the BBC1 current affairs programme *24 Hours*, and later the first controller of Radio 4, before his death, aged just forty-five, in 1975. Joy Whitby, who had joined the BBC before her husband, became a leading pioneer in children's television.

The Whitbys tried hard in the late 1950s to fix Butler up with a girlfriend. Among a few young women they invited to dinner with him was the young Biddy Baxter, who was then a producer on schools' programmes, working for Joy Whitby. She later achieved fame as editor for twenty-five years of the famous children's programme *Blue Peter*. But Baxter wasn't interested.

So they tried again, with a couple of bright young BBC news producers, Denise Cremona and Marilyn Evans. This time they invited both David and his former Nuffield flatmate Zbigniew Pelczynski to come to the theatre with the two young women. Their thinking was that Marilyn would be best suited for Zbigniew, while David might prefer Denise. But, as things progressed, first with a play in the Haymarket, then on to dinner at a restaurant in Marylebone, the evening proved astonishingly successful, though not quite as planned. For Zbigniew immediately fell for Denise, while David found Marilyn the more interesting. At the end of the evening, Butler offered to take her back to her home in south-west London, explaining that it wasn't far from where his mother now lived in Richmond. David doesn't seem, however, to have been bowled over by this first encounter. 'I just knew she was an extremely nice and agreeable person and I wanted to pursue her acquaintance,' he says.[15]

Marilyn Evans had been born in 1937, so was twelve years younger than David. She was the daughter of Trevor Evans, who served as industrial correspondent and then industrial editor of the *Daily Express* for an astonishing thirty-seven years between 1930 and 1967. He was not just a daily reporter, but an influential columnist, too – a senior figure in British journalism at a time when industrial editors were important players; when politics was dominated by poor labour relations; and the *Express* was a paper to be reckoned with. Evans so impressed the proprietor, Lord Beaverbrook, that he appointed him to the board of Beaverbrook Newspapers. He was eventually knighted in 1967. When Evans died in 1981, both Jim Callaghan and the then Labour leader Michael Foot delivered eulogies at his funeral, and one of them claimed that during the war Evans had acted as a conduit between Beaverbrook, who was then Production Minister, and Ernest Bevin, the Minister of Labour, who refused to talk to each other. 'Wow, I knew Grandpa was important,' remarked one of Butler's sons, 'but I didn't know he'd won the war!'[16]

Trevor Evans was born to a family of Welsh-speaking miners in the pit village of Abertridwr, just north of Caerphilly in South Wales. When Trevor was only eleven, the area suffered Britain's worst ever mining disaster, when 440 men were killed in the mine in the neighbouring community. Nonetheless, when Trevor left school three years later he became an electrician at the Abertridwr colliery, where he joined the miners' union, the NUM. But then he switched to being a journalist on local papers, which paid him a penny a line. 'He was always a Labour man,' says his son Richard, who became political correspondent on the *Financial Times*. 'He instilled in Marilyn and me a lot of Labour views. The whole family was left-of-centre. Marilyn was quite strongly left.'[17] The milieu of political discussion and argument in the Evans household was fuelled by the piles of newspapers and books around the place, and the presence of senior Labour and trade union figures whom Trevor Evans often invited home. Trevor's wife, born Margaret Gribbin, boasted even stronger journalistic blood in her background: her father and several other relatives held prominent posts on various national newspapers.

The Evans family lived in Kingston-on-Thames in south-west London, chosen because it was served by trains which left Waterloo after 4 a.m., when the last edition of the *Express* went to press. But the family spent the war years in New Quay, a fishing town on Cardigan Bay in south-west Wales, where the young Marilyn learnt fluent Welsh, and where Dylan Thomas was also living at the time (though there is no record, alas, of any encounter). Indeed, New Quay is said to be Thomas's model for Llareggub ('bugger all' backwards), the fictional village in his drama *Under Milk Wood*. In later life, Marilyn always spoke of how she 'acquired a permanent sense of Welshness from a childhood spent on this coast, with its long sandy beaches and spectacular caves'. Some Evans cousins lived further inland, where they ran a pub and a small farm. 'Memories', she said, 'included falling off a haystack, luckily accompanied by a bale of hay, feeding swill to pigs and (illegally) drinking warm milk from the cow.'[18] Schooling was in Welsh and English, and Marilyn was clearly very bright. Her cousin Val Atkinson later recalled how she and Marilyn often shared a bed. 'After "lights out" she would serialise books she had read for me. I remember *The Three Musketeers*. I realise now she could only have been seven.'[19] Marilyn would later describe these war years in West Wales as the happiest time of her childhood.

On returning to London, Marilyn became a brilliant pupil at

Wimbledon High School. At the age of only eleven, she beat the rest of the school – including girls many years her senior – in a general knowledge quiz, and the school honours board still displays the exhibition she won to St Hilda's College, Oxford in 1955 – only the second person in her family to attend university (after her brother Richard). Marilyn had originally planned to read history or PPE, but suddenly switched to English after seeing an inspiring production of Shakespeare's *Coriolanus*. She'd decided the 'artistic representation of history' was fascinating, whereas simple history itself was 'so straightforward by comparison, just like newspapers'.[20] But journalism and history nonetheless remained important themes in her future career.

Marilyn later wrote of how she 'found Oxford dreamlike, medieval and utterly ravishing. I think I was forty before I grew out of my teenage infatuation with the place.'[21] She wrote film reviews for the student magazine *Isis* and news features for the newspaper *Cherwell* and worked backstage on several student plays. She joined the Critical Society, where young dons and students supplemented the traditional university teaching by meeting informally to discuss papers and argue with each other about more modern literary issues, such as why literature mattered to wider society. 'This was an outer layer of education no prospectus mentioned,' she once said.[22]

Marilyn was also active in the Socialist Club (which was left of the Labour Club), whose members had been energised by the big events of 1956 – Suez and the Soviet invasion of Hungary, which had caused many people to leave the Communist Party. It meant a ringside seat at the very start of what became known as the New Left – a group of intellectual socialists who were 'unsatisfied by the welfare state and hostile to the Cold War'.[23] They had no time for Stalinist communism, or for the staid and timid Labour Party, many of whose policies were barely distinguishable from those of their Conservative opponents.

She was 'not a student radical', her contemporary Stuart Hall once said, 'but very, very intelligent'.[24] Marilyn was especially close to a high-powered group which included the historian Raphael Samuel and Canadian philosopher Charles Taylor. Another member, Gabriel Pearson, who later became a Professor of Drama and Film at Essex University, was Marilyn's boyfriend for a spell.

Marilyn later said of her student days: 'My social life, my love life and my education all coalesced after Suez, and made a kind of sense of the rest of my time at Oxford.'[25] On Good Friday 1958, having gone to an anti-nuclear rally in Trafalgar Square, Marilyn suddenly found herself, without notice, setting off on what would be the first Aldermaston march. She'd gone into London unprepared, with nothing in her handbag except her purse and a copy of *Paradise Lost*, but was then persuaded to join the four-day protest walk. 'She would have hated it, as she was totally non-athletic,' says one of her sons. 'Her idea of a walk was a mile or two, and she didn't like camping.'[26]

Pearson, Hall, Samuel and Taylor were the four original co-editors of the journal they founded in 1957, *Universities and Left Review*, which three years later became the famous *New Left Review*, which tried to connect politics with art and culture, and whose approach became a major influence on Marilyn's later academic career (though not her politics). 'Theirs was a style of criticism,' she said, 'which was more historical and sociological than the "close reading" or "new criticism" I had been taught.'[27]

Marilyn didn't just get a first-class degree in 1958, but a rare 'congratulated' degree where, by tradition, the examiners invite the student to see them, and then rise to their feet and applaud their work. Marilyn then taught English for a year at the Perse Girls' School in Cambridge, before, in 1960, she became a trainee producer with the BBC, working in the newsrooms in London and Manchester. It was there she met Tony Whitby, who immediately realised Marilyn was something special.

After the match-making evening organised by the Whitbys,

David initially made no effort to contact Marilyn – partly because he went to America for several weeks that spring, but also, one suspects, because he was shy with women. By happy circumstance, however, she was working on the BBC local election results programme in May 1961 where David was appearing in his usual role as analyst. Over drinks after the programme, he seized his chance and invited Marilyn to lunch. That was followed by a second date; and then he invited her to a summer ball in St John's College, Oxford, a few weeks later. It was there, around 4 a.m., on what was only about their fifth encounter, that Butler proposed to her. But the story goes that Marilyn had terrible menstrual cramps that night, so wasn't too enthusiastic when she suddenly found David, in evening dress and down on one knee, asking her to marry him. 'Don't be so bloody silly, David,' she reportedly replied.[28] It was 'much, much too soon', David himself recalls her saying. 'I suppose I hadn't thought things through,' he says. 'There was a certain amount of impulse.'[29]

David didn't propose to Marilyn again that summer, but he knew he was in with a chance when, over dinner on his birthday in October, in a small restaurant near the BBC, Marilyn said she was 'coming round' to the idea of marriage. Butler gave her something of an ultimatum, however, explaining how anyone he married would have to share his love of America, and he suggested she must decide by the following March when he was due to go on a US lecture tour.

Another important factor, according to their son Dan, was a small incident late one night in Oxford. While getting in David's sports car, they heard a man calling for help to get his girlfriend over the wall of a nearby college, since the college lodge was locked by that hour. Even though as dean of Nuffield he was in charge of discipline in his own college, David duly helped the woman over. Marilyn was impressed.

Butler spent Christmas with the Evans family in Kingston. Marilyn left early on Boxing Day to go to work and over the breakfast washing-up David boldly announced to Trevor Evans: 'I want to marry your daughter.' When Marilyn met David for lunch that day, she told him her father had phoned to congratulate her and to say he was delighted. There was no dissent from Marilyn, so David happily assumed they were now engaged.

After a skiing holiday in Kitzbühel in Austria with the Whitbys, the couple were married on 3 March 1962. He was thirty-seven; she was twenty-five. Much to Margaret Evans's disappointment, since Marilyn was her only daughter, it was a very basic ceremony at Kingston Register Office accompanied by just four guests: Marilyn's parents, David's mother and his brother Michael. It was Marilyn's decision. Indeed, the wedding took place so quietly and secretively that many people assumed the bride must be pregnant. She wasn't. After a two-night honeymoon in Brighton, they set off on David's American lecture tour, but before leaving they posted invitations for two celebration parties to be held on their return, one in Oxford, the other in London, which for many friends and relatives was the first they knew of the marriage. One invitation went to the other couple from the Whitbys' match-making evening. But, remarkably, Zbigniew and Denise had beaten the newlywed Butlers to it, having married just before Christmas. (They remained together until Denise's death in 2013 – so in one evening the Whitbys had produced two marriages which lasted over 100 years in total.)

Marriage to David provided Marilyn with a good opportunity to return to academic life back in Oxford – a choice she always insisted was of her own volition, rather than that of a dutiful wife. (In later years it would pain her that of her five closest friends from St Hilda's, none returned to professional life after marrying and having children.) Originally the plan was that back at St Hilda's she would do a DPhil on Jane Austen and politics, but David suggested that too many people did research on Austen, and he came up with another subject. David's sister Christina, who had married the Oxford architectural historian Howard Colvin, had been working in the Bodleian Library on the papers of their great-great-aunt, the Anglo-Irish nineteenth-century novelist Maria Edgeworth, since the archive was at that time in Oxford on loan from Dublin. Indeed, David has suggested the Edgeworth connection may even have been a small carrot in his courtship of Marilyn. She seized on the idea and, working with Christina's help, completed her DPhil in 1966. She greatly benefited from the access to more than 4,000 letters written to and from Edgeworth, and members of her immediate family, most of which had never been researched or cited publicly before. Earlier scholars had depended on the very limited Edgeworth correspondence published in the late nineteenth century.

Marilyn also took English tutorials for several colleges, but finding a full-time post wasn't easy. When she'd applied to Brasenose College, she was the first woman to be shortlisted for a teaching job at what was then an all-male college, and several Brasenose dons were so horrified that they refused to come and watch her interview. 'The St Hilda's fellows were outraged by the way Brasenose behaved,' she later claimed, and so in 1970 they made her a junior research fellow at their college instead.[30] Her DPhil was turned into her first book, which both revived Maria Edgeworth's rather neglected reputation and also put Marilyn on the path to becoming one of the leading scholars of the radical and 'Romantic' English literature of the late eighteenth and early nineteenth centuries.[31] She and David's sister were together awarded the Rose Mary Crawshay Prize by the British Academy for their joint work on Edgeworth (Christina having simultaneously edited and published many of the collected letters).

Marilyn was applauded for her lively, entertaining writing, which seemed to be influenced by her journalistic background and was refreshingly free of the impenetrable language of many scholars. Her handwriting may have been 'a virtually illegible ant's crawl', in the words of a friend, but her work was far from indecipherable.

'Her style is clear, highly readable and jargon-free,' a fellow English don wrote years later. 'Arguments are delivered as stories, literature a series of narratives.' Marilyn once described her populist, direct style and refusal to use theoretical language as the product of 'the daughter of a man who wrote for 12 million people every day'.[32]

The thesis and book were ten years in the making because the Butlers had quickly begun having children – three boys, born at roughly eighteen-month intervals: Daniel – Dan – in November 1963, who arrived eight days after the assassination of John F. Kennedy; Gareth, born in May 1965; and Edmund – Ed – born in January 1967.

Marilyn was heavily pregnant with Edmund at the time she completed her thesis. Her examiners were slow to arrange her viva, the formal occasion where doctoral students are interviewed about their theses. David happened to meet one of them at a lunch in Oxford and – without wishing to breach propriety – mentioned the delay, since he feared it might go beyond the date the baby was due. The examiners swiftly got their act together. Here were two male dons in 1966 questioning a heavily pregnant woman – men who weren't used to dealing with pregnant women in their work. So they handled her with kid gloves, afraid they might induce labour while the viva was taking place. But the thesis was brilliant, and her viva was easily concluded.

The family lived in the bottom half of a large house owned by Nuffield at 151 Woodstock Road, where they would stay for the next forty-eight years. They initially rented the property from the college, but in 1972 Nuffield sold them the entire house for £11,000, in what is now one of the richest neighbourhoods in Britain. The building had enjoyed some distinguished occupants in its time, including the young Hugh Gaitskell and his family in the early 1900s and, immediately after the war, John Hicks, the economist who later won the Nobel Prize. Owning the whole building allowed David and Marilyn to work in their own separate studies, and for each boy to enjoy his own bedroom (and they often let part of the house to other academics).

In addition, inspired by David's happy memories of his grandparents' house in Birdlip, in 1966 the couple also bought a small home in the Oxfordshire countryside. After visiting a couple of dozen possible properties, they found a cottage in the village of Taston, seventeen miles north of Oxford, not far from Chipping Norton, and also close to Charlbury, with its picturesque station on the Cotswold line between Oxford and Worcester. Ridge Cottage enjoys a ten-mile view down the valley, and when the trees are in leaf there's no sign of any other human habitation. It was a place for the couple to write their books, to invite friends and colleagues, and where the boys could run wild in summer.

David and Marilyn often called each other 'best beloved', the phrase used by Kipling to address the reader in his *Just So Stories*, which the couple read to the boys when they were young.[33] To others, David would often refer to 'my dear wife', and he meant it. People would sometimes notice them holding hands. His partnership with Marilyn was remarkably loving and successful, especially in an era when almost half of marriages ended in separation or divorce. Their relationship 'could appear one of chalk and cheese, academically and emotionally', wrote Dennis Kavanagh, who got to know the family through writing books with David over several decades. 'If he was optimistic, impetuous and gregarious, she was sceptical, cautious and longed for peaceful study. Where he would lecture from a few scribbled notes and dash off his writing, she would "slow burn" perfectly constructed articles. Yet they were always drawn to each other, admiring each other's strengths.'[34]

'She would agonise over things,' Kavanagh adds. 'David would never agonise over anything.'[35] Where Marilyn worked slowly and solidly on one big project, David would speedily tackle numerous tasks at once.

David himself thinks Marilyn was 'a little frustrated by me not being an intellectual', and claims she told one of their sons that he had 'no inner life'.[36] 'She … is an intellectual who plays with ideas, with extreme concentration,' he once remarked. 'I'm just a hereditary academic. I follow the family trade, like a carpenter, and produce academic books and live in an academic world.'[37]

Their oldest son, Dan, thinks his father had 'an intellectual crush' on Marilyn, 'and really admired her brain-power'. They would be teasing each other and sparring, 'in a way friends found difficult to understand', Dan says. 'They'd never stop playing devil's advocate to each other. Dad is a persistent optimist, thinking things are going to get better. Mum would think things were going to get worse.'[38]

And whereas David would go to bed very early each night, Marilyn tended to stay up very late. 'Dad would go to bed about ten o'clock and would yawn very, very loudly as a way of hinting it was time to go to bed as well.'[39] Marilyn found it hard to get to sleep and David sometimes woke in the middle of the night to find the bedside light on, with his wife jotting down her 'night thoughts' on a pad she kept on the bedside table. 'In the morning,' says Dan, 'Dad would bring her coffee and half a grapefruit, and she would work until she had to get up, which might not be until 11 a.m.'[40] David wouldn't take work with him when abroad on holiday, while Marilyn, in contrast, felt guilty if she spent more than a few hours without returning to her books, and had a bad conscience about all the things she hadn't completed.

While Marilyn was finishing her DPhil on Edgeworth, the Butlers employed a Welsh nanny who worked four or five hours a day as she concentrated on her studies. And Marilyn once observed how Austen was a good subject for someone who was a busy, distracted mother. Her books were not too long, she said, and were confined to 'finite chapters' that could easily be read and analysed in the limited periods between taking the boys to and from school.[41]

Socially, David could often be clumsy. On one occasion, early in their marriage, Marilyn had invited some of her friends – left-wing liberals from Essex – over to Oxford. David asked the guests what train they were planning to catch home. Not having considered the matter, they suggested 5 p.m., and so well before then, around 4 p.m., Dan recalls, 'he started shepherding them into the car, and they took offence at it. And she got very, very cross about it. He'd taken the 5 p.m. literally.'[42]

Yet surprisingly for someone so immersed in literature, Marilyn shared David's lack of interest in music. Most of their tiny collection of records had political themes. Marilyn collected historical folk music from the early Jacobite period; there was a collection of US campaign songs dating back to the early twentieth century; a recording of *Politics and Poker*, a Broadway musical about the New York Mayor Fiorello LaGuardia; and LPs of the satirical singer Tom Lehrer, who was extremely popular on American and British campuses in the 1950s and '60s. At times David's unmusicality could be embarrassing, as when the Butlers attended a university concert given by the Russian pianist Vladimir Ashkenazy. David reportedly fell asleep during the performance and snored, and at the official reception afterwards he couldn't come up with anything to say. 'What do you think about when you're playing?' David is said to have asked. 'Mum wanted the ground to swallow them up,' says Dan.[43]

It was quite remarkable, given his extraordinary workload and the norms of the time, how much David Butler plunged into the life of a family man. When the boys were babies he happily changed their nappies; later, on most evenings he would cycle home for their bath-time. Yet one of his Nuffield students, Helen Rushworth (later Wallace), recalls a sense that:

> other fellows thought that David was really a bit soft in the head, because at the end of his five o'clock seminars, at 6.30 p.m., he would go off to phone his sons, to talk to them before they went to bed. That was not entirely appreciated by some of his colleagues.[44]

Sometimes when away from Oxford, Butler's determination to get home for the boys' 7 p.m. bath-time caused him to drive at top speed. 'It nearly killed me,' says a colleague, 'and in the end my wife forbade me from driving with David any more.'

And his attempts to be a good husband and enthusiastic DIY expert, not always with great success, have generated a wealth of family anecdotes. In the basement at Woodstock Road, the boys liked putting on theatrical shows. So David built a miniature stage, and wired it up with dimmer switches, which were quite unusual at that time. During the work he managed to give himself several electric shocks, before deciding it might be best to turn off the electricity first. David also tried to renew the wiring and electrical fittings for the whole house in Woodstock Road, with the result that fuses kept tripping. Butler was slightly offended when professional electricians kept asking, 'What idiot did this dreadful work?' and in the end Marilyn banned her husband from any more electrical handiwork.

The house and garden in Taston are full of David's DIY efforts, including garden walls he once built and, inside the front hallway, a long rope light-switch with loops, which stretches up to the top floor. Surprisingly perhaps, for a man whose professional career was based on precision and measurement, he didn't believe in using tape measures or spirit levels. Instead, he just used his own judgement on whether something was the right length, straight or balanced. There were 'no two parallel lines', one colleague was heard to say of Butler's efforts at Woodstock Road.

On another occasion at Taston, while Marilyn was away working in Oxford, David was engaged in a DIY task which required him to drill some metal. Rather than use the vice in his workshop, he held the metal himself and ended up with the drill bit going all the way through his hand. Butler was carried on the back of the neighbours' moped, without a helmet, to the cottage hospital in Chipping Norton, and Marilyn returned home to find six-year-old Dan babysitting his two younger brothers.

David was a great delegator, of course, and in later years he would often try to enlist whoever was present at Taston to help him with what the boys thought were 'bewilderingly pointless tasks'. The future actor Toby Jones, who was a school friend of the teenage boys, would cause much mirth by imitating Butler's smart voice as he tried to recruit them to his DIY work: 'Ah yes, I'm glad you're here. I was just hoping to move the cottage two feet to the right, and thought you might be able to help.'[45]

Just after the war, Butler had acquired a whole batch of original prints of cartoons by the late eighteenth-century caricaturist James Gillray, and years later he decided to frame and display them about the house. 'For picture framing,' says Dan, 'you are supposed to use both glue and nails, but he'd just use one or the other. So there would be an explosion in the middle of the night, as one of his framed pictures came off the wall.'[46]

When the family acquired a new dishwasher in the late 1960s, David managed to flood the ground floor. 'It was just a tidal wave,' says Dan. 'He'd rush round and do a Corporal Jones impression. He'd say "Don't panic!" and "Stop shouting at me!"'[47]

Bel Crewe, who got to know the Butlers as Dan's partner and the mother of his two children, recalls how they were generous with their time and trying to find out more about her. But the house was 'chaotic', she says: 'All they would do is read and write and think. There were books and papers everywhere. I don't think I had met academics like my traditional stereotype of an academic. Piles of books about to fall over, and the fridge full of food that was past its sell-by date.'[48]

Neither parent was known for their cooking skills. David 'was always pulling out instant pizzas from the freezer and shoving them in the oven', says Ed, 'and he wouldn't notice if he'd left a fork in there. For him, eating was a chore to be overcome. He could eat a small Findus pizza in four mouthfuls. He's not a gastronome and would happily eat cheap foods.' His appreciation of wine was no better. 'He will boast that he can't tell the difference between a good and a bad wine, so he might as well drink the bad.'[49]

That may explain why Butler's attempts at brewing his own wine were not met with universal acclaim. 'He started with various hedgerow wines,' says Dan. 'Most were peculiarly horrible.' David made elderflower wine every autumn, but later moved on to rice wine, 'and he made gallons and gallons of it. The whole of the larder was lined with at least fifty demijohns.' This was served to his Nuffield students when they visited Woodstock Road for Butler's parties. 'He'd think it was drinkable, but it was repulsive,' says Dan.[50] Ed recalls the elderflower wine as equally disgusting. 'He made tons of it, but he was never great at sterilising stuff. My first foray into alcohol, age twelve, was drinking Dad's wine. I went to the toilet as quickly as I could.'[51] Fortunately, family and guests were rescued around 1980 when changes in excise duty made buying wine much cheaper.

At one time, the Butlers' parties might be enlivened by one of the pet ferrets that Dan kept in the back garden at Woodstock Road. Around 9 p.m., David sometimes encouraged his son to go and get one to entertain the guests. 'Tony Benn took to the ferret rather well,' he recalls. 'Shirley Williams cuddled it and thought it was quite nice.'[52]

In 1973, Marilyn Butler moved from St Hilda's to become fellow and tutor at St Hugh's (which was about to take the young Theresa May, née Brasier, though she read geography). Two years later, Marilyn brought out what would become probably her best-known work, *Jane Austen and the War of Ideas*, which helped establish her as one of the world's leading authorities on Austen.[53] The book put Austen in her historical context, and showed that, far from being apolitical, the novelist was hugely but subtly engaged in the political tussles of the early nineteenth century. The book 'utterly transformed critical understanding of Austen', says her colleague Jeri Johnson, 'and began Marilyn's piecemeal dismantling and gradual reassembly of the terrain of the Romantic period'.[54]

The book's importance, says Nigel Leask, Regius Professor of English at Glasgow University, 'lay in its historically contextualised and political readings of the novels, skilfully demonstrating how Austen gave flesh to the ideological values of British conservatism' during the anxiety in British politics sparked by the French Revolution.[55] Marilyn believed that literature is rooted is history, and that novels and poetry were not written in isolation, but among the political arguments and forces of the world around them. A book, she felt, 'is made by its public'.[56] Marilyn also wanted to widen the number of writers who were analysed and taught, and deliberately wrote to make scholarly criticism accessible to the much wider audience who still read the novels. 'Her books, especially on Jane Austen and the Romantics,' says her friend Heather Glen, 'reached a stream of the reading public that did not usually read literary criticism, but they wanted to think seriously about literature.'[57]

Two other books soon followed: *Peacock Displayed* in 1979, a literary life of the nineteenth-century novelist, poet and satirist Thomas Love Peacock; and then, in 1981, *Romantics, Rebels and Reactionaries: English Literature and its Background 1760–1830*, which combined much of Marilyn's research over the previous two decades into the literature and history of the Romantic period.[58] 'It was brief and accessible,' says Heather Glen, 'but it was underpinned by massive scholarship. And, as reviewers noted, it was quietly revolutionary.' Glen adds that this 'seminal' book 'stressed the interconnections between writers, and brought their writing to life by showing how they were responding to one another and to a larger history'.[59] The Romantics title is still included on university reading lists and, along with the Jane Austen book, is still widely read.

Marilyn Butler was also a committed feminist, and this was strongly reflected in her work. Several of her prime subjects were women, notably, of course, Maria Edgeworth and Jane Austen (and later Mary Wollstonecraft), and she also argued that 'students of literature, like readers of novels, are predominantly female, a demographic fact which male producers of literary criticism forget at their peril'.[60] Butler became closely involved in establishing a paper on women's writing as part of the Oxford English course. In her own career, and in her encouragement of others, she would later be credited with 'having inspired women academics to challenge the barriers that still effectively block female advancement'.[61]

By the mid-1980s, as Marilyn Butler approached the age of fifty, she had good reason to feel that she had succeeded all round. For twenty years she'd had to balance the needs of her family with her studies, her writing and her teaching. All three Butler sons had gone as day boys to Abingdon, the private school south of Oxford, and then they passed the Oxbridge entrance exams, but each chose Cambridge rather than their home-town university.

Now, at last, she would be able to concentrate more fully on her own academic career.

CHAPTER TWELVE

WHICH IS BUTLER? WHICH IS STOKES?

Not everyone was impressed by the new science of psephology that David Butler and his colleagues had created. To some, it took the romance out of elections. Other scholars argued that it belittled the role of the historian, marginalising the contextual knowledge necessary for an appreciation of elections and the build-up to them. The idea that election results could be broken down scientifically – or even forecast – by polls and calculations of swing seemed to undermine the idea that everyone has a democratic choice, which they make for themselves, and to destroy the belief that parties can persuade voters by their campaigns, their past record and policies. Of course, David Butler had long been interested in such questions. Throughout the late 1940s and '50s, whenever asked what he was working on, he would often reply, 'The study of political behaviour.'

But he had formidable critics. The Oxford historian and polemicist A. J. P. Taylor had led the charge, in his column in the *Daily Herald* during the 1955 election. Under the headline 'Down with Psephology', Taylor wrote:

> The whole business of a General Election is run for the benefit of the psephologists. We are like so many ants being observed in a laboratory. The real question in a General Election is no longer

> who is going to govern the country in the next five years, but how accurately the experts can forecast the results. *I'm against this so-called science with its chance and its percentages and its cube rule. We are the people of Britain, not dots on a card* ... it is time for us to kick back. There is a joker in the pack. And it is called human free will. The people of the United States revolted against the Pollsters in 1948. The experts said that Truman was going to lose. So the American people gave him a big majority just to prove them wrong. That will happen here one of these days. And I hope it happens soon. Let the experts prophesy about everything else, but not about you and me.[1] [Emphasis in the original.]

The practitioners of politics – the politicians and campaign organisers – had rather more immediate reasons for suspicion. Many MPs and candidates were uncomfortable with David Butler's ideas about uniform swing, because they suggested a politician's personal qualities made no difference, and that voters were incapable of discriminating between good and bad candidates. Party agents were equally sniffy at the belittling implication that their campaign efforts made little difference to the outcome, and that all would be swept in or out by the unstoppable pendulum of the national swing between the parties.

In December 1959, the Prime Minister Harold Macmillan weighed into the argument when he gave a short speech at the unveiling of a bust of himself at the Oxford Union. Macmillan used similar language to A. J. P. Taylor:

> One of the latest so-called sciences is one called psephology – flourishing in one of those new Colleges – the study of how the people voted last time, how they will vote next time; all apparently capable of mathematical calculation, irrespective of the electoral campaign or the issues at stake.
>
> This sort of political Calvinism (of which Dr Gallup is the

> founder) is only redeemed by the recent discovery that their predetermined anticipations are generally proved wrong. The electors do show, from time to time, a regrettable outbreak of political Free Will.[2]

Macmillan loved mischief, and in making this outburst, albeit light-heartedly, the 'new' college he obviously had in mind was Nuffield, located about 200 yards away. Macmillan may also have known that Britain's most famous psephologist, David Butler, was a cousin of his great Tory rival Rab Butler.

Yet Butler and his co-author Richard Rose could not resist using his lines on the very first page of their study of the general election that Harold Macmillan had won just two months before. They went on to defend their trade. Psephology was not primarily about forecasting, they insisted. 'A psephologist, like a cricket correspondent, should be judged by his success in enhancing his readers' knowledge and understanding of the game far more than by the accuracy of any forecasts he may make. Election majorities are not predictable; and there is no likelihood of their becoming so.'[3]

There may have been elements of playful daring on both sides, since Macmillan's family firm, Macmillan & Co., had been bringing out the Nuffield election studies – complete with 'mathematical calculation' and polling analysis – since 1950. Indeed, Harold Macmillan had still been heavily involved in the firm's work when they commissioned the first Nuffield book they published. And for many years his brother Daniel Macmillan and his son Maurice (by then a Conservative MP) personally handled David Butler and the Nuffield election series.

After Macmillan resigned as Prime Minister in 1963, he returned to the family firm to serve as company chairman for ten years, while they published several more of Butler's books on elections. More important, Macmillan & Co. also commissioned the Butler book that is widely regarded as the most influential and pioneering psephological book ever published in the UK: *Political Change in Britain*. That in turn led to a permanent rolling survey of voting behaviour, the British Election Study, which continues to this day.

It could be argued that its roots lay early in Butler's career. In his introduction to the first Nuffield study he wrote, *The British General Election of 1951*, Butler confessed there were 'two large gaps' in studying elections. The first gap he identified – 'the inner history of the decisions made by the party leaders' – would, of course, be partly be remedied by the interviews that Anthony King and Butler started conducting with senior politicians and their advisers in the early 1960s. Butler's second gap was the 'motives which drove the voters to behave as they did'.[4] In time, Butler would fill that gap too.

The idea for what became *Political Change in Britain* arose while Butler was attending the 1960 annual gathering of the American Political Science Association (APSA) at the University of Michigan in Ann Arbor, accompanied by the Warden of Nuffield, Norman Chester. One of the star turns at that year's APSA conference was a panel of political scientists from the Survey Research Centre (SRC) at Michigan – including Warren Miller and Donald Stokes – who had just published the first detailed analysis of voting behaviour in the United States. The statistical approaches they employed stood in stark contrast to the more narrative style of Butler's own work, published in 1958, *The Study of Political Behaviour*. It was probably the most theoretical book Butler ever wrote, and it examined the various methodological approaches to political science. Interestingly, in the light of what was to come, he expressed scepticism about the possibility of studying behaviour through polling and surveys. 'It is plain that sample surveys have been far more useful in gathering facts than in gathering opinions,' he wrote, and he queried the cost and efficiency of carrying out surveys with people before and after an election if it turned out that only a small number of them had changed their minds.[5]

The SRC in Michigan, however, had been conducting investigations since 1948 into why Americans voted the way they did. The 1948 survey, of just 577 people, redoubled its efforts after the notoriously inaccurate forecasts by pollsters – endorsed at the time by most other experts and commentators – that Thomas Dewey would triumph over Harry Truman. So, having interviewed people before the election, the SRC team went back to question them again afterwards. They carried out larger surveys around the presidential elections of 1952 and 1956, and began biennial surveys in 1958, so that their pioneering book *The American Voter*, published in 1960, was based on interviews and re-interviews with thousands of citizens across the United States over more than a decade. The Michigan team asked detailed questions about people's voting records, the strength of their party identification, their social background and even their families' voting histories. It concluded that long-term forces were most important in partisan identification, not least the way one's parents voted. Such sociological studies were not new – Alfred Kinsey's famous reports into human sexuality in 1948 and 1953 took a similar approach – but this was the first time a panel had been used for electoral politics.

These Michigan Election Studies would radically transform academic, media and public understanding of why Americans voted the way they did. They have continued ever since, known today as the American National Election Studies.

'Why not do a similar exercise in Britain?' Butler suggested to Norman Chester. 'And perhaps do it in conjunction with Michigan?' It would be an obvious activity for the college, a complement to the regular Nuffield election books, which were good at analysing the immediate factors behind individual elections, but weak in terms of understanding how public attitudes changed over long periods of time – even though the Nuffield books always argued long-term factors were more important in determining elections than short bursts of campaigning at the end of each parliament. So, Butler and Chester approached members of the Michigan team to ask if anyone would be willing to bring their expertise to help a similar exercise in Britain. Initially, Warren Miller agreed to assist Nuffield, but eventually Donald Stokes, the most junior member of the group, took on the job.

Donald Stokes – known to most colleagues as Don, but whom Butler invariably called Donald – was a patrician Quaker from Pennsylvania, and two years younger than Butler. Always well-mannered and smartly dressed, he was a lifelong Democrat and a man of the left. But whereas Butler always spoke very fast and seemed in a tearing hurry, Stokes chose his words slowly and with great thought. It summed up their relationship.

Stokes was reluctant at first to become a co-author. He preferred instead to offer his advice and know-how in exchange for access to British research data to use for his own comparative work in Michigan. But gradually Stokes warmed to the idea. The initial working title of the expected book was *The British Voter*, a simple reworking of the American original. Butler's colleague Herbert Nicholas joked over sherry that they call it *Swinging Britain*. The eventual title was less colourful: *Political Change in Britain: Forces Shaping Electoral Choice*.

The project was a prime example of how in the 1960s and 1970s, the years when David Butler was at his peak, he nearly always worked in collaboration with a co-author. Butler believes his work was 'much better done' in partnership with someone else, and that working as part of a couple would spur him on to get the project finished. 'I don't like letting other people down. And if I'm in collaboration, I will make a boast: "I'll let you have this by such and such a time," and though I don't always keep it completely, I don't break the deadlines – these self-imposed ones – by very much.'[6]

With *Political Change in Britain*, the partnership proved extremely successful, producing what is probably the biggest and longest-running survey ever carried out in the British social sciences, a groundbreaking analysis of why voters pick the parties they want to govern us. Yet it came close to disaster, and tested Butler's mastery of deadlines as never before. The book was extremely slow in the making – nine years – slightly longer than it took to fulfil John F. Kennedy's famous pledge, at around the same time, for America to put a man on the moon. Donald Stokes and his family arrived at Nuffield in January 1963, in the midst of the big freeze of that year, and they stayed in north Oxford for nine months. Butler and Stokes then initiated their first survey, in the knowledge that a general election was due by the autumn of 1964.

Stokes returned to Britain for the general elections of 1964 and 1966, staying several months each time, and in 1964 he and Butler even visited Harold Macmillan, the man who had mocked psephology so roundly five years earlier, at the offices of Macmillan & Co. Butler in turn visited Ann Arbor about once a year, generally for two or three weeks on each visit, though for a six-month spell in the second half of 1965.

Stokes's expertise in surveying, statistics and computing was way beyond Butler's own limited knowledge. Butler is always effusive in his debt to Stokes and the leading role he played in their eventual book. 'All the good ideas in it', says Butler,

> came from Donald Stokes, who was just very clever, very courteous, a wonderful American. I was a good manager and book producer. He was a perfectionist … He was such a good and nice man. I never really quarrelled with him, but I got very angry at the way it dragged on.[7]

Between 1963 and 1966, Butler and Stokes commissioned three nationwide studies of voters before and after the two British general elections of that decade, in 1964 and 1966. They conducted 2,009 interviews between 24 May and 13 August 1963; 1,830 interviews between 18 October and 4 December 1964; and 2,086 interviews between 4 April and 4 June 1966.

No fewer than 1,380 of the interviewees took part on all three occasions, which meant that rather than simply obtaining snapshots of how people thought at any one moment – as normal opinions polls did – they were getting the first evolving picture of how views changed over time. The interviews, conducted by the British Market Research Bureau, lasted about an hour, and each involved about 150 questions. The 1963 interviews began with what newspaper people read; attitudes to each of the main parties; the party leaders; the Common Market; nuclear weapons; nationalisation; relations with America; and their views on all sorts of other policies. Then voters were asked whether they saw themselves as Conservative, Labour or Liberal, and how strongly they did so. Next came questions about how their parents had voted in the past, and how they themselves had voted at the previous election, in 1959. Were they active in politics? Could they name their MP? (Fifty-five per cent of respondents could.) What class did they think they belonged to? When did they leave school? Did anyone in the family belong to a union? And what was their religion?

The 1964 and 1966 surveys posed similar questions, but also new ones tailored to the elections in those two years.[8] The replies were coded by graduate students at Nuffield and punched onto Hollerith computer cards, which were then sent to Ann Arbor for detailed computer analysis by Donald Stokes and his colleagues at the Survey Research Centre.

This kind of panel survey – returning repeatedly to the same group of people – wasn't entirely new to British political science. Around the 1950 general election, a team from the LSE had interviewed a panel of voters in Greenwich in south-east London about their political preferences. A similar exercise was carried out in North East Bristol in 1951 and 1955. But these were local panels, and it was impossible to say how far the findings in these places were representative of Britain as a whole. Now Butler and Stokes had embarked on a nationwide panel survey.

While David Butler – and many of his colleagues – regard the resulting book, *Political Change in Britain*, as his greatest work, it was also probably his most frustrating to produce. The battles he waged over several years to get the book finished illustrate some of Butler's weaknesses as an author – he was dependent on Stokes both for designing the survey questions and for the subsequent hardcore statistical and polling analysis. Yet without Butler's leadership – cajoling and disciplining Stokes, while also placating their exasperated publishers – the book might never have reached the shelves. Donald Stokes was temperamentally unsuited to deadlines and wanted continually to strive for a more perfect product, sitting on chapters indefinitely while tinkering and redrafting them. For Butler, in contrast, deadlines were important; he had a reputation for sticking to them, and he felt they should be respected even sometimes at the expense of quality. Donald Stokes had to juggle the book with numerous other commitments – summer schools, his normal teaching, and other writing. But Butler probably had an even more diverse and busy workload, which included two volumes on the 1964 and 1966 elections, the first three editions of *British Political Facts*, and, in 1967, his first trip to Australia (which lasted six months), as well as the responsibilities of Butler's new family – all three of his sons were born while the book was in progress.

It was also the biggest project that David Butler had ever undertaken, with at least ten research assistants on both sides of the Atlantic, many of whom were coding data. Several private firms were employed on the highly expensive task of gathering and processing the data. This led to disputes over billing, and the project was further hindered when some data cards disappeared. Nor were matters helped by having two publishers – Macmillan in Britain and their sister firm, St Martin's Press, in New York. And the manuscript was constantly buffeted and remoulded by extensive feedback from pre-publication readers in both countries. In Britain, these included the Cabinet minister Richard Crossman; the pollster Humphrey Taylor; Butler's Nuffield colleagues Philip Williams and

A. H. 'Chelly' Halsey; and his co-author on the election books, Anthony King. All this was being done in a world without email, text messages or word-processing, and where substantial exchanges depended on airmail letters, which could take a week to cross the Atlantic. The phone bill for David Butler's room in Nuffield was huge.

Though most chapters seem to have been drafted by Donald Stokes, it would be wrong to assume the authorship primarily belonged to him. There is plenty of evidence that both men made substantial contributions to the writing, and Butler also provided key research questions, perspective and background context.

Originally, Butler and Stokes hoped to complete their manuscript by May 1966. Then Harold Wilson called an election for 31 March that year, which inevitably caused several months' delay and prompted another round of interviews with voters. Gradually the book slipped later and later. 'I must confess my dismay at what is happening to our timetable,' Butler wrote to Stokes at the start of February 1967 when he had received drafting notes from Stokes on only one of the seven chapters he was expecting. 'I cannot but be filled with the blackest forebodings about what, at this rate, is going to befall all our hopes for completing the project.'[9]

A week later, having heard from an American contact that Stokes had gone to Japan without telling him, Butler wrote in despair, and secretly, to Stokes's Michigan colleague Warren Miller about 'a situation which I find very shattering', suggesting that the whole very costly enterprise might be in jeopardy. 'I am very deeply upset,' Butler told Miller.

> A collaboration must be a collaboration – Donald seems to me to have violated the decencies of trust and frankness almost beyond recall … I am answerable to Nuffield … for the expenditure of very large sums of money … I really have to decide on my whole future timetable – and it seems impossible to arrange anything in terms of any assurance from Donald.[10]

A fortnight on, Butler wrote to Stokes setting out what he saw as the fundamental problem between them: 'The difference between us is that you enjoy doing things and I enjoy having done them; I have a deeper sense of obligation to time and to people, you have a deeper sense of obligation to academic perfection.'[11] Stokes, keen to build a book of great importance, clearly thought the manuscript needed substantial revision and felt a 'deepening of the argument would often be required if the book were really to be faithful to the project in which we had invested much'.[12] Butler feared revision might simply spoil the text and was keen to respect their commitment to a new deadline of spring 1967. 'Obviously I like deadlines and find them productive,' he cuttingly observed. 'You dislike them and find them counter-productive.'[13]

The bickering continued. It was always very courteous, though, with the authors taking trouble to enquire in their letters about the well-being of each other's families. Stokes regretted that they had ever 'gotten into the business of deadlines' and 'the sense of dishonoured pledges which you express so strongly'.[14] Butler started to lay down the law. They had to finish by the end of June 1967, he said. Continuing work on the manuscript beyond mid-summer 'cannot be contemplated', Butler insisted. 'I have only one life to live and I am not prepared to go to Australia with further drafting hanging over my head.'[15]

June came, and June went, and Butler did have to cope with further revisions while in Australia. Stokes admitted the thought of 'having a substantially finished manuscript by summer's end' had 'evaporated'.[16] Butler replied that the delays meant he had 'lost all moral authority to bully' Macmillan over his other project, *British Political Facts*, on which the publishers had made serious printing errors in the proofs.[17] By December 1967, they were talking about finishing the following March. Yet by February 1968, that had slipped to the end of 1968, although the publishers knew the fault wasn't Butler's. 'If the chain has a weak link, then it is Stokes – and the fact of his living overseas,' wrote Tim Farmiloe of Macmillan to Phillip Martin of St Martin's Press in New York. 'We know from our experience ... that we can rely with complete confidence on Butler to keep to a very tight schedule.'[18]

In the end, an almost-complete manuscript was submitted only in February 1969. By now the schedule was so tight that Butler and his assistant Phyllis Thorburn had to drive over to the printers in Bungay in Suffolk on a Sunday to deliver the corrected index and check the revised proofs. *Political Change in Britain* was finally published simultaneously in Britain and America in October 1969.

The bill for the research work was enormous – £50,000, or £825,000 at 2018 prices – largely met by Nuffield College, with help from the Nuffield Foundation (a separate institution from the college), and from other research foundations.

The book demolished many of the assumptions that had dominated academic and media analysis of elections since 1945: for instance, that people are more inclined to vote Conservative as they grow older; and that the deaths of older voters and the advent of new generations of younger voters have a negligible effect on election results. Before Butler and Stokes's work, nobody knew how many people changed their votes between elections, though the overall party totals, of course, suggested the picture was quite stable. The pair demonstrated that there was, in fact, a considerable amount of 'churn' between elections, and that the final outcome was the net change after millions of people had switched their party support in opposite directions, in many cases cancelling each other out.

For years, people had argued that class was by far the most important factor in voting choice, and that the better-off half of the population clearly voted Conservative, while the worse-off plainly voted Labour. Butler and Stokes examined the concept of class in British politics from many different angles, and in huge depth. 'Neither prior nor subsequent studies of the class alignment came near to the richness of their treatment,' said the academic William Miller more than thirty years later.[19]

Butler and Stokes argued that class had peaked as a factor in voting. They also claimed that how somebody's parents had voted was, in fact, a better pointer than class in determining votes. In a decade when teenage rebellion was all the rage, it was hard to appreciate, they argued, how much people's politics were influenced by what their parents did. Butler and Stokes's surveys showed that where people were brought up in homes in which both parents voted Labour, or both voted Conservative, almost 90 per cent of them voted the same way their parents had voted when they were growing up. These habits, passed from parent to child even in the face of class traditions, were the most powerful indicator of political allegiance. The famous lines from Gilbert and Sullivan's comic opera *Iolanthe* 'That every boy and every gal / That's born into the world alive / Is either a little Liberal / Or else a little Conservative!' held true, they said, almost ninety years after the song was written (albeit with Labour replacing the Liberals).

One of the most radical moves Butler and Stokes made was to explore the effect of births and deaths on the politics of the electorate. First, there was what they called 'differential fertility' – varying birth rates among different groups. Families with strong Labour traditions tended to have more children than households where the habit was to vote Conservative. This was not simply a matter of class, they stated, for Conservative working-class couples tended to have 25 per cent fewer children on average than Labour working-class families.

Their other new concept was 'selective death', and the fact that groups which tended to favour the Conservatives – middle-class people, and women – also tended to live longer. This, they calculated, meant that Conservatives on average had the chance to vote in thirteen general elections over their lifetimes, but Labour supporters in only twelve contests.

The book was much anticipated, and not just in academic circles, but the pressure and sense of expectation may have caused the product to be oversold. *Political Change in Britain* was heralded a month ahead of publication with a substantial 2,000-word summary of Butler and Stokes's work – under their bylines – spread over a page and a half of the *Sunday Times*. This article argued, a lot more forcefully than the book did itself, that long-term demographic changes in the electorate – the death of elderly Conservatives and the coming of age of young socialists – would tend over time to favour Labour. As an example of this trend, they maintained that only 14 per cent of Labour's success in returning to power in 1964 could be attributed to people who voted Conservative in 1959 switching to Labour five years later. The turnover of the electorate through deaths and new voters, in contrast, accounted for 40 per cent of Labour's success. Indeed, they argued that 'if the 1964 vote had been cast by those who composed the electorate in 1959, the Conservatives would have been returned for the fourth successive time with a quite adequate majority'.[20] This trend, Butler and Stokes asserted, would continue for another thirty years, as most of the people due to die in the '70s, '80s and '90s would have grown up in the early twentieth century, before Labour had established itself as an equal player with the Conservatives, and so this generation had been less likely to inherit the habit of voting Labour. So, the year-by-year demographic transformation of the electorate in Labour's favour, they maintained, was 'bound to continue'. Butler and Stokes were careful to stress that this phenomenon did not 'predict disaster for the Conservatives', but the headline above their article – LABOUR'S SECRET STRENGTH – suggested otherwise. That headline was probably written by a sub-editor on the paper, not the authors themselves, along with the summary that their book predicted that 'these underlying demographic changes will increasingly favour Labour'.[21]

The newspaper did much to promote the article, and Butler was surprised, when walking through Piccadilly Circus one Saturday, to see his name on a *Sunday Times* billboard. What seems to have happened is that the newspaper originally paid to serialise extracts from the book, but when they read it and saw how academic the text was, the editors realised it would be hard to find suitable sections to reprint for a mass audience. So instead they persuaded the authors to write a summary of their findings, and in the process the points about Labour's rosy future were pumped up.

With hindsight, of course, the headline, summary and article look extremely rash, if not foolhardy. Only eight months later, in June 1970, the Conservatives returned to power, despite a large influx of younger people onto the voting register with the 1969 reduction in the voting age from twenty-one to eighteen. Indeed, in the seven general elections held over the twenty-five years after 1969, Labour won the popular vote only once – in October 1974 – and for much of that period, during the four successive Thatcher/Major victories of 1979 to 1992, there was much talk of Labour being in terminal decline rather than on an inexorable rise. Butler and Stokes's analysis, and the presentation and interpretation of it, serves as a warning to those who have predicted in 2017 and 2018 that the steady death each year of Conservative and pro-Brexit older voters will soon produce a strong and permanent Labour majority among the electorate, who will also want to return to the European Union.

The *Sunday Times* article prompted a satirical piece by John Wells in *The Spectator* in which he combined Butler with the zoologist Desmond Morris, who had just published *The Human Zoo*, a sequel to *The Naked Ape*, his immensely popular book on human behaviour:

> Best-selling author Dr Desmond 'Fatty' Butler, of the Nuffield Free Money Distribution Centre at Oxford, is probably as well known for his television appearances during general elections as 'David', the scatter-brained slide-rule expert, as he is for books,

> in which he compares the human being to a machine, dwelling at length on the mechanics of sexual and emotional response, and winning for himself lavish serialisation in the more colourful Sunday papers. In his latest work, 'The Human Tool', published by Accles and Pollock at 300s [shillings], Dr Butler paints an exhilarating picture of a major Labour renaissance during the next few years, culminating in the total destruction of all rival parties by the end of the century … By the year 2000, with the Labour family producing an average of 6.35 children a year more than the comparable Conservative family, the Socialists should have a majority of 613 seats in Parliament. That the Labour Party should continue in such circumstances to advocate abortion and the contraceptive pill merely underlines a truth to which psephologists have drawn attention again and again – that politicians know very little about politics.[22]

Perhaps because of the inaccurate representation – or 'hyping' – of the book through the *Sunday Times* article and its promotion, *Political Change in Britain* got off to a terrible start when it finally came out four weeks later. On the day of publication, the Conservative shadow Chancellor Iain Macleod famously savaged the book in a long review in *The Times*. 'It will give birth to a hundred PhD dissertations and a thousand footnotes. It is admirably presented,' Macleod wrote. The effort, however, 'that has been put into documenting the obvious is enough to make angels weep … my verdict is uncompromising. It is of negligible interest except to its own private world.'

Macleod was unhappy that Butler and Stokes's three surveys – in 1963, 1964 and 1966 – were all conducted at a time when things were looking 'disastrous' for the Conservatives (though the authors acknowledged this problem in the book). Similar research in late 1966, after devaluation in 1967 and after the Budgets of 1968 and 1969, Macleod argued, would have produced very different results – a claim that had merit. The work was a 'temple' built on 'sand', he went on, which partly depended on loaded questions. He believed the authors were far too reliant on opinion polls when polls had often shown themselves to be inaccurate, and 'any rookie political agent of either party could have told them' some of their conclusions. 'I think little of this work,' Macleod concluded. 'I offer Abraham Lincoln's comment on a book: "People who like this sort of thing will find this the sort of thing they like."'[23] Five days later, the *Times* political editor David Wood seemed so embarrassed by what Macleod had written in his paper that he rode to Butler and Stokes's defence. 'The academic growth industry of political science in alliance with opinion polling', Wood wrote:

> has put all politicians in its debt … they have fashioned techniques of electoral measurement which are not only far superior to the guesswork and hunch of members of the Macleod school like me, but which slowly progress towards unveiling the mystery of the human forces [to] make and unmake governments … After reading Dr Butler and Professor Stokes I am much nearer to understanding my trade than I should have been unaided.[24]

Six years later, the political columnist David Watt accused Iain Macleod of 'spluttering like an Indian colonel' and claimed the politician subsequently admitted his outburst had been 'motivated in part by anger at a recent article by David Butler, apparently hostile to the Tory Party'.[25]

Gerald Kaufman, then a member of Harold Wilson's 'kitchen cabinet', was even less kind than Macleod. Kaufman explained that seven years earlier he'd tried to 'put paid … to the public credibility' of Butler and 'his psephological sibling Dr Robert McKenzie' with a long article in the *New Statesman* entitled 'The Witch Doctors'.[26] Since then, he admitted, he'd been 'won over' to them. But *Political Change in Britain*, Kaufman wrote in *The Listener*, contained 'some of the most turgidly indigestible prose ever assembled between two hard covers', and 'breaking up at intervals this impenetrably massed letterpress are diagrams of an almost uniquely incomprehensible nature'.[27] The *Economist* review condemned its 'disappointingly turgid prose'.[28]

More cutting still was the review in *The Observer*, simply because of who wrote it. The book would have 'a seminal influence' on the study of politics, said Bob McKenzie, but he found it 'highly unsatisfactory'. He thought Butler and Stokes had exaggerated the benefits to Labour of Conservative voters dying out year by year, and he found the conclusions 'extremely disappointing'. The authors, McKenzie said, had made no attempt to give a 'theory' of electoral behaviour or political change.[29]

The early reviews weren't all negative, however. Under the heading 'Make a Baby for Labour', Alan Watkins in the *New Statesman* called it 'the most important contribution to the study of elections published in Britain since the war', though he then added that it contained 'more pointless little diagrams than I have seen since my five-year-old daughter brought her drawing book home'.[30] 'With this book the study of voting behaviour in this country has at last come of age,' wrote the Labour MP David Marquand. 'Everyone interested in British society or politics must at all costs read it.'[31] For the *TLS* it was a work of 'high importance and lasting value'.[32]

More light-hearted, though highly pertinent, was a satirical sonnet written by Christopher Hollis for *The Spectator*, asking which author contributed exactly what to the book, with the last four lines especially telling:

> Which is Butler? Which is Stokes?
> Which of them put in the jokes?
> And the statistics, which again?
> Nuffield or Michigan?
> Alas, alas, and no one knows

Whose the jargon in the prose
When the jokes are rather subtler,
Is it Stokes? Or is it Butler?
Who first dared survey the range
Of political chop and change?
And will the pattern always be
Just the sort that they foresee?
Youth, says Shakespeare, won't endure.
What's to come is still unsure.[33]

Academic reviewers were rather more positive, particularly in America. 'An absolutely unavoidable work for anyone seriously interested in its subject,' wrote Richard Lyman, the president of Stanford University.[34] The distinguished French political scientist Jean Blondel called it a 'landmark in the understanding of the "forces which shape electoral change" … an almost perfect example of rigorous analysis … where both survey findings and statistical techniques are used with great elegance'.[35] In 1970, *Political Change in Britain* won the American Political Science Association's annual Woodrow Wilson Foundation Award for the best book on government, politics or international affairs. 'It will leave its mark for many years to come,' read the citation at the award dinner in Los Angeles, where the authors received a prize of $1,000.[36]

They were in esteemed company, for previous winners of the award included James MacGregor Burns, Henry Kissinger and Richard Neustadt (for his book *Presidential Power*). Nowadays, the work remains one of only sixteen books for which there is an individual entry in *The Oxford Companion to Twentieth-Century British Politics*.[37]

Nonetheless, almost five years after it was first published, *Political Change* was the subject of a damning 45-page academic analysis in the *European Journal of Political Research*. What made the critique all the more serious was that it came from 28-year-old Ivor Crewe, who had been a colleague of David Butler's at Nuffield between 1969 and 1971, before moving to Essex University. Indeed, Crewe had even co-written an appendix to the 1970 election book, and during the campaign travelled with Butler to observe activities in north-west England, where the pair stayed overnight with Crewe's parents in Didsbury. Crewe argued that 'the conceptual framework' that Butler and Stokes adopted in *Political Change in Britain* was 'inadequate, indeed distinctly unhelpful' when it came to other forms of political change, which Crewe said their book had 'chosen to ignore'.

The three most important changes cited by Crewe included the decline in turnout, a fall in the combined support for the two main parties, and a growing volatility in swings between them. For example, in 1951, there were only two seats in which the number of non-voters exceeded the vote of the winning candidate. By 1970, that had grown to eighty-nine seats. In 1951, almost 80 per cent of the electorate voted Labour or Conservative; in 1970, it was less than 65 per cent. In the space of just twenty years, the established parties had become far less trusted, and these trends were to continue very markedly over the next four decades. 'It is the loss of popular appeal by *both* parties', said Crewe, 'rather than the relative appeal of each which stands in need of explanation', and this, Crewe argued, was 'a more important political change than the one on which Butler and Stokes concentrated'.[38]

Butler and Stokes, Crewe claimed, had failed to explain either the gradual fall in turnout in elections or 'the growing flux in party support over recent years'. Nor, he said, had they provided 'a systematic analysis of the floating voter', nor analysed why some voters rather than others switch parties.[39]

It wasn't just the powerful nature of Crewe's critique – under the bold title 'Do Butler and Stokes Really Explain *Political Change in Britain*?' – which was striking, but the way he carried out his attack. Crewe admits to having had 'all the experience and maturity of a 25-year-old. It was arrogant of me to write it. It is perfectly understandable that he should have been annoyed.'[40] Although Butler calls Crewe's article 'a slashing attack', he says he and Stokes never quarrelled with Crewe, and that they remained friends over the years.[41]

Ivor Crewe's article proved rather more prescient than Butler and Stokes's forecasts of gradually increasing Labour strength. It was published in the year the revived Liberal Party obtained almost a fifth of the vote in the February 1974 election, and other trends identified by Crewe would continue for the next few decades. Support among the electorate as a whole for the Conservatives and Labour combined eventually fell to just 44.6 per cent in 2015 (though revived to 56.7 per cent in 2017 with the decline of Ukip). Turnout would reach a low point of 59.4 per cent in 2001, though gradually recovered after that, and reached 69.0 per cent in 2017.

Today, however, Ivor Crewe – now Sir Ivor, a former Vice-Chancellor of Essex University and a major figure in the 'Essex school' of British political science – acknowledges a big debt to Butler and Stokes. '*Political Change in Britain* shaped my generation, and the way we thought about elections. It was pivotal … Modern political science is descended from Butler and Stokes … But if it hadn't been for the Michigan School, Butler couldn't have written *Political Change in Britain*.'[42]

In 1969, Butler and Stokes had obtained a major grant of £35,760 from the Social Science Research Council – the equivalent of about £250,000 today – to enable them to continue their voting surveys beyond the 1970 election. As a result, the second edition of *Political Change* came out in January 1975, though it went to press well before the October 1974 general election. The new volume argued that social class was rapidly declining as an influence on the way people voted. They also tempered their assertion from 1969 that long-term demographic trends favoured Labour, with more emphasis on the greater volatility of the electorate, a greater willingness among voters to move away, at least for a while, from their natural home party. This was combined in the new work with more stress on upward social mobility – a lot more working-class people were becoming middle class than moving the other way.

Butler and Stokes said that their work in the 1960s and early 1970s should be merely the start of periodic, sustained research, with a rolling programme of Michigan-style interviews with voters at regular intervals. So, they pioneered a process which has continued for almost sixty years and is the longest-running survey in the social sciences in the UK, what John Curtice calls 'part of the central architecture of the academic study of voting behaviour in the UK'.[43] Like the TV series *Doctor Who*, which started around the same time, it has changed its cast at regular intervals and taken several guises. In the early 1970s, David Butler happily relinquished the survey, and in 1974 it was taken on by Ivor Crewe and Bo Särlvik at Essex University, who formally called it the British Election Study (BES), and analysed trends around the two elections of 1974 and that of 1979. The 1983 book based on Crewe and Särlvik's work, *Decade of Dealignment*, was a deliberate riposte to Butler and Stokes, and the Essex pair published several articles along similar lines.[44] Earlier, Crewe had used some of their conclusions – that party and class ties had grown significantly weaker – to encourage Labour MPs to found a new centre party, and this eventually led to the new Social Democratic Party (SDP).

In 1983, the BES was awarded to a team loosely based at Oxford, comprising Tony Heath, Roger Jowell and John Curtice. They worked in cooperation with a body called Social and Community Planning Research (the forerunner of NatCen) to produce the book *How Britain Votes*.[45]

From 2001 to 2010, the BES moved back to Essex, under David Sanders and Paul Whiteley, who worked with a team at the University of Dallas in Texas. More recently, the BES has been run by Jane Green and Ed Fieldhouse of Manchester University, leading a consortium which includes Nuffield and Nottingham (though in 2018, Green was appointed to take David Butler's old fellowship at Nuffield). The modern BES has carried out extensive surveys before and after the general elections of 2015 and 2017, the Scottish referendum of 2014 and the European referendum of 2016. The survey database now contains a wealth of data from the past fifteen British general elections, which is made available to all scholars.

Butler and Stokes's work was truly pioneering. In 2010, the Political Studies Association (PSA) in Britain conducted a poll of members to decide on the most important book published in their field since the PSA was founded in 1950. *Political Change in Britain* was declared the winner.

David Butler always says *Political Change in Britain* was 'much the best and most long-lasting book with which I have been associated'. The problem was that Butler's greatest intellectual achievement would always be qualified by questions about how much he owed to his extraordinary professional marriage with Donald Stokes. Butler himself is generous in expressing his debt to Stokes, who died in 1997 at the age of sixty-nine. He was the 'cleverest man I have ever worked with', says Butler, 'and the honours which the book has won must be attributed to him, an intellectual perfectionist'.[46]

In his obituary of Donald Stokes, Anthony King summed up the collaboration between the pair. Butler's motto, he wrote, 'was the wartime engineer's "The second best tomorrow". Stokes' seemed to be, "Perfection, even if it takes forever." The combination was perfect. Stokes stalled. Butler nagged. Together they produced a classic. Neither could have done it without the other.'[47]

CHAPTER THIRTEEN

AN ENGLISH DON ABROAD

David Butler calculates – in a typically Butler-ish way – that he has spent at least five years of his life outside Britain. From 1947 until the 1960s, most of his foreign ventures were to the United States, with long spells in America in 1947–48 and 1955–56, almost annual trips for summer schools or lecture tours, and substantial visits to observe most of the presidential election contests. He also enjoyed a few brief trips to Ottawa.

The advent of a wife and children restricted Butler's foreign travel, and after 1962 he vowed not to spend more than a month overseas without taking the family with him. In July 1967, the Butlers set out on a journey to the other side of the world that was substantially to change and expand David Butler's career and academic outlook and enabled him to export his expertise to two leading members of the Commonwealth, first to Australia and later to India.

Butler had been invited to the federal capital, Canberra, to become a visiting fellow at the Australian National University (ANU), one of the country's top universities. So David took Marilyn and the three boys too, which can't have been easy, since Edmund was barely six months old and Daniel and Gareth were only three and two respectively, but they also took the family nanny, Ann Read.

ANU provided the Butlers with a flat in Canberra, and Marilyn was appointed a part-time lecturer in the university's English department. 'I didn't expect to fall for Australia or its way of life,'

Butler wrote later. 'Yet that is what happened ... we found ourselves entranced.'[1]

Although Butler loved US politics and regarded America as his second home, he felt comparative studies of the British and US political systems didn't really work – there were too many differences between the parliamentary and presidential models of government. Australia was another matter. 'I suddenly had an enormous enlightenment,' he said, 'because comparative politics *did* work. As long as I wasn't an imperial figure trying to impose British answers on Australia, British questions were good questions to ask there.'[2] He quickly acquired a feel and fascination for Australian politics, rapidly grasped what was going on, devoured the history, and picked up the names of the key players. During the 1970s, when the British economy was in trouble, Butler even spoke of emigrating there if things got really bad.

Butler had been encouraged to go to Canberra by two men who had been at Nuffield and would go on to become senior figures in Australia. Creighton Burns had been at Oxford in the early 1950s, where he helped Butler on his election books, driving him around the country to conduct interviews, and had also been one of his studio assistants on BBC election night in the early '50s. He went back to a university career in Australia, before becoming a senior correspondent and, later, editor of the *Melbourne Age*.

But David's Butler's official sponsor at ANU was Don Aitkin, one of his Oxford protégés who had similarly helped with both the BBC results programme in 1964 and the subsequent election book. Aitkin then volunteered to do computer coding on the Butler and Stokes election survey and ended up working for the project for a few months in Michigan. Aitkin had ambitious plans for the same kind of study in Australia, based on the questions devised by Butler and Stokes. Aitkin's work developed into the Australian National Political Attitudes Survey, in which he questioned three cohorts of voters between 1967 and 1979. Their rolling studies continue today as the Australian Election Study, an accumulated archive covering almost as long a time span as the studies in the United States and the UK.

Don Aitkin was becoming something of a 'telly don' himself in his native country, combining academic work with broadcasting, especially during elections. And Aitkin would provide his mentor with introductions to many people in both Australian politics and the media. With Canberra as his base, Butler moved around the state capitals, rapidly immersing himself in the country's politics, giving seminars and lectures comparing the two systems, and visiting the political science departments of the dozen or so Australian universities that existed at that time. 'What smoothed his passage everywhere', says Aitkin, 'was his appetite to know, and his self-confidence, plus, increasingly, his connections. I was surprised at how many people he knew whom I didn't know.'[3] He also slotted in a fortnight's tour of New Zealand universities, organised by his Nuffield colleague Austin Mitchell.

Burns and Aitkin were examples of how David Butler's impressive list of contacts had partly been assembled through the Antipodean Rhodes Scholars and other graduate students he had met and taught over the years. John Stone, one of his PPE students at New College in the early 1950s, was now rising rapidly within the Australian Treasury (where he eventually became the top civil servant). Another Oxford contact was Rupert Murdoch, whom he'd met occasionally when the Australian was studying PPE at Worcester College in the early 1950s, and on the 1967 trip the Butlers drove out to Cruden Farm, the Murdoch family's beautiful country house and garden, an hour's drive south of Melbourne. By 1967, Murdoch had launched his new upmarket newspaper *The Australian* but was still on the left of politics. Sitting at the Murdoch dinner table, Butler felt slightly uncomfortable. 'I really was a fascist beast,' he jokes. 'I am middle-of-the road, and was then middle-of-the-road, but Murdoch and his then wife [Anna], and my dear wife, were certainly to the left of me.'[4] A year or two later, Butler thought of inviting Murdoch to a college feast at Nuffield, but thought the better of it when he saw how Murdoch had turned the *Melbourne Truth* newspaper into what he regarded as a scandal sheet.

The Australian political system was originally based on the Westminster model, of course, but then developed in its own ways. Yet not much had been written about it. As with British election statistics twenty-five years earlier, Butler found himself to be something of a pioneer, and had the area almost to himself. Having read the basic and limited literature on Australian government which was then available, Butler had the 'challenge in a fairly empty field, to ask basic questions: how do you do this?'[5]

He frequently did what he had done so successfully in America twenty years before: simply ring people up out of the blue and ask to go and see them. Few said no. 'David Butler's status went before him,' says the Australian psephologist Malcolm Mackerras.[6] And it probably helped, too, that Butler was an independent outsider. 'I found it very easy to talk to people,' he says. 'Many people outside Canberra had a distaste for Canberra, a quiet contempt for it, and a contempt for the study of Australian politics.'[7]

It was an 'exciting, mind-blowing time', and especially interesting as Australia had not long emerged from the sixteen-year rule of Liberal leader Sir Robert Menzies, Australia's longest-serving Prime Minister. The country was starting to loosen its ties with Britain, following the Wilson government's withdrawal of forces from East of Suez, and the UK's attempts to join the Common Market. Canberra itself was only just fully developed physically as the nation's capital, with the flooding of the artificial Lake Burley Griffin in 1964.

David Butler was exploring a country of great size, but of only 12 million people (half the population today), where the study of government and politics was fairly primitive compared with Britain and America. Perhaps, Butler suggested a few years later, it was because 'so many Australians still cherish the illusion that theirs is only a small country' and not worth bothering about. And yet, Butler concluded, 'it is easy to find interesting and original things to say about it'.[8]

Butler immediately found himself in popular demand. It was an era when Australia was still much more deferential towards Britain – the 'Mother Country' – and well-disposed towards British visitors, as exemplified by Menzies, who had famously described himself as 'British to the bootstraps'. 'It was a plus to be a Pom,' says Butler, 'whereas later on it was not a particular plus at all.'[9]

It was a period when Australia still lacked self-confidence and suffered from what Australians call 'cultural cringe', the phenomenon first identified in the 1950s whereby they feel a sense of inferiority, and assume that anything produced in their own country is of lower quality to work produced in Britain or Europe.

Australian universities and broadcasters felt honoured by the presence of an English don who'd come to observe their political system and elections. And Butler became a regular commentator for the ABC – the Australian Broadcasting Commission (later Corporation), on its evening news analysis programme *This Day Tonight*, which liked interviewing foreign commentators because they could often make more pungent observations than their own in-house and domestic pundits.

Just before the Butlers were due to return to England, in December 1967, David agreed to speak to *This Day Tonight*'s aggressive young Canberra reporter Mike Willesee for a kind of farewell assessment. Now that he'd been studying Australian politics for six months, Willesee asked Butler, how would he compare an Australian political XI with a British one? Butler replied something to the effect, he recalls, that 'You clobber us at tennis and usually beat us at cricket, but I'd back a British XI to win at politics.'[10]

So who were the 'bright lights', Willesee asked, and whom would he pick for an Australian political XI? Butler threw up a few well-known names, but Willesee immediately spotted that he had omitted several others, not least the Prime Minister, Harold Holt. 'One thing I have learnt in Australia', Butler replied, 'is to use the word "rubbish" as a verb. I do not wish to rubbish people on TV.'[11]

'Come off it, David,' Willesee insisted. 'What do you think of the Prime Minister?' Butler replied that he was a 'profound disappointment', adding that Holt was 'not quite up to the full scale of the job'.[12]

Butler apologised to the ABC producers afterwards for being so forthright. The TV company didn't mind, of course: they thought his remarks were excellent.

> But I knew that there was trouble. I was, briefly, to become unwittingly famous. That evening, and over the next 48 hours, I had thirty doorstep and telephone interviews. The headline stories, to my surprise, were not 'INSOLENT POM INSULTS P.M.', but 'BRITISH EXPERT SAYS P.M. NO GOOD.' It seemed that I was the little boy who said out loud that the Emperor had no clothes.[13]

Butler tried to explain to journalists afterwards that he had been speaking in the spirit of being questioned as a sports or drama critic, but also elaborated that he 'had never seen Mr Holt do anything just right'. The nearest, he said, had been in Holt's TV address two weeks earlier explaining his decision for Australia to follow Britain in devaluing its currency.

Just nine days later, Harold Holt suddenly vanished. He had been swimming in rough seas off the coast of Victoria. His body was never found, prompting a flurry of conspiracy theories as to what had happened, though the consensus is that Holt, an experienced swimmer, had simply misjudged how dangerous the water was. Speculation that he had committed suicide was dismissed as out of character. The first David Butler heard of the tragedy was while stopping in India on his way home, 'and telegrams arrived from friends, suggesting that I had driven him to it'.[14] 'I don't think I felt guilty,' says Butler. 'He'd just over-rated himself as a swimmer.'[15]

It was a highly unfortunate episode, although nobody seems publicly and seriously to have suggested that Butler's remarks drove Holt to take his own life. But the interview had the unintended consequence of adding to David Butler's fame in Australia. After all, many people, especially journalists and academics, had shared his low opinion of Harold Holt. Only they hadn't dared say so in public.

There had been no full federal election during Butler's first visit to Australia, only a half-election to the Australian upper house, the Senate, in November 1967, when Butler was employed as an expert on the ABC's results programme. This wasn't easy, for the ABC usual analyst was jealous and suspicious, and kicked up quite a row. It was wrong, he argued, for an English visitor to be commenting on the results. Afterwards, Butler wrote a report for the ABC on the televising of Australian elections, drawing on his experience of Britain and America, in the vein of the reports he had written for Grace Wyndham Goldie at the BBC in the 1950s. But Butler's analysis for the ABC, which he also published in an academic journal, was more hard-hitting, with much emphasis on how *not* to cover an election. Although it offended some established broadcasters, Butler had the backing of Don Aitkin and several other young Australian academics, who felt their country's approach to elections was years behind the kind of professional and insightful coverage they'd seen in Britain and America.

Butler would return to Australia to observe each of the fourteen full elections over the next three decades, from 1969 to 2001 (Australian elections occur more often because each parliament lasts a maximum of three years). In 1969, he again worked for the ABC results programme, on his first Australian federal election, but for later contests over a couple of decades Butler became the in-house boffin on election night for various commercial stations. 'That's what paid for my air fares,' he recalls.[16] One excerpt of the Network 10 results programme from the 1983 election shows Butler reeling off the names of crucial seats in full flow as if he had lived Down Under all his life, and peppering his remarks with details of candidates and aspects of their local constituencies in the way that was so familiar to British viewers. After each programme he would again spend time – often on the plane home – writing to a senior figure at the TV outlet for whom he had been working, explaining where the broadcast had succeeded, but also with plenty of suggestions for improvement.

Butler would often be treated as a mini-celebrity, with the occasional public mockery that entails. This report comes from the anonymous 'Gang Gang' diary column in the *Canberra Times* in 1977:

> There are lots of ghastly things about Australian elections, but to me the most unspeakable spectacle is always that moment when Dr David Butler, the Cambridge [*sic*] psephologist, arrives at Sydney Airport and is besieged by idiot Australian reporters all asking him who is going to win.
>
> This is cultural cringe at its worst.
>
> At the moment of his arrival, the greying don knows less about the election than most Australian household pets do, and far, far less than anyone of the umpteen Australian political scientists who are keeping a lonely vigil in Australian universities, their noses pressed against their office windows as they hanker for the glimpse of an approaching journalist come to plumb their expertise.
>
> Dr Butler comes to all our federal elections, bless his heart.
>
> His arrival at an Australian airport guarantees that there is to be an election, just as surely as the appearance of a vulture is an infallible sign that some poor creature is about to give up the ghost.[17]

And it was true that on some of these early visits, Butler might find reporters greeting him at the airport, seeking his wisdom on the coming contest. One reporter, Ian Warden – who was probably the anonymous 'Gang Gang' diarist – suggested in the same paper that Butler seemed only to have brought one blazer on his trip. 'I have seen him several times and he has always worn this rather unpleasant orangey-brown creation.' Worse followed.

> I can also reveal that he wore sandals, with socks! Yes, truly! Would I tell you a lie? What a nation we are, letting an Englishman who wears sandals with socks come and lecture to us about our elections! Put him on the first plane home. That's what I say. And his sandals too...[18]

Warden was, in fact, himself an immigrant from Britain.

Over the years, Ian Warden seems to have mellowed and gradually grown fond of the English visitor. In 1987, he reported on Butler's presence in the National Tally Room, the hall in Canberra where the Australian Electoral Commission collates all the results as they are declared. 'This is my ninth Australian federal election,' Butler told him, and Warden noted how his 'eyes (behind thick glasses) scoured the giant tally board for any hint of a swing to anyone which might be a harbinger of some national trend. He was like some old sea-dog, examining the firmament for some portent of a storm.'[19] Indeed, Butler's own personal tally of elections – proudly introduced into every conversation and every newspaper article – seemed almost as important as the actual results.

By 1994, Warden was joking that, rather than bothering with candidates going out campaigning, and people going to vote, the result should instead be decided by a political scientist of international standing.

> The obvious choice is Dr David Butler of Nuffield College, Oxford, a man who is not only very familiar with Australia ... but who, as an Englishman and a don, a gentleman, and a scholar,

> would be too principled to accept the huge bribes that [the] Labour Party would surely offer him to blot his psephological escutcheon by cooking the books.[20]

One Australian reporter once overhead Butler on the phone begging the ABC not to call him 'Dr'. It sounded 'pompous', he argued.

> In England it's not necessary to have a doctorate to go up the academic ladder as it is in the United States. In fact, at one time, having a doctorate was considered a sign that you couldn't get a job for the time being. There's a kind of inverted snobbery that having a doctorate was something to keep quiet about.[21]

Marilyn and the family joined Butler on a second six-month visit in 1972, though the boys resented having to go to a local Australian school in what would have been the summer holiday back home. But the family went skiing and visited the Barrier Reef, and there was much excitement, says Ed, 'encountering a deadly redback spider in our loo in Canberra'.[22]

Butler continued to enjoy the freedom to be slightly more scathing in his analysis of Australia than he might have been at home, relishing life in a country where politics is more combative than in Britain. He frequently lambasted as 'duds' the three elected PMs who had succeeded Sir Robert Menzies. Harold Holt he dismissed as 'bumbling'; John Gorton as 'erratic', and William McMahon as 'ageing'. In contrast, he saw the up-and-coming Labour leader Gough Whitlam, who was elected Prime Minister in 1972, as 'charming, erudite, witty, brash, egotistical, arrogant. He has total self-assurance and great command of detail.'[23]

In 1973, Butler published *The Canberra Model*, which was the product of his second spell at ANU the year before.[24] One of the few books Butler didn't write with a co-author, it mostly comprised articles he had written during his visit, and much of the content seems unremarkable. It did identify, though, many of the problems that Gough Whitlam's Labour Party would face having come to power after twenty-three years in opposition, and which they didn't know how to resolve. 'What a pity they did not read it and take it seriously,' suggests academic Pat Weller.[25] Yet at the time the book came as a bit of a thunderbolt within the small community of Australian political scientists, largely because of its introduction, where Butler was blunt in admonishing most of his Australian colleagues for not taking Australian politics seriously enough as a subject. 'I found my time in Canberra ... so intellectually rewarding that I was baffled at the absence of other academics from the field,' he wrote:

> The pages of the Australian journals and the shelves of Australian libraries are singularly void of writing on the contemporary machinery of government ... The great shortage of reflective analysis about the working of the Canberra system constitutes a reproach to the Australian political science community; its members cannot shrug off responsibility ... The corridors of Canberra are paved with gold, ready to be picked up by any academic prospector. The world of political science is the loser for the non-existence of an Australian gold rush.[26]

For too long, Australian political science departments had neglected their own country, Butler believed. The best graduate students quickly went to America or Britain to study politics, while Australian government and politics were often given only small parts on the university curriculum at home. Butler argued that there was much to learn from the 'Canberra model' of government. After the United States, Australia was the best example of federal government in the world, he said, and after Britain, the best example of parliamentary government. One colleague recalls Butler telling him that when he addressed a class of graduate students in Melbourne about Australian politics, 'They treated me with the condescension of a group of nuclear physicists listening to an electrician telling them about the wiring of their houses!'[27]

David Butler was giving his Australian colleagues a kick up the backside, telling them to be more confident about covering their own world, and assuring them that it was just as interesting as Britain or America, if not more so.

It worked. Australian political science developed rapidly over the next couple of decades. 'David's work had an immense influence,' says Ian McAllister, one of the leading academics on Australian politics for the past forty years. 'Before he wrote *The Canberra Model*, it was generally only the odd American political scientist who had taken an interest in Australian politics. David's book galvanised a generation of research and lifted it from a slightly parochial interest into a serious intellectual endeavour.'[28]

The extent of Butler's writing on Australian politics was impressive, especially for an outsider. He wrote regular columns for Rupert Murdoch's *Australian*, for several other publications, and also in academic journals. And in the mid-1970s Butler extensively explored the constitutional issues of what happened in November 1975 – the biggest political drama in Australian history, what became known as 'The Dismissal'. The Governor-General, Sir John Kerr, theoretically deriving his authority from the Queen, took action in a way the Queen would almost certainly never have done in the UK. He sacked the Labour Prime Minister Gough Whitlam on the grounds that there was budgetary deadlock after the Australian Senate refused to pass his tax measures. Kerr immediately replaced Whitlam with the Liberal leader Malcolm Fraser, on the understanding that Fraser would be a caretaker PM and call an immediate election (which he duly did, and duly won by an overwhelming majority). Butler concluded that Sir John Kerr had appeared 'profoundly partisan' in his action, even though he had not breached the Australian Constitution or any past Privy Council judgments. 'The principle is surely that twentieth century heads of State under the Westminster model shall do their utmost to keep clear of party political controversy and that if, in the very last resort, they have to intervene, they shall do their utmost to make plain the neutrality of their action.'[29]

In broad terms, David Butler was doing in late 1960s and early 1970s Australia what he had done in Britain a quarter of a century before. Just as in Britain in 1945, Australian election analysts didn't look at constituency results in percentage terms. Butler also helped export the concept of two-party swing to Australia, a country where it was especially helpful because changes in party votes had been remarkably uniform at elections over the years. In these years, Butler also helped the young psephologist Malcolm Mackerras develop a version of his Swingometer for the ABC.

In some ways Mackerras was an Australian version of David Butler, only twice as eccentric and obsessive, and a lot more gauche. Butler regarded him as 'a kind of joke-figure but enormously industrious', and 'one of those monomaniacs who are the salt of the earth'.[30] With Butler's help, Mackerras achieved a national fame which matched that of his brother, the renowned conductor Sir Charles Mackerras. Spotting that Mackerras had a big ego, Butler suggested that he call his new device 'The Mackerras Pendulum', which was readily accepted, and Butler made the term public in an article for *The Australian* in 1972.[31]

Mackerras says Butler advised him he could go much further than the BBC Swingometer because the Australian Parliament had far fewer MPs in its lower house (125 at that time), compared with five times that number in Britain. 'He pointed out to me that under Australian conditions, it would be possible to place *names* [of constituencies] in a pendulum. He felt sorry for himself because all his Swingometer could do is record mere *numbers* of seats.' Mackerras concludes that 'those thoughts, plus my own work, is what made me famous'.[32]

So Mackerras listed all 125 seats in order of marginality around the outside of his pendulum, which was a more complicated process because it had to encompass the Australian system of preferential voting. It meant David Butler had founded two different versions of the Swingometer in two different countries. It's a sign of his generosity that in both cases he allowed others to take the credit. On his visit for the 1969 Australian election, Butler also described Mackerras as Australia's leading psephologist.[33] The description soon caught on and, with a lot less modesty than Butler himself, Mackerras often used the term himself, until Antony Green of the ABC assumed the mantle a few years ago.[34] Indeed, one colleague suggests that Mackerras effectively became 'the country's official psephologist' when, in 1990, the Australian Government Publishing Service published *The Mackerras Federal Election Guide*.[35]

The Mackerras Pendulum remains a major feature of Australian elections – much more than the Swingometer in Britain – and Mackerras reckons he must have produced around 150 versions of it over the years. These days, the Mackerras Pendulum is not normally a physical device with a moving arrow, but a range of charts which are frequently used in TV graphics and published in leading Australian newspapers. The chart isn't a semicircle like the BBC Swingometer, but a tall diagram shaped like a test tube, partly to reflect the U-shaped seating layout in the Australian lower house. The Pendulum diagram has constituency names listed down each side, with the most marginal seats fanned out around the curved section at the bottom.

Malcolm Mackerras was also involved in the directory *Australian Political Facts*, first published in 1990. Ian McAllister, the principal co-editor, happily admits it was 'very much modelled' on the similar title Butler had founded in the UK nearly thirty years before. McAllister says he 'shamelessly' used Butler's 'framework and style' on the Australian version, though he gave Butler due acknowledgement.[36]

Back in Oxford, David maintained his daily interest in Australian affairs and elections by instituting in 1973 an Australian politics lunch, to which Rhodes Scholars and others were invited, and which was held in the Welsh Pony pub near Nuffield. He saw it as something of a thank-you to Australians for all the generous hospitality he had received when he was in their country. Australian members over the years included many who have returned to distinguished careers in the Australian academic world and politics. They include Kim Beazley, the former leader of the Australian Labour Party; Geoff Gallop, former premier of Western Australia; George Brandis, a senior minister in several Liberal governments, who became High Commissioner to London in 2018; Neal Blewett, a former High Commissioner who was a minister under Bob Hawke and Paul Keating; and Tom Harley, a leading businessman who was the great-grandson of the country's second Prime Minister, Alfred Deakin, and who has acted as a back-room powerbroker in Liberal politics in Australia.

Butler had helped Tom Harley get into Oxford, and they became close friends. Butler would often stay with him on visits to Australia, and Harley would use a Butler visit as the excuse for a 'terrific party'. 'I'd get all sorts of people together, such as Zelman Cowen [former Governor-General] and Malcolm Fraser and grandees from the Melbourne business community.' In conversation with such guests, Harley says Butler would often 'ask very simple challenging questions, such as "What difference will it make who wins?" They weren't insightful questions, but basic. And he would get interesting reactions. It was wonderful.'[37]

Butler couldn't get enough of Australia. 'The informality of life appealed to him,' says his old friend Don Aitkin:

> and the simplicity of getting around (by air) and the connectedness of the society – no matter what state or territory he was in, people would network for him, and quickly and effectively, too. Not to mention picnics, wine and food. The weather enabled lots of picnics, and the bush was close, and very different.[38]

In 2002, in a ceremony at Australia House in London, Butler's contribution to political science and the study of government in Australia was recognised by the award of the Medal of the Order of Australia (OAM). The OAM is the lowest of four ranks in the Australian honours system, roughly equivalent to an OBE or MBE in Britain. It was unusual in that OAMs are very rarely awarded to people who are not Australian citizens.

But the influence exerted by Butler between the two political systems worked both ways, and he used his Australian experience to argue for reforms back home, notably for a version of the Australian Electoral Commission, the independent statutory body established in 1984 (and preceded for a decade by the Australian Electoral Office) to regulate and oversee elections. Butler also argued that Britain could learn much from the Australian process of redrawing constituency boundaries, which takes only a few months compared with many agonising years in the UK.

On the other hand, Butler used his experience of Australia and Britain effectively to argue caution against a growing campaign in Australia in the early 1970s, led by Gough Whitlam's Labour Party, (and to a lesser extent in Britain) for what would soon be known as Freedom of Information in high places. 'It is worth stressing that certain kinds of secrecy are essential to the working of ministerial government on the pattern that we know,' he wrote.

> The fact that secrecy has been carried to ludicrous extremes, and has often been prejudicial to the public interest, does not mean that, in its right place, it cannot contribute mightily to good government ... There is a quite separate case for secrecy which has nothing to do with individual rights or national security: it is to enable ministers and civil servants to reach decisions in a sensible way.

He concluded that 'any Government, in Canberra or London, that insisted on exposing all its deliberations to instant view would not enjoy a successful life – let alone a long one'.[39]

* * *

Australia was not the only example of David Butler carrying considerable influence between political systems that were thousands of miles apart. On the family's return from their first trip to Australia, the Butlers stopped for several days in New Delhi, where they were looked after by the former Nuffield economist Jagdish Bhagwati. David was immediately captivated by this brief glimpse of India. He was keen to return, but it would be more than fifteen years before the chance arose.

In 1982, Butler was visited by two economists, both in their early thirties, from the Delhi School of Economics, who had travelled over to England specially to see him. Prannoy Roy and Ashok Lahiri explained that they were interested in developing in their own country the kind of psephology that was now well-established in Britain, America and the West, and which Butler had done so much to promote. The pair had already been playing around with Indian election statistics and sought advice from the man they regarded as the master. Could he help?

Prannoy Roy, who had an Indian father and Irish mother, had been educated in England, at Haileybury and then London University, but was 'totally Indian in spirit', says Butler.[40] Today, he is a highly significant player in Indian television, both as boss of large independent production company NDTV (New Delhi Television), which he jointly owns with his wife, and as a charismatic on-screen presenter for NDTV. Ashok Lahiri has also gone on to greater things, too, as chief economic adviser to the Indian government, and now as a member of the Finance Commission.

'I still well remember that first meeting,' says Lahiri. 'He was extremely warm and encouraging and his enthusiasm was infectious. He readily agreed to come to India and help us.'[41] The pair had already stored past election results in digital form on a computer, but a major problem was that the names of Indian constituencies frequently changed when the boundaries were radically redrawn after each ten-year census. 'David encouraged us to link the constituencies over time and produce tables that showed how the voting patterns changed across the elections,' says Lahiri. Butler wasn't actually able to visit Roy and Lahiri until the following year, but together the three then managed to edit the country's first psephological directory, *A Compendium of Indian Elections*.[42] The book largely comprised tables of election results and statistics, dating back to India's first election in 1952. It was rather poorly printed, but it was a start.

The 1983 visit gave Butler the chance to witness the state assembly elections in the eastern province of Andhra Pradesh. Ashok Lahiri was impressed at how Butler 'roughed it out in fairly trying conditions ... without losing his enthusiasm to ask the most pertinent questions'. On his 1983 visit, Butler visited Hyderabad to witness the new voting machines in action, an experience which later encouraged him in urging the Commons Home Affairs Committee to recommend their use in Britain.

Butler returned to India in December 1984 for the general election which followed the assassination of Indira Gandhi, and was accompanied by Paul McKee, who had developed on-screen computer graphics for ITN in London. By then, Roy and Lahiri had persuaded India's only TV channel, the state broadcaster Doordarshan, to let their research think tank, with Butler's help, run the election results service. Doordarshan was taking a bit of a risk, since it was the first time they'd farmed out their results coverage to an independent production company, and initially it was fairly chaotic. Researcher Lolita Bam recalls that lino was still being laid on the floor when they moved into their office at the TV station. Until that time, coverage of elections on Indian television had been very primitive, at roughly the same stage as the BBC's output had been when Butler started working on results programmes in the early 1950s. Part of the problem was that politics in India was substantially more complicated than in Britain, with one dominant party, Congress, and dozens of smaller parties, many of which were based on region or caste. Butler helped the Indians produce up-to-date computerised statistics and modern on-screen graphics. 'We spent hours each day sitting on the lawns of the India International Centre near Lodi Gardens in Delhi discussing elections,' says Lahiri. 'He would bring out his index cards with a question or an issue on each card. With the cards he broke down the general election into bite-sized pieces which, even as relative novices, Prannoy and I could handle.'[43]

Doordarshan didn't even have a rolling results programme in 1984. Instead, the team worked on regular bulletins which would break into the normal output. Butler's main work was behind-the-scenes analysis of the results, passing notes to Prannoy Roy, who filled the Dimbleby role as presenter. However, Butler also did a few stints as on-screen commentator, fielding Roy's questions. The problem was that after everything Roy and Butler said in English, it had to be repeated by another presenter in Hindi.

Indians were astonished at Butler's ability to predict the outcome on the basis of a handful of early results which had seen substantial swings. 'I said, "Without doubt Congress is going to win," and nobody believed it,' says Butler. 'When they did, they were just frightened of saying it, and impressed when I did.'[44]

India quickly became the third great overseas love of David Butler's career and gave him a new lease of life when his star in Britain started to wane in the '80s and '90s. He quickly identified with Indians' 'universal zest for politics' and 'their enthusiasm for voting, the demand to express a popular verdict'. 'Politics, like cricket,' he wrote, 'is a major spectator sport.' The long-standing BBC correspondent Sir Mark Tully remembers how Butler would come and have breakfast in his garden and lap up the politics and the statistics. 'The thing I loved was his huge enthusiasm for these strange elections in a strange country. He had a never-ending fascination for Indian politics – that's why our breakfasts were so enjoyable.'[45]

However, Butler witnessed the dark side of Indian politics, too. 'For the first time in a life of election-watching,' he wrote in a despatch to *The Times*, 'I saw votes being stolen, crudely and brutally.' On polling day in 1984, a Delhi BBC journalist had taken him forty miles north to the Baghpat constituency in western Uttar Pradesh of the former Prime Minister Charan Singh, where they visited five local polling stations. In four, the fraud was 'blatant'. At one station he saw a leader of the locally dominant Jat caste intimidating overawed lower-caste Harijans by demanding to inspect their ballot papers.[46]

But such trips were exceptional. Unlike Australia, where he travelled the country, Butler largely confined himself to the capital, New Delhi. And his interest was pretty much limited to Indian elections and voting statistics. It would have been far too difficult to immerse himself in the complexities of Indian politics and government in the way Butler had in Australia – not least because of the language barriers. He didn't deal much with Indian academics. Nor did he have much time to go sightseeing or take an interest in Indian culture and cuisine.

Ed Butler, who accompanied his father on trips to India in 1989 and 1991, says the two to three weeks of preparation before polling day involved drawing up cards on each of the more than 500 seats. 'The days of prep were coloured by a challenging diet of curry, and inedible versions of Western food, which frequently led (for both of us) to protracted bouts in the loo, but Dad just waved aside such adversity, charging on with typical energy and his uniquely blithe fortitude.'[47] Producer Lolita Bam recalls how Butler would scribble things down on scraps of paper overnight, 'and return to work the next morning to ask us to research and find out the answers to his queries'.[48]

With Butler's considerable help, the dynamic Prannoy Roy was effectively the pioneer of election television in India. 'I owe every bit of any psephology I know to David,' he says.[49] When Roy and his wife set up their own production house, NDTV, in 1988, Butler and Paul McKee went to work there on election nights instead. They initially produced election bulletins to be inserted into Doordarshan's regular output, followed, after 1991, by full-length election programmes for the state broadcaster, and subsequently results programmes for NDTV's own news channel. 'Their standards by comparison with Indian TV in-house were extremely modern,' says Mark Tully. 'What was remarkable was the level of information and the speed of the output.'[50]

Ed Butler says the 'wonder' of David's relationship with his Indian hosts was that:

> Prannoy was already an accomplished academic and TV personality, but he always had this very gracious and genuine reverence for Dad's experience in how to portray overall, in graphic and statistical terms, the drama of an election night, which had never really been done in any meaningful way in India before.[51]

NDTV's professionalism on elections and other journalistic output quickly helped the company become a major player. And Butler's contribution was especially generous given that he was paid very little for his time in India beyond travel and hotel expenses. Although he was almost entirely off-screen after 1984, he went to India to help on the next seven elections up to 2004, when the former Nuffield student Manmohan Singh became Prime Minister. But Butler felt that, just as in Australia, his contributions became less helpful over the years, as Indian analysts rapidly advanced their own understanding, methods and professionalism. 'I knew I was useful in '84,' Butler says. 'I was moderately useful in 1989. After the third time I wrote and said, "You're better than me."'[52]

Because of India's great diversity, psephology there was a lot more complicated than simply applying the methods that Butler and colleagues had developed elsewhere. Roy and Lahiri couldn't find uniform national swing of the kind seen in Australia or Britain, but did find that uniform swing worked if India was divided into 'homogenous swing zones' – areas which ran across state and even constituency boundaries, but where voters always seemed to swing together. 'For some reason,' Roy wrote, 'the electorate in these zones tended to show swings of a uniform size in the same direction election after election.'[53] Another problem was that unlike the two-party system in Britain, and its variant in Australia, India in the 1980s had the dominant Congress Party against numerous smaller opposition parties, which made television presentation very tricky. So, David Butler helped Prannoy Roy and Ashok Lahiri design what they called the Index of Opposition Unity, which was essentially a measure of the opposition to the Congress Party.

Butler, Roy and Lahiri subsequently updated their directory of election statistics several times, with the title *India Decides*, published jointly with the news magazine *India Today*.[54] While Butler wrote analysis chapters at the front, Roy and Lahiri constructed tables of figures at the rear. But Butler claims managerial credit, too. With echoes of his work with Donald Stokes, he says the guides 'wouldn't have been published but for me, as I had the drive, and we met our deadlines'.[55]

Even after his last trip to help NDTV with its election coverage, in 2004 (in his 80th year), Butler sent Prannoy Roy and his colleagues a detailed two-page memo complimenting them on what had worked, and gently suggesting where matters might be improved – snippets of wisdom and advice on making earlier forecasts; getting messages through to the right people on the team; better on-screen graphics; the need for more rehearsals; outside commentators; more detailed statistics; and even the division of duties between staff. Just as with his lengthy memos to Grace Wyndham Goldie at the BBC half a century before, Butler was still acting as though he were a TV producer.

Ed Butler says his father loved being treated 'as a kind of psephological rock star' in India, though without being vain about it, at a time when he was no longer in such demand at home. He also observes 'a very natural if perhaps surprising fit' between his father and India:

> There is this constant, almost exhausting, passion of the Indian people for politics and elections – and Dad is the same – his tiggerish drive, and I guess that kind of innate certainty he always imparted (to me anyway) that in this democratic ritual something is being solved, wrapped up, finessed, inexorably improved upon by the electorate. There is a kinship there, even if the ugliness and alien-ness of the religious and ethnic politics was definitely beyond his normal scope.[56]

But India was never like America or Australia. Despite making around fifteen to twenty visits over the years, spending perhaps a year in the country altogether, David Butler never really explored India, didn't speak Hindi and couldn't claim a real feel for India's rich culture and history. 'I don't know India,' he once said. 'I just know something of Indian television. Nonetheless the subcontinent greatly enlarged my horizons.'[57]

And, in turn, David Butler made a substantial contribution to introducing psephology to the country where arguably it was most needed. The Indian political system, despite its well-known corruption and voting irregularities, could nonetheless claim broadly to be democratic. After all, Indian governments *were* regularly ejected by the voters. Just as he had done in Britain in the 1950s, 4,000 miles away Butler had helped explain election statistics and trends to the hundreds of millions of Indian television viewers, participants in the largest democracy the world has ever known.

CHAPTER FOURTEEN

ACADEMIC ENTREPRENEUR

Peter Cook seems an unlikely pollster. In 1970, the comedian collaborated with John Cleese and Graham Chapman, two stars of the new *Monty Python* TV show, to bring out a satirical film about the burgeoning election industry, called *The Rise and Rise of Michael Rimmer*. It was the idea of the young David Frost, who'd been inspired by the Hull North by-election in January 1966, where a good result for Labour prompted Harold Wilson to call the general election for nine weeks later.

The Rise and Rise of Michael Rimmer had a stellar cast. As well as Cook, Cleese and Chapman, it also included Arthur Lowe (of *Dad's Army* fame), Ronnie Corbett and even the playwright Harold Pinter. Michael Rimmer (Peter Cook) is a young man who wheedles his way into a sleepy advertising agency. He then starts manipulating opinion polls to get elected as a Conservative MP. Rimmer quickly ends up as Prime Minister, and after bombarding people with hundreds of referendums, he's voted in as president-for-life, on the promise of no more referendums. Sadly, the film didn't get many votes at the box office, yet its themes were highly topical.

The election industry was under attack in the late 1960s, with growing disquiet over whether voters and elections could be manipulated by slick advertising and clever marketing men, and fears that elected politicians were being outflanked by ever more powerful pollsters and psephologists. Using polls to analyse past elections was one thing, but there was a fear of the misuse of polls to influence current or future contests. In 1967, a Speaker's Conference had even recommended – unsuccessfully – that opinion polls be banned for the final seventy-two hours of a campaign. David Butler had become one of the leading embodiments of the election industry. It was a role he relished, but in the long term his academic career probably suffered for it, too.

The real-life drama of the 1970 general election, when Butler was at the height of his fame, only fuelled the disquiet about the industry, especially on the left. For weeks, every poll suggested Harold Wilson would win comfortably. Only one opinion poll during the entire campaign – the day before voting – forecast a Conservative victory, though the surprise wasn't quite on the scale of Thomas Dewey's defeat in the US presidential election of 1948.

On the BBC election night programme – the first to use colour – the pollsters came up with another novelty: Britain's first ever exit poll. It was conducted in Gravesend in Kent, which was selected by David Butler's team at Nuffield as the 'most ordinary constituency in England', with an electorate typical of the country as a whole. People were asked how they'd voted as they left the polling stations, prompting the BBC, on the basis of this one seat, to forecast, against expectations, a Conservative victory nationwide, even before the first actual result from any constituency. This was then confirmed by the first real declarations, in Guildford and Cheltenham. So unprepared was the BBC for any substantial swing to the Tories that just after midnight came a famous symbolic shot of a man with a brush painting extra figures onto the Conservative side of the board behind the Swingometer while Bob McKenzie was speaking. Around 2 a.m., after Harold Wilson told the young David Dimbleby (on the ground in the Prime Minister's Merseyside seat) that it could still be 'very close', David Butler immediately responded from the studio in London: 'I hate to disagree with a fellow member of the Royal Statistical Society, especially as he's still Prime Minister, but I don't think there can be any doubt at this stage about the outcome.'[1] And Butler was right, of course. Labour lost.

By the early 1970s, David Butler was one of the best-known 'egg-heads' in Britain. His overnight TV appearances explaining why people voted the way they did – from council elections to general elections – and his fast-talking mastery of extraordinary detail made him a familiar face to a large section of the general public, in an era when Britain still had only three TV channels and such programmes attracted large audiences. In the aftermath of 1970, though, Butler became something of a public scapegoat, despite his success with the exit poll. When he and his co-author Michael Pinto-Duschinsky published *The British General Election of 1970* the following spring, they got unfriendly reviews from several big names on the left.

There was some anger that the pollsters' and commentators' confident forecasts of a Labour victory may have made some Labour voters presume the result was in the bag, and that they didn't need to bother going to the polling station. The former Cabinet minister Barbara Castle wrote that 'the study of elections has become so sophisticated that the politicians have almost been elbowed out ... the pollsters and psephologists have been moving in'. And she attacked Butler for again suggesting that any campaign work made very little difference: dedication in politics was now at a discount, she said. 'All that mattered was THE SWING, almost Calvinistic in its fatalistic overtones. And the key to the swing lay in the statistical analyses of which the psephologists were the high priests.'[2]

Castle's colleague Richard Crossman accused the authors of letting their 'desk-psephology' defy the experience of participants in the campaign, and he challenged their view that the quality of a candidate makes little difference to the number of votes his party gets. Crossman said that by concentrating on 'the national swing', which evens out all the differences between seats, Butler 'fails to see the trees for the wood. This is as fatal an attitude in psephology as it is in forestry. When it comes to tending them (or cutting them), it is the individual trees that matter: the wood is an abstract statistical or geographical concept. So is the swing.'[3]

Likewise, the left-leaning commentator Anthony Howard, who was close to both Crossman and Castle, wrote a review entitled 'Taking the Life out of Politics', in which he accused the authors of a 'sterilising process of converting politics into a kind of statistical panel game'. Repeating Castle's analogy, Howard argued that 'Dr Butler' was 'the high priest in the temple – a temple in which the politicians themselves had long since ceased to serve as anything but the humblest acolytes'.[4]

Despite this left-wing onslaught on his sorcery, David Butler would remain the 'high priest' on BBC election nights throughout the 1970s, probably the most exciting decade of post-war political history. In February 1974, Edward Heath narrowly lost to Harold Wilson after calling a snap election over the miners' strike. This left a hung parliament, which led to a second election seven months later, as Wilson sought an outright majority. The two results programmes in 1974 were presented by Alastair Burnet, who was aided behind the scenes by a 25-year-old journalist from *The Economist*, Andrew Neil, whose official job was to keep Burnet supplied with information about seats and candidates, and whose unofficial role was to keep him supplied, too, with tots of whisky. David Butler, who required no such pepping up, had, as usual, a promising Nuffield student 'feeding' him figures and other material: this time it was the 22-year-old Gus O'Donnell, who would go on to become Cabinet Secretary thirty years later.

In 1970, Butler's dark suit and tie did little to test the new colour television output, but his 1974 appearances seemed to reflect the trends of the times – in February he even wore a more casual beige suit with salmon-pink shirt. And on both broadcasts there was a lively rivalry with Alastair Burnet, one of the few people in the kingdom whose memory for parliamentary seats, MPs and their majorities matched Butler's. Burnet was willing to compete with Butler much more than Cliff Michelmore or Richard Dimbleby ever did.

Both 1974 elections produced close, nail-biting drama on election night, and it wasn't until late the following afternoon that it became clear what the final tally would be. (Indeed, in the first 1974 election Wilson didn't become Prime Minister until the Monday evening.) Butler spent much of the BBC programmes speculating about the problems of hung parliaments and minority government, something Britain hadn't experienced for more than four decades. The new situation, and his recent experiences in Australia, meant he was starting to think in much more constitutional terms. On the morning after election night, he urged fresh analysis:

> I do think that precedents mustn't be preserved too long. A lot of British government has been confused by people citing Victorian precedents simply because the situation hasn't arisen for eighty years. You do have to make your rules again … I don't feel I can forecast the future by extrapolating from the past, as to some extent I do with the computer and election results![5]

Although Butler maintained that he and Bob McKenzie were always good friends, their relationship seemed more strained than ever – perhaps not helped by McKenzie's negative review of *Political Change in Britain*, though Butler was never a man to bear grudges. BBC colleagues couldn't help noticing the frostiness. 'Certainly,' recalls Chris Long, who was a BBC computer expert in the 1970s, 'at meetings or debriefs they kept their distance from each other, and certainly that spilled over onto the screen. Off air I don't think I ever saw them chatting together.'[6]

Dennis Kavanagh, a politics lecturer who worked as McKenzie's aide on the 1979 results programme, thinks he had grown envious of Butler and irritated by him. 'He described David to me as a "boy scout". Bob thought that they were underpaid and knew that David would do it for nothing. He was also jealous of David getting more air time … [Bob] was constantly moaning to me and demanding to be called in.' Kavanagh also recalls that McKenzie had a very poor knowledge of British geography. 'I used to send McKenzie little cards … With places like Bolton and Bury, he asked me, could I write on what part of England they were in, as the viewers might not know. He himself didn't know, whereas David was very good on his geography.'[7]

While this television work established David Butler's reputation with the general public, the two editions of *Political Change in Britain* (the second in 1975) did more than anything to help establish David Butler as a serious scholar. At Oxford, when Butler wasn't overseas, PPE students would flock to his Friday night seminars with visiting bigwigs. And there was his extraordinary outpouring of books, what his Nuffield colleague Nevil Johnson disparaged as the 'David Butler book factory'. 'David was turning out these books like a Xerox machine,' says one of his many co-authors. The 1970s saw his output grow to almost frenzied levels. Alongside *The Canberra Model* (1973), the revised edition of *Political Change in Britain*, and further versions of *British Political Facts* (1975 and 1980), the 1970s spawned no fewer than six more volumes of Nuffield election studies. With politics in ferment, he seized every opportunity to provide the first drafts of history.

His output was all the more remarkable given that this was an age of typewriters and carbon copies rather than word-processors and email. His long-serving secretary at Nuffield, Audrey Skeats, had to type and retype his manuscripts and, rather like Winston Churchill, Butler would often dictate his chapters, as well as a constant stream of articles, for both the press and academic journals. Co-authors and junior colleagues would sometimes be asked to check the facts or insert correct details.

His co-author on the 1970 election book, Michael Pinto-Duschinsky, was not to blame for the hostile reviews, but Butler decided they were not an ideal team and couldn't write together again. They'd spent too much time arguing and Butler couldn't put up with Pinto-Duschinsky's habit of expressing his strong political views (he was a Conservative councillor in Oxford). Pinto-Duschinsky bore no hard feelings; he said he never expected nor wanted to do a second book.

Searching for a new collaborator for the next election (due by 1975), Butler consulted Richard Rose, who suggested Dennis Kavanagh. As it happened, Butler had been an external examiner a few years before on Kavanagh's doctoral thesis about constituency campaigning. He rang Kavanagh and they agreed to meet at the Oxford and Cambridge Club. Ten days later, Kavanagh recalls Butler ringing to ask if he'd 'accepted' the proposal. 'I didn't know he'd offered me the co-authorship,' Kavanagh says.[8] Anyway, he agreed.

It was the start of the longest and most prolific partnership of Butler's career. Within weeks, the pair were plunged into the February 1974 election. Kavanagh came down to Oxford to work in Butler's office. 'I was just a northern boy,' says Kavanagh,

> but what hit me when I came down to Oxford, visiting Nuffield and a few other colleges, was how jealous they were of David – his high media profile, his low teaching load, and the way he had a lot of resources from his college, which they were reluctant to share in those days. And I used to get the backlash because I was working with him. There was jealousy of Nuffield, the institution.[9]

When the election produced a hung parliament, both the authors and the publisher, Macmillan, resolved to publish the book very quickly. Harold Wilson, having soon settled the coal strike, was expected to call a second election later in the year. What's more, Butler could only spend a few weeks in Oxford before returning to

Australia to cover the May 1974 federal election there. As a result, Kavanagh wrote much of the text, but it suffered from the tight timetable. The book felt rushed: it was full of typographical errors and factual mistakes.[10] Butler himself has said February 1974 is the least substantial of the fifteen Nuffield general election studies he edited or co-edited. Yet the story provided a more exciting read than many more predictable contests. The lively, haphazard nature of the short campaign produced a drama full of unusual incidents, such as Enoch Powell's advice to vote Labour, which he considered the only party which might take the country out of the Common Market.

David Butler and Dennis Kavanagh initially worked well as a team, though Kavanagh would often grumble to others that he bore most of the workload. Butler subsequently described himself, much as he had with Donald Stokes, as the 'business manager' of the partnership:

> I know how to get the book done. I raise the money and I arrange with contributors and push the ones who are recalcitrant. I'm the entrepreneur. Dennis is a very quick, easy writer, and he does think very fast, organising things ... When I'm with him and he's challenging me, then ideas flow out.[11]

They tended to conduct major interviews together. Butler, who was much more likely already to know the people they visited, tended to ask the questions, while Kavanagh took notes. 'Given his quick-fire approach, David is a remarkably good interviewer of politicians,' Kavanagh once wrote.

> He has a knack of asking the right questions and getting people to confide in him. He is straight-forward about his approach. As he once said to me: 'I've never believed in aggro-interviewing. The politicians are doing us a favour, and the least we can do is

> to show interest in and sympathy for their problems.' In other words, rapport is essential, or 'they need a little love.' … David would describe to me Douglas Hurd, Chris Patten and Shirley Williams as 'pure gold', but of others to whom he had listened politely he would mutter afterwards, 'a lot of guff there'.[12]

Butler and Kavanagh's interviews were conducted on the basis that the subjects would not be quoted by name, but the pair were sometimes criticised as being too discreet, accused of being over-protective and not making enough of what they had been told. The respected *Sunday Times* columnist Hugo Young, who himself spent several hours each week lunching and interviewing high-level political sources, wrote that if the 1983 edition had a fault:

> it lies, as it has before, in the very refusal of the authors to play up the quality of the information to which they have access. One knows from experience how good their contacts are in the party organisations, and how freely their sources will speak to them, relieved, no doubt, not to be confronted by menacing and unreliable journalists.[13]

What Butler and Kavanagh were doing was in some respects more akin to journalism than scholarly research, and in 1975 the political editor of *The Times*, David Wood, pointed out how Butler seemed to be thriving on the very methods he had decried in the early 1960s, when he complained that British reporting of politics was substantially inferior to its American equivalent: 'It is ironic that an academic who began as an unsparing critic of British political reporting should have developed into one of the best political reporters of his time, using exactly the so-called "Lobby" or "non-attributable" methods that he once condemned.'[14]

Wood praised it as 'political journalism of hindsight with a value all its own', since Butler and Kavanagh would go back to the election battlefield and talk to the generals whether they had won or lost.[15] Butler's friend Tony Benn also employed a military analogy for their regular background interviews. 'His visits to me rank with an inspection by a Field Marshal.'[16]

In contrast to almost any journalist, however, Butler and Kavanagh would often send chunks of their draft manuscripts to their sources, not to give them a veto over the text, but to correct any factual mistakes and in the hope that, having seen the broader account, sources might offer additional titbits of detail. The Conservative official Sir Michael Fraser, for example, would sometimes reply with dozens of pages of notes. The obvious danger, of course, was that having seen this instant history in typescript, subjects might try to withdraw or tone down what they had previously said. 'You usually can satisfy them by giving in to them one tenth,' Butler once explained. 'But on the other hand, you do get so much extra input, and quite often you elicit documents from them.'[17]

* * *

In 1976, when Norman Chester announced he would be standing down as Warden of Nuffield two years later, after a remarkable twenty-four years in the post, David Butler hoped to succeed him. For many years in the late 1950s and early 1960s when he was dean and senior tutor, Butler had effectively been Chester's deputy and close adviser, the 'ageing dauphin', says one colleague. To many in the outside world, he would have been an obvious choice, too. If the general public and people in the media had heard of anyone at Nuffield College, it was probably David Butler. And nobody could question Butler's devotion to the college. It had been his academic home for almost thirty years – as graduate student, research fellow, dean, senior tutor and, briefly, in the year 1976/77, domestic bursar. Over that time, Butler had often been sounded out about professorships and other academic posts around the world, but had always turned them down for the college he loved. His hopes of becoming Warden were dashed, however, when nobody in college gave him any encouragement. So he gave up, and instead ran the campaign of the sociologist Chelly Halsey, though the job eventually went to an outsider, the historian Michael Brock. Butler would later credit Brock with doing a good job.

'It's such a pity he was not Warden of Nuffield,' says the former Labour minister Andrew Adonis, who was at the college from 1985 to 1991.

> David was a serious academic entrepreneur. He never lost his boyish enthusiasm for his subject. Most academics have lost their enthusiasm by their forties or fifties. David's so good at encouraging people to do things. He's positive and bouncy. He almost single-handedly connected Nuffield to the real world. He would have turned the place into a kind of salon. He would have given it prestige.[18]

According to Janet Morgan, who was at Nuffield in the early '70s:

> There was a feeling among some colleagues that David was a snob because he was not interested in the boring things they were interested in. David was a happy man. Here was David so enjoying what he was doing, and being on TV was not thought a good thing. David was joyful and boyish.[19]

'I would say they despised him,' says one long-standing colleague. 'Because of the intellectual disdain for him he would never have been elected Warden.'

It probably didn't help that Butler's range of academic interests was quite exclusive. Despite his prolific output over the years, he wasn't particularly interested in political philosophy, policy-making or international relations. Perhaps, as Isaiah Berlin had discovered long ago, he was too atheoretical. Chelly Halsey told the BBC in 1983 that he thought the problem was:

> David Butler is a man who sees it as necessary to be excellent in a relatively narrow way, so as to be quite sure that he *is* excellent. He determined to become someone who was a sort of walking encyclopaedia-cum-computer about all things to do with electoral politics and he's an unrivalled authority in that way. And yet I like to tease him and say he knows nothing of politics – he doesn't understand politics at all; that politics is really about moral issues. It has to be about the feelings and preferences of people, and not about the adding up of numbers with respect to elections and by-elections and majorities and so on.[20]

If some colleagues thought David Butler's range of interests was too narrow, his concerns had nonetheless widened during the 1970s. His fascination with the democratic process had not just taken him to Australia (and subsequently to India), but the turmoil of British politics during that time led Butler to explore several new topics. These included the first ever British referendum in 1975 – the vote on whether the UK should remain a member of the European Economic Community (EEC), otherwise known as the Common Market. Butler wrote his account of the contest – as part of the Nuffield election series – in collaboration with his colleague Uwe Kitzinger, a German refugee who had studied PPE with him at New College just after the war, before becoming an economist for the Council of Europe and an early champion of Britain joining Europe. Once Britain joined the EEC, Kitzinger became adviser to one of the first European Commissioners, Sir Christopher Soames.

The referendum itself was the idea of another of their New College PPE colleagues, Tony Benn, who wanted out, having grown increasingly hostile over the years to the idea of Britain belonging to the community. He proposed a public vote on the issue as early as 1970, well before Britain joined in 1973 – partly to help resolve Labour's internal divisions.

Butler and Kitzinger divided the chapters quite amicably and made very few alterations to each other's manuscripts. The biggest argument was over whether to include a risqué cartoon from the French satirical newspaper *Le Canard enchaîné* which showed Harold Wilson in bed having sex with a woman who is wearing a crown marked 'Europa', with Wilson's face pressed against her large exposed breasts. The caption has her saying, '*Entrez ou sortez, mon cher Wilson, mais cessez ce va-et-vient ridicule…*' ('Come in or get out, my dear Wilson, but stop this ridiculous coming and going…')[21] In a way, that summed up the dispute between the two authors over the cartoon. 'I wanted it in,' says Kitzinger, 'and David was too strait-laced for that. I had great difficulty in persuading him … because it struck me as expressing exactly what the feeling of the French was – and of course today that cartoon is even more relevant. It was almost over his dead body that the cartoon got in.'[22]

Britain voted to remain inside the EEC by just over two to one – 67.2 per cent Yes, to 32.8 per cent voting No. With the Labour government promising further referendums on its planned devolution proposals for Scotland and Wales, and the practice growing elsewhere too – though not quite on the scale of the satirical Michael Rimmer – it was a suitable moment for Butler to work with the renowned American scholar Austin Ranney on a book of scholarly essays by several international authors about referendums around the world.[23]

The decisive result in the EEC referendum was a major setback for its instigator, Tony Benn, and Harold Wilson used the defeat to demote the left-winger within Cabinet, from Industry Secretary to Energy.

Benn's rapid move to the left during the late 1960s and early 1970s also placed a strain on his friendship with David Butler. Benn still regularly came to the Friday night seminars, but clearly didn't enjoy his visits. In his diary in 1971, Benn tells how he 'attacked the way politics was taught in Oxford ... This didn't go down very well.'[24] Two years later, Benn dismissed the seminar as 'a completely Conservative audience' (which seems rather unlikely). 'I find Nuffield College a complete washout. They are so rich, they have so much money and are so remote from real life, it was extremely unattractive.'[25] A few weeks later, the criticism got more personal: 'What is interesting about David Butler and all these academics ... is that they have absolutely forgotten what democracy is about, as coming from the people.'[26]

During the February 1974 election prompted by the miners' strike, Butler apparently told Benn that he feared a Conservative landslide, and that the 'consensus politics' that Labour had stood for in the past would not survive. Butler was 'deeply depressed and pessimistic', Benn recorded after their meeting, which he interpreted as 'sure symptoms of the right-winger'.[27]

Butler, in turn, began to think Benn had become a bit mentally unbalanced and 'intoxicated by his meetings', he recorded during the October 1974 election, and Butler wasn't frightened to say this to Benn.[28] During the EEC referendum, Benn's diary records Butler telling him he had 'never known anyone so absolutely drunk by public meetings as I was during the referendum'. Benn admitted, 'I don't deny it.'[29] A year later, Benn complained that Butler's 'idea of politics is now so remote from my own', and then declared shortly afterwards that Butler had become a Conservative.[30] 'He's pretty close to the Tories, doesn't like Mrs Thatcher, thinks she's putting people in the middle of the road off, but it won't put David Butler off from being a Tory even though he may not vote.' Butler is 'an ageing, consensus man', Benn wrote, an 'old academic who ... is really out of touch with reality'.[31]

Despite Tony Benn's regular internal attacks from the left, the Labour government of 1974–79 proved to be extraordinarily resilient. Only for a brief spell, between the October 1974 election and the summer of 1975, did Labour have even a tiny majority in the Commons. Yet Harold Wilson and his successor Jim Callaghan managed to overcome by-election losses and defections to survive as a minority government for another four years. This was largely thanks to the thirteen Liberal MPs who, for eighteen months in 1977–78, agreed to the famous Lib–Lab Pact where they pledged to support the government on confidence votes in return for ministers adopting various Liberal policies. During the first half of the twentieth century, periods of one-party majority government were the exception, yet for almost thirty years after 1945, the two-party, first-past-the-post system always gave the Conservatives or Labour more than half the seats in the Commons (though in 1950, 1964 and 1974 the government majorities were very small).

Butler calculated that Britain was likely to return to coalition government eventually. The slow revival of the Liberals, the growing success of the nationalists in Scotland and Wales, and the increasing independence of Northern Ireland politicians from their British partner parties suggested it would get progressively harder for either Labour or the Conservatives to secure majorities. Hence the book which Butler edited in 1978, *Coalitions in British Politics*. It was a collection of essays by some of the most distinguished historians of modern politics, including A. J. P. Taylor, Robert Blake and Kenneth O. Morgan, examining how coalitions, quasi-coalitions and minority governments had worked in Britain over the previous two centuries.[32]

It proved premature, for after the industrial disputes of the 1978–79 Winter of Discontent, and the Labour government's failure to secure a sufficient majority in the referendum on Scottish devolution in March 1979, the Callaghan government finally fell, ushering into power a revolutionary new player in British politics.

CHAPTER FIFTEEN

CONSENSUS PINKO

Margaret Thatcher had proved good value when David Butler and Dennis Kavanagh interviewed her in November 1974, just after the Conservatives' second election defeat of that year. The Nuffield co-authors found her 'surprisingly relaxed and forthcoming', Butler reported.

> I was struck at how eager she was to get in her delicately phrased barbs against Ted [Heath] and his entourage. But she is a fiercely intelligent woman, shrewd, quite generous in her praise of the other side. I certainly take her very seriously indeed. She was rather warmer than on my previous encounter, but she still is a rather cold fish, and she gives no trace of any sense of humour.[1]

Twelve weeks later, Thatcher was elected party leader in place of Heath. But the Conservative leader was rather less friendly when both Butler and Kavanagh visited her in early August 1978, ahead of an election expected that October (but which Jim Callaghan famously postponed). They found her tidying her room at the Commons – ready to move into Downing Street, she told them; and she revealed she had even defrosted her fridge that morning before going on holiday. 'She started off very charmingly and easily,' according the authors' account, 'but as the interview progressed she became much more aggressive, picking up individual words or phrases that we used and throwing them back at us and demanding to know what we really meant by them.' The worst example came when Butler suggested there was a new 'consensus' between the two main parties on economic policy (following the spending cuts imposed on Labour by the International Monetary Fund in 1976), and she 'pounced on our use of the word consensus'.[2] Dennis Kavanagh later wrote that:

> The atmosphere changed immediately, and she unleashed a barrage of hostile questions. 'What do you mean by consensus?' After a three-second pause she offered five different definitions of the term and challenged him to say which one he [Butler] referred to. I knew that he was floundering. After further exchanges, in which he may have been using well-worn phrases about the need for compromise and the politics of the possible – with an implicit rebuke for her style – she returned to the attack: 'Do you realise what you are saying?' and 'Do you consider yourself fit to hold an academic appointment?' All this was said with deliberate Thatcher emphasis and hostility on the key words. The lady was on the warpath and the atmosphere was extremely uncomfortable. A by-now shaken collaborator looked to me for support, perhaps to begin a new line of questioning. I am afraid to report that I was no use to him; I simply looked the other way. Some ninety minutes later she escorted us out of the office and said, 'You do understand me, don't you?'[3]

'Pontius Pilate was my name that day,' Dennis Kavanagh now recalls. 'David and I went to St James's Park to recover. The two of us were shattered and exhausted … It was such a powerful performance.'[4] So David Butler found himself under attack from both Tony Benn on the left and Margaret Thatcher on the right as a representative of their dreaded 'consensus'. A few years later, Thatcher's close adviser Tim Bell would tell Dennis Kavanagh that she regarded David Butler as a 'pinko', by which she meant someone in the middle. Bell explained that Thatcher saw David Butler as a journalist as well as an academic, 'and as such she did not like pinko journalists, like Hugo Young and Adam Raphael. She thought that a journalist should be either for her or against her.'[5]

Conversely, as Tony Benn reached his peak as leader of the Labour left in the early 1980s, and seriously challenged for the leadership, his diary entries on Butler got ever more critical and personal.

> David Butler's way of teaching politics is to persuade everybody to stand on the side-lines and look at the gossip. There is no hard analysis there, no involvement, and it is the most extraordinary way of teaching politics, a slightly deeper version of the media approach to politics where the gossip is fun but there is no cutting edge of any kind.[6]

The irony was, of course, that the Benn diaries were full of gossip.

And five months later Benn wrote of Butler: 'Considering he's a serious student of a political scene, he's got no grasp of what is happening or what might happen. It's not really worth arguing with him because I'll never shift his view.' Benn felt that Butler was now 'in the category of people working in a university entirely bought over and influenced by commercial forces', and even cited the fact that his college had been founded by the wealthy Lord Nuffield.[7]

The suspicion of Butler's politics continued during the 1983 election. 'David is an old friend,' Benn wrote, 'but seeing him is really like being parachuted for half an hour into the SDP–Liberal Alliance camp.'[8] Butler's view of the same meeting was that Benn, 'when intoxicated by the enthusiasm of his own audience … moves some way from reality'.[9]

Six days later, Margaret Thatcher increased her majority to 144, while the Labour vote fell to under 8.5 million – or 27.6 per cent, the party's lowest share of the vote since 1931. But Benn's verdict was that eight and a half million people had voted for socialism. A month later, Benn was even more scathing of Butler: 'He is basically a Tory wet and looks at the world through the eyes of Francis Pym and says that Mrs Thatcher is not extreme whereas the Labour Party is, and I got rather more crabby with him than I should have done.'[10] Butler himself reported that, 'Once more, as so often in Anthony's house, I had a sense of amiable non-communication. Anthony lives in a private world of wishful thinking.'[11] Yet the affection remained. 'Nowhere in this hour and a half', said Butler, 'was there any sign of decrepitude in Anthony although he does wear his deaf aid. He was the lively enthusiastic zealot that I have always known.'[12] Every time he went back to Nuffield, Benn complained a year later, he felt 'more and more remote' from his 'old mates', but 'I have chosen the other side in the class war'.[13]

The tensions between Benn and Butler reflected the growing bitterness within British politics during the early 1980s, especially on the centre-left after Roy Jenkins, Shirley Williams and others broke away from the Labour Party in 1981 to form the Social Democratic Party. The SDP promised to 'break the mould of British politics', and polls from the early '80s suggested that the SDP, working with the Liberals in what became the Alliance, might actually succeed in that aim. Indeed, many polls in late 1981 and early 1982 suggested that, in combination, the SDP and the Liberals were more popular than either the Conservatives or Labour, and it looked likely that the next general election would produce a hung parliament. So, David Butler and Vernon Bogdanor convened a couple of private one-day conferences at Nuffield College, similar to those in the past on the broadcasting of elections. Politicians and senior civil servants were invited to discuss the repercussions if Britain was again to enter a period, like much of the inter-war years, where no party had a majority.

The conferences produced the book *Governing Without a*

Majority, published at the start of 1983, and which David Butler – the sole author, unusually – considered one of his most important works. In some ways, it was also one of his most personal books, and showed his increasing interest in moving beyond elections to political scenarios in a hung parliament. Butler warned that just because the country had experienced one-party rule since 1945, it might not carry on that way, and he forecast that a future hung parliament would radically alter large parts of the British constitution. 'The rules of the game in British politics are deeply intertwined with the assumption that one party will win a clear majority and rule the roost,' he wrote. 'If that assumption is no longer valid, a very large proportion of the normal conventions of government would come under challenge.' The book examined not just the British precedents for minority and coalition government in the past, but also overseas experience.[14]

Within weeks of publication, though, the book looked embarrassingly redundant, as Margaret Thatcher boosted her majority to 144 seats in the May 1983 election. Yet the book's significance was maintained. Before nearly every election for the next thirty years, as the votes for minor parties gradually rose – and thus the number of seats not held by the two main parties – there would be speculation that there might be a hung parliament next time round. Butler's book was updated before the 1987 election and it came to be treated within politics and government as something of a handbook on the constitutional precedents and options. Yet, surprisingly, every general election until 2010 produced a majority for one party or the other (though for a spell in the mid-'90s John Major lost his majority). In the late noughties, however, with Gordon Brown looking set to lose his majority at the next election, but with David Cameron and the Conservatives looking not quite strong enough to win outright, the speculation grew. A report prepared by the Institute for Government in 2009 contained several citations of Butler's book, even though the latest edition was more than twenty years old.[15]

June 1979 had another big constitutional innovation when Britain took part in the first ever direct elections to the European Parliament. Even though Butler was in the midst of writing his account of the 1979 general election, which had occurred only a month before, Nuffield and Macmillan agreed he should write a separate history of these first European elections, which he did in collaboration with the former Labour MP David Marquand (who had given up his Commons seat to become an adviser to Roy Jenkins, Britain's only ever President of the European Commission).[16]

Books on the European elections were never likely to be great bestsellers, or to make much money for Macmillan, and it would be an incomplete series. Butler wrote further volumes to cover the 1984 Euro elections, written with Paul Jowett, and for the 1994, 1999 and 2004 European contests, written with Martin Westlake, but the 1989 campaign, and those of 2009 and 2014, which involved the historic rise of Ukip, would go uncovered. (When Butler retired from writing, there was no obvious successor; nor were the resources available.)[17] A major problem was that, apart from occasional trips to academic conferences in France, David Butler had never taken much interest in politics or elections in the rest of Europe, nor studied how politics worked within the European Community. So, broadly speaking, for all three volumes Butler wrote the British end of the account – events in Westminster and Whitehall and the campaigns in Britain – while Marquand, Jowett and Westlake dealt with the European angles: developments in Brussels and the contests in other EU states.

Meanwhile, the main books in the Nuffield series – those on general elections by Butler and Dennis Kavanagh – started to face competition from other books on elections, and these were often written by former colleagues on the Nuffield series. In 1976, the Washington DC think tank, the American Enterprise Institute for Public Policy Research, initiated the 'Britain at the Polls' series of books on each general election, and Anthony King and Ivor Crewe played leading roles in several of the volumes. Through various publishers, these have analysed every British election since February 1974, with the exceptions of 1987 and 2015.

After the 1979 election, the pollster Robert Worcester and the Political Studies Association had convened a one-day conference on the contest, at Essex University. This spawned the book *Political Communications: The General Election Campaign of 1979*, which included chapters from numerous academics based on their conference papers, and focusing, as the title suggests, on media aspects of the campaign.[18] Similar books, based on similar PSA conferences, have been published after every subsequent election.

Another competitor came in the shape of Richard Rose, Butler's co-author in 1959, and Ian McAllister. In *The Nationwide Competition for Votes: The 1983 British Election*, they argued that the books in the Nuffield series were 'centralist, concentrating upon a few square miles around Parliament' (though it would have been harder to make such a charge before 1970, when each Nuffield book had several chapters on individual constituencies). Rose and McAllister's account therefore focused considerably more than Butler's books ever had on the election in distant parts of England, and with separate chapters on Scotland, Wales and Northern Ireland.[19]

In a fascinating article on their working relationship, published in 1992, Dennis Kavanagh cited David Butler's 'optimism and his sheer busyness' as among his many great virtues:

> Having so many activities in hand has meant that, if he was disappointed in one task, he could proceed to the next. Also remarkable is his energy, indeed hyperactivity. He always seems to be bustling and rushing somewhere … I have known him arrive at Heathrow at 9 in the morning from a flight from Australia (having written an article for the *Spectator* on the flight) and a few hours later give a promised talk to students in Oxford. This illustrates both his concern about punctuality and his determination to carry out

> commitments, regardless of personal inconvenience ... David talks and lectures at high speed. In conversation, he sometimes seems to be thinking of his next question before you have answered the last one. His welcome for deadlines and apparent relish for working in a breathless hurry were, of course, additional reasons why some academics, forever sniffing out superficiality, held him in suspicion. His desire for haste has sometimes got the better of him.[20]

These observations by Dennis Kavanagh were first published in a book of essays called *Electoral Politics*, which he edited to mark David Butler's retirement from Nuffield in 1992. The book included a photo of Butler as a frontispiece, and contributions from many of his closest colleagues and co-authors over the years. Yet even here, in a laudatory profile, were hints of the strains in their relationship. Kavanagh revealed that 'nothing irritated me more' about working with Butler 'than his weakness for the telephone', which he suggested would be his co-author's one luxury on *Desert Island Discs*, or several phones perhaps (though, as someone with no interest in music, Butler was hardly likely to be invited onto the programme). Kavanagh recalls how his daughter Jane, who helped in Butler's office on the 1987 book, 'didn't understand his mania for being on the phone all the time', even when deadlines were fast approaching. 'He was waiting for calls from the Beeb, or for gossip. He'd look bewildered at the phone, willing it to ring. "Oh, well I'll have to do some work, then," he'd say. If it had been David's wish, it would have been to have two phones going off simultaneously.'[21]

Much more scathing in academic terms was Kavanagh's remark that Butler learnt 'more by conversation than by keeping up with the literature of a subject'. If forced to choose, Kavanagh said, Butler would 'prefer to learn about his subject by talking to politicians than reading books'.[22] It was a fair point, for Butler had acknowledged in his diary when he was a young man how he never found time to read books. He once observed to his colleague Vernon Bogdanor that politics was a language and that one had to 'mix with those who spoke it' – politicians, officials and journalists. 'He was probably right,' Bogdanor says.[23]

Some of Butler's Nuffield colleagues were rather more disdainful, especially when talking in private. 'Mere journalism' is how politics fellow Nevil Johnson, who occupied the adjacent room to Butler in college, would dismiss his activity. 'Nevil Johnson had a kind of phobia about David,' says the former Labour minister and Nuffield alumnus Andrew Adonis, who recalls Johnson saying Butler 'never does more than float above the surface'.[24] 'Johnson was a clever man,' Butler recalls, 'but extraordinarily difficult.'[25]

The college's long-standing and highly distinguished sociologist John Goldthorpe – a famously blunt Yorkshireman – had conducted many social surveys over the years. Goldthorpe and his Nuffield colleague Chelly Halsey were especially interested in occupational and social mobility, which was not far removed from some of the work that Butler and Donald Stokes did in the '60s and '70s for *Political Change in Britain*. Goldthorpe was a great admirer of Stokes but felt that Butler relied on the American too much, and that he didn't understand statistics beyond basic arithmetic. He didn't know how to design proper surveys, Goldthorpe thought, and didn't understand the work that others were doing on class and voting behaviour. 'I don't think David was interested in intellectual issues,' Goldthorpe says. 'His worlds are politics, media and government.'[26]

Relations between Goldthorpe and Butler were always cordial, but the sociologist was especially annoyed by a debate in the college's governing body in the late 1970s involving the Indian economist and future Nobel prizewinner Amartya Sen, then an Oxford economics professor based at Nuffield. Sen has always been interested in issues that straddle the borders between economics and philosophy – in particular, welfare economics – and he suggested to his senior colleagues that Nuffield should introduce a fellowship for philosophy. But Butler was worried that having a philosopher on the books would probably mean one fewer politics fellow. Nuffield was a specialist college, he argued, and its narrow range of specialisms worked well together. 'David's view prevailed,' John Goldthorpe recalls. 'So Amartya left and moved to be chair of economics in association with All Souls. It was a great loss to the college and cost us a Nobel laureate.'[27]

At the start of the BBC results programme in 1979, David Butler proudly told David Dimbleby, who'd replaced Alastair Burnet as presenter, that he'd been starring on election nights since 1950. He did not know it then, but it would be his last such show for the BBC. Although he was still only fifty-four, Butler's shock of grey hair made him look rather older. Around 1980, he was taken to lunch in Charlotte Street by the editor put in charge of the subsequent programme, David Dickinson, and told he would not be used on BBC TV next time round.

It was an understandable decision. Television producers like to balance heavyweight experience with fresh faces. There was a feeling that the coverage in past years had been too academic, and occasionally went over the heads of some viewers. 'Nobody doubted his expertise,' says the former BBC head of current affairs Chris Capron, 'but he came over dryly and without very much sense of humour. And on general election night, programmes really thrived on having a sense of humour.'[28]

The death in 1981 of Butler's on-screen sparring partner Bob McKenzie meant that the BBC's 1983 election had two new psephologists, Anthony King and Ivor Crewe from Essex University, who had both contributed to the Nuffield election studies and came, in a way, from the David Butler 'stable'.

In subsequent years, BBC TV would employ two other psephologists on election night whom one might call members of the 'David Butler school'. Peter Kellner had known and admired Butler since he was an economics student at Cambridge in the late 1960s. During one term, Butler was contracted to come over from Oxford to deliver a series of eight lectures on British politics on Friday mornings, since, remarkably, Cambridge had no real politics course or academics at that time. To save time, Butler gave the lectures in four pairs. He drove over early in the morning and delivered one lecture at 9 a.m. and then the second at 11 a.m., before driving back to Nuffield. Kellner recalls the lectures were 'hugely popular', and how during the hour-long break between them, Butler would sit in the Sidgwick Buttery, where he would happily chat over coffee to the more eager students, and 'regale us with his insights'.[29]

John Curtice (who in 2018 became Sir John) remembers staying up as a ten-year-old schoolboy to watch Butler and McKenzie on the 1964 results programme, and later he used a book token awarded as a school prize to acquire the first edition of Butler and Stokes's book *Political Change in Britain*. Years later, in the late 1970s, Butler supervised Curtice's DPhil at Nuffield and quickly spotted his potential, appointing him in succession to Gus O'Donnell in the 'feeder' role on the 1979 BBC results programme, when Curtice remembers witnessing the on- and off-screen rivalry-cum-friendship between Butler and Bob McKenzie.

Butler also asked Curtice to join Michael Steed in the same role that had given him his great career break back in 1945: writing the statistical appendix to the 1979 Nuffield book. Curtice recalls being surprised that Butler didn't really explain what the appendix should focus on. 'It was never clearly laid out. He wasn't somebody thinking in terms of a broad intellectual structure, and "Here are the three things I'd like you to answer."' Curtice has been involved in the Nuffield appendix ever since and remains grateful to Butler for advising him very early in his psephological career to get to grips with the latest computing methods and technology. 'I'm too old and I'll never do it,' Butler reportedly told Curtice. 'You need to go and get statistically trained and learn how to use computers.'[30] Butler teamed Curtice up with Clive Payne, the Nuffield computer wizard, and Curtice's career never looked back.

Payne also worked on BBC election nights and suspects Butler's departure from the TV programmes may have in some small way been connected to the arrival of Angela Rippon, the first woman on a BBC election programme. Her job was to summarise the results at regular intervals. Payne recalls that the two established pundits regarded her as a mere newsreader who knew nothing about elections. He particularly remembers an occasion during a rehearsal in 1979 when Rippon inadvertently reversed a couple of figures. 'He shouted out across the studio, "That's rubbish!" After that, he didn't appear on BBC TV as a commentator again.'[31]

Having been told that he was no longer needed on screen, David Butler was hurt by the BBC decision. He'd done ten successive BBC general election broadcasts dating back to 1950, plus innumerable special programmes on by-elections and local government elections. The news came without any warning from senior executives, some of whom he regarded as friends. 'I was slightly shocked that I was being sacked from a position I had for twenty-nine years, just slightly carelessly by a relatively middle-level producer over a lunch,' he says.[32]

But Butler wasn't dropped by the BBC entirely, and he was switched to become a studio analyst for the overnight Radio 4 programmes for the next three contests – 1983, 1987 and 1992 – working alongside Brian Redhead, and under the editorship of his former researcher Anne Sloman, who until the mid-'80s was still co-author of *British Political Facts*. His friend Paul McKee also arranged for him to be employed as a regular analyst on elections and by-elections for ITN's fledgling evening news programme *Channel 4 News* (which is how the author got to know him).

Indeed, far from Butler's output reducing as he moved into his sixties, it seemed to expand yet further. He also began writing regular analysis columns for *The Times*, usually commissioned by George Brock, the son of the Warden at Nuffield, Michael Brock. And in 1982, Butler also helped found the international academic journal *Electoral Studies* and served as co-editor for the next ten years (along with Bo Särlvik from Essex). It was a useful addition to scholarly literature, as Butler's own work over the years, writing for a patchwork of different journals, showed there was an obvious gap in the market for a journal on elections. *Electoral Studies* was truly international, both in its editorial board (twenty-eight members from seventeen countries), and in its subject matter. It was unfortunate, though, that like so many academic journals at that time, it was published by Pergamon, the firm owned by the crooked Oxford-based businessman Robert Maxwell.

In the late 1970s, David Butler also convened a regular discussion for politics dons throughout the university. Butler enjoys lunching and dining clubs and they met, like the Australia group, once a month in the Welsh Pony pub, where colleagues were encouraged to talk about any book they'd read in the past month, or any developments in their field.

Apart from becoming Warden of Nuffield, Butler says his only other real ambition was to achieve the highest professorship in the university's politics department. By the late 1970s it was pretty unusual for an academic of his age, distinction and wider reputation not to be a professor. The Gladstone Professor of Government and Public Administration was founded only in 1944, and is attached to All Souls College, the most eminent academically of all the colleges at either Oxford or Cambridge. The three previous Gladstone professors had been Kenneth Wheare, Max Beloff and the brilliant and charismatic Samuel Finer, who held the job until 1982. Butler says Sammy Finer encouraged him to go for the position on the basis that he had the greatest international reputation of any politics don at Oxford. Among others to apply in 1984 were Vernon Bogdanor, Butler's protégé at Brasenose; Bernard Crick, the politics professor at Birkbeck College, London; and Butler's neighbour at Nuffield, Nevil Johnson. Butler was never even interviewed, which must have been especially galling given that his close friend Philip Williams was on the selection panel.

In the end, the committee went for Peter Pulzer, a don at Christ Church. Pulzer was probably seen as the safer choice, though shortly afterwards he orchestrated the famous and controversial vote in which Oxford dons rejected Margaret Thatcher for an honorary degree.

Butler's bid for the Gladstone professorship may have been hindered by his wanting the post to be transferred to Nuffield College, at a time when his college's pre-eminence was resented by many people in Oxford social sciences. They thought the college was spoilt and that Nuffield fellows spent too much time trying to make a name for themselves in the outside world. There was no better example, they probably felt, than David Butler.

'I thought it very unjust,' says Vernon Bogdanor, who says he didn't really expect the job himself.

> It was mean to deny him a chair, especially when he was an international figure, and also so good with students. He was probably the figure best-known in that area of politics, and the best person to succeed Sammy Finer. I think he took it quite hard, though he never showed it, and never showed any malice to anyone about it.[33]

On reflection though, Butler says it was just as well he didn't get the Gladstone professorship. He doesn't think he would have enjoyed life at All Souls (even though several ancestors had gone there). It is probably the greatest 'ivory tower' of them all – indeed, unlike most colleges, its towers are genuinely ivory-coloured. All Souls has no students and consists entirely of fellows, and it has a forbidding reputation for the high level of intellectual and cultural discussion at its illustrious formal dinners. 'I wouldn't have been very good in the range of subjects – political theory being quite outside my subject,' Butler said later. 'To be the leading figure in politics [at Oxford] wouldn't have been my scene.'[34] Nor, Butler suspects, would he have enjoyed the responsibility of administering the Oxford politics syllabus, and trying to modernise it in a federal university where change was notoriously slow and much power still lay with the individual colleges. There was an attempt, in 1989, to make Butler the Professor of Politics, but the post went to Archie Brown instead. The university could have found Butler a chair of some kind, of course, but his colleagues chose not to do so. So, like the historian A. J. P. Taylor – and probably for similar reasons – David Butler never became an Oxford professor.

Instead, in 1986, Butler spent a term at the University of Virginia in Charlottesville. He enjoyed it considerably, and the university made him and Marilyn a very attractive offer (though David says it was really Marilyn they wanted). Would they both like to take up professorships in Virginia? The Butlers effectively accepted and even started looking for somewhere to live in Virginia. But then came the offer of an academic post which was just as distinguished as the Gladstone professorship, if not more so.

CHAPTER SIXTEEN

THE RECTOR'S HUSBAND

The news came out of the blue from Margaret Thatcher's Downing Street – not to David, but to his wife. The Prime Minister, she was told, with the approval of the Queen, would like to confer on her the role of King Edward VII Professor of English Literature at Cambridge University. It is one of the most illustrious positions in higher education in Britain. Founded and endowed by the great newspaper baron Lord Rothermere in 1910, and officially in the gift of the Crown, the post is regarded in all but name as one of Britain's historic Regius professorships. Marilyn Butler was thrilled. The job had 'a special aura', she felt, 'partly because England (unlike Scotland) has no other Regius chair in English', and 'partly because of the high standing of Cambridge English'.[1]

Previous incumbents of the chair had included the renowned literary critic Sir Arthur Quiller-Couch, who held it from 1912 to 1944. Frank Kermode and Christopher Ricks were more recent incumbents. But Marilyn Butler would be the first woman ever to hold the professorship. Nevertheless, it took her several weeks to decide whether to accept the job. Apart from the offer from Virginia, there was now the prospect of the couple living apart, but in the end she accepted. Plans to move to America were abandoned, even though it entailed some financial sacrifice given the substantially higher salaries both Butlers would have earned in America.

Marilyn had succeeded where David had failed. Perhaps it was partly because she had played the game in academic terms, while he hadn't. By the 1980s, university scholars were increasingly and narrowly judged on their peer-reviewed articles in learned journals. It was considered rather old-fashioned for an academic to concentrate on books, especially books for commercial publishers, as David had done. Despite editing *Electoral Studies*, the journal he had co-founded, David's output of scholarly articles over the previous forty years had been pretty erratic. Marilyn had also written a few books, of course, but put much more of her effort into writing articles not to be devoured by ordinary people, but to feed the increasingly self-referential and claustrophobic world of academic publishing. Each journal article had to be approved before publication, anonymously by a group of fellow academics. Then she, like tens of thousands of university colleagues around the world, would partly be rated according to the number of times her work was cited in articles and books by other academics. That was never a world in which David was comfortable, though the citation record from his book output would nonetheless have been impressive.

People were immediately struck by David's immense pride in his wife's achievement. He was not just content, but positively delighted that from now on Marilyn would hold the more high-powered and academically prestigious job. It was agreed they would commute weekly from Oxford to Cambridge, though at different times and in separate cars. Marilyn would leave on Monday morning and return on Friday night. David, however, drove over to Cambridge on Wednesday evening and returned to Oxford on Friday as well. Still only sixty-one, David was keen to carry on working at Nuffield. He had no plans for immediate retirement, and had learnt from the example of his father, who had died of cancer of the liver at the age of seventy-two in 1951, when David was only twenty-six. 'I resented his dying. I liked him,' Butler later wrote in 2005.

Perhaps the cancer was inevitable – but I suspected that he died

> because, though quite contented, he had nothing more to do. I resolved that in retirement I would have a full agenda and that, when I died or became incompetent, I would still have things piled up, waiting for me to read or write.[2]

Marilyn's new role also fitted in neatly with the rest of the family. By 1986, the Butlers' two oldest sons, Daniel and Gareth, had finished studying at Cambridge. Gareth, who got a first in history from Caius, was working as a researcher to two Labour MPs, Denis Healey and Tom Clarke, with thoughts of perhaps going into politics himself one day. Of the three boys, Gareth looked most like his father, and took the most interest in David's work; he displayed the same trainspotterish love of facts. Indeed, while Gareth was still at Cambridge, his father appointed him to succeed Anne Sloman as his co-editor of *British Political Facts* (starting on the sixth edition, published in 1986). David was always closest to Gareth, whom he once called 'the most talented of my sons'.[3]

When Rab Butler had retired as Master of Trinity College, Cambridge in 1978, *The Times* had carried a valedictory profile pointing out that he was the last of a continuous line of Butler dons in Cambridge dating back to 1794. Hope of continuing the dynasty, the writer suggested – in Oxbridge terms at least – rested with David Butler in Oxford. 'He has already done his best by marrying another Oxford don and producing three sons. It remains to be seen whether they will make sure that the name of Butler is as well known in academic circles in future generations as it has been in the past.'[4] The boys were understandably embarrassed.

In fact, none of the three thought of following their parents into the scholastic life, and David made great efforts to find them employment elsewhere. Dan, who got a 2:2 in history from Trinity College (where another Butler relative, Henry Montagu, had also once been Master), spent several months with the polling firm MORI, then joined the British Retail Consortium before becoming a journalist at Haymarket Publishing. These posts were all thanks in turn to his father's contacts with the pollster Bob Worcester (with whom Dan later fell out), the former MP Tom McNally and Haymarket owner Michael Heseltine.

The only son for whom Marilyn's new job was a slight problem was Ed, who was still a student at Queens' College, Cambridge, and actually reading his mother's subject, English Literature. He dutifully attended her classes and lectures.

By convention, any Cambridge professor also becomes a fellow of one of the colleges, upon which a Regius professor can confer great prestige. Newnham, an all-women college, sought Marilyn's presence, but she was reluctant to join a place that hadn't yet resolved whether to admit men. She'd had enough of such arguments at St Hugh's in Oxford, where she'd upset some colleagues by switching sides after concluding that the admission of men would only reduce the opportunities for women.

Jesus College offered her a whole house, but she didn't think the family could cope with a third house on top of their two homes back in Oxfordshire. Christ's offered her rooms in the college, but they were too small for two people. 'I've got a husband, too,' she told them. 'Oh no, you can have a lover,' they apparently replied, 'but not a husband.'[5] King's College offered a set of rooms with perfect views: 'one way facing Clare and the Cam', says David, 'the other way, Queens' and another bit of the Cam'. Indeed, they could just about see Ed's room in Queens'.[6] So King's it was.

There were private mutterings that Marilyn Butler had been the beneficiary of positive discrimination, that she only got the job because she was a woman, but few would complain about her seven years in office. She was taking a bit of a risk, however, since the English faculty at Cambridge had a reputation as something of a snake-pit. Her predecessor but one, Frank Kermode, had resigned in 1982 after a very public row between younger and older factions over whether to employ the young theorist Colin MacCabe. Yet

Marilyn decided to be refreshingly individual from the start, surprising members of the faculty when she devoted her inaugural lecture to the poetry of Robert Southey, the overlooked member of the Romantic trio that included Wordsworth and Coleridge. One colleague says some were 'evidently perplexed' by her interest in such a subsidiary writer, and he suggests 'there might have been some mischief in her choice – she certainly had an entertainingly naughty streak'. But Marilyn maintained that Southey's works had once been 'admired by the most knowing of his contemporaries and that was good enough reason for us to return to them'.[7]

Her former Cambridge colleague Nigel Leask remembers how she would be an 'energetic presence' at colleagues' seminars and lectures, 'insisting on always asking at least one question'. Leask noted her habit (rather like David) of scribbling notes on filing cards, 'upon which she would subsequently draw for her lectures and articles'.[8] Her classes would often stray beyond the official time, and afterwards Marilyn might take students round to the pub to continue the discussion. Indeed, she was well-known for her sociability and love of conversation. One former colleague recalled how on an evening flight back from America, Marilyn talked through the night.

For seven years Marilyn convened a regular Cambridge seminar on intellectual history with her colleague Stefan Collini. The English professor John Mullan, who was then at Cambridge, has said research students from that era remember her:

> utterly refreshing effect on the somewhat stolid world of eighteenth-century and Romantic studies at the university. Here was a senior academic for whom seminars were also social gatherings, who seemed actually to enjoy talking to students and was warm in her encouragement of those at the beginning of their academic careers.[9]

'She was always approachable and eager to listen,' Nigel Leask recalls, 'and willing to share her insights and opinions – even the latest faculty gossip – with graduate students and early career researchers: this was in marked contrast to some others of her rank and academic celebrity, who often left us tongue-tied, preferring to cultivate a remote charisma rather than intellectual sociability.'[10] 'She loved gossip, but with her it was never malicious,' remarked her friend and close colleague Heather Glen. 'Her shrewd sense of what was going on in a situation was always tempered by a sense of its comedy.' Underpinning everything, Glen said, was Marilyn's 'sense of academic work as a collaborative process, of the intellectual life not as a competition but as conversation: a conversation that she found endlessly fascinating'.[11]

Marilyn Butler would describe the Cambridge chair as the most stimulating time of her professional career, 'but in scholarly terms also the most frustrating' because of the administrative and professional responsibilities which the post involved, and her writing output inevitably diminished. Quite apart from the regular classes and lectures a King Edward professor has to give, she had to consider book proposals (as an editor for the Cambridge University Press), read the work of her graduate students and provide references for students and colleagues to obtain jobs. Her duties also included numerous university and English faculty committees, in an era when education was rapidly becoming more bureaucratic and cost-conscious, and senior scholars, she said, were 'diverted into vastly amplified systems of appraisal and assessment'.[12]

Meanwhile David, who reached his 65th birthday in October 1989, maintained his extraordinary workload well into the next decade. In 1991 he was awarded a CBE, public recognition which was surprisingly late given his important contributions over the years to several fields. There was an effort to get him a knighthood instead, but the proposal was dismissed, it's rumoured, by a rather snobbish senior civil servant on the grounds that Butler had never held any top academic post of sufficient stature: he'd never been head of an Oxbridge college, nor a full-blown professor.

Butler formally retired from his duties as a fellow of Nuffield College at the age of sixty-seven, when the college made him an emeritus fellow. The event was marked by several profiles in the national press around the time of his final Friday seminar, after thirty-three years, in March 1992. He was presented with a book containing letters of congratulation from three former Prime Ministers and three former Cabinet Secretaries, including a poem from one of them, Lord (Robert) Armstrong. The seminars were split into two forms thereafter. In Hilary term, until the early 2000s, Butler and Vernon Bogdanor acted as co-convenors of similar politics seminars at Brasenose College. And in Trinity term ever since, Nuffield has hosted media and politics seminars in conjunction with the Oxford Reuters Institute for the Study of Journalism. They continue to this day, and the seminar room where they are held has been renamed the Butler Room, and is adorned by several of his Hogarth prints which he donated to the college.

Lord Armstrong, while Cabinet Secretary in the 1980s, had also been the driving force behind another of Butler's ventures over the years, the Redcliffe-Maud Club, which brought together Oxford academics and senior civil servants to share thinking and expertise in quiet seclusion. It was named after Lord (John) Redcliffe-Maud, the ultimate super-brain mandarin, whose long career as a top civil servant was sandwiched between spells at Oxford, and who is perhaps best known for his report on English local government. The club, of around ten dons and ten mandarins, met several times a year in various Oxford colleges over a period of about twenty years. After drinks and a good dinner, members would listen to one of their number introduce the discussion on a major issue, and then chew things over for an hour and a half.

Around the time of his Nuffield retirement, Butler stepped down from the editorship of *Electoral Studies* after a decade, but almost immediately took on the chairmanship of the Hansard Society, which promotes democracy and parliamentary institutions at home and overseas. He used the post as a platform to campaign for his long-standing view that Britain needed an Electoral Commission, which he'd already promoted in 1991 as vice-chairman of a Hansard Society committee on election campaigns chaired by the former Conservative minister Christopher Chataway.[13] After both Labour and the Liberal Democrats committed themselves to the idea in their manifestos in 1997, Butler now reiterated the case in a second pamphlet for the society.[14] He also presented his argument to the Commons Home Affairs Committee, who agreed with Butler that 'experience in other countries, notably Australia and India, has shown the value of a permanent body in charge of electoral matters'.[15]

But when a new Electoral Commission was set up by the Blair government in 2000, Butler declined to serve as a commissioner himself, as he felt it would constrain his other work and his ability to make public statements. However, he did chair a seminar for the new commission to advise those who had agreed to serve as commissioners. In 1997, when the Labour government established an inquiry under Roy Jenkins – known as the Jenkins Commission – to look at alternatives to the first-past-the-post voting system, the former SDP leader recruited Butler to convene a group of academic experts to advise on the technical aspects of different systems. In 2002, in similar vein, Butler and the journalist Peter Riddell chaired an independent commission for the Constitution Unit at University College London, which examined the various forms of proportional representation that had been introduced around the UK, especially since 1997.

Alongside regular updated versions of *British Political Facts*, Butler remained co-author of the Nuffield election studies, which developed into a fairly routine operation in which several chapters were written by contributors who would do the same job for many editions, including John Curtice and Michael Steed on the statistical appendix. Dennis Kavanagh started taking extensive notes during interviews, rather than wait until afterwards, as had been Butler's practice, and he also persuaded Butler that not all the material had to be used unattributably. Instead, the co-authors agreed that sources could be quoted by name providing that they approved the quotes before publication.

In the 1992 volume, Butler and Dennis Kavanagh were the first people, it seems, to publish the term 'New Labour' to describe leader Neil Kinnock and the group around him – including Peter Mandelson, Gordon Brown and Tony Blair – who wanted to make the party more attractive to middle-class voters. 'By 1990,' Butler and Kavanagh wrote:

> Labour was now perhaps divided less on traditional left-right lines than between old Labour and new Labour. Old Labour was identified with the values and interests of the past, with high taxes, public ownership, trade unions, council housing, heavy industry and the north. New Labour sought to identify the party with skills training, new ways of working, improved public services, greater rights for women and families, and protection of the environment.[16]

David Butler extended his 'instant history' work with an account of one of the most disastrous decisions ever taken by a British government: the poll tax (or community charge) introduced by the Thatcher government in the late 1980s and then abolished with great haste once John Major became Prime Minister in 1990. The book, which like the Nuffield election studies was based on interviews with nearly all the major players, scotched several long-standing myths about the poll tax. Not least of these was that Thatcher herself had initiated the idea with the help of friends in ideological think tanks such as the Adam Smith Institute; on the contrary, the authors showed, the main instigators were left-wing Tories such as William Waldegrave, George Younger and Kenneth Baker. It was written jointly with the LSE local government specialist Tony Travers and the former Nuffield fellow and future Labour minister Andrew Adonis. They called it *Failure in British Government*, as they felt the phrase 'poll tax' on the spine might not help it sell, and rather than list themselves alphabetically on the cover, they put Butler's name first in the hope that his reputation would boost sales.[17]

While David was still pursuing his interests in Oxford, Marilyn Butler was finding Cambridge University rather grand – 'a succession of huge palaces', she once said – in contrast to Oxford's 'medieval row of little houses', a university which had begun as a place for ordinary folk who were interested in ideas.[18] It was perhaps inevitable that David and Marilyn would return in time to Oxford, especially as they went back there most weekends anyway. In 1993, Marilyn started thinking about becoming an Oxford head of house, at a time when only five colleges had ever appointed a woman to the job – and those were all colleges which were historically women-only: Lady Margaret Hall, Somerville, St Hugh's, St Hilda's and St Anne's. It was clear that three headships would become vacant in the summer of 1994: Keble, Merton and also Exeter, the fourth oldest college in the university. College governing bodies like to spend at least twelve months on the selection process, and Marilyn had already applied for Keble and Merton when, in June 1993, the Rector of Exeter College, Richard Norman, suddenly died in office.

More than four decades earlier, in 1952, David had applied to become politics tutor at Exeter, only to be pipped for the job by Norman Crowther-Hunt, who went on to become a minister in the Wilson government of the 1970s, and later Rector of Exeter himself (just before Richard Norman). It may have been just as well Butler did not get the tutor's job, for Nuffield had given him what he later told people was a 'forty-year sabbatical', with the freedom to write books, to travel overseas and to pursue the issues that interested him. As a tutor at Exeter, Butler would have been burdened with a heavy timetable of tutorials and university lectures.

Under Exeter's statutes, the college was obliged to appoint a successor by the end of the summer vacation, at the start of October. Jeri Johnson, an English fellow at Exeter who had known Marilyn at St Hugh's, approached her to see if she would allow her name to be put forward. She would. Among other attractions, Marilyn liked the fact that Exeter was so close to the Bodleian Library. But the election was 'distressingly contentious', Johnson later said, though that is often the case in such appointments. Marilyn's main rival was David Vaisey, a former Exeter undergraduate who was now a fellow of the college, having also become head of the Bodleian Library. He was a popular, genial figure, and seen as the 'safe' candidate. The Exeter governing body – about forty people – interviewed the candidates, both formally and informally, chatting to them over a long dinner accompanied by lots of drink. Marilyn 'scandalised more than one fellow', says Johnson, when she was asked whether she believed in God. 'In reply, she gave a brief account of her adolescent reading of Bertrand Russell, after which, she said, the rest was at best agnosticism.' But the bursar was impressed that Marilyn had such a good grasp of the college's accounts. She later admitted that David had given her a special tutorial in the matter. When the fellows met privately, they couldn't agree, so it went to a secret ballot. 'Marilyn won in the first round,' recalls Johnson, 'much to the astonishment, I believe, of many in the room.'[19]

David was staying with Don Aitkin in Canberra when Marilyn rang to tell him. Aitkin picked up the house phone and chatted to Marilyn for a few moments, before passing the phone to David. 'I think she's got it,' David recalls him saying.[20]

As with the Cambridge professorship, it was a highly symbolic achievement. By persuading Marilyn to start early, Exeter became the first previously all-male college at either Oxford or Cambridge to appoint a female head. A few weeks later – by coincidence, or maybe not – Keble and Merton chose women as their new heads too, although they didn't take over until the summer of 1994.

Marilyn started at the end of 1993, after a term when she doubled up as Rector-elect while also serving out her notice in Cambridge.

Jeri Johnson subsequently revealed there had been a serious division by age: while most of the Exeter fellows under forty-five had supported Marilyn, she reckoned, those over forty-five mainly hadn't. 'Marilyn was to assume the rectorship of a college riven,' she later said.[21] Yet Marilyn Butler soon managed to heal the internal divisions. Indeed, she displayed similar generosity to that which David had often shown at Nuffield. Marilyn's 'delight in people and conversation' was not limited to the academic fellows, says Jeri Johnson. 'It extended without interruption to staff, to scouts, to her beloved housekeeper and her PA, indeed to everyone.'[22] She occasionally taught English undergraduates, and also become well-known for making witty speeches.

When Marilyn and David moved into the college at the start of 1994, they were invited by the bursar for a drink with the architect who'd been renovating the buildings in the main quadrangle. To their surprise, they were taken out into Turl Street and invited to look up at a row of thirteen grotesques stretching southwards along the street – small sculptures which had recently been carved by the stonemasons on the site, each of which represented a different letter of the new Rector's name – a marigold for the 'M', an archer for the 'a', followed by rondels, the eye of God for the 'I', then a lion; a yew; and Neptune. Her surname comprised carvings of bells, a unicorn, twins, a lamb, an Episcopal figure and a Roman nose. In addition, a grotesque of Marilyn's face was placed inside the main quadrangle, high above the porters' lodge. 'It was a complete surprise,' says David. 'We had no prior knowledge they were being done.'[23] Although the college would later commission David Cobley to paint a fine portrait of Marilyn to sit alongside past rectors in the dining hall, this was a more amusing, more public and more permanent welcoming gesture to the college's first female rector, in keeping with the medieval traditions of much of central Oxford.

By convention, Oxbridge heads of house are made honorary members of the Oxford and Cambridge Club in London, the base where David often conducted background interviews for his books, yet any woman at that time was restricted to becoming just an 'associate member'. So Marilyn ignored the invitation, at a time when many members and senior figures within the two universities were growing increasingly angry about the club's discrimination against women. At the start of 1995, David resigned from the Oxford and Cambridge Club in protest, and kicked up a public fuss by getting *The Times* to publish his resignation letter. It was quite a sacrifice for a man who was so conscious of his ancestry, for his great-grandfather George Butler had been a founding member of the club in 1817, and he himself had enjoyed membership for forty-three years of the club and its predecessor (the United University Club).

The club had balloted its members on the issue in 1993. They voted 76 per cent to 24 per cent to accept women as full members, but club rules required more than 50 per cent of the *entire* membership to vote for any change, and the reformers were seventy votes short. Under the rules, the question could not be raised again until 1998, which Butler felt was too long to wait. Some Oxbridge college heads had already resigned in quiet protest, Butler claimed, along with several other distinguished members. 'One does not lightly give up association with so comfortable and civilised an institution,' he wrote to *The Times*:

> But the action – or the inaction – of the club committee has made it impossible for a self-respecting Oxford don to remain involved with a body that remains so flagrantly impervious to the will of its members or to the norms of contemporary British society ... It is all so silly ... The problems associated with going mixed are negligible. The advantages are great. In 1995 it no longer seems civilised to remain a member of an institution in which the responsible general committee seems determined to retain every existing barrier to the equal treatment of women.[24]

Butler's protests received considerable attention. He was interviewed by the *Today* programme on Radio 4, and for a few days he became something of a feminist hero. He later wrote of how his 'open letter from an unimportant don resigning from a relatively unimportant institution' had 'thrust upon me a strange, if very transitory, prominence ... simply because I ventured to say publicly that, even to a moderate, middle-of-the-road character, it was distasteful to continue association' with a club 'which excluded almost half the members of those universities ... The article struck a reverberating chord.' Not everyone was supportive, though. 'I want to drink in peace,' one angry member wrote to him. 'I don't wish to be surrounded by headmistresses and female dons. Do you? ... I do wish women did not try to run everything. They should restrict that to their families and homes.'[25] Characteristically, the club never replied to Butler's letter and article.

A few weeks afterwards, the two vice-chancellors of Oxford and Cambridge, together with all but four of the seventy or so heads of house, signed a statement accusing the club of 'offensive' and 'discriminatory' policies towards women. They disassociated themselves from the club and threatened legal action if it continued claiming links with the two universities.[26] A year later the Oxford and Cambridge Club finally agreed to admit women as full members.

Butler didn't resume his membership, however. Conveniently, perhaps, the row had occurred just after he had found another comfortable London base which was even better placed for Westminster and Whitehall, and which had lower fees. In 1994, he had been elected a fellow of the British Academy, a rather less formal institution which acts as a kind of West End club for senior university academics, though it was surprising perhaps that Butler had to wait until his 70th year before he was elected.

At Exeter College, in contrast to how they treated their own two houses, the Butlers made a real effort to refurbish the Rector's lodgings; they acquired William Morris wallpaper, new curtains and pictures for the main reception room, and sculptures for the college gardens. They also obtained a bas-relief of the Victorian social reformer Josephine Butler, whose husband George – David's great-uncle – had been a fellow of Exeter in the mid-nineteenth century. David Butler diligently acted as Marilyn's consort – like Denis to Margaret Thatcher, someone remarked – behaving unobtrusively at most of the formal occasions the Rector has to attend, including high table dinners and chapel services (though David was even less of a believer than his wife). He was the first rectorial spouse to be elected as a member of the senior common room (SCR), though he was careful not to abuse his position, making sure, for example, not to hog the SCR's daily copy of *The Times*. He also assisted occasionally with PPE teaching, and unofficially helped supervise a few of the college's graduate students. And his willingness to help wasn't confined to students at Exeter. Chris Ballinger, who was then studying at Queen's College, decided he wanted to write on Australian politics for his mini-dissertation for his PPE degree, with a view to travelling to Australia to do some of the research. Ballinger's tutor advised him to seek Butler's help, though the student was wary.

> This was the great David Butler. I was extremely nervous. I didn't have an academic background. I approached him at a seminar and asked if I could talk to him about Australian politics. He said, 'Come with me now. Are you busy?' He took me back to Exeter, to the Rector's lodgings. We traipsed around darkened corridors, and he gave me an awful lot of books. I was tottering along holding them all. He said, 'When you've read that lot, come back and we'll talk.'[27]

So began yet another of David Butler's mentorships and friendships. Butler agreed to act as Ballinger's supervisor for the dissertation; he wasn't paid for it, though he would have been perfectly entitled to a modest fee for the equivalent of giving eight tutorials. Butler also provided his new student with 'dozens of names' of people in Australian politics, as well as academics at ANU in Canberra who could help him gain access to the National Library. 'The David Butler card gave me the confidence to navigate Australia,' Ballinger says, and:

> a real sense that this world is navigable. I'm a boy from rural Sussex, whose father was a bus mechanic, mother a provincial civil servant. Neither had been at university, and politics was not my world. When I approached him, he didn't know who I was – why should he care? He was six years retired.[28]

Butler had always had a good eye for scholarly talent. As soon as Ballinger's finals were over, he recruited him as a researcher for the 1999 European elections book, and then for the Nuffield book on the 2001 general election, which – apart from the famous Prescott punch – was perhaps the dullest campaign in a hundred years, with Tony Blair being returned with almost exactly the same majority as Labour achieved on coming to power in 1997.

David Butler was still touring the country visiting by-elections and local campaigns with all the gusto he'd displayed fifty years before; rattling off statistics and historical quirks to anyone who'd listen; dashing across busy streets weaving between traffic; and terrifying passengers in his car as he raced from one location to the next. Butler 'appeared more concerned with his stories and observations than our speed or position on the road, which often seemed to wander towards the right-hand side', Ian St John, one of his 1997 researchers, wrote in his diary. 'He drives quickly, and often down narrow country lanes, with one hand on the steering wheel, and with a propensity to overtake on bends.'[29] Yet he never showed any sign of boredom or sense that he'd seen and done it all before. And at the turn of the new millennium, candidates, agents and organisers were happy to talk to this supposedly retired academic, as much as they had in 1950. Indeed, they were talking to an election legend.

Nonetheless, his co-author on the Nuffield election studies, Dennis Kavanagh, felt Butler wasn't pulling his weight enough, and that he himself was having to do too much of the writing, and most of the interviews. It was agreed that the 2005 edition, written when Butler was eighty, would be his last. It had been an extraordinary span, stretching back fifteen editions to 1951, before Tony Blair or most other party leaders of the noughties had even been born. Yet Kavanagh insisted that this time his name should come first on the cover. 'In 2005, we once again worked very hard together,' it was explained in the preface, 'but the burden fell more heavily on Dennis Kavanagh. It therefore seems appropriate, as David Butler bids farewell to the chronicling of general elections, that this final joint venture should be marked by a reversal of names.'[30] The 2005 edition is the shortest of all the Nuffield studies, reflecting another dull campaign, but also perhaps Butler's diminished contribution. Several friends think the 2005 book was 'one Nuffield study too far', though, as we shall see, Butler had other distractions diverting his energy and attention in the summer of 2005, and no longer had the resources he'd enjoyed in the past.

More than fifty years earlier, of course, Winston Churchill had unexpectedly asked the young David Butler whether he had become a handicap to his party. Now, perhaps, as he had so judiciously told Churchill in 1951, David Butler too, after a similar innings of half a century, was no longer the asset to colleagues that he once was.

Yet Butler still displayed extraordinary drive in other respects. As David rushed up a London Underground escalator on his way to a lunch one day, he passed his son Gareth, who was standing while chatting to a BBC colleague. 'Look at him,' Gareth remarked. 'He's eighty, and he still thinks standing on the escalator is immoral.'[31]

Way back in 1987, David Butler had, 'on the spur of the moment', told the governing body of Nuffield that he planned to write a personal history of the college. It was a retirement project on which he did an increasing amount of work after 1992. He collected material and did a few interviews, but 'made little progress', partly, Butler said, because unlike most books he wrote, this project 'never had a deadline'.[32] Later he drafted several chapters and even teamed up with the sociologist A. H. 'Chelly' Halsey to make it a joint effort. Butler went so far as to distribute a questionnaire to all past members of the college, but the project collapsed, though there are different explanations as to why. Butler says Halsey pulled out of the partnership, though he also says he himself realised it was never going to work. 'Chelly thought differently about things – we really had a difference of style of thought, and I knew it was going to get difficult.'[33] But according to another account, 'Chelly Halsey drafted chapters and held meetings with David, but all David would do is talk.' Halsey sought advice as to how other co-authors worked with Butler, but 'gave up, flabbergasted'. The journalist Robert Taylor, who'd been a Nuffield student in the 1960s, took over Butler's work and quickly turned it into his own personal history, which was published in time for the 50th anniversary of the Royal Charter in 2008.[34]

David Butler also kept up the television punditry on election nights. After three elections for Radio 4, the director-general John Birt marked his retirement from the BBC with a big lunch at which Butler was presented with a model ballot box, complete with baby Swingometer and a plaque. Yet for the 1997 election Butler found himself with a berth back on television on ITV's overnight results programme. 'I was amazed that the BBC would let go of the man who I always regarded as the best person on BBC election nights,' says former ITN editor Stewart Purvis.[35] Butler now sat alongside his third Dimbleby – David's younger brother Jonathan – though his appearances during the broadcast were nothing like as frequent as they had been in his BBC heyday. In 2001, Butler switched again, to Sky News, where he made occasional contributions from a 'virtual'

Commons chamber located away from the main action. Sky employed him again in 2005 as one of a panel of analysts, the sixteenth successive election that Butler had worked on an overnight election programme on either TV or radio.

The Butlers left Exeter College in the summer of 2004 when Marilyn, now sixty-seven, retired after ten and a half years as Rector. In the months leading up to her retirement, though, there were signs that, mentally, Marilyn was having problems. 'She always had the ability to discourse in epicycles,' says Brian Stewart, a former maths don, 'but found it increasingly hard to bring the process to a conclusion – and David would rescue her very skilfully and patiently.'[36] Marilyn also kept forgetting things, and the following Christmas, spent with the Evans family in Kingston, Dan recalls his father, just before dinner, leaning across and saying, 'Mum might have Alzheimer's.'[37] Dan then told his brothers and their partners about the problem when the younger generation of the family all went for a walk in Richmond Park. But when they got back, Dan recalls that his father 'hastily' warned him not to tell anyone, not even his two brothers, though it was too late, of course:

> This might seem like a tiny detail, but I think it's symptomatic of their attempt over the next two to three years to cover everything up. 'We don't want anyone to know,' he said. 'If people think you've got dementia, it's dreadful. Invitations dry up and you get cut out.' I feel, with the benefit of hindsight, that was a mistake. How could they expect to socialise in academic circles, surrounded by people whose job it is to weigh up intellects, without it being spotted?[38]

In March 2005, Marilyn was tested, and her dementia was confirmed. David and Marilyn continued to keep it secret, though that only aroused people's suspicions and curiosity. Marilyn's decline was very gradual, says David: 'We had four more or less very normal years.'[39] Family photos show them happily holidaying together through the mid-2000s. It meant, however, that David faced being the carer for his younger wife, rather than enjoying the years of semi-retirement together that he had envisaged, in which they would have continued their daily routines of reading and writing, and more relaxed scholarship. David had always assumed that he would predecease his wife and typically he had even made actuarial calculations of how long each of them could expect to live, and had refurbished their home accordingly.

Then, from an unexpected direction, came even worse tragedy. The Butlers' middle son, Gareth, had enjoyed a reasonably successful career in broadcasting. After joining the BBC World Service as a producer at Bush House, he moved to Anne Sloman's current affairs team at Radio 4, working on programmes such as *Law in Action* and *The Week in Westminster*. He then moved to *The World at One* and *The World This Weekend*, before two years as assistant to Tony Hall, the then head of BBC News. In 2002, Gareth was also made deputy editor of the new *Politics Show* on Sunday mornings on BBC1.

Over the years, Gareth always found a role in Radio 4's election programmes, even following his father in appearing occasionally as an on-air analyst. He was eventually put in charge of what to him was the dream job – editing Radio 4's election night programmes, which in the early noughties encompassed two general elections as well as one US presidential contest and broadcasts for the European and local elections. Gareth loved the overnight programmes' 'spirit and edgy drama', the presenter Jim Naughtie later said.

> He understood how to sift the trivial from the important and how to spot a rogue poll, or a glib analysis, at a hundred paces. The most extraordinary facts would always be at his fingertips. For a presenter his memory was a godsend, and his statistical skill and confidence a relief.[40]

In so many ways, Gareth was like his father. 'He held in his head facts and figures, policy details and statistical quirks that never ceased to amaze,' said BBC presenter Jon Sopel. 'Who needed Google when Gareth was in the office?'[41] It was the same at home. On long car journeys, Gareth would ask his children to suggest any year since the end of the Middle Ages, and he would respond with an interesting or quirky fact about the year in question.

In contrast to David, however, Gareth was known around the BBC for being very laid-back. Indeed, some felt he could be too relaxed, and easily distracted by his passion for football and cricket. His shifts on *The World This Weekend* included gaps on Saturday afternoons while he went to watch Arsenal, and in the office, politics might be reduced to second place while he followed a tight Test match on television.

Gareth's personal life was less smooth. He and his first wife Lucy Anderson, a solicitor who later became a Labour councillor and then an MEP, had two children, Joel and Sacha. But the couple divorced and in 2007 Gareth married Jessica Asato, another Labour activist who often appeared in the media supporting the Blairite cause in the party (and stood unsuccessfully for the marginal seat of Norwich North in 2015).

At the start of 2008, after twenty years with the BBC, Gareth had decided to take voluntary redundancy. He began seeing potential employers and weighing the options – possibly a job with a think tank, or a consultancy, or in polling. On the last day of February, only a few weeks before he was due to leave the BBC, he took a short stroll along the street from the Westminster studios in Millbank for an interview at the Electoral Commission. Suddenly, during the discussion, he collapsed. It was a fatal heart attack. He was rushed to St Thomas's Hospital, but never regained consciousness. He was just forty-two.

His father and both brothers all spoke at Gareth's funeral service, along with Jon Sopel, Jim Naughtie and the actor Toby Jones.

David paid further tribute to his lost son by retaining his name as co-author on the cover of *British Political Facts* when a new edition came out two years later. It was the first time that David Butler had known unexpected tragedy in his life and must have been all the more difficult for him as Marilyn's dementia was now quite advanced. She understood about Gareth's death, though, and told Heather Glen that the death of a child was something no parent should have to bear.

That summer, on holiday with his extended family, David Butler wrote to himself:

> I am sitting in a scented garden in Eastern Portugal, surrounded by seven grandchildren, two sons, three daughters-in-law, and, above all, a wife. Everything should be very pleasant, but this year we have lost Gareth. Marilyn has aged – and so have I. It has been a bad year, our first bad year. To have got so far in life without tragedy is fortunate. Those whom we loved left us in the fullness of years, without trauma or misery. But now, with not many years left, we face miseries that most of the human race have to confront far earlier and far more often than us.
>
> At eighty-three, after a happy childhood, a long and fulfilled academic career and a splendid expanding family, I must not complain about the diminution of my existence … We sit back adequately pensioned, waiting for our gradual descent into oblivion, grateful for a lifetime of good fortune. But, if only Gareth were here…[42]

And before long, Marilyn's mental state had degenerated too far for David to look after her at home, and David and the boys found a very attractive care home in Summertown in north Oxford. On the day in 2009 when it came to move her there, they guided her down the steps at the front of 151 Woodstock Road. By this stage, Marilyn did not seem to remember much, and said very little that made sense, but as she got to the bottom of the steps there came an 'ultra-poignant' moment for everyone.

Marilyn clearly knew what was happening, for she turned to glance back at the house, then remarked, 'We had a good life here, didn't we?'[43]

CHAPTER SEVENTEEN

THE RULES OVERTURNED

Marilyn often had days out from her new residential home in Summertown, when she was able to go out to lunch or was taken to visit the old family home at 151 Woodstock Road, but eventually the care home was no longer able to handle her worsening condition. So the family moved her to the Headington Care Home in east Oxford, a couple of miles away, which specialises in looking after with people with dementia. 'That's when I lost her,' David said.[1]

He would visit Marilyn there almost every day for the rest of her life. He'd talk to her about what he was doing, about the family, and what was going on in the wider world; he'd read the newspaper to her; and, until the last couple of years, he would also take her out for walks and other activities. 'Only twice did I see her acutely depressed,' says David. Often, she smiled at him sweetly. 'It was not as sad a time as you might think.'[2] Even towards the end, when Marilyn could no longer talk, David would notice the occasional 'very strong flash of understanding when I talked to her about somebody she knew'.[3] Dennis Kavanagh admired Butler's 'stoicism and lack of self-pity' at this time. 'He coped with Marilyn's abrupt and long-term decline without complaint,' he says.[4]

Butler realised that 151 Woodstock Road was far too big for him on his own, especially now he was in his mid-eighties. Fortunately, he managed to secure a lease in a rather special block of modern sheltered flats just off the Banbury Road in north Oxford. The building has a full-time warden and communal facilities, notably the canteen where lunch is served every day. It's distinguished by the residents, who include the former MP and philosopher Bryan Magee; the former history don Leslie Mitchell; journalists Robert Taylor and Godfrey Hodgson; and Eleanor Brock, widow of Michael Brock, the former Warden of Nuffield. The calibre of conversation round the lunch table can be formidably high, not least because many of the tenants are retired Oxford dons. But for other meals, and at weekends, residents cater for themselves.

The Butlers sold Woodstock Road in 2011 for almost £2 million. Butler held a big leaving summer party in the garden and tried to persuade friends and colleagues to relieve him of some of his and Marilyn's many thousands of books, for there was room for only a few hundred of his most cherished volumes in his new flat.

Eventually Butler had to give up the Peugeot car in which he drove every day to see Marilyn. 'We were so relieved,' says Marilyn's brother Richard Evans, who recalls David's lifelong reputation for terrible driving. 'Every panel was bashed, and it got to the stage when people wouldn't get in the car with him.' David could never understand why every clutch he had seemed to fail before long.[5] Instead of booking taxis, he took the bus every day up Headington Hill to see Marilyn. Butler has always been rather frugal.

In late 2009, without his knowledge, another effort was made to get Butler a knighthood. Letters of recommendation were secured from five leading figures, including a very senior executive at the BBC; a leading newspaper commentator; and three of Britain's foremost psephologists, including Peter Kellner, the president of the polling firm YouGov. 'He has done more than anyone else to coax journalists, broadcasters and politicians to think about politics in a more rigorous way – and to coax political scientists to apply their skills to the actions of current and not merely past politicians,' Kellner wrote to the honours secretary at the Ministry of Justice, the department who were handling the nomination (because of their role overseeing election administration).[6]

Two months earlier, Kellner had even suggested Butler be knighted during day two of the BBC election results programme when, around lunchtime, David Dimbleby interviewed Butler in the studio about the advent of a hung parliament. A few minutes afterwards, Kellner, one of the main BBC pundits, said it was 'wonderful' to see Butler there. 'Forty-four years ago,' Kellner said, 'his lectures inspired me to go into political number-crunching. If the new government wants to do something that nobody will object to, and which the union of number-crunchers will applaud, it will be to give David a knighthood which is long overdue.'

Dimbleby turned to Butler. 'I don't know if you heard that encomium?' he asked.

'Yes, it was rather embarrassing.'

'Yes,' said Dimbleby, 'very embarrassing, but nonetheless true.'[7]

Six months later, Butler unexpectedly received a letter from the Cabinet Office announcing that, if he had no objection, the Prime Minister would be submitting his name to the Queen. It would be announced in the 2011 New Year's Honours list.

Butler did actually have a few doubts about becoming 'Sir David'. Also, what would the left-wing Marilyn have thought about being 'Lady Butler'? (*Who's Who* even updated her entry to give her title in parentheses.) Sadly, David felt she was too far gone for him to consult her. 'I wasn't sure that she would approve,' he says, even though her own father had also been knighted.[8] And there was some family precedent:

> My grandfather Pollard had been offered a knighthood: for services to history in 1930 by Ramsay MacDonald, whom he'd known as a young man. Anyway, my grandfather would have deserved it. But he rejected it on the grounds that it would put up the bills, and it was a medieval nonsense.[9]

And Butler remembered how his mother had reacted when she heard of Trevor Evans's knighthood in 1967, remarking that she hoped none of her family so disgraced themselves. On the other hand, Butler's brother-in-law, the architectural historian Howard Colvin, had been inclined to reject his knighthood, too, but was persuaded by Oxford colleagues that he should accept for his profession. Butler similarly told himself that 'for the sake of my much cleverer successors it is my duty to accept the first such honour for psephology'. (John Curtice would receive the second such knighthood in 2018.)[10] 'I don't think I was as genuinely reluctant as Howard, but I wouldn't in the least have minded if my family had said, "Don't do it." I would have been obedient to the family. Anyway, they didn't disapprove, and my grandchildren enjoyed coming to the Palace.'[11]

The nomination may well have been given a nudge by the Cabinet Secretary Sir Gus O'Donnell – his BBC election programme 'feeder' from 1974 – who sent Butler a handwritten note of congratulation on the day it was announced. 'It was a delight to see your name emerge at the Main Honours Committee,' O'Donnell wrote, 'and I am sure there are many Nuffield students, like myself, who owe you a personal debt of gratitude.'[12]

The Queen herself conferred the knighthood, somewhat fittingly given that her reign coincided almost exactly with David Butler's own public career. Indeed, he'd been working on the proofs of his first Nuffield book when he heard news of the death of George VI in February 1952. 'You invented that swingy thing,' the Queen is reported to have said just after she placed her sword on his shoulder. 'More or less,' replied the now Sir David. 'And it still works, doesn't it?' 'More or less,' he said again.

This was a period when people wanted to laud him. There was the Political Studies Association award in 2010, of course, for *Political Change in Britain*, voted by PSA members as their most important book of the previous sixty years. The same year, Nuffield and the

Oxford University Reuters Institute honoured him with a Friday night seminar where for once Butler was the guest visitor. Many in the sixty-strong audience were former students and colleagues who'd attended the regular seminars over the years, including Anthony King, Vernon Bogdanor, Uwe Kitzinger and the former Cabinet minister Margaret Jay. The Reuters Institute also teamed up with the BBC to celebrate the new Sir David by instituting annual Butler Lectures to be broadcast on the BBC Parliament Channel, though the series petered out after three years.

As he approached his tenth decade, David Butler looked a slightly shabby figure, though also at times quite debonair when he tucked a paisley cravat into the top of his shirt. His clothes were often scruffy, his eyebrows untrimmed and tufty, and he didn't always shave under his chin. But he remained remarkably active. He would frequently go into Nuffield College, chat to old colleagues and attend the media seminars on Friday evenings. He travelled to London a lot, where he would stay with his son Ed or base himself at the British Academy. Every six weeks or so he attended a lunch of the Pebble Club, a group of journalists and psephologists which has been convened for more than twenty years by the former BBC polling analyst David Cowling and always meets in a restaurant in a corner of Fitzrovia. Butler would always contribute to the discussion, often with comments based on his long experience, or by asking a very basic question, as had long been his style. In 2013, he even travelled with his son Dan to Australia, for a lavish conference at ANU in Canberra to mark forty years since the publication of *The Canberra Model*. The Butlers were fêted in grand style, though it was mainly older and retired academics who attended; the younger generation of Australian politics scholars didn't know his work. Later the same year, he flew with Ed to India, where Prannoy Roy arranged his swansong appearance for NDTV.

Marilyn Butler died in March 2014, at the age of seventy-seven. David had found it reassuring that even in her final week she often understood things he was saying and smiled at him. Marilyn received full obituaries in all the broadsheet papers, and a big memorial service at Exeter College six weeks later. She had been 'without doubt *the* outstanding Romanticist of the last quarter of the twentieth century', the Romantic scholar Michael Rossington said in the service programme. 'She was also the most wonderful, generous, witty, sharp and honourable intellectual that I have ever met.'[13] Her ashes were scattered at Ridge Cottage in Taston, just as Gareth's had been. It was a dreadful time for David. Having lost his wife of fifty-two years, he learnt three days later that Tony Benn had also died. Despite their differences during the 1970s and '80s when Benn was at his peak as a left-wing force, their friendship had always remained strong.

Marilyn's academic influence lived on, though. When going through her papers, her friend Heather Glen found the manuscript of an unfinished book about a group of eighteenth-century English poets and the politics and culture in which they lived. Glen decided that with much editing the manuscript would be perfectly publishable, and *Mapping Mythologies* came out eighteen months after her death, to positive reviews.[14] Later that year, a group of scholars organised a two-day conference on Marilyn's work at a country house in Hampshire, part of which David attended.

Partly to cheer him up, and to mark his 90th birthday in October 2014, Nuffield College held a day-long programme of activities. These included a political seminar; a lecture on television interviews given by David Dimbleby; and a dinner in hall in Nuffield, where Butler gave a brief speech recounting his visit to Winston Churchill back in 1950.

David Butler is surrounded by friends and neighbours in his sheltered block, where social life centres on the lunches served in the communal dining hall on weekdays, but it can often be quite a lonely existence, especially at weekends. 'One can spend Friday, Saturday and Sunday without talking to a single soul,' he says, 'and one does get depressed.'[15] The walls of his flat are decorated with some of the old political cartoons he bought in 1945, a drawing of his great-great-grandfather Edgeworth's family at his 60th birthday party dating from 1804, and a painting by Ozias Humphry of a teenage girl which may be – or may well not be – one of the few known portraits of Jane Austen. A dispute over the portrait has raged for twenty-five years. 'I think I am now 95 per cent certain that this is indeed Jane in 1789, aged thirteen,' Butler says. 'The evidence seems to me fairly compelling, but I am not a scholar in that area. I merely listen to expertise.'[16]

He reads *The Times* every day with the help of a magnifying machine, occasionally sends emails from his computer, and watches a lot of cricket and news and current affairs on television, though he has to peer close up to the screen to read any captions. Some weekends, Butler still visits Taston, where the cottage is now owned by Ed and his wife; or goes to see Dan and his family in a remote part of mid-Wales where his son runs courses guiding people as to which fungi in the woods are edible. In 2017, his family took him back to the Rhine on a cruise.

During the 2015 general election, Butler made a few media appearances, and on the morning of the BBC results programme, he was interviewed in the studio by David Dimbleby – the two old warhorses of TV election broadcasts. It was the last of a string of live election night contributions dating back to 1950. David Butler never expected to experience another general election. Indeed, he often told people that he only expected to live for another year. He was quite prepared for death, he announced, and as an atheist he didn't expect an afterlife. 'I have no visions of hell,' he said. 'I'm just going to disappear.'[17]

But Butler was about to have a new lease of life, for then came the shock result of the EU referendum in 2016, followed by David Cameron's resignation, the advent of Theresa May, and her doomed attempt to boost the Tories' small Commons majority. The 2017 election was arguably the most fascinating of his entire life, and Butler was again keen to get involved. For once, he didn't appear on any results programme, but nonetheless he had plenty of other opportunities to comment on the 2017 campaign while it was in full swing. The most notable was a five-minute recorded interview with Emily Maitlis, which was given great prominence almost at the very start of an edition of *Newsnight* two weeks before polling day. As he and Maitlis sat with glasses of iced juice in an empty restaurant, Butler declared that the 'movement of opinion recorded in the polls is a bigger movement than has occurred in any previous election … Something has happened out there.'[18]

At the age of ninety-two, Butler also entered the age of new media when, about four weeks before polling day, this author suggested to Dan and Ed Butler that perhaps they should persuade their father to join Twitter. His sons loved the idea. David didn't really appreciate what Twitter was, and his eyesight was too poor by now really to see it in operation. But over the remaining days of the campaign David and the boys together devised more than eighty tweets, compressing into 140 characters interesting bits of historical election trivia or observations which compared 2017 to past campaigns (resurrecting his reputation as the facts man). Then one of the boys would post them. Within a few hours of his first tweet he had 1,200 followers, and by polling day he had reached almost 16,000. 'It was fun,' he says. 'The reaction was good. I didn't get anyone saying I was a pompous old fart. I was a puppet of my sons on the whole.'[19] On 22 May, after Theresa May had radically changed the Conservatives' social care policy, announced in the manifesto only four days before, Butler tweeted that he couldn't recall 'a U-turn on this scale', a comment which made the news headlines on Radio 4 that evening. The day after the election, however, Butler announced he would be tweeting no more. 'Learning to tweet at 92 has been fun. But my musings should now be confined to elections, so I am signing off,' he wrote, then teased, '…until next year?'[20]

The 2017 election was quite a shock to Butler. On the day Theresa May called it, there was much talk of her boosting her majority from twenty-six to well over a hundred. Seven weeks later, the Conservatives had no majority at all, and although they were still easily the largest party, May faced the miseries of pushing Brexit legislation through a hung parliament. It was the biggest election turnaround in modern political history and overturned so many of the rules of elections which Butler had famously established over the years. Butler had always argued that the events of the campaign didn't make much difference; what mattered were the years of build-up. Clearly that didn't apply in 2017. Jeremy Corbyn and Labour reduced a 21.5 per cent Conservative lead in the polls at the start to just 2.4 per cent at the ballot box. The idea of uniform swing was further eroded with contradictory results next door to each other: for example, Walsall North saw a 6.1 per cent swing to the Conservatives, and Walsall South a 2.9 per cent swing to Labour. Young people – the 18–24 group – voted in much stronger numbers than for many years, and even the class trends seemed to have broken down. In October 1974, Labour had been 37 per cent behind the Conservatives among middle-class voters (ABC1s); in 2017, it was just 12 per cent behind. Yet Labour's 35 per cent lead among semi-skilled and unskilled working-class people (DEs) had fallen to just 9 per cent over the same period.[21] Nothing seemed to make sense any more.

It was a baffling outcome for a man who'd spent his whole life trying to understand elections, and to explain to mass audiences why people voted the way they did. In 2017, he wasn't sure he knew what had happened, though nobody else could really explain the election either. Everywhere around the world, models of political behaviour were being overturned. It was exciting still to be involved in elections, if only in very small ways by the mid-2010s, but privately David Butler said he wished he hadn't lived long enough to see it.

'The rules in the game of politics have changed very substantially from the world that I lived in,' he told a podcast for *Prospect* magazine in May 2018, again demonstrating his use of new media.

> I could go on commenting on election after election, assuming broadly speaking that the future would resemble the past ... It was a repetitive operation watching elections from 1950 to 2010 and I think since then it has been very significantly more unpredictable. I suppose I'm therefore relieved to be out of the game and the opportunity of making a fool of myself.[22]

CONCLUSION

A LIFE TO THE FULL

Psephologist and scholar, historian and journalist, broadcaster and teacher, pioneer and explorer, mentor and father, David Butler has made the most of his nearly five score years.

And he's made an impact. Before Butler, public discussion of British politics was innumerate. Until the twenty-year-old undergraduate returned to New College after the war and, at a bit of a loose end before the start of term, turned the 1945 constituency results into percentages, there had really been no statistical study of elections beyond a few articles in obscure journals half a century before. Butler then promoted the concept of swing and the idea of uniform national swing as yardsticks for the public to understand election results. That was aided by his use of the new word psephology, and the rediscovery of the Cube Law (which held good until the early 1970s). Few academics manage to start their own discipline, but Larry Sabato, one of the best-known and most eminent political scientists in the United States, acknowledges Butler as 'the father of popular psephology, not just in the United Kingdom but around the world'.[1]

Scholars and journalists had, of course, analysed election results in the past, but it was David Butler the broadcaster who, more than anyone in the 1950s and 1960s, helped explain them to the new mass audience which had started watching television, most notably through the BBC's deployment of Butler's famous Swingometer, though he rarely performed with the device himself. And David Butler also played an important role in 1958 in ensuring that British TV and radio journalists were first allowed to cover election campaigns in the way we know today.

Butler was also a pioneer in contemporary history through his leadership of the Nuffield election studies for over fifty years. He understood the value of instant history – gathering documents while they were still available, talking to hundreds of players in the campaign process, and then using this material to improve and amend the record of events that political journalists had first produced on the day.

Butler the scholar, seeking to explain how people thought about politics and why they voted as they do, helped recruit Donald Stokes from America. Together they founded the rolling panel analysis of political behaviour – the British Election Study – which continues to this day, with an ever-growing database of voter opinion over more than five decades and counting.

Butler the explorer then took much of what he had learnt and developed in Britain and America to Australia and to India – where, in different ways, he made a major impact on the understanding of politics and elections in these modern parliamentary democracies.

Butler the teacher didn't just tutor two or three generations of Oxford undergraduates, but also scores of graduate students from Britain and abroad. Many have gone on to fame and eminence in politics and government, or in journalism and academic life. In numerous cases, their first steps in the outside world were taken with Butler's active help as he used his network of contacts to help place students in employment. Butler the mentor always had a sharp eye for scholarly talent, and took a delight in encouraging the success of his protégés.

He could be gauche, of course. He rarely tells jokes, or laughs at them. He has an unfortunate habit of not looking people in the eye, but focusing instead on a spot on their forehead. At parties he would be on constant lookout to talk to someone more important. But these social weaknesses hide a kindness and generosity; a shy young guest might then be introduced to the newly arrived VIP and given the most lavish, and often highly exaggerated, testimonial. His former research assistant Lewis Baston credits him, behind his awkward exterior, with 'a wisdom and emotional intelligence'.[2]

Colleagues carp, of course. David Butler never wrote one *big* book on his own, they often complain. Donald Stokes, they argue – and Butler readily admits this – was the real brains behind his most famous and influential book, *Political Change in Britain*. Throughout his career Butler was undoubtedly dependent on the collaboration of numerous colleagues, almost to the point of exploiting them. And it's true that of the forty titles in Butler's name listed in the bibliography of this book, he wrote just seven on his own. Most of those were fairly short volumes; four of them were published very early in his career, during the 1950s. Butler is derided for admitting he gets far more excited by facts than by ideas, and that he prefers to learn and research through conversation rather than reading. Colleagues were disparaging of a man who loves the next call from the BBC, who seems happier in the TV or radio studio than in a lecture hall – a glorified journalist, they said, who likes to concentrate on quick newspaper columns rather than agonise over considered contributions to learned journals.

Yet many academics would be proud to have written even seven books. What's more, Butler is far better at writing books and articles than most scholars. His work is easily readable to a lay audience. He uses plain, fluent prose, with few adjectives, and refreshingly free of the buzzwords and incomprehensible jargon which does so much damage to the reputation of higher education. Where so many of his Nuffield colleagues failed to reach the pre-war aims of William Morris and Sandie Lindsay in making the college's work relevant to public life and the wider public, David Butler succeeded abundantly. His record would have been highly impressive in the modern era, where 'relevance' has become a key measure of the success of university research in today's REF assessment process.

Harold Wilson famously used to say he went into politics because he couldn't stand the intrigue of university life. Yet unlike many academics, David Butler has never shown malice towards colleagues, spoken disparagingly of people, or been much involved in plots. 'David is incapable of intrigue,' says his colleague Vernon Bogdanor. 'I never heard him do or say anything vindictive, about anyone. He doesn't understand bad people or really nasty people.'[3] On the contrary, David Butler always treated colleagues with courtesy and hospitality, even people who were quietly bad-mouthing him. Throughout his career, he went out of his way to share his work with others – as still shown when he invites outside historians and writers to make good use of the extensive archive of Nuffield election interviews.

And far from feeling exploited, most of his many collaborators speak fondly of working with Butler. One former co-author, Paul Jowett, identifies a 'David Butler Club' – an army of people spread throughout public life, government, politics, journalism and the universities who feel a debt and will always defend him. Many don't know one other, but when they meet and discuss the link, they feel an immediate affinity and 'end up liking each other'.[4] They may amuse themselves talking about his idiosyncrasies and foibles, but there's an extraordinary warmth within the 'David Butler Club', as witnessed at regular lunches of the Pebble Club.

All this while enjoying a happy and active family life. Many men who are as frantically busy and internationally successful as David Butler would neglect their wives and offspring. Not him. David Butler found love late in life, but his private notes and letters to Marilyn over the fifty years of their marriage clearly show it was an intense, loving and enduring relationship.

David Butler undoubtedly broke new ground. He excelled and pioneered in several media, across four continents, in eight decades.

He started out before most of his rivals, and was still toiling long after they retired or expired.

If most of us managed just a tenth of David Butler's achievements, and enjoyed our lives half as much, we'd have been pretty successful.

APPENDIX

FROM ACADEMIC ARISTOCRACY

This appendix should be read in conjunction with the Butler Family Tree on pages 358–9.

In 1955, the historian Noel Annan wrote a famous essay on 'The Intellectual Aristocracy' – what at least one member of David Butler's family calls the 'The Stud Book'.[1] Annan identified an academic elite which for more than two centuries had dominated England's great universities: a network of fellows, professors and heads of colleges at Oxford and Cambridge. Annan explored the extraordinary family relationships between these dons, whom he separated into nine great intellectual families. These academic dynasties, intricately connected with each other by extensive intermarriage, included the Trevelyans and the Wedgwoods, the Huxleys and the Darwins. Among their number were the Butlers, whom Annan describes as being 'in full flower between the wars'.[2] 'We stretch back a long way academically,' David Butler once said, 'and really there were no near relatives who weren't dons … Being an academic was a solid part of the background.'[3]

'The point to emphasise', says David Butler's youngest son Ed, 'is how much the family tradition was clearly an important part of Dad's life. As his encyclopaedic memory of all these ancestors indicates, he was profoundly aware of a lineage and a tradition … and he's always been very keen that we boys are equally aware of them all.'[4]

David (Henry) Edgeworth Butler counts well over a dozen Oxbridge dons among his ancestors and cousins, including several fellows of All Souls College, a handful of Oxbridge heads of house, and headmasters of three of England's great public schools. And because the Butlers in David's direct line tended to marry late in life, this academic family tree covers an extraordinary span of time in just a few generations. 'My father was born before the invention of the internal combustion engine,' Butler likes to tell people. 'My grandfather was born before the 1832 Great Reform Act, and my great-grandfather was born before the American Declaration of Independence.'[5]

The Butlers can trace their ancestry back to **Richard Butler** (d. 1547) of Claines, a village just north of the city of Worcester, where the family carried out legal duties for the medieval cathedral. Seven generations later, **Weeden Butler** (1742–1823), David Butler's great-great-grandfather, achieved some fame as a clergyman and writer, and was a friend of the great statesman and philosopher Edmund Burke. Weeden's second son was **George Butler** (1774–1853) – the great-grandfather who was born before America declared independence. He was a fellow of Sidney Sussex College, Cambridge, headmaster of Harrow for twenty-four years (1805–29) and later Dean of Peterborough. It is with George Butler and his children that the Butler family began to excel.

One daughter, **Louisa Galton** (1822–97), married Francis Galton, the statistician and polymath who invented fingerprinting. Having been inspired by Charles Darwin, his half-cousin, Galton was also an early pioneer of the controversial science of eugenics – a term he himself invented. Interestingly, given the themes of this book, Galton also developed the idea of surveys and questionnaires to collect information on human activity and behaviour. George Butler also had four sons, three of whom followed similar careers.

One of these sons, **Arthur Gray Butler** (1831–1909) – David Butler's grandfather – was a fellow of Oriel College, Oxford, and then in 1862 became the first headmaster of Haileybury College in Hertfordshire, and we will return to him later.

George's first son, the **Rev. George Butler** (1819–90), was also an Oxford don – at Exeter College – then, from 1866 to 1882, principal of Liverpool College, and subsequently Canon of Winchester. His wife, **Josephine Butler** (1828–1906) (whose father was a cousin of the Whig Prime Minister Earl Grey), was even more distinguished. As one of the great Victorian social reformers, she pursued successful campaigns against child prostitution and the trafficking of women and children into the sex trade. Josephine also played a leading part in the early agitation for votes for women. In 2006, she became the only member of the family to have a college named after her – Josephine Butler College at Durham University.

Henry Montagu Butler (1833–1918) was a successor to his father as headmaster of Harrow, taking the position at the age of only twenty-six, and he held the job for twenty-six years (1859–85). He and his father remain the two longest-serving Harrow headmasters since 1730. Henry Montagu Butler then served for thirty-two years (1886–1918) as Master of Trinity College, Cambridge, the longest-serving head of the college since 1742. Henry Montagu Butler was a legendary character in Cambridge, who caused a big stir at the age of fifty-five when he married a 21-year-old girl who had come top of the Classical Tripos the year before.

Of Henry Montagu Butler's three sons, **Sir James 'Jim' Butler** (1889–1975) was very briefly MP for Cambridge University (1922–23) before becoming Regius Professor of Modern History (1947–54) and Vice-Master of Trinity College (1955–60). His brother **Sir Neville Butler** (1893–1973) became British ambassador to the Netherlands.

George Butler's other son, **Spencer Perceval Butler** (1829–1915) – David Butler's great-uncle – was a conveyancing solicitor. His three daughters and ten sons all had good careers and indeed four of his sons were knighted. One of these was **Sir Montagu Butler** (1873–1952), who was governor of the central provinces of India from 1925 to 1933 before becoming Master of Pembroke College, Cambridge (1937–48).

Sir Montagu was the father of **Richard 'Rab' Austen Butler** (1902–82), who had an extremely distinguished political career which included the 1944 'Butler' Education Act, and spells as Chancellor, Home Secretary, Foreign Secretary and Deputy Prime Minister, though never Prime Minister. Rab spent twenty-five years in office, which was, according to *British Political Facts* (written, of course, by his second cousin David), the second longest ministerial career of the twentieth century (after Winston Churchill, who spent twenty-nine years as a minister). From 1965 to 1978, Rab Butler followed his great-uncle as Master of Trinity.

Rab's son **Sir Adam Butler** (1931–2008) was Parliamentary Private Secretary to Margaret Thatcher when she was opposition leader, and later served six years as one of her junior ministers.

The line from Spencer Butler and Sir Montagu Butler has further distinction. Rab Butler's sister **Iris Portal** (1905–2002) was the mother of **Jane Welby (now Williams)** (b. 1929), who was Churchill's personal secretary during the early 1950s. Jane's son **Justin Welby** has been the Archbishop of Canterbury since 2013.

Spencer Perceval Butler's fourth son was **Sir Geoffrey Butler** (1887–29), a history don who helped found the Cambridge University Conservative Association, and also played a major role in developing Conservative thought in the early twentieth century with his seminal book *The Tory Tradition*, which was based on a series of lectures he gave in 1914. In 1923, Geoffrey Butler was elected Conservative MP for Cambridge University, defeating his cousin James, who was also a Cambridge history don. James had been elected as an Independent for the university at the 1922 general election but stood as an Independent Liberal in 1923. This is thought to be the only case in modern British history of cousins opposing each other for the same parliamentary seat (which Geoffrey retained until his death in 1929).

An astonishing seven members of the Butler family served as president of the Cambridge Union over the seventy years from 1855 to 1924, as follows: Henry Montagu Butler (1855); Montagu Butler (1895); Arthur Butler (1897); James Butler (1910); Geoffrey Butler (1910); Gordon Butler (1914); and finally Richard 'Rab' Butler (1924).[6] In addition, Spencer Perceval Butler was secretary and treasurer of the Cambridge Union in the early 1850s, while Arthur Gray Butler was president of the Oxford Union in 1853. In the 200 years since the Oxbridge Unions were founded in the early nineteenth century, no other family has so dominated their elections (the closest is perhaps the Foot family, who had five Union presidencies in the mid-twentieth century – four at Oxford, one in Cambridge).

It is in their great scholarly careers at Cambridge, however, that the Butlers most excelled. Indeed, for almost 200 years, from 1794 until Rab Butler stood down as Master of Trinity in 1978, there was always at least one Butler don within the university. And for fifty of the ninety-two years between 1886 and 1978 a Butler was either Master or Vice-Master of Trinity, then the largest Cambridge college. 'No other family can claim such a galaxy of academic stars,' a *Times* article claimed at the time of Rab's retirement, under the headline 'Cambridge without a Butler: like a master without a servant'.[7]

Yet these distinguished and long-serving Cambridge dons were mostly cousins to David Butler. His direct ancestry descends, as mentioned above, from the other notable son of George Butler – Arthur Gray Butler (1831–1909), the grandfather born before the Great Reform Act – who is perhaps best remembered today for an athletic achievement from his schooldays at Rugby, shortly after the headship of the great Thomas Arnold. Butler's Leap was an especially difficult jump from a road across an adjacent brook which was often attempted by successive generations of Rugbeians, and is today commemorated by a gastropub and a street of that name nearby. At Haileybury, the school he helped found, Arthur Gray Butler is acknowledged as a highly influential figure, even though he was headmaster for only five years. He was later dean and tutor of Oriel College, Oxford, where he taught Cecil Rhodes (and later he helped ensure that the university benefited from Rhodes's will, through endowing the famous Rhodes scholarships, many of whose holders would be taught by his grandson David).

In 1877, Arthur Gray Butler married **Harriet Edgeworth** (1851–1946), who came from a wealthy family whose estates were based around Edgeworthstown in County Longford in Ireland, and who were linked by marriage to the Pakenhams – the family of the Earls of Longford. Harriet's aunt was the distinguished novelist **Maria Edgeworth** (1768–1849), who wrote literature for both adults and children in the 1790s and the early nineteenth century. A cousin was the philosopher, economist and statistician **Francis Edgeworth** (1845–1926). Both of these renowned Edgeworths play important but very different roles in David Butler's own life story.

Arthur and Harriet's only son, **Harold Edgeworth Butler** (1878–1951), was David Butler's father. Harold Butler went to Rugby and then got a scholarship to New College, Oxford, where, in 1899, he won the Newdigate Prize for poetry. At twenty-three, Harold was appointed a lecturer at New College, and then became a fellow, and spent a decade teaching and researching in Oxford before moving to University College London to succeed the poet A. E. Housman (of *Shropshire Lad* fame) as Professor of Latin. Harold Butler held the job for thirty-two years.

Two of Harold's three sisters, Ruth and Violet – David Butler's aunts – were fellows of St Anne's College, Oxford. **Ruth Butler** (1881–1982), who became Vice-Principal of the college, lived to be 100. **Violet Butler** (1884–1982) wrote an influential book in her twenties about social conditions in working-class and poor districts of Oxford, before spending more than thirty years as an economics tutor at St Anne's. She lived to be ninety-eight.[8] The third sister,

Olive Butler (1879–1971), was warden of the Lady Margaret Hall Settlement, a community charity in south London.

In 1917, towards the end of the First World War, Harold Butler married one of his students, **Margaret 'Peggie' Pollard** (1895–1982), who was seventeen years his junior, and thereby linked the Butlers to another important strand of academic ancestry. Peggie's father was **A. F. 'Albert' Pollard** (1869–1948), the well-known Tudor historian who was Professor of Constitutional History at the University of London (1903–31), as well as a fellow of All Souls, Oxford (1908–36). Pollard founded the Historical Association in 1906 and was also a leading contributor to the *Oxford Dictionary of National Biography (DNB)* (which may partly explain why more than two dozen of David Butler's relatives feature in the directory!). Pollard's wife, **Catherine 'Katie' Lucy** (1869–1934) – David's grandmother – whom he married in 1894, was the daughter of **William Lucy** (1837–73), an Oxford industrialist after whom was named the well-known ironmongery manufacturers Lucy & Co., owners of the famous Eagle Works in Jericho, north Oxford, next to the Oxford Canal and Birmingham railway. The firm manufactured the radically new mobile shelving for the book stacks under the Radcliffe Camera, where David did much of his early psephological work. The Lucy factory was not demolished until 2007, and in commemoration a new road on the site was named William Lucy Way. Not all David Butler's Oxford antecedents are academic.

William Lucy died in 1873, at the age of only thirty-five, but his widow Alice – David Butler's great-grandmother – lived for another sixty-four years, dying at the age of ninety-six in 1937. Alice was the daughter of **George Jennings** (1811–82), one of the great Victorian pioneers of sanitary equipment. David Butler recalls, as a child in the 1930s, talking to Alice, whom he says was 'very frail and very small', but 'had a sweet smile'. Alice told him, in particular, how she and her sister had been among the estimated one and a half million-strong crowd which watched the grand and colourful procession for the state funeral of the Duke of Wellington in November 1852. Her father had bought his daughters expensive seats in a special stand erected for the occasion near Marble Arch. Alice explained to the young David that her stepmother had complained that the ten shillings which each of the girls' tickets had cost – at least £50 at 2018 prices – was extravagant, but Alice's father had told his wife: 'No, my dear. Not extravagance. It is something they will remember all their lives.' 'And I have, David, haven't I?' Alice reportedly remarked to her great-grandson.[9]

Indeed, David Butler may well be the only person still alive who has heard a first-hand account of the funeral of the victor of the Battle of Waterloo.

The year before Wellington's funeral, David's great-grandmother had also visited the 1851 Great Exhibition at the Crystal Palace in Hyde Park, where her father, George Jennings – David Butler's great-great-grandfather – had persuaded Prince Albert to let him install the first ever public lavatories in Britain. Users had to put a penny coin into a slot – hence the euphemism 'spend a penny' – and, as well as a clean seat, they were also provided with a towel, a shoe-shine and a comb. Initially, when the Crystal Palace was moved to south London, they planned to do without Jennings's lavatories. 'Persons would not come to Sydenham to wash their hands,' it was said, but Jennings won the argument and his loos produced an income of £1,000 a year. The advent of public lavatories was largely down to him.[10]

But in 1851 the ten-year-old Alice Jennings seemed more interested in the ingenious neighbouring attraction at the Great Exhibition – an 'alarm bed' which was designed to tip the sleeper out at a set time. 'Granny Lucy', David says, 'remembered many hours playing delightedly on the bed as an exhibit of a sluggard being ejected onto the floor.'[11]

One more relative on Butler's maternal side is worth a mention – David's uncle **Graham Pollard** (1903–76), who was the only other child of A. F. Pollard and his wife Katie. At Oxford, Pollard was famous for winning an unofficial half-blue in 'spitting', reportedly by defeating Evelyn Waugh over a distance of ten yards. His place in the *Oxford DNB* was secured, however, through his work as a bibliographer and the owner of a well-known bookshop in Bloomsbury.

In 2017, it was revealed that Graham Pollard had led an extraordinary double life. While a member of the Communist Party in the 1920s and '30s, and as a staff writer on the *Daily Worker*, he had also been working for the British security services MI6 and then MI5. His marriage in 1924 to the prominent left-wing activist **Kay Beauchamp** had been part of his cover.

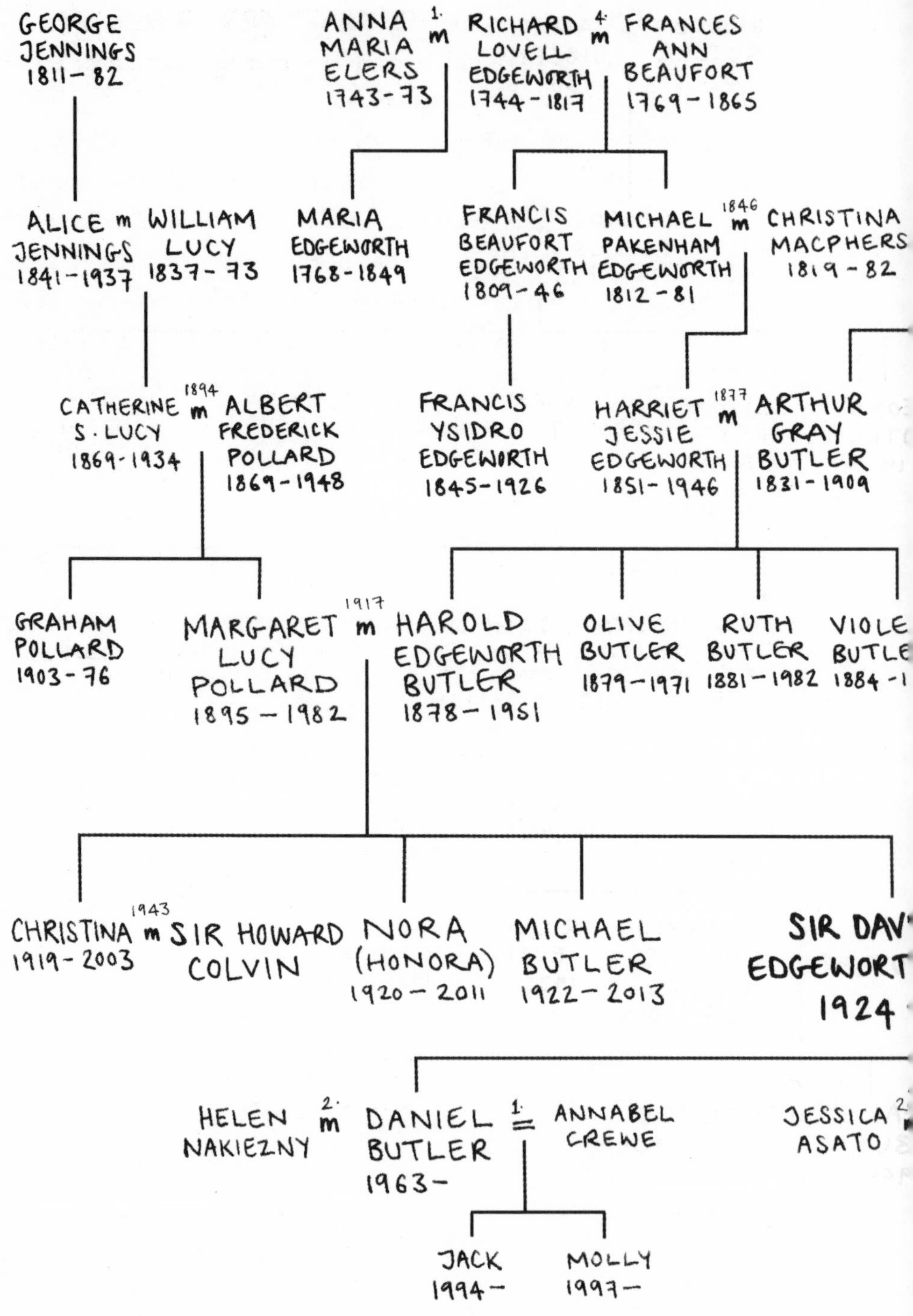
GEORGE JENNINGS 1811–82
ANNA MARIA ELERS 1743–73
1. m
RICHARD LOVELL EDGEWORTH 1744–1817
4. m
FRANCES ANN BEAUFORT 1769–1865
ALICE JENNINGS 1841–1937
m
WILLIAM LUCY 1837–73
MARIA EDGEWORTH 1768–1849
FRANCIS BEAUFORT EDGEWORTH 1809–46
MICHAEL PAKENHAM EDGEWORTH 1812–81
1846 m
CHRISTINA MACPHERS 1819–82
CATHERINE S. LUCY 1869–1934
1894 m
ALBERT FREDERICK POLLARD 1869–1948
FRANCIS YSIDRO EDGEWORTH 1845–1926
HARRIET JESSIE EDGEWORTH 1851–1946
1877 m
ARTHUR GRAY BUTLER 1831–1909
GRAHAM POLLARD 1903–76
MARGARET LUCY POLLARD 1895–1982
1917 m
HAROLD EDGEWORTH BUTLER 1878–1951
OLIVE BUTLER 1879–1971
RUTH BUTLER 1881–1982
VIOLE BUTLE 1884–
CHRISTINA 1919–2003
1943 m
SIR HOWARD COLVIN
NORA (HONORA) 1920–2011
MICHAEL BUTLER 1922–2013
SIR DAV EDGEWORT 1924
HELEN NAKIEZNY
2. m
DANIEL BUTLER 1963–
1. =
ANNABEL CREWE
JESSICA ASATO
JACK 1994–
MOLLY 1997–

THE BUTLER FAMILY TREE

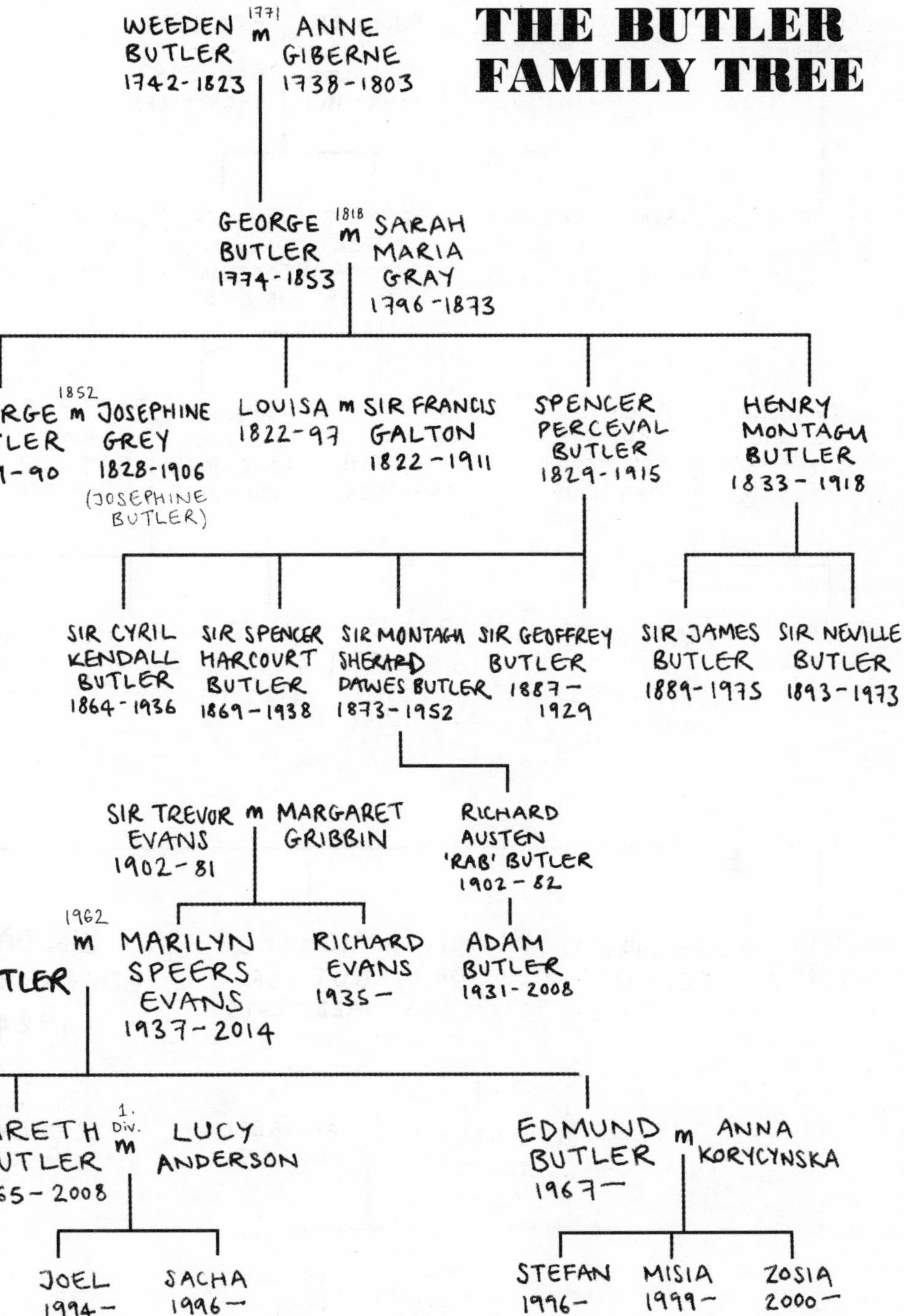

WEEDEN BUTLER 1742-1823
1771 m
ANNE GIBERNE 1738-1803
GEORGE BUTLER 1774-1853
1818 m
SARAH MARIA GRAY 1796-1873
ORGE TLER 19-90
1852 m
JOSEPHINE GREY 1828-1906 (JOSEPHINE BUTLER)
LOUISA 1822-97
m
SIR FRANCIS GALTON 1822-1911
SPENCER PERCEVAL BUTLER 1829-1915
HENRY MONTAGU BUTLER 1833-1918
SIR CYRIL KENDALL BUTLER 1864-1936
SIR SPENCER HARCOURT BUTLER 1869-1938
SIR MONTAGU SHERARD DAWES BUTLER 1873-1952
SIR GEOFFREY BUTLER 1887-1929
SIR JAMES BUTLER 1889-1975
SIR NEVILLE BUTLER 1893-1973
SIR TREVOR EVANS 1902-81
m
MARGARET GRIBBIN
RICHARD AUSTEN 'RAB' BUTLER 1902-82
UTLER
1962 m
MARILYN SPEERS EVANS 1937-2014
RICHARD EVANS 1935-
ADAM BUTLER 1931-2008
ARETH BUTLER 965-2008
1. DIV. m
LUCY ANDERSON
EDMUND BUTLER 1967-
m
ANNA KORYCYNSKA
JOEL 1994-
SACHA 1996-
STEFAN 1996-
MISIA 1999-
ZOSIA 2000-

BIBLIOGRAPHY

Adeney, Martin, *Nuffield: A Biography*, Hale, 1993.

Agenda for Change: The Report of the Hansard Society Commission on Election Campaigns, Hansard Society, 1991.

Aitkin, Don, *Critical Mass: How the Commonwealth got into Funding Research in Universities*, Don Aitkin, 2017.

Andrews, P. W. S. (Philip) & Brunner, Elizabeth, *The Life of Lord Nuffield: A Study in Enterprise and Benevolence*, Basil Blackwell, 1955.

Annan, Noel, *Our Age: Portrait of a Generation*, Weidenfeld & Nicolson, 1990.

Annan, Noel, *The Dons: Mentors, Eccentrics & Geniuses*, HarperCollins, 1999.

Attenborough, David, *Life on Air: Memoirs of a Broadcaster*, BBC Books, 2002.

Benn, Tony (ed. Ruth Winstone), *Years of Hope, Diaries, Papers & Letters, 1940–62*, Hutchinson, 1994.

Benn, Tony (ed. Ruth Winstone), *Out of the Wilderness, Diaries, 1963–67*, Hutchinson, 1987.

Benn, Tony (ed. Ruth Winstone), *Office Without Power, Diaries, 1968–72*, Hutchinson, 1988.

Benn, Tony (ed. Ruth Winstone), *Against the Tide, Diaries, 1973–76*, Hutchinson, 1989.

Benn, Tony (ed. Ruth Winstone), *Conflicts of Interest, Diaries, 1977–80*, Hutchinson, 1990.

Benn, Tony (ed. Ruth Winstone), *The End of an Era, Diaries, 1980–90*, Hutchinson, 1992.

Blewett, Neal, *The Peers, The Parties and The People: The General Elections of 1910*, University of Toronto Press, 1972.

Bogdanor, Vernon & Butler, David (eds), *Democracy and Elections: Electoral Systems and Their Political Consequences*, Cambridge University Press, 1983.

Briggs, Asa, *The History of Broadcasting in the United Kingdom, Vol. IV: Sound and Vision*, Oxford University Press, 1978.

Briggs, Asa, *The History of Broadcasting in the United Kingdom, Vol. V: Competition*, Oxford University Press, 1995.

Butler, David, *British General Elections since 1945*, Basil Blackwell, 1989.

Butler, David (ed.), *Coalitions in British Politics*, Macmillan, 1978.

Butler, David (ed.), *Elections Abroad*, Macmillan, 1959.

Butler, David, *Governing Without a Majority: Dilemmas for Hung Parliaments in Britain*, Collins, 1983.

Butler, David, *The British General Election of 1951*, Macmillan, 1952.

Butler, David, *The British General Election of 1955*, Macmillan, 1955.

Butler, David, *The Canberra Model: Essays on Australian Government*, Macmillan, 1973.

Butler, David, *The Case for an Electoral Commission – Keeping election law up-to-date*, Hansard Society, 1998.

Butler, David, *The Electoral System in Britain 1918–51*, Oxford University Press, 1953.

Butler, David, *The Study of Political Behaviour*, Hutchinson, 1958.

Butler, David, Adonis, Andrew & Travers, Tony, *Failure in British Government: The Politics of the Poll Tax*, Oxford University Press, 1994.

Butler, David & Butler, Gareth, *British Political Facts 1900–1985*, 6th edn, Macmillan, 1986.

Butler, David & Butler, Gareth, *British Political Facts 1900–1994*, 7th edn, Macmillan, 1994.

Butler, David & Butler, Gareth, *Twentieth-Century British Political Facts 1900–2000*, 8th edn, Macmillan, 2000.

Butler, David & Butler, Gareth, *British Political Facts Since 1979*, 9th edn, Palgrave Macmillan, 2005.

Butler, David & Butler, Gareth, *British Political Facts*, 10th edn, Palgrave Macmillan, 2010.

Butler, David & Cain, Bruce E., *Congressional Redistricting: Comparative and Theoretical Perspectives*, Macmillan USA, 1991.

Butler, David & Freeman, Jennie, *British Political Facts 1900–1960*, Macmillan, 1963.

Butler, David & Freeman, Jennie, *British Political Facts 1900–1967*, 2nd edn, Macmillan, 1968.

Butler, David & Freeman, Jennie, *British Political Facts 1900–1968*, 3rd edn, Macmillan, 1969.

Butler, David & Halsey, A. H. (eds), *Policy and Politics: Essays in Honour of Norman Chester*, Macmillan, 1978.

Butler, David & Jowett, Paul, *Party Strategies in Britain: A Study of the 1984 European Elections*, Macmillan, 1985.

Butler, David & Kavanagh, Dennis, *The British General Election of February 1974*, Macmillan, 1974.

Butler, David & Kavanagh, Dennis, *The British General Election of October 1974*, Macmillan, 1975.

Butler, David & Kavanagh, Dennis, *The British General Election of 1979*, Macmillan, 1980.

Butler, David & Kavanagh, Dennis, *The British General Election of 1983*, Macmillan, 1984.

Butler, David & Kavanagh, Dennis, *The British General Election of 1987*, Macmillan, 1988.

Butler, David & Kavanagh, Dennis, *The British General Election of 1992*, Macmillan, 1992.

Butler, David & Kavanagh, Dennis, *The British General Election of 1997*, Macmillan, 1997.

Butler, David & Kavanagh, Dennis, *The British General Election of 2001*, Palgrave, 2002.

Butler, David & King, Anthony, *The British General Election of 1964*, Macmillan, 1965.

Butler, David & King, Anthony, *The British General Election of 1966*, Macmillan, 1966.

Butler, David & Kitzinger, Uwe, *The 1975 Referendum*, Macmillan, 1976.

Butler, David, Lahiri, Ashok & Roy, Prannoy, *A Compendium of Indian Elections*, Arnold-Heinemann, 1984.

Butler, David, Lahiri, Ashok & Roy, Prannoy, *India Decides: Elections 1952–1989*, Living Media India, 1989.

Butler, David & Low, Donald (eds), *Surrogates for the Sovereign: Constitutional Heads of State in the Commonwealth*, Macmillan, 1990.

Butler, David & Marquand, David, *European Elections and British Politics*, Macmillan, 1981.

Butler, David, Penniman, Howard & Ranney, Austin (eds), *Democracy at the Polls: A Comparative Study of Competitive National Elections*, American Enterprise Institute for Public Policy Research, 1981.

Butler, David & Pinto-Duschinsky, Michael, *The British General Election of 1970*, Macmillan, 1971.

Butler, David & Ranney, Austin (eds), *Electioneering: A Comparative Study of Continuity and Change*, Oxford University Press, 1992.

Butler, David & Ranney, Austin (eds), *Referendums: A Comparative Study of Practice and Theory*, American Enterprise Institute, 1978.

Butler, David & Rose, Richard, *The British General Election of 1959*, Macmillan, 1960.

Butler, David & Sloman, Anne, *British Political Facts 1900–1975*, Macmillan, 1975.

Butler, David & Sloman, Anne, *British Political Facts 1900–1979*, Macmillan, 1979.

Butler, David & Stokes, Donald, *Political Change in Britain: Forces Shaping Electoral Choice*, Macmillan, 1969.

Butler, David & Westlake, Martin, *British Politics and European Elections 1994*, Macmillan, 1995.

Butler, David & Westlake, Martin, *British Politics and European Elections 1999*, Macmillan, 2000.

Butler, David & Westlake, Martin, *British Politics and European Elections 2004*, Macmillan, 2005.

Butler, Marilyn, *Jane Austen and the War of Ideas*, Oxford University Press, 1975.

Butler, Marilyn, *Mapping Mythologies: Countercurrents in Eighteenth-Century British Poetry and Cultural History*, Cambridge University Press, 2015.

Butler, Marilyn, *Peacock Displayed: A Satirist in His Context*, Routledge and Kegan Paul, 1979.

Butler, Marilyn, *Romantics, Rebels and Reactionaries: English Literature and its Background 1760–1830*, Oxford University Press, 1981.

Butler, C. Violet, *Social Conditions in Oxford*, Sidgwick & Jackson, 1912.

Carpenter, Humphrey, *The Inklings: CS Lewis, JRR Tolkien, Charles Williams and their friends*, Unwin Paperbacks, 1981.

Carter, John & Pollard, Graham, *An Enquiry into the Nature of Certain Nineteenth-Century Pamphlets*, Constable, 1934.

Chester, Norman, *Economics, Politics and Social Studies in Oxford 1900–85*, Macmillan, 1986.

Cockerell, Michael, *Live From Number 10: The Inside Story of Prime Ministers and Television*, Faber, 1988.

Cox, Geoffrey, *See It Happen: The Making of ITN*, Bodley Head, 1983.

Crewe, Ivor & Särlvik, Bo, *Decade of Dealignment: The Conservative victory of 1979 and electoral trends in the 1970s*, Cambridge University Press, 1983.

Dancy, John, *Walter Oakeshott: A Diversity of Gifts*, Michael Russell, 1995.

Donoughue, Bernard, *Downing Street Diary: With Harold Wilson in No. 10*, Jonathan Cape, 2005.

Donoughue, Bernard, *Downing Street Diary, Vol. 2: With James Callaghan in No. 10*, Jonathan Cape, 2008.

Durant, Henry, *Behind the Gallup Poll*, News Chronicle, 1951.

Gilbert, Martin, *Never Despair: Winston S. Churchill 1945–1965*, Heinemann, 1988.

Glyer, Diana Pavlac, *The Company They Keep: CS Lewis and JRR Tolkien as Writers in Community*, Kent State University Press, 2007.

Goldie, Grace Wyndham, *Facing the Nation: Television and Politics, 1936–1976*, Bodley Head, 1977.

Grist, John, *Grace Wyndham Goldie: First Lady of Television*, Authors Online, 2006.

Gunther, John, *Inside USA*, Hamish Hamilton, 1947.

Halsey, A. H., *Essays on the Evolution of Oxford and Nuffield College*, Nuffield College, 2012.

Hayward, Jack, Barry, Brian & Brown, Archie (eds), *The British Study of Politics in the Twentieth Century*, Oxford University Press/British Academy Scholarship Online, 2003.

Hazell, Robert & Paun, Akash (eds), *Making Minority Government Work: Hung parliaments and the challenges for Westminster and Whitehall*, Institute for Government, 2009.

Heath, Anthony, Jowell, Roger & Curtice, John, *How Britain Votes*, Pergamon, 1985.

Herken, Gregg, *The Georgetown Set: Friends and Rivals in Cold War Washington*, Knopf, 2014.

Higgins, Charlotte, *This New Noise: the Extraordinary Birth and Troubled Life of the BBC*, Guardian Books, 2015.

Hood, Christopher, King, Desmond & Peele, Gillian (eds), *Forging a Discipline: A Critical Assessment of Oxford's Development of the Study of Politics and International Relations in Comparative Perspective*, Oxford University Press, 2014.

Johnson, R. W., *Look Back in Laughter: Oxford's Postwar Golden Age*, Threshold Press, 2015.

Kavanagh, Dennis & Butler, David, *The British General Election of 2005*, Palgrave Macmillan, 2005.

Kavanagh, Dennis (ed.), *Electoral Politics*, Oxford University Press, 1992.

Kavanagh, Dennis, *Politics and Personalities*, Macmillan, 1990.

Keynes, John Maynard, *The Economic Consequences of the Peace*, Macmillan, 1919.

Lloyd, Trevor Owen, *The General Election of 1880*, Oxford University Press, 1968.

Mackerras, Malcolm, *Mackerras Federal Election Guide*, AGPS Press, 1989–95.

Mayne, Richard, *The Copper Stick: An Autobiography*, Matador, 2015.

McAllister, Ian & Rose, Richard, *The Nationwide Competition for Votes: The 1983 British Election*, Frances Pinter, 1984.

McCallum, R. B. & Readman, Alison, *The British General Election of 1945*, Oxford University Press, 1947.

Milne, Alasdair, *DG: The Memoirs of a British Broadcaster*, Hodder & Stoughton, 1988.

Mitchell, Austin, *Calendar Boy*, Pen & Sword Politics, 2014.

Mortimore, Roger & Blick, Andrew (eds), *Butler's British Political Facts*, Palgrave Macmillan, 2018.

Nicholas, H. G., *The British General Election of 1950*, Macmillan, 1951.

Parkinson, Stephen, *Arena of Ambition: A History of the Cambridge Union*, Icon, 2009.

Priest, Joan, *Scholars and Gentlemen: A Biography of the Mackerras Family*, Boolarong Press, 1986.

Ramsden, John (ed.), *Oxford Companion to Twentieth-Century British Politics*, Oxford University Press, 2005.

Robinson, Nick, *Live from Downing Street: The Inside Story of Politics, Power and the Media*, Bantam Press, 2012.

Rodger, Gary, *SWING: A brief history of British General Election Night broadcasting*, (e-book) Kindle, 2015.

Rose, Richard, *Learning About Politics in Time and Space*, ECPR Press, 2014.

Russell, A. K., *Liberal Landslide: The General Election of 1906*, David & Charles, 1973.

Salter, F. R., *St. Paul's School 1909–1959*, Arthur Barker, 1959.

Stannage, Tom, *Baldwin Thwarts the Opposition: The British General Election of 1935*, Croom Helm, 1980.

Taylor, Robert, *Nuffield College Memories: A Personal History*, Nuffield College, 2008.

The Times Guide to the House of Commons, all editions, 1906 to 2017.

Thorpe, Andrew, *The British General Election of 1931*, Clarendon, 1991.

Underhill, D. F., *Queen's Own Royal Regiment the Staffordshire Yeomanry: An account of the operations of the Regiment during World War II, 1939–1945*, Staffordshire Yeomanry Museum, 1994.

Worcester, Robert & Harrop, Martin (eds), *Political Communications: The General Election Campaign of 1979*, Allen & Unwin, 1982.

Wright, Lawrence, *Clean and Decent*, Routledge and Kegan Paul, 1960.

ENDNOTES

In the endnotes below, 'Butler intv.' refers to several dozen interviews and conversations which I had with David Butler between June 2015 and July 2018 – some conducted face to face, others over the telephone. 'Butler (MSC) intv.' and 'Butler (ST) intv.' refer to interviews and conversations Butler had with Margaret Crick and Seth Thévoz respectively over the same period.

I have also relied heavily on two other interviews which David Butler has conducted in the past. The first was with Brian Harrison as part of his research for Volume 8 of *The History of the University of Oxford* (covering the twentieth century). Butler's other extensive interview was with Paul Thompson, split over two days in September and October 2014, as part of the Pioneers of Social Research Project at the British Library. These are denoted below as 'Butler (Harrison) intv.' and 'Butler (Thompson) intv.'.

All interviews with other people were conducted by the author, except those specified as being with Margaret Crick (MSC) or Seth Thévoz (ST).

The word 'ana' in the footnotes refers to a series of short autobiographical memoranda which Butler has written over the years, relating his memories of individuals or of particular events. They range in length from a short paragraph to several pages. Some were written contemporaneously, although most were drafted or rewritten by Butler in the 2000s. Some of these have titles; others don't.

'Butler Diary/Letter' refers to one of the many letters which Butler wrote during his 1944–45 war service, and subsequent spells in the United States in the 1940s and '50s. These letters, sent to his parents (or just his mother after his father's death in 1951), took the form of a daily diary. Where possible the dates refer to the day described, not the day the letter was sent.

Butler also made numerous efforts to write a proper diary, though these usually ceased after only a few weeks. This was sometimes called his 'Commonplace book', though it is denoted here simply as 'Diary'.

Notes to Introduction: You Haven't Much Time!, pages vii–xi

1 Butler notes of visit to Winston Churchill, 6 February 1950.
2 Butler (Thompson) intv.
3 *Economist*, 7 January 1950.
4 Butler notes, op. cit.
5 Butler (Thompson) intv.
6 Butler notes, op. cit.
7 Ibid.
8 Butler (Harrison) intv.
9 Transcript of final Butler Nuffield seminar, 4 June 2010.
10 *Times Literary Supplement*, 7 June 1947.

Notes to Chapter One: Born to Elections, pages 1–17

1 Butler intv.
2 Reproduced in Noel Annan, *The Dons: Mentors, Eccentrics and Geniuses*, HarperCollins, 1999, pp.304–41.
3 *Times*, 9 June 1951.
4 *Independent on Sunday*, 15 July 2015.
5 Butler intv.
6 Ibid.
7 Ibid.
8 Butler ana, 'Memories', undated.
9 Butler intv.
10 Ibid.
11 Butler (Thompson) intv.
12 Ibid.
13 Butler ana, 'Elections and me', 21 May 2002.
14 Nicholas Parsons intv.
15 Butler ana, 'Elections and me', 21 May 2002.
16 Butler intv.
17 *Daily Telegraph*, 28 March 1936.
18 Butler intv.
19 David Butler, *The Glass Bird*, unpublished manuscript, 1936.
20 Butler (ST) intv.
21 Denis Gildea, *Memoirs*, unpublished manuscript, 2002, p.31.
22 Richard Mayne, *The Copper Stick*, Matador, 2015, p.62.

23 Butler intv.
24 Mayne, op. cit., pp.59–60.
25 Butler intv.
26 Butler (Thompson) intv.
27 Gildea, op. cit., p.31.
28 John Allport, 'Some Notes on St. Paul's School During the Second World War', 1999, archive, St Paul's School, London.
29 Gildea, op. cit., p.41.
30 Butler intv.
31 *The Pauline*, December 1940.
32 *The Pauline*, July 1941.
33 *The Pauline*, November 1942.
34 School Reports, December 1942, archive, St Paul's School, London.
35 Harold Butler to L. G. Wickham Legg letter, 18 December 1942, archive, New College, Oxford.

Notes to Chapter Two: Gung-Ho for War, pages 19–34

1 Butler personal papers.
2 Butler (Thompson) intv.
3 Butler Diary/Letter, 15 November 1944.
4 Butler Diary/Letter, received 20 November 1944.
5 Butler Diary/Letter, 17 November 1944.
6 Butler Diary/Letter, 19 November 1944.
7 Ibid.
8 Butler Diary/Letter, December 1944.
9 Butler (Thompson) intv.
10 Butler personal papers.
11 Butler (Thompson) intv.
12 D. F. Underhill, *An account of the operations of the Regiment during World War II*, Staffordshire Yeomanry Museum, 1994, p.33.
13 Staffordshire Yeomanry, 'C' Squadron, War Diary, 6 February 1945.
14 Butler (Thompson) intv.
15 Ibid.
16 Ibid.
17 Staffordshire Yeomanry, 'C' Squadron, War Diary, 23 March 1945.
18 Underhill op. cit., & Staffordshire Yeomanry, 'C' Squadron, War Diary, 23 March 1945.
19 Draft article by D. F. Underhill, May 1945, archive, Staffordshire Yeomanry Museum.
20 Staffordshire Yeomanry, 'C' Squadron, War Diary, 25 March 1945.
21 Underhill article, op. cit.
22 Butler intv.
23 Butler (Thompson) intv.
24 Butler intv.
25 Butler ana, 'Coat-hanger', 20 September 2000.
26 Butler ana, 'War', 2000.
27 Staffordshire Yeomanry, 'C' Squadron, War Diary, 23 May 1945.
28 Ibid., 28 May 1945.
29 Butler intv.
30 Staffordshire Yeomanry, 'C' Squadron, War Diary, 5 & 18 June 1945.
31 Ibid., 20–24 June 1945.

Notes to Chapter Three: In the Absence of Cricket, pages 35–54

1 Butler intv.

2 Despite extensive research, I have not been able to find any examples, and it was several years after DB's work on the 1945 election that the main reference directories added percentage figures.
3 R. B. McCallum to Richard Rose letter, 12 October 1966, archive, Nuffield College, Oxford.
4 John Maynard Keynes, *The Economic Consequences of the Peace*, Macmillan, 1919, p.67.
5 Keynes, op. cit., p.69.
6 McCallum to Rose, op. cit.
7 Butler, McCallum lecture, 1 November 1997.
8 *Parliamentary Affairs*, Vol. 8, No. 4, January 1954.
9 McCallum to Rose, op. cit.
10 Ibid.
11 Ibid.
12 Transcript of final Butler Nuffield College seminar, 4 June 2010.
13 McCallum lecture, op. cit.
14 Butler (Thompson) intv.
15 R. B. McCallum & Alison Readman, *British General Election of 1945*, Oxford University Press, 1947, pp.277–92.
16 Ibid., pp.293–5, and pull-out.
17 Ibid., p.277.
18 Ibid., p.278.
19 Ibid., p.290.
20 Ibid., pp.290–91.
21 Ibid., p.291.
22 In 1951, Labour's 231,033 vote advantage would have been much smaller had four Ulster Unionists (then regarded as part of the Conservative tally) not been elected unopposed in Northern Ireland – in seats where the party got 166,400 votes in total in 1955. The Tory total in 1951 was probably reduced by a further 50–60,000 by the party's decision to withdraw in three seats – Bolton West, Huddersfield West and Dundee West – to give the Liberals a straight run against Labour.
23 McCallum & Readman, op. cit., p.292.
24 Dennis Kavanagh (ed.), *Electoral Politics*, Oxford University Press, 1992, p.5.
25 *Manchester Guardian*, 10 April 1947.
26 *Journal of the Royal Statistical Society*, Vol. 61, No. 3, September 1898.
27 Butler lecture, 'The Evolution of British Electoral Studies', LSE, 20 March 2014.
28 *Journal of the Royal Statistical Society*, op. cit. In 1896, Jervoise Baines wrote a long analysis of the two general elections of 1892 and 1895, in which he had calculated percentages seat by seat, but only for the amount by which the winning candidate's majority exceeded the vote of his main rival. *Journal of the Royal Statistical Society*, Vol. 59, No. 1, March 1896.
29 McCallum & Readman, op. cit., p.264.
30 Butler LSE lecture, op. cit.
31 *Journal of the Royal Statistical Society*, Vol. 69, No. 4, December 1906.
32 Henry Durant, 'Behind the Opinion Polls', News Chronicle pamphlet, 1951.
33 Butler to Henry Durant letter, 10 December 1946.
34 *Independent*, 7 November 1997.
35 Butler ana, 'Berlin', 2000.
36 Ibid.
37 Butler intv.
38 Butler undergraduate file, archive, New College, Oxford.
39 Butler intv.
40 Ibid.
41 Butler undergraduate file, op. cit.
42 Frank Smith (MSC) intv.
43 Butler (Harrison) intv.
44 Butler intv.

Notes to Chapter Four: Surveying America, pages 55–78

1 Butler intv.
2 Butler Diary/Letter, 30 August 1947.
3 Butler Diary/Letter, 31 August 1947.
4 Ibid.
5 Butler Diary/Letter, 10 September 1947.
6 Butler Diary/Letter, 20 September 1947.
7 Butler Diary/Letter, 31 October 1947.
8 Butler Diary/Letter, 3 November 1947.
9 Butler Diary/Letter, 10 November 1947.
10 Butler Diary/Letter, 11 October 1947.
11 Butler (Thompson) intv.
12 Butler Diary/Letter, 14 October 1947.
13 Butler Diary/Letter, 8 December 1947.
14 Butler personal papers.
15 Butler Diary/Letter, 15 October 1947.
16 Butler Diary/Letter, 13 December 1947.
17 Butler Diary/Letter 17 October 1947.
18 Butler Diary/Letter, 16 November 1947.
19 Butler personal papers.
20 Butler Diary/Letter, 20 November 1947.
21 Butler Diary/Letter, 21 November 1947.
22 Butler Diary/Letter, 20 January 1948.
23 Butler Diary/Letter, 29 January 1948.
24 Butler Diary/Letter, 17 February 1948.
25 Butler Diary/Letter, 6 February 1948.
26 *Time and Tide*, 14 May 1948.
27 Butler Diary/Letter, 17 May 1948.
28 Butler Diary/Letter, 28 April 1948.
29 Butler Diary/Letter, 10 May 1948.
30 Butler Diary/Letter 11 June 1948.
31 Butler ana, 'Frankfurter', 13 November 2006.
32 Butler Diary/Letter, 3 May 1948.
33 Butler Diary/Letter, 10 June 1948.
34 *Time and Tide*, 3, 24 & 31 July 1948.
35 Butler Diary/Letter, 26 July 1948.
36 John Gunther, *Inside USA*, Hamish Hamilton, 1947.
37 Butler (ST) intv.
38 Butler Diary/Letter, 27 July 1948.
39 Butler Diary/Letter, 13 August 1948.
40 Butler Diary/Letter, 13 August 1948.
41 Butler Diary/Letter, 8 April 1948.
42 Butler Diary/Letter, 12 June 1948.
43 Butler Diary/Letter, 27 July 1948.
44 *Time and Tide*, 30 October 1948.
45 Ibid.
46 Butler Diary/Letter, 20 September 1948.
47 Butler Diary/Letter, 21 September 1948.
48 Butler Diary/Letter, 2 November 1948.
49 Ibid.
50 Butler Diary/Letter, 11 November 1948.
51 Butler Diary/Letter, 25 October 1948.

52 Butler Diary/Letter, July 1952.
53 Butler Diary/Letter, 7 September 1952.
54 Butler Diary/Letter, August 1952.
55 Butler conversation with Tony Benn, Hansard Society, 16 November 2004.
56 Butler Diary/Letter, 15 July 1952.
57 Butler Diary/Letter, 29 July 1954.

Notes to Chapter Five: Into the Family Trade, pages 79–95

1 Robert Taylor, *Nuffield College Memories: A Personal History*, Nuffield College, 2008, p.23.
2 Martin Adeney, *Nuffield: A Biography*, Hale, 1993, p.168.
3 Nuffield College Newsletter, Summer 2005.
4 Butler (Harrison) intv.
5 Nuffield College Newsletter, Summer 2005.
6 Butler, *The Electoral System in Britain, 1918–51*, Oxford University Press, 1953.
7 Butler (ST) intv.
8 *Time and Tide*, 2 April 1949.
9 Butler lecture, 'The Evolution of British Electoral Studies', LSE, 20 March 2014.
10 *Economist*, 7 January 1950.
11 Royal Commission on Systems of Elections, Minutes of Evidence, Cmnd. 5352, pp.77–86.
12 *Economist*, 7 January 1950.
13 *British Journal of Sociology*, September 1950, p.185.
14 Ibid., pp.193–4.
15 Butler notes of visit to Winston Churchill, 6 February 1950.
16 Ibid.
17 Ibid.
18 Ibid.
19 Ibid.
20 Ibid.
21 Ibid.
22 Ibid.
23 Ibid.
24 Ibid.
25 Ibid.
26 Ibid.
27 Ibid.
28 Ibid.
29 Ibid.
30 Ibid.
31 Ibid.
32 Ibid.
33 Butler (Thompson) intv.
34 Zbigniew Pelczynski intv.
35 Ibid.
36 Butler ana, 'Political Neutrality', 2000.

Notes to Chapter Six: Telly Don, pages 97–121

1 Arthur Burrows to Reuters, 20 October 1924, BBC Archive, R28/81/1 News Gen Elec Results File 1A 1923–29.
2 Grace Wyndham Goldie, *Facing the Nation*, Bodley Head, 1977, p.61.
3 Grace Wyndham Goldie memo to Cecil McGivern, 16 January 1950, BBC Archive, T32/172, TV Talks, GE.
4 Goldie, op. cit., pp.61 & 63.

5 David Attenborough, *Life on Air: Memoirs of a Broadcaster*, BBC Books, 2002, p.14.
6 Alasdair Milne, *DG: The Memoirs of a British Broadcaster*, Hodder & Stoughton, 1988, pp.8 & 175.
7 John Grist, *Grace Wyndham Goldie: First Lady of Television*, Authors Online, 2006, p.78.
8 Milne, op. cit., p.8.
9 The Invention of General Election Broadcasting, BBC website.
10 Ibid.
11 Goldie, op. cit., p.64.
12 Goldie to Butler letter, 26 January 1950, BBC Archive, TV Art 1 1950–59.
13 Ibid.
14 Butler letter to Paul Johnson, 29 April 1949, BBC Archive, Talks RConti File 1, 1949–62, Butler, David.
15 Anthony Wedgwood Benn memo to Miss Arbuthnott, 16 January 1950, BBC Archive, Talks RConti File 1, 1949–62, Butler, David.
16 Butler letter to Goldie, 31 January 1950, BBC Archive, TV Art 1 1950–59, TV Talks General Election 50, Butler, David.
17 Ibid.
18 Goldie to McGivern, op. cit.
19 Butler (Thompson) intv.
20 Norman Collins memo to Goldie, 31 January 1950, BBC Archive, R34/545 Policy, Polit. Broadcasting GE 47–50.
21 Goldie, op. cit., p.65.
22 Ibid., p.66.
23 Ibid., p.64.
24 *Manchester Guardian*, 24 February 1950.
25 *Listener*, 9 March 1950.
26 Grist, op. cit., p.77.
27 Goldie, op. cit., p.67.
28 Butler letter to Goldie, 26 February 1950, BBC Archive, TV Art 1 1950–59, Butler, David.
29 Goldie letter to Butler, 27 February 1950, BBC Archive, TV Art 1, 1950–59, Butler, David.
30 Butler letter to Churchill, 5 February 1951, Churchill papers, 2/109.
31 Churchill telegram to Butler, 7 February 1951.
32 Butler Diary, 8 February 1951.
33 Tony Benn (ed. Ruth Winstone), *Years of Hope, Diaries, Papers & Letters 1940–62*, Hutchinson, 1994, p.144 (19 March 1951).
34 Transcript of final Butler Nuffield seminar, 4 June 2010.
35 Benn, op. cit., pp.158–9 (31 October 1951).
36 Butler letter to Goldie, 23 July 1951, BBC Archive, T32/173 TV Talks, GE51, Dated Papers 1951.
37 Butler letter to Goldie, 20 May 1951, quoted in Asa Briggs, *History of Broadcasting in the United Kingdom, Vol. IV*, Oxford University Press, 1978, p.608.
38 Butler report to BBC, 14 June 1951, BBC Archive, T16/510.
39 British Broadcasting Corporation Annual Report and Accounts for the Year 1954/55, HMSO, 1955.
40 *Radio Times*, 21 October 1951.
41 Ibid.
42 Ibid.
43 Butler (Thompson) intv.
44 *Manchester Guardian*, 27 October 1951.
45 *Yorkshire Post*, 27 October 1951.
46 *Glasgow Herald*, 27 October 1951.
47 *Daily Herald*, 27 October 1951.
48 Butler Diary, 17 November 1950.

49 Ibid.
50 Butler Diary, 22 November 1950.
51 Butler Diary, 14 November 1950.
52 Butler Diary 23 November 1950.
53 Butler Diary, 18 December 1950.

Notes to Chapter Seven: A Speedometer Type Device, pages 123–142

1 Butler memo to Goldie, May 1950, BBC Archive, TV Art 1 1950–59, Butler, David.
2 Butler memo to Goldie, 31/5/1950, BBC Archive, TV Art 1, Butler, David.
3 Butler Diary, 14 November 1950.
4 Viewer Research report, Men of Authority, 29 November 1950, BBC Archive, R9/7/2.
5 Ibid.
6 4 December 1950, VR50/310-50/534; & 9 January 1951, BBC Archive, R9/7/3.
7 Butler Diary, 15 December 1950.
8 Viewer Research Report, Men of Authority, 9 January 1951, BBC Archive, R9/7/3 VR51/1-51/276.
9 Butler Diary, 28 November 1950.
10 Butler intv.
11 Butler Diary, 23 November 1950.
12 Butler (Harrison) intv.
13 Ibid.
14 Butler intv.
15 David Butler, *The British General Election of 1951*, Macmillan, 1952, p.1.
16 Ibid.
17 R. B. McCallum letter to Alison Readman, 12 July 1949, Wright family papers.
18 I am grateful for the help of Inklings scholars Diana Glyer and David Bratman on this matter.
19 *The Quest: A Quarterly Review*, Vol. 3, p.194, 1912. The algebraic use of these words hasn't ever been recognised by the Oxford English Dictionary, but they were used occasionally in this context from the 1910s to the 1930s, and there was even one instance as recently as 2013: Andrew Gregory, *The Presocratics and the Supernatural*, Bloomsbury, 2013.
20 *Oxford Magazine*, 17 May 1951.
21 Butler letter to mother, 22 August 1952.
22 *New York Herald Tribune*, 8 August 1952.
23 *Time* (US), 18 August 1952.
24 *Daily Express*, 30 September 1952.
25 *The Twentieth Century*, July–December 1955.
26 *Parliamentary Affairs*, Vol. 8, No. 4, January 1954.
27 Butler letter to Maurice Macmillan, 22 August 1952, archive, Macmillan, Basingstoke.
28 Butler ana, 'Psephology', 26 September 2010.
29 Butler (Thompson) intv.
30 David Butler, *The British General Election of 1951*, Macmillan, 1952, p.9.
31 *Public Administration*, Vol. 33, Summer 1955.
32 Butler (ST) intv.
33 Remarkably, of the thirty-five general election programmes broadcast by the BBC or ITV since 1950, almost half – sixteen – have been presented by a member of the Dimbleby family.
34 Peacock letter to Butler, 24 January 1955, BBC Archive, TV Art 1 1950–59, Butler, David.
35 Butler letter to Peacock, 25 January 1955, BBC Archive, TV Art 1 1950–59, Butler, David.
36 Butler letter to Peacock, 19 February 1955, BBC Archive, TV Talks, GE 1955, Studio Commentators, T32/734.
37 Butler letter to Goldie, 10 March 1955, BBC Archive, T32/734, TV Talks, GE 1955, Studio Commentators.

38 Butler letter to Goldie, 5 May 1955, BBC Archive, T32/734, TV Talks GE 1955.
39 *Radio Times*, 22–28 May 1955.
40 BBC election results programme, 26–27 May 1955.
41 Butler intv.
42 BBC election results programme, 26 May 1955.
43 BBC election results programme, 27 May 1955.
44 *Observer*, 29 May 1955.
45 *The Star*, 27 May 1955.
46 *Scotsman*, 28 May 1955.
47 Peacock letter to Butler, 3 June 1955, BBC Archive, TV Art 1 1950–59, Butler, David.
48 Butler letter to Peacock, 6 June 1955, BBC Archive, TV Art 1 1950–59, Butler, David.
49 Goldie letter to Butler, 8 June 1955, BBC Archive, TV Art 1, 1950–59, Butler, David.
50 Ibid.
51 Butler memo on 1955 election programme, 31 May 1955, BBC Archive, TV Art 1, Butler, David.

Notes to Chapter Eight: Gilded Year in Georgetown, pages 143–159

1 John Carter & Graham Pollard, *An Enquiry into the Nature of Certain Nineteenth-Century Pamphlets*, Constable, 1934.
2 Recording of Butler lunch with Peter Marshall & Margaret Crick, 13 June 2017.
3 Ibid.
4 Butler ana 'Suez', 2 November 2006.
5 Butler–Marshall lunch, op. cit.
6 Virginia Shapiro (née Makins) interview.
7 Butler ana, 'Makins', undated.
8 Butler–Marshall lunch, op. cit.
9 Butler ana 'Makins', op. cit.
10 Butler–Marshall lunch, op. cit.
11 Butler ana, Makins, op. cit.
12 Ibid.
13 Butler Diary/Letter, 29 May 1956.
14 Butler–Marshall lunch, op. cit.
15 Butler Diary/Letter, 21 May 1956.
16 Butler Diary/Letter, 22 May 1956.
17 Gregg Herken, *The Georgetown Set*, Knopf, 2014, p.7.
18 Ibid., p.7.
19 C. David Heymann, *The Georgetown Ladies' Social Club*, Atria Books, 2003, pp.10–11, cited in Herken, op. cit., p.7.
20 Butler Diary/Letter, 23 February 1956.
21 Butler Diary/Letter, 24 February 1956; Herken, op. cit., p.24.
22 Herken, op. cit., opening page.
23 Butler ana, 'Frankfurter', 13 November 2006.
24 Butler Diary/Letter, 21 December 1955.
25 Butler Diary/Letter, 7 January 1956.
26 Butler Diary/Letter, 22 January 1956.
27 Butler Diary/Letter, 4 April 1956.
28 Butler Diary/Letter, 16 June 1956.
29 Butler Diary/Letter, 23 February 1956.
30 Butler Diary/Letter, 3–4 December 1955.
31 Butler Diary/Letter, 19 December 1955.
32 Butler Diary/Letter, 15 April 1956.
33 Butler Diary/Letter, 29 March 1956.
34 Ibid.

35 Butler Diary/Letter, 4 April 1956.
36 Butler–Marshall lunch, op. cit.
37 Peter Marshall, *Churchill in Number Ten, Eisenhower in the White House, and the 'Makins Mission'*, unpublished memoirs, 2014, p.13.
38 Butler Diary/Letter, 1 May 1956.
39 Butler Diary/Letter, 6 May 1956.
40 *Washington Sunday Star*, 13 May 1956.
41 Ibid.
42 Butler intv.
43 Marshall, op. cit., p.13.
44 Butler ana, 'Makins', op. cit.
45 Butler–Marshall lunch, op. cit.
46 Butler Diary/Letter, 9 & 11 April 1956.
47 Butler–Marshall lunch, op. cit.
48 Butler Diary/Letter, 25 April 1956.
49 Butler–Marshall lunch, op. cit.

Notes to Chapter Nine: Buccaneering Butlers, pages 161–181

1 Martin Gilbert, *Never Despair*, Heinemann, 1988, p.510.
2 H. G. Nicholas, *The British General Election of 1950*, Macmillan, 1951, pp.101–2.
3 Ibid.
4 David Butler, *The British General Election of 1951*, Macmillan, 1952, p.79.
5 Butler letter to mother, July 1952.
6 Butler–McKenzie memo, BBC Archive, R34/562/1, Policy, Political Broadcasting, Party Conferences File 1, 42–54, November 1953, p.1.
7 Ibid., p.2.
8 Ibid., p.3.
9 Ibid., p.5.
10 Ibid., p.7.
11 Ibid., p.9.
12 Ibid., p.10.
13 Ibid., p.11.
14 Butler letter to mother, late August 1954.
15 Goldie letter to Butler, 6 September 1954, BBC Archive, T32/268 TV Talks, Party Conferences, Conservatives, 1954.
16 Goldie memo, 26 August 1954, BBC Archive, T16/146/1 TV Policy Political Broadcasts, Party Conferences File 1, 1950–54.
17 David Butler, *The British General Election of 1955*, Macmillan, 1955, p.64.
18 Geoffrey Cox, *See It Happen*, Bodley Head, 1983, p.114.
19 Butler (Harrison) intv.
20 Harman Grisewood letter to Butler, 3 & 7 January 1958, BBC Archive, R78/1, 193/1 Management; Political Broadcasting/Nuffield College Conferences B415-1-5.
21 Grisewood on interview with Butler, 19 December 1957, BBC Archive, R78/1, 193/1 Management; Political Broadcasting/Nuffield College Conferences B415-1-5.
22 Tony Benn (ed. Ruth Winstone), *Years of Hope, Diaries 1940–62*, Hutchinson, 1994, p.260 (10 January 1958).
23 Benn, op. cit., p.261 (10 January 1958).
24 Butler (Harrison) intv.
25 Report of Nuffield conference, 11 January 1958.
26 Butler intv.
27 The Invention of Election Broadcasting, BBC website.
28 *Manchester Guardian*, 20 January 1958.

29 Asa Briggs, *The History of Broadcasting in the United Kingdom, Vol. V*, Oxford University Press, 1995, p.242.
30 Report of Nuffield conference, 11 January 1958.
31 *Manchester Guardian*, 20 January 1958.
32 Cox, op. cit., p.116.
33 Ibid.
34 David Butler & Richard Rose, *The British General Election of 1959*, Macmillan, 1960.
35 Transcript of final Butler Nuffield seminar, 4 June 2010.
36 *Radio Times*, 2 October 1959.
37 Butler was paid 500 guineas (£525) for his work, plus a 100 guinea (£105) bonus, compared with just 180 guineas (£189) in 1955. Even allowing for inflation, these were not large sums considering the many days' work involved and compared with what an election expert would be paid today.
38 BBC election results programme, 10–11 October 1959.
39 CBS presidential election results programme, 8–9 November 1960.
40 Butler intv.
41 Sir Paul Fox intv.
42 Ibid.
43 BBC election results programme, 15–16 October 1964.
44 Ibid.
45 Ibid.
46 *New Statesman*, 5 October 1962.
47 Ibid.

Notes to Chapter Ten: College Man, pages 183–206

1 Butler (Harrison) intv.
2 Scott Housley email to author.
3 Jonathan Seagrave email to author.
4 Sheila Dunleavy email to author.
5 Stephen Brooks intv.
6 Butler ana, 'Edward Heath', revised 2013.
7 Butler ana, 'Crossman', 21 May 2002.
8 *Sunday Times*, 19 May 1963.
9 Butler (Harrison) intv.
10 Ibid.
11 Transcript of final Butler Nuffield seminar, 4 June 2010, & Butler (Harrison) intv.
12 Butler (Harrison) intv.
13 Jagdish Bhagwati email to author.
14 Butler (Harrison) intv.
15 Ibid.
16 Butler standard letter, 'University Seminar: British Politics', Nuffield College, 1992.
17 Transcript of final Butler Nuffield seminar, 4 June 2010.
18 Ibid.
19 Butler (Harrison) intv.
20 *Observer*, 12 June 1960.
21 *New Zealand Journal of History*, Vol. 2, 1968.
22 Ibid.
23 Lord (Oliver) Poole, intv., 7 July 1964, election study archive, Nuffield College, Oxford.
24 Rab Butler intvs, 3 February & 30 June 1964; Poole, op. cit., election study archive, Nuffield College, Oxford.
25 Butler & King, *The British General Election of 1964*, Macmillan, 1965, p.45.
26 *Harper's Magazine*, 1 May 1963.

27 'Political Reporting in Britain', BBC Third Programme, 27 July 1963, reproduced in *The Listener*, 15 August 1963.
28 *New Zealand Journal of History*, Vol. 2, 1968.
29 Ibid.
30 Austin Mitchell, *Calendar Boy*, Pen & Sword Politics, 2014, p.77.
31 Trevor Lloyd, *The General Election of 1880*, Oxford University Press, 1968; Alan Russell, *Liberal Landslide: The General Election of 1906*, David & Charles, 1973; Neal Blewett, *The Peers, The Parties and The People: The General Elections of 1910*, University of Toronto Press, 1972; Andrew Thorpe, *The British General Election of 1931*, Clarendon, 1991; Tom Stannage, *Baldwin Thwarts the Opposition: The British General Election of 1935*, Croom Helm, 1980.
32 Butler letter to Rex Allen, 9 June 1960, archive, Macmillan, Basingstoke.
33 Ibid.
34 Butler (Harrison) intv.
35 David Butler & Jennie Freeman, *British Political Facts 1900–1960*, Macmillan, 1963, p.xii–xvi.
36 *Profile*, BBC Radio 4, 27 May 1983.
37 Butler (ST) intv.
38 Anne Sloman intv.
39 Ibid.
40 David Butler & Jennie Freeman, *British Political Facts*, 2nd edn, Macmillan, 1968, pp.xviii & xix.
41 PC Thompson email to author.
42 Cook and Brendan Keith published a volume for 1830–1900; then Cook and John Stevenson produced volumes for 1760–1830, and 1688–1760. *British Political Facts* also influenced *British Election Facts*, started in 1975 by F. W. S. 'Fred' Craig, which was later taken over by Plymouth University psephologists Colin Rallings and Michael Thrasher.
43 Roger Mortimore & Andrew Blick, *Butler's British Political Facts*, Palgrave Macmillan, 2018.

Notes to Chapter Eleven: The Love of His Life, pages 207–228

1 Grace Wyndham Goldie letter to Butler, 8 June 1955, BBC Archives, TV Art 1, 1950–59, Butler, David.
2 Butler Diary/Letter, 28 November 1948.
3 Butler intv.
4 Benedicte Hjejle (MSC) intv.
5 Butler Diary/Letter, 7 June 1957.
6 Butler Diary/Letter, 5 July 1957.
7 Butler Diary/Letter, 10 July 1957.
8 Butler Diary/Letter, 7 July 1957.
9 Benedicte Hjejle email to MSC.
10 Benedicte Hjejle (MSC) intv.
11 Butler Diary/Letter, 15 October 1957.
12 Butler Diary/Letter, 27 April 1958.
13 Butler Diary/Letter, 23 July 1958.
14 Joy Whitby intv.
15 Butler intv.
16 Ed Butler email to author.
17 Richard Evans intv.
18 Marilyn Butler, unpublished auto-obituary, May 1996 (eighteen years before her death), archive, St Hilda's College.
19 Programme for Memorial Service for Marilyn Butler, Exeter College, Oxford, 24 April 2014.
20 *Times Higher Education Supplement*, 15 September 1995.
21 Marilyn Butler, unpublished memoir, undated, archive, St Hilda's College, Oxford.
22 Marilyn Butler auto-obituary, op. cit.

23 Marilyn Butler memoir, op. cit.
24 *Times Higher Education Supplement*, 15 September 1995.
25 Marilyn Butler memoir, op. cit.
26 Dan Butler intv.
27 Nigel Leask in *Biographical Memoirs of Fellows of the British Academy, XVI*, British Academy, 2017, p.89.
28 Dan Butler intv.
29 Butler intv.
30 Marilyn Butler (MSC) intv. (in 2003).
31 Butler intv.
32 *Times Higher Education Supplement*, 15 September 1995.
33 Bel Crewe (MSC) intv.
34 *Independent*, 20 March 2014.
35 Dennis Kavanagh email to author.
36 Butler (Thompson) intv.
37 Butler (Harrison) intv.
38 Dan Butler intv.
39 Ibid.
40 Ibid.
41 *Times Higher Education Supplement*, 15 September 1995.
42 Dan Butler intv.
43 Ibid.
44 Helen Wallace (ST) intv.
45 Ed Butler email to author.
46 Dan Butler intv.
47 Ibid.
48 Bel Crewe (MSC) intv.
49 Ed Butler intv.
50 Dan Butler intv.
51 Ed Butler intv.
52 Dan Butler intv.
53 Marilyn Butler, *Jane Austen and the War of Ideas*, Oxford University Press, 1975.
54 Jeri Johnson address, Memorial Service for Marilyn Butler, Exeter College, Oxford, 24 April 2014.
55 Leask, op. cit., p.92.
56 *Times Higher Education Supplement*, 15 September 1995.
57 Heather Glen address, Memorial Service for Marilyn Butler, Exeter College, Oxford, 24 April 2014.
58 Marilyn Butler, *Peacock Displayed: A Satirist in his Context*, Routledge, 1979; *Romantics, Rebels and Reactionaries: English Literature and its Background 1760–1830*, Oxford University Press, 1981.
59 Heather Glen address, op. cit.
60 Marilyn Butler, *Jane Austen and the War of Ideas*, Oxford University Press, 1975, reprint, 1987, p.xxvi.
61 Leask, op. cit., p.86.

Notes to Chapter Twelve: Which Is Butler? Which Is Stokes?, pages 229–251

1 *Daily Herald*, 17 May 1955.
2 David Butler & Richard Rose, *The British General Election of 1959*, Macmillan, 1960, p.1.
3 Ibid., p.4.
4 David Butler, *The British General Election of 1951*, Macmillan, 1952, pp.4–5.
5 David Butler, *The Study of Political Behaviour*, Hutchinson, 1958, pp.66–7.
6 Butler (Harrison) intv.

7 Butler (Thompson) intv.
8 David Butler & Donald Stokes, *Political Change in Britain*, Macmillan, 1969, pp.464–81.
9 Butler letter to Donald Stokes, 1 February 1967.
10 Butler letter to Warren Miller, 8 February 1967.
11 Butler letter to Stokes, 20 February 1967.
12 Stokes letter to Butler, 20 February 1967.
13 Butler letter to Stokes, 20 February 1967.
14 Stokes letter to Butler, 28 February 1967.
15 Butler letter to Stokes, 7 March 1967.
16 Stokes letter to Butler, 3 August 1967.
17 Butler letter to Stokes, 1 September & 11 October 1967.
18 Tim Farmiloe letter to Philip Martin, 3 October 1968, archive, Macmillan, Basingstoke.
19 Jack Hayward, Brian Barry & Archie Brown (eds), *The British Study of Politics in the Twentieth Century*, British Academy Scholarship Online, 2003, p.242.
20 *Sunday Times*, 28 September 1969.
21 Ibid.
22 *Spectator*, 3 October 1969.
23 *Times*, 30 October 1969.
24 *Times*, 3 November 1969.
25 *Financial Times*, 24 January 1975.
26 *New Statesman*, 5 October 1962.
27 *Listener*, 20 November 1969
28 *Economist*, 1 November 1969.
29 *Observer*, 2 November 1969.
30 *New Statesman*, 31 October 1969.
31 *New Society*, 30 October 1969
32 *Times Literary Supplement*, 13 November 1969.
33 *Spectator*, 15 November 1969.
34 Annals of the American Academy of Political and Social Science, January 1971.
35 *Political Science Quarterly*, March 1972.
36 Butler & Stokes file, archive, Macmillan, Basingstoke.
37 John Ramsden (ed.), *Oxford Companion to Twentieth-Century British Politics*, Oxford University Press, 2005.
38 *European Journal of Political Research*, Vol. 2, 1974.
39 Ibid.
40 Sir Ivor Crewe intv.
41 Butler intv.
42 Crewe intv.
43 Christopher Hood, Donald King & Gillian Peele (eds), *Forging a Discipline*, Oxford University Press, 2014, p.127.
44 Ivor Crewe & Bo Särlvik, *Decade of Dealignment*, Cambridge University Press, 1983.
45 Anthony Heath, Roger Jowell & John Curtice, *How Britain Votes*, Pergamon, 1985.
46 Butler lecture, 'The Evolution of British Electoral Studies', LSE, 20 March 2014.
47 *Guardian*, 29 January 1997.

Notes to Chapter Thirteen: An English Don Abroad, pages 253–275

1 *Listener*, 1 January 1970.
2 Butler (Harrison) intv.
3 Don Aitkin emails to author.
4 Butler intv.
5 Video intv. by John Uhr, Australian National University, April 2013.
6 Malcolm Mackerras email to author.

7 John Uhr intv., op. cit.
8 David Butler, *The Canberra Model*, Macmillan, 1973, p.3.
9 Butler intv.
10 Butler ana, 'Harold Holt 1967', checked 2013.
11 *Sydney Morning Herald*, 9 December 1967.
12 Butler ana, 'Harold Holt 1967', op. cit.; *Sydney Morning Herald*, 9 December 1967; *Canberra Times*, 9 December 1967.
13 Butler ana, 'Harold Holt 1967', op. cit.
14 Ibid.
15 Butler intv.
16 Ibid.
17 *Canberra Times*, 27 October 1977.
18 *Canberra Times*, 12 December 1977.
19 *Canberra Times*, 12 July 1987.
20 *Canberra Times*, 2 January 1994.
21 *Canberra Times*, 18 October 1969.
22 Ed Butler intv.
23 *New Statesman*, 24 May 1974.
24 David Butler, *The Canberra Model*, op. cit., 1973.
25 Pat Weller email to author.
26 David Butler, *The Canberra Model*, op. cit., pp.3–12.
27 Weller email to author.
28 Ian McAllister email to author.
29 *Parliamentary Affairs*, Vol. 29, No. 2, Spring 1976, p.207.
30 Butler intv.; *Australian*, 9 September 1972.
31 *Australian*, 9 September 1972.
32 Mackerras letter to author.
33 *Canberra Times*, 18 October 1969.
34 Mackerras email to author.
35 Malcolm Mackerras, *Mackerras Federal Election Guide*, AGPS Press, Canberra, 1989–95.
36 McAllister email to author.
37 Tom Harley intv.
38 Aitkin email to author.
39 *Parliamentary Affairs*, Vol. 26, No. 2, June 1973, pp.406–9 (In 1975, Butler wrote to *The Times* expressing reservations about full publication of the Crossman Diaries. 'Open government and efficient government are both desirable goals,' he wrote. 'But they are not wholly compatible.' *Times*, 12 July 1975.)
40 Butler intv.
41 Ashok Lahiri email to author.
42 David Butler, Ashok Lahiri & Prannoy Roy, *A Compendium of Indian Elections*, Arnold Heinemann, 1984.
43 Lahiri email to author.
44 Butler intv.
45 Sir Mark Tully intv.
46 *Times*, 27 December 1984.
47 Ed Butler email to author.
48 Lolita Bam email to author.
49 Prannoy Roy email to author.
50 Tully intv.
51 Ed Butler email to author.
52 Butler intv.
53 *India Today*, January 1985.

54 David Butler, Ashok Lahiri & Prannoy Roy, *India Decides: Elections 1952–1989*, Living Media India, 1989.
55 Butler intv.
56 Ed Butler email to author.
57 Transcript of final Butler Nuffield seminar, 4 June 2010.

Notes to Chapter Fourteen: Academic Entrepreneur, pages 277–291

1 *Election 70*, BBC1, 18 June 1970.
2 *New Society*, 15 April 1971.
3 *New Statesman*, 16 April 1971.
4 *Observer*, 18 April 1971.
5 *Election 74*, BBC1, 28 February–1 March 1974.
6 Chris Long email to author.
7 Dennis Kavanagh intv.
8 Ibid.
9 Ibid.
10 David Butler & Dennis Kavanagh, *The British General Election of February 1974*, Macmillan, 1974.
11 Butler (Harrison) intv.
12 Dennis Kavanagh, *Electoral Politics*, op. cit., pp.8–10.
13 *Times Literary Supplement*, 22 June 1984.
14 *Times*, 6 November 1975.
15 Ibid.
16 Dennis Kavanagh, *Electoral Politics*, op. cit., p.11.
17 Butler (Harrison) intv.
18 Lord (Andrew) Adonis intv.
19 Janet Morgan intv.
20 *Profile*, BBC Radio 4, 27 May 1983.
21 David Butler and Uwe Kitzinger, *The 1975 Referendum*, Macmillan, 1976, p.44.
22 Uwe Kitzinger intv.
23 David Butler & Austin Ranney (eds), *Referendums Around the World: The Growing Use of Direct Democracy*, American Enterprise Institute, 1978.
24 Tony Benn, unpublished diary, 27 January 1971.
25 Ibid., 6 June 1973.
26 Ibid., 6–7 July 1973
27 Ibid., 10 February 1974.
28 Tony Benn intv., 8 October 1974, election study archive, Nuffield College, Oxford.
29 Tony Benn, unpublished diary, 23 July 1975.
30 Ibid., 9 October 1976.
31 Ibid., 3 November 1977.
32 David Butler (ed.), *Coalitions in British Politics*, Macmillan, 1978.

Notes to Chapter Fifteen: Consensus Pinko, pages 293–307

1 Margaret Thatcher intv., 21 November 1974, election study archive, Nuffield College, Oxford.
2 Margaret Thatcher intv., 9 August 1978, election study archive, Nuffield College, Oxford.
3 Dennis Kavanagh, *Electoral Politics*, op. cit., p.10.
4 Dennis Kavanagh intv.
5 Tim Bell intv., 8 July 1983, election study archive, Nuffield College, Oxford.
6 Tony Benn, unpublished diary, 1 February 1980.
7 Ibid., 2 July 1980.
8 Tony Benn (ed. Ruth Winstone), *The End of an Era, Diaries, 1980–90*, Hutchinson, 1992, p.290 (3 June 1983).

9 Tony Benn intv., 3 June 1983, election study archive, Nuffield College, Oxford.
10 Tony Benn, unpublished diary, 8 July 1983.
11 Tony Benn intv., 9 July 1983, election study archive, Nuffield College, Oxford.
12 Ibid.
13 Tony Benn, unpublished diary, 19 October 1984.
14 David Butler, *Governing Without a Majority: Dilemmas for Hung Parliaments in Britain*, Collins, 1983.
15 Robert Hazell & Akash Paun (eds), *Making Minority Government Work: Hung parliaments and the challenges for Westminster and Whitehall*, Institute for Government, 2009.
16 David Butler & David Marquand, *European Elections and British Politics*, Macmillan, 1981.
17 David Butler & Paul Jowett, *Party Strategies in Britain: A Study of the 1984 European Elections*, Macmillan, 1985; David Butler & Martin Westlake, *British Politics and European Elections, 1994*, Macmillan, 1995; David Butler & Martin Westlake, *British Politics and European Elections, 1999*, Macmillan, 2000; David Butler & Martin Westlake, *British Politics and European Elections, 2004*, Macmillan, 2005.
18 Robert Worcester & Martin Harrop, *Political Communications: The General Election Campaign of 1979*, Allen & Unwin, 1982.
19 Ian McAllister & Richard Rose, *The Nationwide Competition for Votes: The 1983 British Election*, Frances Pinter, 1984, p.7.
20 Dennis Kavanagh, *Electoral Politics*, op. cit., pp.20–21.
21 Dennis Kavanagh email to author.
22 Dennis Kavanagh, *Electoral Politics*, op. cit., p.17.
23 Bogdanor email to author.
24 Adonis intv.
25 Butler intv.
26 John Goldthorpe intv.
27 Ibid.
28 Chris Capron (MSC) intv.
29 Peter Kellner intv.
30 Sir John Curtice intv.
31 Clive Payne intv.
32 Butler intv.
33 Vernon Bogdanor intv.
34 Butler (Thompson) intv.

Notes to Chapter Sixteen: The Rector's Husband, pages 309–331

1 Marilyn Butler, auto-obituary, op. cit.
2 Butler ana, 'Age', 28 March 2005.
3 Butler (Thompson) intv.
4 *Times*, 24 July 1978.
5 Butler intv.
6 Ibid.
7 *Guardian*, 13 March 2014.
8 Leask, op. cit., p.99.
9 *Guardian*, 13 March 2014.
10 Leask, op. cit., p.100.
11 Heather Glen address, op. cit.
12 Marilyn Butler, auto-obituary, op. cit.
13 *Agenda for Change: The Report of the Hansard Society Commission on Election Campaigns*, Hansard Society, 1991.
14 David Butler, 'The Case for an Electoral Commission – Keeping election law up-to-date', Hansard Society, 1998.

15 Fourth Report of Home Affairs Select Committee, 1997–98, HC768–11.
16 David Butler & Dennis Kavanagh, *The British General Election of 1992*, Macmillan, 1993, p.61.
17 David Butler, Andrew Adonis & Tony Travers, *Failure in the British Government: The Politics of the Poll Tax*, Oxford University Press, 1994.
18 *Times Higher Education Supplement*, 15 September 1995.
19 Jeri Johnson address, op. cit.
20 Butler intv.
21 Jeri Johnson address, op. cit.
22 Ibid.
23 Butler intv.
24 *Times*, 11 January 1995.
25 *Times*, 24 January 1995.
26 *Times Higher Education Supplement*, 24 February 1995.
27 Chris Ballinger intv.
28 Ibid.
29 Ian St John, unpublished diary, 6 & 24 April 1997.
30 Dennis Kavanagh & David Butler, *The British General Election of 2005*, Palgrave Macmillan, 2005, p.xii.
31 Rhodri Jones intv.
32 David Butler, 'History of Nuffield', lecture, 6 March 1999.
33 Butler intv.
34 Robert Taylor, *Nuffield College Memories: A Personal History*, Nuffield College, 2008.
35 Stewart Purvis email to author.
36 Brian Stewart email to author.
37 Dan Butler intv.
38 Dan Butler email to author.
39 Butler (Thompson) intv.
40 *Independent*, 6 March 2008.
41 *Guardian*, 4 March 2008.
42 Butler ana, 'Portuguese reflections', July 2008.
43 Dan Butler email.

Notes to Chapter Seventeen: The Rules Overturned, pages 333–342

1 Butler (ST) intv.
2 Butler intv.
3 Butler (Thompson) intv.
4 Dennis Kavanagh email to author.
5 Richard Evans intv.
6 Peter Kellner letter to Ministry of Justice, 2 July 2010.
7 *Election 2010*, BBC1, 7–8 May 2010.
8 Butler intv.
9 Ibid.
10 Butler ana, 'DEB', 21 November 2010.
11 Butler intv.
12 Sir Gus O'Donnell letter to Butler, 30 December 2010, personal papers.
13 Programme for Marilyn Butler Memorial Service, Exeter College, Oxford, 24 April 2014.
14 Marilyn Butler, *Mapping Mythologies: Countercurrents in Eighteenth-Century British Poetry and Cultural History*, Cambridge University Press, 2015.
15 Butler (ST) intv.
16 Ibid.
17 Butler intv.
18 *Newsnight*, BBC2, 26 May 2017.

19 Butler intv.
20 @SirDavidButler.
21 'How Britain Voted Since October 1974', ems-ipsos-mori.com website.
22 *Prospect* podcast, 4 May 2018.

Notes to Conclusion: A Life to the Full, pages 43–347

1 Larry Sabato email to author.
2 Lewis Baston (ST) intv.
3 Vernon Bogdanor intv.
4 Paul Jowett (MSC) intv.

Notes to Appendix: From Academic Aristocracy, pages 349–357

1 Reproduced in Noel Annan, *The Dons: Mentors, Eccentrics and Geniuses*, op. cit., pp.301–41.
2 Noel Annan, *Our Age*, Weidenfeld, 1990, p.7.
3 Butler (Thompson) intv.
4 Ed Butler email to author.
5 Butler intv.
6 Stephen Parkinson, *Arena of Ambition: A History of the Cambridge Union*, Icon, 2009, pp.26–7, 341, 348–9, 352–3 & 355.
7 *Times*, 24 July 1978.
8 Violet Butler, *Social Conditions in Oxford*, Sidgwick & Jackson, 1912.
9 Christina Colvin, David Butler & Francis Butler, *A Miscellany for the Butler Family*, private publication, 2014, p.19.
10 Lawrence Wright, *Clean and Decent*, Routledge, 1960, pp.200–201.
11 Colvin et al., op. cit.

ACKNOWLEDGEMENTS

This book was initiated by Nuffield College, Oxford, in 2015, and the college has given significant financial help to the project over the past three years. I am grateful to the Warden, Sir Andrew Dilnot, for his continuing encouragement, and to Neil Fowler for overseeing the venture, though it should be stressed that the college gave me complete freedom over what I have written.

This is the first biography I have written with the cooperation of the subject, and Sir David Butler could not have been more helpful. Not only did he spend many hours during numerous interviews and conversations on dozens of occasions chatting to me about his life and career, but he also dealt patiently with my numerous follow-up queries and provided me with many papers from his personal archive with no restrictions on use.

I have also had the benefit of substantial information and advice from David's sons Dan and Ed. Every exchange between us seemed to yield new memories and anecdotes. David's niece Ann Addison was also a great help, along with Dan's former partner Bel Crewe.

My research has also benefited from the know-how of two people who are both successful published authors in their own right. Seth Thévoz has been a wonderful companion these past three years in exploring the Butler story. Seth's extraordinary knowledge and understanding of modern history, and his instinctive feel for both politics and the academic world, have been a huge asset to the project, along with his eye for quirky and amusing detail. As a successful historian, or maybe as a journalist, or both, Seth Thévoz is a future name to watch.

My former wife, Margaret Crick, is one of the best researchers in the business, who displays astonishing ability and persistence in tracking down documents and unearthing new material, but also a great skill in getting people to open up in interviews. I also had the research help of another future star, Adele-Momoko Fraser. My daughter Catherine drew the complicated Butler family tree.

Chris Ballinger, who knows David Butler better than almost anyone, would have been ideally placed to write this book himself. Instead, he went to extraordinary lengths to assist me. The manuscript is sprinkled with Chris's personal memories of working with David, and laced with fond examples of David's idiosyncrasies and generosity, as well as the benefit of Chris's expertise as an Oxford politics tutor. I owe him a great debt, and a very fine lunch.

Lucy Hetherington twice went through my manuscript in deep and considered detail, and suggested all sorts of excellent improvements. David Cowling, Susan Lipton, Caroline Morgan and Neil Fowler all read drafts of the text and suggested corrections and helpful amendments.

At Nuffield we received considerable help from the bursar, Tom Moore; the registrar, Justine Crump; the communications manager, Catherine Farfan; the IT director, Mark Norman; the former librarian Elizabeth Martin and the acting librarian, Tessa Tubb; the assistant librarian, Diana Hackett, and former assistant Clare Kavanagh; and the Warden's personal assistant, Claire Bunce. Thank you to a great college team.

Matthew Chipping at the BBC Archives in Caversham gave us immense help in tracking David Butler's work for the BBC over the decades, but most notably during the early years of television. We also received vital assistance from several other archivists: Valérie Nolk at Colet Court; Alexandra Aslett at St Paul's School;

Jennifer Thorp at New College, Oxford; Amanda Ingram at Pembroke College, Oxford; Jenny Wood at Brasenose College, Oxford; Alysoun Sanders of Macmillan Publishers; Jeremy McIlwaine, who looks after the Conservative Party archives in the Bodleian Library, Oxford; and members of staff at the Weston Library at the Bodleian. For David Butler's brief war career, we were helped by Joanne Peck, the efficient researcher at the Staffordshire Archives, and Joanna Terry, the head of archives and heritage.

Other people who have provided significant help during our journey are Neil Braggins of Newsquest; Maria Montas of CBS News; Ian Moore at the British Library; Diana Gower of *The Guardian*; Nathalie Wilks of New College; Viera Ghods at St Paul's School; Adam Green of Trinity College, Cambridge; and the staff of *Private Eye*.

I am grateful to Josh Benn and Ruth Winstone for providing extracts about David Butler from the extensive unpublished parts of Tony Benn's famous diary. Alison Readman's daughter Daphne Wright and R. B. McCallum's son Andrew were both hugely helpful in giving us access to their parents' correspondence on the early years of psephology. Charles Hollis kindly granted permission to reprint his father's poem.

Gary Rodger, author of the ebook *Swing: A brief history of British General Election Night broadcasting*, was always patient, prompt and cheerful in responding to our regular requests for more information. Malcolm Mackerras went to great lengths to explain David's part in developing public and scholarly understanding of elections in Australia, and his role in the Mackerras Pendulum, an Australian version of the famous Swingometer.

With one exception, the only people to refuse my requests for interviews did so on the grounds of infirmity or age. I am enormously grateful to the following people for speaking to us, or for going out of their way to be helpful in other ways: Lord (Andrew) Adonis, Don Aitkin, Lucy Anderson, David Andrews, Jessica Asato, Tim

Bale, Lolita Bam, Owen Barder, Michael Barratt, Lewis Baston, Lord (Alan) Beith, Hilary Benn, Jagdish Bhagwati, Jennifer Blaker, Vernon Bogdanor, John Bowis, George Brandis, David Bratman, Daniel Brittain-Catlin, Stephen Brooks, Edward Brown, Chris Capron, Penny Carleton-Smith, Andrew Carroll, Peter Catterall, Keith Clement, David Cowling, Patrick Cowling, Sir Ivor Crewe, Byron Criddle, Sir John Curtice, Jenny Davies, David Dimbleby, Lord (Bernard) Donoughue, Keith Dowding, Tony Drake, Sheila Dunleavy, Liz Elton, David Ensor, Richard and Maria Evans, Maya Even, Jan Fairer, Tim Farmiloe, Marya Fforde, Liz Fisher, Sir Paul Fox, Tam Fry, Paddy Garrett, John Garth, Robert Gildea, Diane Glyer, John Goldthorpe, Brian Gosschalk, Jane Green, the late John Grist, Phil Harding, Henry Hardy, Tom Harley, Brian Harrison, Martin Harrison, Michael Herman, Nick Hillman, Benedicte Hjejle, Godfrey Hodgson, Neil Hogben, Scott Housley, Baroness (Margaret) Jay, Paul Jowett, Sunder Katwala, Dennis Kavanagh, Peter Kellner, Paul Kelly, Raza Khattak, the late Tony King, Uwe Kitzinger, Ashok Lahiri, Lord (Nigel) Lawson, Chris Long, Liz Lorrimer, Ian McAllister, Iain McLean, Douglas McWilliams, Don Markwell, Peter Marshall, Diane Mauzy, Peter Menneer, Avrion Mitchison, Janet Morgan, Roger Mortimore, Ron Neil, Malcolm Newbury, Stephen Parkinson, Nicholas Parsons, Clive Payne, Michael Peacock, Gillian Peele, Zbigniew Pelczynski, Michael Pinto-Duschinsky, Stewart Purvis, Graham Pyatt, George Richardson, Peter Riddell, Dermot Roaf, Richard Rose, the late Robert Rowland, Prannoy Roy, Pat Ryan (née Vickerman), Larry Sabato, Ian St John, Joseph Santamaria, Len Scott, Mark Scott, Jonathan Seagrave, Colin Seymour-Ure, Virginia Shapiro, Audrey Skeats, Anne Sloman, Frank Smith, Daniel Snowman, Liam Spender, Michael Steed, Susan Stokes, Janice Taverne, Robert Taylor, Tony Teasdale, Paul Thompson, P. C. Thompson, Tony Travers, Sir Mark Tully, John Uhr, Nancy Walker, Helen and Lord (William) Wallace, Frances and John Walsh, Lord (Gordon) Wasserman, Helen

Watanabe, Lord (Alan) Watson, Pat Weller, Peter Wells, Martin Westlake, Joy Whitby, Lord (Stewart) Wood, Sir Peregrine Worsthorne and Peter Wynne Davies.

Olivia Beattie at Biteback did a superb job chivvying me towards my deadlines, editing the text and pressing me on factual details. I am also hugely grateful to Iain Dale for taking on the project in the first place.

INDEX

THE POLITICS OF THE POLL TAX

PAY NO POLL TAX

DAVID BUTLER
ANDREW ADONIS
& TONY TRAVERS

David Butler and Dennis Kavanagh

THE BRITISH GENERAL ELECTION OF 1992

LABOUR 35%
CONSERVATIVE 43%
LIBERAL 18%

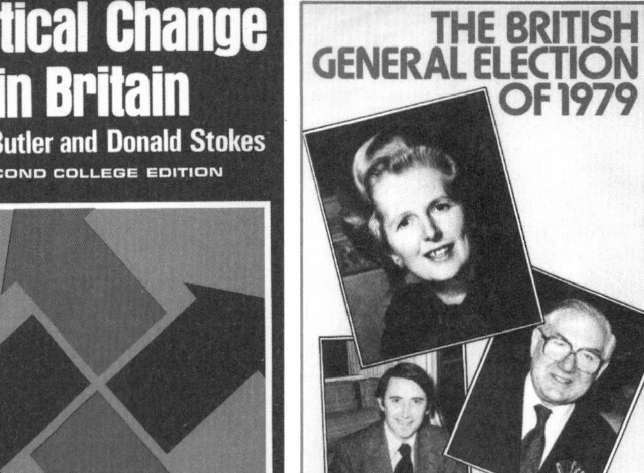

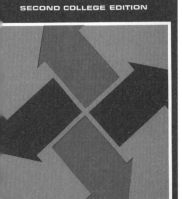